Building Network Capabilities in Turbulent Competitive Environments

Practices of Global Firms from Korea and Japan

Series on Resource Management

Building Network Capabilities in Turbulent Competitive Environments: Practices of Global Firms from Korea and Japan
by Young Won Park and Paul Hong
ISBN: 978-1-4398-5068-8

Integral Logistics Management: Operations and Supply Chain Management Within and Across Companies, Fourth Edition
by Paul Schönsleben
ISBN: 978-1-4398-7823-1

Lean Management Principles for Information Technology
by Gerhard J. Plenert
ISBN: 978-1-4200-7860-2

Supply Chain Project Management: A Structured Collaborative and Measurable Approach, Second Edition
by James B. Ayers
ISBN: 978-1-4200-8392-7

Modeling and Benchmarking Supply Chain Leadership: Setting the Conditions for Excellence
by Joseph L. Walden
ISBN: 978-1-4200-8397-2

New Methods of Competing in the Global Marketplace: Critical Success Factors from Service and Manufacturing
by William R. Crandall and Richard E. Crandall
ISBN: 978-1-4200-5126-1

Supply Chain Risk Management: Minimizing Disruptions in Global Sourcing
by Robert Handfield and Kevin P. McCormack
ISBN: 978-0-8493-6642-0

Rightsizing Inventory
by Joseph L. Aiello
ISBN: 978-0-8493-8515-5

Handbook of Supply Chain Management, Second Edition
by James B. Ayers
ISBN: 978-0-8493-3160-2

Supply Market Intelligence: A Managerial Handbook for Building Sourcing Strategies
by Robert B. Handfield
ISBN: 978-978-0-8493-2789-6

The Portal to Lean Production: Principles & Practices for Doing More With Less
by John Nicholas and Avi Soni
ISBN: 0-8493-5031-3

Building Network Capabilities in Turbulent Competitive Environments

Practices of Global Firms from Korea and Japan

YOUNG WON PARK and PAUL HONG

CRC Press is an imprint of the
Taylor & Francis Group, an **informa** business

CRC Press
Taylor & Francis Group
6000 Broken Sound Parkway NW, Suite 300
Boca Raton, FL 33487-2742

Printed in the United States of America on acid-free paper
Version Date: 20111116

International Standard Book Number: 978-1-4398-5068-8 (Hardback)

Library of Congress Cataloging-in-Publication Data

Park, Young Won.
Building network capabilities in turbulent competitive environments : practices of global firms from Korea and Japan / Young Won Park and Paul Hong.
p. cm. -- (Series on resource management)
Includes bibliographical references and index.
ISBN 978-1-4398-5068-8 (hardback : alk. paper)
1. Information technology--Korea (South) 2. Information technology--Japan. 3. Business networks--Korea (South) 4. Business networks--Japan. 5. Social networks--Korea (South) 6. Social networks--Japan. I. Hong, Paul. II. Title.

HD30.2.P3697 2012
658'.044--dc23 2011045295

Visit the Taylor & Francis Web site at
http://www.taylorandfrancis.com

and the CRC Press Web site at
http://www.crcpress.com

Contents

SECTION II Case Studies of the Korean IT Industry

SECTION III Infrastructure of IT Capability

Preface

These days it is common to read about the rapid advancement and growth of Korean global firms (e.g., Samsung Electronics, LG Electronics, Hyundai Motor Company) in the global market. After the 2008 financial crisis, many global firms, including those of Japan, struggled to maintain their competitive positions. Yet, Korean firms display an amazing rate of growth and expansion. For a while many Japanese business leaders regarded such growth records of Korean firms as short-lived because their technological capabilities in the past were mostly built by learning or imitating from Japanese firms. However, beyond such quick and easy assessment, the growth rate of Korean firms has not slowed down since the middle of the 1990s, and instead it is accelerating. In view of their impressive performance records, many Japanese firms seriously consider Korean manufacturing practices—particularly the source of their strengths. As of April 1, 2010, the Minister of Economy, Trade and Industry (METI) started the operation of a Korea Department which exclusively focuses on studying about Korean global firms. It is highly unusual that any Japanese government entity establishes a department for the purpose of studying trade and industrial policy of other neighboring countries. METI, through its Korea Department, is committed to thoroughly study about leading Korean global firms in the key industries (e.g., electrical and electronics) and carefully examine their practices. It is well accepted in Japan that the synergy effect of the active role of Korean government and the owner-based management styles enable rapid and effective decision making by Korean firms for aggressive strategic investment decisions in the emerging markets. Besides, a continuous sense of urgency and constructive crisis management are also huge contributing factors for their competitive strengths.

Such interest on Korean firms is not limited to Japan. Academic researchers and business leaders in the United States, China, Brazil, India, and Europe would like to know more about Korean firms. Yet very little is known about the strategic and operational practices of Korean firms. Many do assume that Korean firms are not really different from Japanese firms. A central thesis of this book, therefore, is that there is a real difference between Japanese and Korean firms in terms of business strategy and management practices. Strategic decision making of Korean firms that effectively responds to the changing business environments—particularly in the context of rapid transitions from analog to the digital age—are worthy of further examination. In this sense, this book specifically focuses on the comprehensive *manufacturing strategies* of Korean firms that integrate modular product architecture, global supply chain management, and IT strategy. Based on extensive interviews and fieldwork studies, this book provides case studies that highlight the details of the power of Korean manufacturing firms.

Increasingly, the sustainable competitive advantage of firms requires steady creation and delivery of products and services that meet changing customer expectations. Because these complex products and services involve interconnected business activities across organizational boundaries, there is a great need for research that explores the dynamic relationship mechanisms of organizational networks. In this context, value chain management is a major way to analyze the competitive advantage of a networked firm. Here, value chain refers to all the business activities that supply the flow of information, products, and services, including the acquisition of raw materials, transforming intermediate products, manufacturing and assembling the final products, distribution, sales, and after-sales service. In this book, we use Value Chain Management (VCM) and Supply Chain Management (SCM) interchangeably.

One critical element of value analysis in SCM is product architecture. No firm may control all areas of their supply chain. Product architecture is the basic design philosophy which governs how products are divided in terms of component parts, product functions, and component interfaces through design processes. By product architecture firms may link core components of a product together throughout its value chain. Product architecture determines the details of make–buy components.

Two major classifications of product architecture are modular and integral. Products are located on the opposite ends of a continuum between modular and integral. Even within the same family of products, different architectures may be applied according to diverse product positions and process structures. Products with modular architecture have a one-to-one relationship between function and module so that each component is easily divisible. On the other hand, products with integral architecture show that functions and component parts are integrated as an indivisible unit. Automobiles are a good example of this. The relationship between function and module is not one-to-one but many-to-many. Designers of each module are responsible for the detailed requirements. They also need to collaborate closely for the integrity of the overall product. On the other hand, products with modular architecture are organized by divisible elements of complex products and processes. Explicit design rules are applied in the process of dividing the complex system into semi-independent subsystems based on certain connection rules. Modularity is the process state of dividing a complex system into divisible subsystems. The main characteristics of modular architecture are: (1) the division of complex systems by modules, (2) continuous evolution of the connection rules of modules, and (3) the independent nature of each model from one another.

It is worth noting several merits of modular product design (Feitzinger and Lee, 1997). First, a firm may determine the numbers of basic components according to the needs for the final product. Any component may be added during the assembly process as an option. The product differentiation can occur by postponement (i.e., adding other components in the later stage). Second, a firm may be flexible in attaining any particular modules. Any modules can be configured according to the specific process goals (e.g., reduction of the total production time). Third, product problems are more easily recognizable because even ambiguous product quality issues are more quickly identified.

Modularity is also regarded as a key for logistics cost reduction, lead-time improvement, and customization (Hoek and Weken, 1998). Since modularity usually involves the standardization of component parts and product groups, it facilitates an internal integration of functions within firms. For example, research and development (R & D) pursues efficiency in product design, while manufacturing responds to marketing that demands flexibility and customization requirements for customers. As a result, modularity considers both horizontal and vertical component requirements that include the expectations of the entire supply chain (e.g., procurement and logistics elements). In brief, by applying modular architecture, firms may simplify operations processes and accordingly achieve drastic cost reductions. In this way, the global supply chain is enhanced. Thus, product architecture is regarded as an essential analytical tool that examines how firms create value through complex business processes in the supply chain.

We also use IT strategy to examine the dynamic role of product architecture in supply chain management. Firms are not fixed in their use of product architectures. Rather, according to competitive requirements, they adopt different forms of product architectures. In the analog age firms mostly adopted integral product architecture; in the digital age modular architecture has become the norm. For example, in the analog age most product architecture of electronic products (e.g., VTR, TV) was integral. The competitive position of Japanese firms was superior with their applications of manufacturing (*monozukuri* in Japanese) capabilities which thrive on integral product architecture. However, in the digital age, Japanese firms have quickly lost their competitive advantages.

Interestingly enough, by surpassing Japanese firms it is Korean and Taiwanese firms from the same East Asian region that have built their global competitiveness. Korean firms in particular learned from Japanese firms for their *monozukuri* capabilities in the past. Over the years Korean firms have transformed themselves as global leaders through the combined effects of implementing their own outstanding management practices with the support of Korean governmental policies of business network environment construction. Of course, the changing technological environments certainly impacted their business performance outcomes as well.

In the changing competitive market context, the worldwide adoption of semiconductor chips is a critical component of digital electronic products. Since the software within the semiconductor chips determines the functional capabilities of electronic products, IT applications become quite important for the changing competitive landscape.

In fact, Korean firms thrive on these changing market environments. For example, Samsung achieves its distinct global market position by applying modular product architecture for most of its successful products. The conventional assumption is that the modularized products easily turn out to become commodities that invite easy entry of competitors and thus lose their competitive advantage with stiff price competition and low profit margins. However, Korean firms consistently build and maintain their competitiveness in the global market. What are their secrets? A number of chapters are devoted to address this critical question in this book.

In brief, this book examines the practices of global firms from Northeast Asia (Korea and Japan in particular) from the perspective of how they build network capabilities in turbulent competitive environments. Specifically, this book shows how product architecture (PA), supply chain management (SCM), and IT strategy are dynamically related and affect one another for sustainable competitive advantage in today's Korean and Japanese global firms. For the effective use of this book it would be helpful to first read the summary of each chapter. We sincerely appreciate Taylor & Francis Group, LLC for providing us the opportunity to compile these articles and publish them in the form of a book. We are certainly responsible for whatever deficiencies and imperfections appear in this book. However, we hope that this book might be helpful in stimulating further research in this important arena.

Young Won Park, PhD

Paul Hong, PhD, CMA

About the Authors

Dr. Young Won Park is an associate professor at the Manufacturing Management Research Center at the University of Tokyo, Japan, and an associate professor at the Waseda Institute for Advanced Study at Waseda University, Japan. Dr. Park holds a PhD degree in the Department of Advanced Social and International Studies from the University of Tokyo, Japan. His articles have been published in journals including *Management Decision, International Journal of Production Economics, International Journal of Technology Management, Journal of Business Research, Benchmarking: An International Journal, International Journal of Services and Operations Management, International Journal of Logistics Systems and Management, International Journal of Business Excellence, International Journal of Procurement Management, Akamon Management Review, Japan Academy of International Business Studies, Japanese Society for Science and Technology Studies, and the Japan Society of Information and Communication Research.* He has received research awards including Dissertation Paper Awards from the Japan Association for Social Informatics (JASI), Best Paper Awards from The Japan Society of Information and Communication Research (JSICR), Research Awards of the Social Science Field from The Telecommunications Advancement Foundation (TAF) and Research Students Awards of the Social Science Field from The Telecommunications Advancement Foundation (TAF). His research interests are in technology management, manufacturing and IT strategy, and global supply chain management.

Dr. Paul Hong is a professor of operations management at the University of Toledo, Ohio, in the United States. Dr. Hong holds a PhD degree in manufacturing management and engineering from the University of Toledo. He also holds an MBA and an MA in economics from Bowling Green State University and a BA from Yonsei University in Seoul, Korea. His articles have been published in journals including *Journal of Operations Management, International Journal of Operations and Production Management, International Journal of Production Economics, International Journal of Production Research, Management Decision, Journal of Supply Chain Management, Journal of Business Research, European Journal of*

Innovation Management, Journal of Enterprise Information Management, Journal of Knowledge and Information Management, International Journal of Quality and Reliability Management, Benchmarking: An International Journal, Strategic Outsourcing: An International Journal, Research in International Business and Finance, International Journal of Business Excellence, International Journal of Procurement Management, Korean Journal of Tourism Research, and *Tourism Culture and Science.* His research interests are in technology management, operational strategy, and global supply chain management. He is the International Research Network Coordinator of the Annual Symposium and Workshop in Global Supply Chains. He is also a member of editorial review board for several journals including *Journal of Operations Management* and *Journal of Humanitarian Logistics and Supply Chain Management.* He worked as a guest editor for special issues for journals including *Benchmarking: An International Journal, International Journal of Business Excellence, International Journal of Services and Operations Management, International Journal of Procurement Management,* and *Journal of Purchasing and Supply Management.* He is also US coordinator of International Manufacturing Strategy Survey (IMSS).

Section I

History

1

What is Network Capability? Introduction, Framework, and Contents

This chapter defines network capability based on the existing literature. In the environment of global markets building capabilities is an important concern. The business environment in three countries in North East Asia (Japan, Korea and China) shows dynamic growths, changes, and challenges. This book deals with the topic of building network capabilities in turbulent global environments. As network concepts are employed in business management, the term "network capability" now refers to systematic connectivity between a focal company and all the interrelated entities that form a vital stakeholder group for the shared goals and mission. As technology environment changes from the analogue period to the digital age, global business environment requires accelerating speed management. No firm can maintain its competitive advantage with its single efforts alone. Chapter 1 examines global business environment in 21st century and literature in detail about "network capability" which continues to develop and enhances core competencies and global competitive advantage by the interrelated socio-technological collaborative infrastructures.

1.1 TWENTY-FIRST CENTURY GLOBAL BUSINESS ENVIRONMENT

1.1.1 Changing Product Architecture with the Transition from Analog to Digital

The competitive business environment of the twenty-first century reflects enormous change with the transition from analog to digital generation.

Open supply chains in the digital generation have transformed the global business environment into a borderless world. The embedded mechanisms in all products using semiconductors and firmware impacted firms to adapt their product architecture from integral to modular type. Such architectural change is in a sense the primary change agent for the economic system from closed specialization to open collaborative internationalization. The PC was the first technology module that adopted the micro processor unit (MPU). In the beginning, the speed of the processor was very slow. Increasingly, the small-scale innovative venture business groups started developing much faster MPUs and made them available in the open business environment (Ogawa et al., 2009). Besides, a series of the open innovation policy of the U.S. government in the 1980s changed the PC industry from closed specialization to interorganizational open collaboration. From the middle 1990s, the PC industry adopted the modular type as its standard product architecture. Thus, the global PC industry transformed itself toward open collaborative internationalization. The PC, which first adopted MPU as technology module in the world, also introduced open international collaboration into the world. This facilitated the widespread realization of global supply chains.

Although the need for interfirm functional specialization (i.e., dividing the scope and roles of value creation and delivery among firms) became better accepted, advanced nations with a solid manufacturing base (e.g., the United States and Europe) dominated the business leadership. However, rapid modularization of product architecture allowed firms to implement complete turnkey-solution types of production processes in the form of international interfirm functional specialization. Here, firms from NIEs (Hong Kong, Korea, Singapore, and Taiwan)/BRICs (Brazil, Russia, India, and China) take assembly function of semifinished products based on modular type technologies or product modular type cost-driven products and while advanced countries focus integral type products for high premium values. The modular type of products have low barriers to entry, and thus the speed of technology diffusion is quite rapid. In contrast, the speed of transferring integral type technology is very slow. From product architectural perspective the twenty-first century international functional specialization is about spectrum diffusion in the global market through two types of product architectures with quite different technology diffusion speeds. Such business structure requires a new kind of infrastructure (i.e., global supply chain).

In the twenty-first century, the product design core of almost all electronic products contains the MCU/Large scale integration (LSI) system.

Functional specialization among firms from NIEs/BRICs and those from North America and Europe utilize the global supply chain for more open international functional specialization. Thus, the previous business model of vertical integration is gradually replaced by the new business model of the global supply chain, which develops a huge employment pool in the industries of NIEs/BRICs. Mutual dependence between firms from NIEs/BRICs and other Western nations has become more critical than ever before. In this regard, MPU and system LSI not only control functionality, quality, and cost but also impact the supply chain, the pattern of international cooperation, and changes the global social structures. Therefore, it is important to learn about the patterns of catch-up of NIEs global firms. Korean and Japanese firms in particular provide rich insight on how the global business environment has evolved with these product architectural changes.

1.1.2 Network Capability: A New Condition for Effective Responses in the Global Business Environment

What do firms do in response to the rapid changes in the global business environment? Two questions are considered here. The first one is, "If product architecture is integral, would manufacturers of finished goods be in an advantageous position?" For open modular product architecture, components suppliers for commodity products are in a better position of strengths (Christensen et al., 2002). In such context, would it be advantageous to keep producing finished goods? Having finished goods in an open modular environment might become a weakness for sustainable competitiveness.

The second question is, "In hardware-based competition, particularly for the open modular products, would differentiation in services and contents be important?" The answer may require multiple perspectives. It is fruitful to study many success and failure experiences of outstanding firms. Take the stories of Intel and Apple, Sony and Samsung. Intel has pursued platform strategy based on product architecture. Its critical question is, "How can we sustain our products as closed integral architecture in an industry environment of open architecture?" Intel has adopted its role as intermediary which does not procure any hardware at all. It did not compete against IBM for finished computer products. Rather, its focus is on component parts, and thus it has concentrated its efforts on leading business interface standardization.

On the other hand, Apple has software power. Yet, Apple has none of its own contents. Instead, it built its strength on software competencies and thus overcame any potential misunderstanding from contents makers. Steven Jobs has paid attention to the daily life of customers. He observed the need to make customers to freely use music contents from Apple's Macintosh. However, this requires persuading the content makers. He visited the content makers to make a point that Apple has excellent software but no contents of its own. He developed iTunes software that strengthens the user interface while respecting the digital rights management (DRM) of the contents makers. At the same time, Apple also developed iPod hardware as well. Apple is outstanding in its utilization of network capability. Based on the core competence of its operating system (OS), Apple is outstanding in its coordinative capability by which it mobilizes global partners for network interfaces. In contrast, Sony satisfied all the conditions in terms of hardware, software, and contents but failed to integrate them. This shows that what matters is not having finished products in the form of software, hardware, and contents; rather, it is about capability that manages network resources. Thus, firms with intermediary function (e.g., Intel) can do as well as those who have software capability or coordination capability that unites its internal and external resources.

Increasingly, the global business environment is moving away from closed integral to open modular. Speed is the key for competitiveness in open modular types of products. It is essential to build network capability that fits to such environmental needs. Most products of Samsung and LG are close to open modular. They achieve synergy effects by integrating the business lines of component parts (with high profit margins) and finished products. In our book we focus on Korean IT firms (e.g., Samsung and LG) which market digital and open modular products. Their catch-up speed with Japanese firms is quite fast; at the same time they are very prone to severe price competition. These Korean firms make every effort for enhancing their product quality and apply a variety of strategies to overcome the limitations of modular products. In the early period of their catch-up, they constructed network environments that quickly transferred the leading-edge technologies of Western and Japanese firms. They developed their core competence in the areas of fast product development system and marketing strategy that differentiated their products from those of the competitors. They also focused on brand strategy by upgrading the level of integration between components suppliers and finished products. Samsung, for example, integrated business lines of component parts (with high profit margins) and those for finished products and achieved tremendous synergy effects. In the case of open modular products, its focus is more on brand value rather than a product's functional differentiation. Samsung's strategic emphasis, therefore, was on brand value enhancement throughout its organizational processes. For this goal, Samsung adopted speedy decision making that is critical for short product development cycle and supply chain management (SCM) facilitation (Kobayashi, 2000).

JY Yoon (CEO of Samsung Electronics) made the following comment on how to respond in the changing global market environment: "If product architecture is open modular, speed matters most. The victory in battles depends on the brand power. Speed is the key for winning performance not only in sashimi sushi but also in commodity products (e.g., mobile phones). No matter how excellent sashimi, after one or two days the value drops drastically. Inventories are deadly for sushi restaurants and digital products makers. Speed is everything." This is the point of digital sashimi strategy (Chang, 2008). Specifically, innovation differentiation is not merely in Product by differentiation but in Price, Promotion, and Place. For the expansion of such a unique business model Samsung has utilized their diverse network capability.

Second, crisis management leadership is important to respond fast by implementing speedy organizational decision making in a rapidly changing business environment. To overcome organizational stagnation and renew organizational ability, firms need to effectively utilize their slack resources and adopt stretch/leverage strategy for building future core competence (Itami, 1987; Hamel and Prahalad, 1994). Japanese firms have utilized such strategy in their catch-up efforts with the global industry leaders. Korean firms also adopted similar strategy. However, in view of their relatively small domestic market, on-going conflicts between the North and South Korea, and the changing global competitive landscape, Korean owners/executives continually managed crisis management to utilize their slack resources fully. Too much strain on people, and organizations may become dysfunctional. However, a reasonable level of stress is healthy for the individual and organizational growth. Many Korean firms have used such crisis management and deployed their network capability for productive purposes. They move forward in the new business world. Korean executives pursue their global strategy based on the 9:1 premise. This means that the portion of the domestic market in the total target market is no more than 10%, and 90% is from the targeted global market. In this sense, Korean firms are quite different from Japanese firms that assume substantial attention on their domestic market share. In this sense, Korean firms are outstanding in their pursuit of global network capability. The critical element of global network capability is the sensing ability of global market opportunities.

Finally, timing is another important concern. The majority of products by Japanese firms or Korean firms have adapted to the dominant designs determined by the Western leader firms. In this case, timing matters. Critiques of Korean Samsung point out that, in an analogy of card games, it shows its cards only after others already showed theirs (Shin and Jang, 2006). However, the traditional product development rule that the first movers are more advantageous than the latecomers does not apply in Samsung's case. In standardization competition, Samsung may arrive one step later, but the game outcome will be quite different if it can cover its minor production introduction timing disadvantage with its superior organizational capability.

Apple's strategic advantage does not lie in its effort of becoming the first mover but in its executing ability of the perfect timing (Choi, 2010). It introduced iPhone in keeping up with the right time for the social network sites. The explosive popularity of iTunes was based on its entry on the proven market. Apple watched carefully how Napster lost all while insisting on its free download policy. As Amazon's Kindle leads the market, Steven Jobs introduced iPad for the much bigger market. Such timing is not about arriving one step late but about taking advantage of the emergence of the growing market potential. Network capability thus includes such sense of timing. The next section briefly overviews the previous literature on network capability and defines our network capability according to the purpose of this book.

1.2 LITERATURE REVIEW ON NETWORK CAPABILITY

1.2.1 Core Competence and Network Capability

Firms' unique resources or superior position determines the competitive advantage of firms (Rumelt, 1984; Wenerfelt, 1984; Barney, 2002). Core competence is particularly important in differentiating with their competitors. The theoretical base of core competence includes classical writings (Smith, 1776; Schumpeter, 1934; Coase, 1937), firm growth theory based on resources (Penrose, 1959), and core competence theories (Hamel and Prahalad, 1990; Morone, 1993). The importance of capability (similar to competence) has frequently been argued for in the past as well (Walsh and Linton, 2002). For example, capability is conceptualized as a base for competitive advantage or long-term business success (Smith, 1776; Schumpeter, 1934; Coase, 1937; Penrose, 1959). Hamel and Prahalad (1990) used both core competence and capability with little distinction. For example, they define core competence as set of skills, technologies, and resources that provide unique value to the customers (Hamel and Prahalad, 1990). Sony's customer advantage, for example, lies in its convenience and ease to possess and carry, and thus Sony has developed its core competence through product minimization. Core competence provides new market opportunities and becomes a resource base which competitors find difficult to imitate. Core competence facilitates coordination and integration of strategic business units (SBU) as well (Javidan, 1998).

Stalk et al. (1992) emphasize the specialized role of core competence in the areas of technological and production functions, while capability is rather extended to the entire value chain. Thus, the terms "competence" and "capability" are somewhat different, and yet this distinction might not be so critically different (Barney, 2002; Park, 2009). In this book, competence and capability are not necessarily distinguished. Rather, core competence or capability of a firm refers to one's unique ability—quite distinct from its competitors'—necessary and essential for its sustainable competitive advantage. One other research stream of capability–competence is learning and knowledge theory (Nelson and Winter, 1982; Levitt and March, 1988; Cohen and Levinthal, 1990; March, 1991; Lippman and Rumelt, 1992; Nonaka and Takeuchi, 1995; Teece, 1998).

Nelson and Winter (1982) suggest that knowledge accumulation is possible through predictable behavioral patterns that are repeated on a daily basis. Such behavioral patterns form organizational routines as embedded knowledge which is compared to DNA for knowledge.

Teece (1998) classified knowledge in terms of codified/tacit knowledge, observable/nonobservable use, positive/negative knowledge, and autonomous/systematic knowledge. Knowledge assets are hard to imitate. All the useful routines that support any specific competence are not easily transferrable, because knowledge assets are inimitable and they require protection by copyright and patent laws. Another defensive wall includes intellectual property regime (e.g., patents, contractual secrets, and trademark). Teece (1998) also notes the value of complementary assets. Most successful innovation for commercialization requires a complementary relationship between specific know-how and other competencies/resources. Some examples of such relationships are: (1) new pharmaceutical innovation and information channel, (2) computer hardware and operational systems (OS) and application software, and (3) game equipment and game contents. Teece (1986) also regards complementary assets in the form of (1) generic assets (i.e., innovation and independent assets for ordinary uses), (2) specialized assets (i.e., innovation and unilateral dependencies), and (3) co-specialized assets (i.e., innovation and mutual dependence). Consider the reasons for business failures of American electronics firms (e.g., RCA): (1) they import technological license from Japanese firms (i.e., lack of innovation); and (2) they discard manufacturing functions (i.e., loss of manufacturing functions as complementary assets). Like Teece (1998), in this book we also emphasize the value of complementary assets in the form of (1) innovation and manufacturing (2) hardware, software, and contents.

According to Nonaka and Takeuchi (1995), Japanese firms create new knowledge within their organization through systematic knowledge creation processes. Embedded knowledge in organizational capability is essential for successful development of new products and services. SECI (socialization, externalization, combination, and internalization) processes are useful to explain how Japanese firms build up organizational shared databases, utilize available external knowledge through innovation-creating systems, combine such external knowledge, internalize field experiences/working knowledge, and thus realize innovation success. They regard middle managers and their decision making style (i.e., middle-bottom and middle-up) as a real source of the sustainable competitive advantage of Japanese firms. Organizational learning ability for new knowledge is important for sustainable competitive advantage. Interestingly enough, many firms that were included in the list of excellent companies by Peters and Waterman (1982) or firms with core competence by Hamel and Prahalad (1994) soon lost their competitive advantage with lack of organizational learning or dynamic capability.

Researchers note that a firm's unique organizational capability requires long-term construction, and thus it might not be flexible enough to respond to the rapid change requirements of the external environment. Thus, each firm needs to reexamine, renew, and reconstruct its core competence for sustainable competitive advantage. Otherwise, current strong core competence may turn into "competence trap," "core incompetence," and "core rigidity" (March, 1991; Leonard-Barton, 1992; Henderson, 1993; Dougherty, 1995; Helfat and Raubitschek, 2000; Dougherty and Heller, 1994; Danneels, 2002).

Abernathy and Clark (1985) distinguish between (1) innovation that reshapes an organizational technological capability and (2) innovation that impacts organizational knowledge of customer requirements. If an organization merely keeps up with regular innovation, organizational knowledge may become an inertia which might lead to organizational rigidity. Based on these findings Henderson and Clark (1990) examine cases of architectural innovation and find that leading firm failures are too often related to problems in communication channels, information filters, and problem-solving strategies. Outstanding environmental adaptation and accumulated organizational resources (e.g., technology, sales performance, and brand power) may be the success factors in the past, and yet in the present they may also become an obstacle for implementing new required changes (Henderson and Clark, 1990; Christensen and Bower, 1996; Christensen, 1997). Other factors such as current core customer pressures, failure to recognize the emerging needs, lack of adaptive capability to changing environment, technological discontinuity, organizational information processing mechanism (structure, recognition, and culture), and organizational routines may all work against the necessary changes. These are some of the reasons why the leading firms in the past are no longer successful in the new market environment.

Abernathy and Clark (1985) also note the strengths of Japanese firms in their comparative study of American and Japanese electronics firms. Hamel and Prahalad (1994) speak of the advantages of Japanese firms. Currently, in view of relatively weak performance of Japanese electronics firms, an increasing research attention is called for more careful study of the strengths of Korean firms as well. Thus, if firms focus on routine innovation, then architectural knowledge embedded in operational routines and work process channels is not easy to reconfigure or create beyond the current level of inertia. Such product architecture, having become so used to the existing information filter mechanism, may no longer be innovative enough to compete against that of its rival firms.

In this context, the theory of dynamic capability has gained much research attention in the 1990s (Teece, 1986; Teece et al., 1990; Utterback and Suarez, 1993; Henderson and Cockburn, 1994; Teece and Pisano,

1994; Teece et. al., 1997; Miller and Morris, 1999; Teece, 2007; Quinn and Dalton, 2009). Henderson and Clark (1990), Henderson and Cockburn (1994), and Teece and Pisano (1994) suggest architectural competence or dynamic capability which is characterized by firm-specific resource (i.e., component competence) plus new resource creation and expansion through strategic integration of intra- and interorganizational resources in response to changing market reality. Such architectural competence and dynamic capability include both specific incremental changes (focusing on management of existing resources) and radical architectural changes (reconfiguring architectural change of the current level of resources).

Teece (1986) suggests that it is possible to build up knowledge assets through innovation. The essence of a firm is to create new knowledge or import from external entities, assemble, or integrate diverse knowledge sources through exploration. Both Hamel and Prahalad's core competence (1994) and Teece's knowledge assets (1986) are visible in products and services. For sustainable competitive advantage it is critical for firms to develop redistribution capability of intra- and interorganizational resources, reconfiguration of knowledge assets, complementary assets and core competence, and prudent selection ability of appropriate organizational structure and system (Roh et al., 2008). In this respect, sustainable competitive advantage requires dynamic capability which is able to keep developing and deploying knowledge assets through these organizational processes.

Because a firm's cumulative knowledge is embedded in management routines and operational processes, these organizational-specific knowledge assets are a source of competitive advantage (Doll et al., 2010; Hong et al., 2011). However, in the context of ineffective organizational governance structure such knowledge assets may not realize their potential, and thus the firm loses its competitive advantage in a matter of time. In this book we examine crisis management governance of Korean global firms for sustaining organizational vitality.

Firms need dynamic capabilities to capture innovation opportunities by connecting to the external network. Dynamic capabilities refer to "organizational ability that develops, realizes, and protects core competence and knowledge assets for sustainable competitive advantage" (Teece, 1986). Sensing abiiity of external environment includes exploring, stretching, and leveraging external opportunities (Hamel and Prahalad, 1994). Such network is the essence of network capability.

Ritter and Gemunden (2003) classify competence as an important factor for organizational innovation. They define competence as (1) possession of resources (e.g., knowledge, skills, and qualifications) and (2) utilization of such resources. Two specific competencies that impact innovation success are network competence and technological competence. Network competence requires innovation network that is so essential for a firm's innovation success. Network competence (1) combines all the resource capabilities of partners and their own (e.g., both technological and organizational) and (2) deploys them toward the goal of shared competitive advantage. Ritter (1999) measures network competence in terms of network management qualifications (coordination of interorganizational relationships) and network risk management performance. Thus, network competence is about a firm's ability to integrate interorganizational resources and apply them. A firm with a high level of network competence tends to adopt relation-driven marketing strategy and implement market-oriented innovation processes for developing and commercializing more innovative products. Thus, the successful organization requires sufficient market knowledge competence for innovation success.

Ritter and Gemunden's technological competence (2002) is an organizational ability that explores, comprehends, and applies emerging or available top-notch technology that is compatible with the internal competence requirements. Such technological competence allows firms to pioneer new markets through new product development and implementation of new product process. Firms with a high level of technological competence have a better chance for innovation success than those with a low level of network competence.

Therefore, network and technological competence is related to Danneels' market and technological competence (2002). Based on the above definitions, in this book we define network competence as "a firm's ability that acquires, combines, and integrates market and technological competence of other organizations with its own resources."

1.2.2 Product Architecture, SCM, and Network Capability

Product architecture is the basic process structure of connecting core components of products (Fujimoto, 2001a). The choice of product architecture governs the essential rules of analyzing product requirement functions, dividing products into component parts, and designing the interfaces of components (Fujimoto, 2003). Two usual classifications of product architecture are modular/integral and open/closed (Ulrich, 1995; Baldwin and Clark, 2000; Fujimoto, 2001). Strategic application of product architecture influences the degree of a firm's competitiveness in the ways it facilitates innovation according to changes in market reality (Henderson and Clark, 1990; Fuimoto, 2004).

Such product architecture is closely related to organizational structure. Baldwin and Clark (2000) argue that product design and organizational design need consistency because product component architecture impacts the firm's organizational architecture. If product component architecture is integral, then organizational architecture should be quite interdependent. On the other hand, modular product architecture requires organizational units to be divided according to specialized functions. Christensen et al. (2002) suggest that, in view of product architecture, firms need to determine organizational structure either as vertically integrated or horizontally specialized.

Based on his long years of field studies Fujimoto (2003) suggests the organizational capability exists not only as the base of organizational routines but also as a primary source of competitiveness in terms of QCDF (quality, cost, delivery, and flexibility). He observes strong correlation between product architecture and organizational capability. Such interrelationship is applicable in the national level of comparative competitive advantage as well.

According to Fujimoto (2006a), alignment patterns between product architecture and organizational capabilities are different. Japanese firms do better with integral products, while Korean firms with their relatively late entry in the market focus on modular products. Korean firms have caught up with Japanese firms in a relatively short time and have shown their increasing prominence in modular products.

A firm's boundary of products and services, its geographical location in its long history, and social environment all influence the extent of its organizational capability. Wakabayashi (2009) defines a network as "a social system which horizontally integrates numerous individuals, groups, and organizations to fulfill common shared purpose and collaborate in relatively decentralized structure and implement an independent decision making process." Such network organization has a high level of innovativeness and quickly adapts to the changes occurring in its external environment. With increasing product complexity the network becomes important because no single firm can handle all the changing market requirements. It is not quite possible for any focal firm to develop and produce all the component parts of a product. It is unreasonable to try vertical integration of all the upstream (e.g., product development and manufacturing) and downstream (e.g., managing entire supply chain and distribution requirements).

Fine (1998) regards strategic decision making as very critical for the integration and specialization linkage of the product–process–supply chain. Christensen et al. (2002) also suggest appropriate decision making, whether a firm's network chooses to be vertically integrated or horizontal specialized according to the changes in product architecture. A vertically integrated networked firm performs better in a market where customer requirements for product quality and functionality are not met. On the other hand, a horizontally specialized networked firm does well in a market with little demand for functionality. Vertically integrated firms occupy leadership positions in the less developed market. However, vertical integration is not so effective in the context that technological progress exceeds customer needs. In a new market where there is a noticeable gap between customer-desired quality and product functionality, then vertically integrated firms find room for growth. As a dominant business model in a market moves from vertical integration to horizontal specialization, producers of the finished products may not generate large profit. Rather, subcomponent parts suppliers take a large share of profits. Christensen et al. (2002) observe that component suppliers usually take more profits in commodity products which have satisfied all known customer needs. In fact, Korean and Japanese IT firms represent such a tendency. For consumer electronic products, component suppliers are more profitable than the manufacturers of finished products. Then, how did Korean firms secure a fair or larger share of profits in such commodity products? This is a key question that will be examined in this book.

After the 1990s, as the concept of strategic outsourcing and strategic alignment became quite popular, the strategic relationship between OEMs and their suppliers has become an important element of business success. Furthermore, SCM is extending beyond a firm's organizational boundaries toward attaining mutual benefits (Demeter et al., 2006), which compels firms to concentrate on their unique and competitive business areas. Therefore, all partners increasingly consider how to contribute to their SCs based on their core competencies (Chiang and Trappey, 2007). Such efforts help firms to culminate their core competencies and to build up cooperative relationships with other firms to strengthen necessary areas.

Once the value chain is established, all partners share a clear vision that unites all constituents into a cooperative value chain within the industry value system. All the members in the value chain need to make efforts to respond to the requirements arising in a rapidly changing market. In a global economy that emphasizes scale and relies on technology, partnership is the driver of the supply chain. Especially, companies in developed countries incline to procure goods and services from suppliers (Liker and Choi, 2004; Liao et al., 2010; Roh et al., 2011).

In the meanwhile, supply chain management considers all the information exchanged and the movement of goods from manufacturer, wholesaler, and retailer to all the suppliers on the extended supply chain. To successfully meet all the requirements of customers, SCM applies the total system in managing information, materials, and services (Chase, 1998; Li and Wang, 2007).

It is possible for focal firms to reduce their innovation expenditures and minimize risk factors through collaboration with the partners in a business-ecosystem (e.g., suppliers with unique technological and manufacturing capability even in other countries). What is critical for competitive advantage is how such focal firms seek, find, and involve these resourceful and competent suppliers in their network. They must combine knowledge assets of many suppliers in their network. Thus, the integrating ability of a focal firm is quite important in any network (Brusoni and Prencipe, 2001; Liao et al., 2010).

However, it is not sufficient to simply bring such suppliers into a network and integrate them as network members. Instead, sustainable competitive advantage requires perpetual network coordinating capability (Roh et al., 2011). In this sense, the coordinating mechanisms of Japanese automobile manufacturers (e.g., encouraging competition among suppliers while promoting long-term trust relationships) have contributed to the formation of successful networks (Asnuma, 1997). Japanese OEMs in the automobile industry often loan their design blueprints/templates and provide technical support to their suppliers with weak development capability. These OEMs also provide their suppliers with different types of technical support step by step according to their current needs (e.g., loan design templates, approve design specifications, and sell design systems). Such network relationships between OEMs and their suppliers do not stop after one particular transaction but continue with long-term relationships.

No OEM ever commits all the component parts to one supplier. At least a two-supplier system is maintained for encouraging a healthy level of competition between them. A network does not end with one business cycle, but expands and grows with the on-going relationship for sustainable competitive advantage. Li and Wang (2007) focus on coordination mechanisms that influence the goals of supply chain members. For example, if firms in a supply chain behave quite independently, the total supply chain is negatively affected. An effective value chain management requires managing incentives within the supply chain (Narayanan and Raman, 2004). Three practical recommendations involve examining any changes of incentives by (1) contract-driven solution, (2) information-based solution, and (3) trust-based solution. Sahin and Robinson (2002) also discuss the value of information and physical flow coordination. On the other hand, in their analysis of the relationship between the U.S. auto manufacturers and their suppliers, Liker and Choi (2004) list six steps for successful supplier relationships: (1) understand the suppliers' practices, (2) encourage competition among suppliers, (3) be directly involved with suppliers, (4) develop the technological capability of suppliers, (5) share information with selected suppliers, and (6) involve suppliers for improvement programs.

In this book we define network capability as a firm's ability to effectively manage its supply chain in keeping with its unique organizational and product architecture for sustainable competitive advantage. Our special focus is on the role of IT as a primary coordination and integration mechanism for one's own organizational resources and those of the entire supply chain.

1.2.3 Innovation and Network Capability

Firms build their competitive advantage based on their own core competence plus a strong network with other firms. A primary source of core competence is innovation capability. A brief discussion in this section covers a few important elements of innovation and their relationship with network capability.

Innovation debates by Shumpeter (1934, 1942) experienced a paradigm shift with Kuhn (1970). Since then, rich streams of innovation research cover both demand and supply sides of innovation. A fair overview of innovation literature must consider (1) incremental innovation and dominant design, (2) path dependence and network exogeneity, (3) disruptive innovation, (4) innovation dispersion, and (5) open innovation.

First, let us start with dominant design and incremental innovation. Tushman and Anderson (1986) characterize technological change as gradual transformation and intermittent discontinuity. Such discontinuity includes ability enhancing discontinuity by existing firms and ability disruptive discontinuity by new entrant firms. Both of these patterns impact environmental factors (i.e., uncertainty and growth potential). Tushman and Rosenkopf (1992) believe technological change occurs not only by internal technological elements but also by nontechnological factors (e.g., organizational relationships, organizational selection criteria). They also offer mutual interactions between technology life cycle and social impact intensity. The four stages of technological development are technological discontinuity, an era of ferment, emergence of a dominant design, and incremental change based on this design. Technological products/systems are comprised of four types: (1) open systems, the most complex form, in which a set of diverse systems are linked together through interface technologies; (2) closed systems, which are the set of subsystems with clear boundaries that form islands of separate autonomy; (3) Simple assembled products, the simplest form, in which standalone automated machines or equipment are grouped together as part of either a closed or open system; and (4) non-assembled products, which are part of simple assembled products that exist in the form of either work-in-process or materials.

Abernathy and Utterback (1978) distinguish product innovation and process innovation. They discuss innovation evolution process in terms of close interrelationships among competitive strategy, production ability, and dependence on organizational structure. In the early fluid stage it is unclear what particular technology would become prominent and thus quite chaotic. With little economies-of-scale effect, the small organization is advantageous with small scale of production–distribution turnovers. In the period of establishment, prominent lead products fix their dominant design. Process innovation occurs in ways to achieve drastic cost reduction and functionality improvement. By this time, economies of scale become important, and thus organization for mass production takes place. Thus, firms are less responsive to the demand pattern changes and technological innovation. Any industry in general passes through three stages (i.e., fluid, transitional, and specific). The rate of product innovation is highest in the early introduction stage. As it moves through fluid, transitional, and specific stages, the extent of innovation becomes increasingly smaller. However, the rate of process innovation slowly increases. By the time of the transitional period, it is the highest, and then it slows down in the specific stage. Such process innovation enables firms to maintain the most appropriate and efficient organizational structure to satisfy the users' requirements. They implement a standardized design format that has passed the market test and satisfies all legal requirements. Thus a particular product that enters in the specific stage achieves optimal conditions in terms of cost, volume, and production capability. In this stage the degree of both product and process innovation becomes quite minimal. With the passing of time the size of customer demand becomes fixed, dominant design is complete, and the product reaches the mature stage in which intense competition occurs in the market. Examples of dominant design are the IBM 360 for computer products, Ford's Model T for automobiles, and the Boeing 747 in the aircraft industry. As a particular dominant design is accepted as the industry standard, a firm's effort is geared toward product differentiation, not radical innovation.

Clark (1985) explains the direction and timing of technological progress based on the A-U model of Abernathy and Utterback (1978). His theory is about examining mutual interactions between design selection and customer choice. It better explains the innovation process compared to the previous theory of natural emergence of technology or theory of customer demand. Focusing on innovation stages, his research questions explore (1) the transitions between the product innovation and process innovation and (2) individual behavioral principles that govern the emerging patterns of particular innovation. Thus, innovation decision making involves influence of organizational hierarchy. Product designers wrestle to determine what specific external factors to consider for product features while customers pay attention to functionality aspects instead. Thus, the interactions between designers and customers are important. Extending these research findings, Henderson and Clark (1990) noticed the frequent failures of many firms even with slight technological change. They then promoted a theory of architectural innovation which examines the interactions between (1) the relational structure among product components and (2) the knowledge system of an organization. They classified the patterns of innovation in terms of *incremental* (strengthening technology linkage requirements and improving previous weak elements), *modular* (linkage elements plus changes in previous structural elements), *architectural* (changing linkage elements and replacing previous structural elements), and *radical* (changing linkage elements and drastic change of structural components). Henderson (1991) observes technological change patterns based on the case study of the semiconductor photolithographic alignment equipment industry. A fruitful study of technological progress patterns requires understanding of both (1) the physical laws governing particular technological mechanisms and (2) the sociological and organizational contexts in which any technology is created and used. Continuous technological progress by dominant design is the result of ongoing interactions between the sociological positioning of customers and the complementary nature of technological elements. Pinch and Bijker (1987) suggest that a study of sociological elements for technology is important just as in any serious research of scientific knowledge. They take an example of the bicycle tire. In the early stage, the front wheel tire of the bike was quite large. In response to the feedback from the diverse sociological groups the dominant design has changed as in the current form. This is the essence of sociological elements. On the other hand, Abernathy and Clark (1985) determine four types of innovation based on technology and market matrix: (1) *architectural* (new market and new technology), *niche creation* (new market and existing technology), *regular* (existing market and existing technology), and *revolutionary* (existing market and new technology). Each type takes different evolution patterns and management environments.

Second, path dependence is important for innovation. Path dependence (David, 1985) and network exogeneity (Kats and Shapiro, 1985) may result in technological constraints in the context of mutually dependent relationships. It may become a dysfunctional mechanism by which any outstanding technology fails to fulfill its value potential. David (1985) explained the historical process of how English keyboard configuration (i.e., QWERTY) was established as a widespread acceptance by using the concept of path dependence theory. He suggests that new keyboard configurations be established using non-economic elements (e.g., intuition and ergonomics), rather than with economic ones (e.g., cost and benefits). With the early mechanical typewriter, the faster the typing speed the greater the chance of getting keystrokes stuck together. To prevent such an undesirable effect, the keyboard configuration was designed to slow down the typing speed. However, with a digital computer keyboard, it is no longer necessary to separate letters that are frequently used in sequence. Even so, the keyboard configuration is still maintained as it was in the past. That is, because keyboard users are familiar with the "QWERTY" configuration, a new configuration of the keyboard is not welcome. Such path dependence prevents people from accepting new innovation. Throughout history such examples are not uncommon. A great paradigm shift requires overcoming such path dependence tendency (Kuhn, 1970). In the course of explaining the relationship between economics and innovation, Arthur (1988) notes that the model of increasing rate of return has multiple equilibrium points. He also used the concept of network exogeneity to show why certain technologies, though not so outstanding at all, survive for a long time. Shapiro and Hal (1999) discuss technological availability as an important competitive factor of standardization decision. A firm may sell its products before its competitors introduce their own in the market. If not, it may spread out rumors to control customers' expectation. Otherwise, it may decide in advance development plans or innovation roadmaps. The key is to manage anticipation to create path dependence in the minds of customers.

Third, disruptive innovation is what shifts this existing paradigm of innovation (Christensen, 1997). This is stronger than incremental innovation in terms of intensity and impact, and thus it disrupts the current organizational system order. Such disruptive innovation works in ways that affect the nature of social economy and firm competitiveness. People are fascinated by these successful innovation stories because outstanding business leaders experience creative destruction in the course of achieving such disruptive innovation.

Fourth, it is critical to identify a target leader through innovation diffusion. Rodgers (1983) argued the innovation patterns as in S-shaped curve because diverse factors (e.g., communication channels, social systems, and time) influence the innovation diffusion intensity rates. Rodgers (1983) classifies the customers into five segments based on the order of selecting new products: Innovators, Early Adopters, Early Majority, Late Majority, and Laggards.

Rodgers (1983) derived the S-shaped bell curve of cumulative frequency distribution that shows how different types of customers impact on diffusion of innovation. Figure 1.1 shows that the 16% line which is the total percentage of innovators and opinion leaders coincides with the very point from which the S-shaped curve rapidly accelerates upward. This shows that successful distribution to opinion leaders is the critical aspect of success of disruptive innovation. The first group among the five patterns that purchases the new products are the innovators, but they account for only 2.5% of potential customers. They are adventurous and less price sensitive, and they do not necessarily follow the social norms. On the other hand, the early adopters are 13.5% of total customers, and they are respected in their belonging group and exercise substantial influence as opinion leaders. These early adopters get access to the product information, purchase the products, make assessments and evaluation, and spread the word around to their neighbors and friends. Their scope of influence thus is quite diverse and broad. They express their opinions saying, "Such and

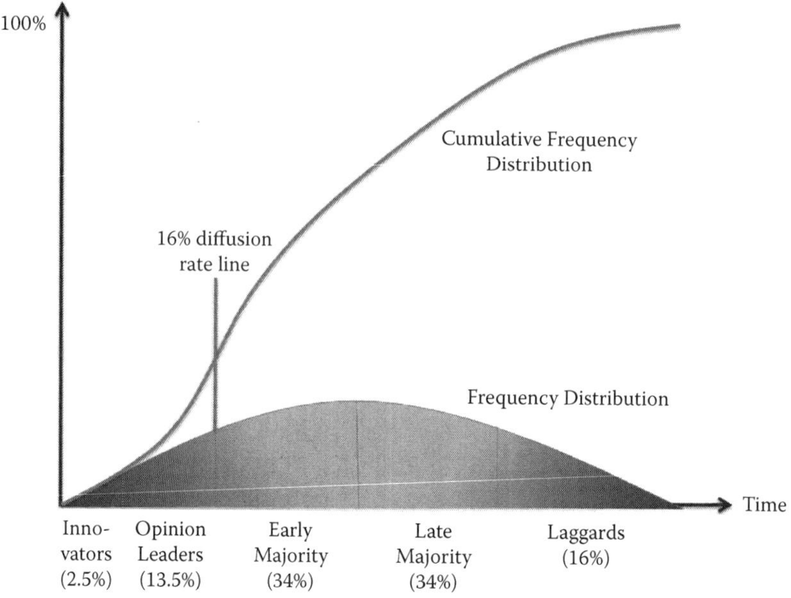

FIGURE 1.1
Innovation diffusion. Adapted from Rodgers (1983).

such product is quite good." Their positive words of recommendation influence enough for the next 34% of the Early Majority so that they are persuaded to try the new products as well. Somewhat indifferent to their income level, these opinion leaders purchase new products they like and derive a tremendous sense of satisfaction. These early adopters emerge as the new customer groups that experience the new products, services, and their technological components. Besides, their opinion matters. They are in a sense prime movers and shakers for creating a new customer base for the innovative products. Among global firms Sony is well known for its effective utilization of early adopters for marketing its new products.

Von Hippel (1986) emphasized the importance of lead users. He argues for market research by involving lead users that have very strong desire for innovative products and services. By analyzing such lead users, it is quite useful to conduct more effective market research for any new products. These lead users too often provide a fresh idea for new products. Their voice is quite important. Patterns of technological progress show S-shaped curves, and in a matter of time firms experience the plateau for any innovative products they introduce in the market (Foster, 1986; Foster and Kaplan, 2001). Firms therefore must anticipate such moments of deteriorating product values and plan in advance for bold investment for developing brand new innovative products.

Fifth, open innovation (Figure 1.2). Change in the business environment is quite rapid. Increasingly, firms accelerate their response to the external market environment. In this context, it is inevitable that firms move away from closed innovation to open innovation (Chesbrough, 2004). Openness refers to pulling knowledge for innovation. This presumes that knowledge contributors may freely access others' sources for necessary input needs. So they may not exercise exclusive rights for their output of their innovation (Chesbrough and Appleyard, 2007).

Values created through open processes are similar to those of public goods. Consumers benefit by these values, and no other users can be excluded. The values of openness are (1) improving the quality of products as users offer ideas and comments; (2) utilizing network effects (Chesbrough and Appleyard, 2007). Open innovation products (e.g., MySpace, YouTube, Wikipedia, and Linux) are different from traditional business strategies in that the ownership of resources value is not limited to particular individuals but to external voluntary contributors. It does not fit to the business model of Porter (1987) in that they do not exclude other users who might imitate or use these products. Google and Yahoo still make enormous profits, although similar search engine technologies are available to others. Microsoft did not stop the rapid growth of Google. The traditional strategy

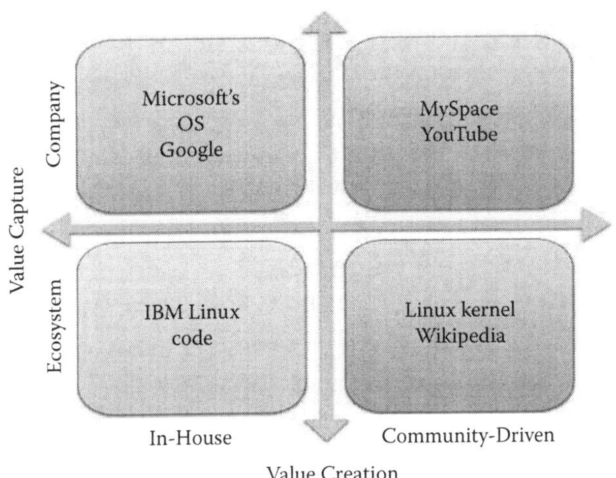

FIGURE 1.2
Open innovation. Adapted from Chesbrough (2007).

theory has focused on ownership, barriers of entry, switching costs, and competition by industry. Thus, open innovation topics such as motivation for individual voluntary participation and the role of community participation, innovation network construction, and ecosystem are somewhat new and different. Some important recent research findings are: (1) the depth and width of pooled knowledge is much bigger than what any individuals can offer (the power of knowledge creation through open invention); (2) sound ecosystems use network effects and open perpetual applications of architecture (the value of ecosystem creation through open coordination); (3) pooling knowledge into system architecture contributes to the creation of superior products and services through open invention and open coordination (the role of open business models in open source software (OSS).

Any firms associated with innovation processes may shut down their own innovation processes and instead exercise their rights on the knowledge assets and acquire the value derived from particular innovation. For example, in the case of Microsoft's source code of operation system (OS), much of the value creation benefit is delivered to particular firms, and the ecosystem that surrounds them also acquires additional benefits as well. Therefore, what is instrumental to coordinate values created through open innovation is an architecture that combines the scattered knowledge. Without proper sense of judgment on how to manage a system, open knowledge may not provide useful solutions for problems. Strategic value of open innovation is achieved by creating and sustaining values while not isolating any individuals, communities, or the participants of the ecosystem.

Many firms adopt open innovation to sustain value creation and knowledge acquisition in contrast to the motivated individuals and communities that take open initiatives. Network capability is thus the ability to form, coordinate, and manage open innovation. In this book, it shows how Korean mobile firms maintain their competitiveness through applying open architecture and building network environments in the era of smart phones. In selecting de jure standard/de facto standard for technological standards, network capability is worthy of careful discussion. For the formulation of de facto standard five patterns are observed: (1) market leadership through monopolistic technology infrastructure; (2) technological monopoly by pooling system; (3) technological standard determination by particular organizations; (4) taking technological initiatives through winning competition in the market; (5) business strategy open technological competition (Shintaku et al., 2000). De facto standard does not mean that the review organization (e.g., ISO or JIS) defines rules and standards, but actual standards that survived in the market competition. De facto standard reflects an element of business strategy that considers intense competition by some dominant design or design rules (Abernathy, 1978; Baldwin and Clark, 2000). Microsoft's OS, VHS in the analog VTR era, and the Blu-ray standard of DVD discs in the digital generation are all examples of de facto standards. De facto standard competition takes market share more seriously than attaining technological superiority. In regard to Microsoft's OS case, it has caught up with GUI GUI-equipped Apple in 1986 through MS-DOS in 1981 and Windows95 in 1995, and since then it has maintained absolute market advantage. The 16% theory by Rodgers (1983) affirms that in any market a new product becomes quite successful when it exceeds the 10% of population acceptance, and then distribution boom is achieved when its acceptance reaches 10% to 30% of the population. However, household electronics show strong commoditization tendency as modular products. Too often de facto standard is established even when the distribution rate of a particular electronic product is no more than 2% to 3% distribution rate in the relevant population.

Compatibility and connectivity between hardware/software also play a critical role for product distribution rate (Shintaku et al., 2000). In the case of VHS standard competition and DVD disc standard competition, the software/contents that are connected to particular hardware quickly attain competitively advantageous distribution rate. HD DVD by Toshiba lost in the disc standard battle to Blu-ray standard organization not by the disc's memory volume but by contents supply side. Toshiba with its $99 model (with half price advantage over Blu-ray standard products) temporarily kept the record sales. In 2007 the sales of Toshiba (HD DVD) were no more than half of Blu-ray Disc, and since then, Toshiba's market performance did not improve. What is important for long-term market success is not just mere sales performance of a particular product at the beginning, but the scope of compatibility and connectivity of software/contents with other products. Therefore, in this book network capability is considered as a critical component for sustainable competitive advantage.

1.3 ORGANIZATION OF THE BOOK

Hamel and Prahalad (1990) explain the relationship between core competence and market (Figure 1.3). Their framework contains dynamic

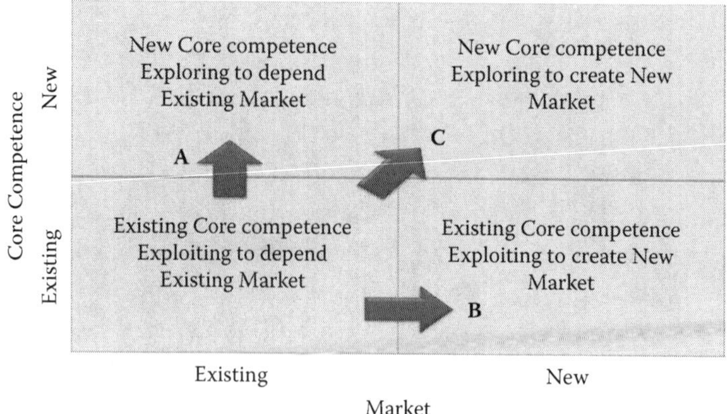

FIGURE 1.3
Renewal of the core competence. Source: Adapted from Hamel and Prahalad (1990).

processes. We adapt their framework to our analytical models of Korean and Japanese firms and offer the characteristics of a network capability. The network competence and technological competence of Ritter and Gemunden (2002) corresponds to the market competence and technological competence of Danneels (2002). In our book we define network capability—as an extension of these above mentioned concepts—as "the unique ability to sense new and emerging market needs and thus to explore and exploit the external resources" (Figure 1.4).

This book is an effort to understand how Korean global firms have built their competitive advantage in a short period of time. With its geographical proximity to Japan, Korea has closely observed how Japan rapidly developed as the number two economic power in the world under inadequate natural resources constraints and unfavorable conditions after World War II. In 1945 Japan had virtually no real industrial technological base. Yet, with vigorous industry development policies of the Japanese government, Japanese firms rapidly acquired the technological know-how of U.S.-based and European firms, built manufacturing (*monozukuri*) and process innovation capabilities, and thus achieved fast economic growth. Japanese firms also benefited through the Korean War in the early 1950s that required rapid deployment of huge amounts of goods, products, and services. Korea learned from these Japanese experiences. Both Japanese and Korean rapid economic growth involved rapid catch-up of technological capabilities plus building of national economic engines through export-driven opportunities. Furthermore, Korean firms observed how U.S. manufacturing firms (e.g., electronics and automobile

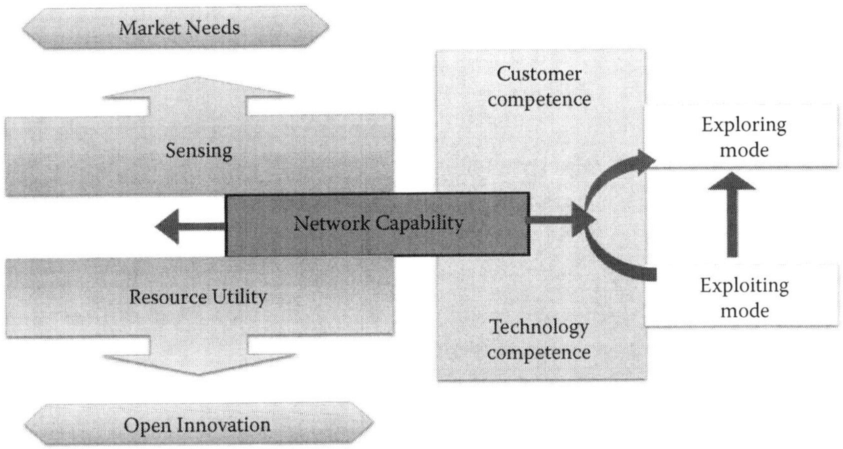

Figure 1.4

Network capability.

manufacturers) have lost their competitive advantage as Japanese firms quickly attained competitive strengths through their effective catch-up practices and sustained process innovations. Some U.S. firms slowed down their vigorous innovation efforts and instead collected royalty fees based on their existing technological patents. In the analysis of why innovating firms or nations are not able to keep reaping economic benefits, Teece (1986) argued for the importance of complementary assets in addition to innovative capabilities. Manufacturing capabilities in particular are emphasized as a main aspect of these complementary assets. U.S. TV manufacturers (e.g., RCA) had offered license to Japanese firms, which in turn achieved the rapid catch-up of both innovative and manufacturing capabilities. Such transitions contributed to the demise of U.S. TV manufacturers. Therefore, any firm that achieves product innovation may soon lose its competitive advantage if it does not secure complementary assets in the forms of manufacturing, marketing, and logistical capabilities. The rival firms may easily catch up with the innovative product features and thus the front innovator soon loses its competitive advantage.

Catch-up time periods may differ depending on the industry architecture. If product architecture is close to modular, the catch-up speed is much faster, because the horizontal industry structure is easy for imitation and replication. The structure of the computer industry (with the emergence of modular product architecture) quickly changed from vertical to horizontal integration (Pisano and Teece, 2007). In similar fashion, in the semiconductor industry analog product development was quickly switched to digital. The industry structure patterns also rapidly changed, and catch-up speed between nations was also affected. In this changing technological environment, it is highly likely that an integral product architecture soon adapts to a modular one. Any firms that depend on their early innovative capabilities soon lose their competitive edge. In this sense, the *monozukuri* capabilities of Japanese firms drove the leading U.S. electronics firms out of the market. Complementary assets in the form of manufacturing capabilities are quite critical for sustainable market advantage. Both the Korean government and Korean firms learned through Japanese examples how to catch up and gain competitive advantage in the global market. Korean firms started focusing on the global market because of its relatively small domestic market. Korean firms soon realized the strategic importance of complementary assets in the form of customer and marketing competence (Danneels, 2002; Christensen et al., 2002). Just as U.S. firms fell into a competence trap with the rapid catch-up of Japanese firms, it seems that Japanese firms also experienced a similar organizational trap in spite of their outstanding technology development and quality in the past (March, 1991).

In view of such competitive contexts, this book examines (1) the learning processes of Korean firms from Japanese counterparts, (2) the role of industry policy of the Korean government, and (3) the critical importance of product architecture in LCD and mobile phones for their global market competitiveness. The role of the Korean government for industry network construction is featured in Chapter 2. Additional historical backgrounds and growth processes of Korean semiconductors, LCD, and mobile phones through case studies are extended up to Chapter 5. Chapter 6 focuses on the Hyundai-Kia case that illustrates the emergence of Korean automobile manufacturers as representative of integral product architecture. Chapter 7 explores further into owner management leadership and IT utilization with case illustrations. Chapters 8 and 9 highlight the differences between Japanese and Korean firms in terms of IT usage in product development through case studies as well. Chapters 10 and 11 explain the differences between Japanese and Korean firms, not only in product development and organizational competence, but also in IT usage competence. Key details of each chapter are summarized as below.

1.3.1 Chapter 1, "What is Network Capability? Introduction, Framework, and Contents"

This chapter defines network capability based on the existing literature. In the environment of global markets building capabilities is an important concern. The business environment in three countries in North East Asia (Japan, Korea, and China) show dynamic growths, changes, and challenges. This book deals with the topic of building network capabilities in turbulent global environments. The definition of "network capability" originally related to (1) broadcast organizations such as TV and radio that utilize regional, national, or international communication networks, (2) interactive task relationships in computerized process management, and (3) social interrelated relationships that are connected for mutual benefits. As network concepts are employed in business management, the term "network capability" now refers to systematic connectivity between a focal company and all the interrelated entities that form a vital stakeholder group for the shared goals and mission. As the technology environment changes from the analog period to the digital age, the global business environment requires accelerating speed management. No firm can maintain its competitive advantage with its single efforts alone. This book particularly examines how Asian global firms and small and medium venture firms not only accomplished rapid catch-up with the leading firms of North America and Europe but also established their global competitive advantage through developing their unique network capabilities. This book examines in detail "network capability" which continues to develop and enhance core competencies and global competitive advantage by the interrelated socio-technological collaborative infrastructures.

1.3.2 Chapter 2, "Korean IT Industry and Network Leadership: A Comparative Study with Japanese Experiences"

There has been substantial discussion in regard to the phenomenal growth of the Korean IT industry. Despite extensive studies on the Korean IT industry, there is very little research that focuses on the complex role of the Korean government. This chapter presents the success factors of the Korean semiconductor and mobile communication industries that represent the Korean IT industry. These Korean examples are compared with examples of their Japanese counterparts. We also examine the impact of Korean governmental policies on network leadership formation, an industry competitive environment, and global technological standardization. Management implications are presented as well.

1.3.3 Chapter 3, "Growth Mechanism and Management of Korean Firms: A Comparative Study with Japanese Experiences"

In this intensive global competitive environment, firms increasingly expand their own resource base and integrate the diverse interorganizational capabilities to create new value chain organizational capabilities. In this context, innovative learning capabilities are essential to effectively respond to the changes of external market reality—particularly customer value transformations.

This chapter shows a growth mechanism of the Korean economy, particularly through the case analysis of two Korean global firms—Samsung Electronics (SE) and Hyundai-Kia Motor Company (HKMC). We present a research model, case history, and the results of in-depth interviews of senior executives of these two firms. We also examine the factors how SE and HKMC have grown as global firms in a relatively short period.

We pay special attention to the role of the owner/CEO in development of organizational capability in a Korean business context. We also discuss how two different firms translate "speedy owner/CEO decision making and large scale of investment" into sustainable competitive advantage through the use of IT and organizational learning from a product architecture perspective.

1.3.4 Chapter 4, "Product Architecture and Technology Transfer: New Catch-Up Patterns in the Digital Era"

This chapter shows relationships between product architecture and technology transfer: New catch-up patterns in the digital era. Rapid modularization of product architecture occurs by firmware (i.e., control software for all digital products) that uses semiconductor CPUs. The technology transfers take place from Japanese firms to Korean and other NIEs nations (Hong Kong, Taiwan, and Singapore). Transitions from analog to the digital era impact catch-up patterns and global technology transfer mode as well. This chapter explains this phenomenon with the illustrative examples of the Japanese CD/DVD industry. These case illustrations of Japanese firms show how firms from Korea and other NIEs nations adopt different patterns of catch-up in the digital era quite different from Japanese firms that learned from firms from the United States and Europe.

1.3.5 Chapter 5, "Korean Semiconductor Industry: A Comparative Study with Japanese Counterparts"

The Korean semiconductor industry has grown with a proactive industrial policy of the Korean government and with the aggressive investment of Korean semiconductor firms. However, the global market share of Korean firms in the memory semiconductor sector is no more than 20%. In this context, it is noteworthy to examine the whole picture of the Korean semiconductor industry from the standpoint both of the memory and non-memory sectors. Particularly, the price drop of the memory semiconductor is closely related to product/business architecture. For this reason, it is meaningful to compare the Korean and Japanese semiconductor industries from the product/business architecture perspective. In the 1990s, Korean semiconductor firms displayed their superior performance over their Japanese counterparts with their competitive strengths; however, in the 2000s, with the specialization of business architecture (i.e., separation of design and manufacturing), Korean firms are drastically losing their competitiveness. Instead, American venture firms that specialize in semiconductor design and Taiwanese foundry firms dominate the global market. In this respect, it is critical for Korean and Japanese firms to learn how to adapt their long-term strategy. In brief, this study compares and contrasts the Korean and Japanese semiconductor industries and provides an insight on how Korean and Japanese firms compete in the evolving semiconductor industry.

1.3.6 Chapter 6, "Korean LCD Industry: Product Architecture and Global Supply Chain Management of LCD"

In the LCD industry LCD panel makers operate in between upstream component suppliers and downstream LCD TV. Since component parts are the larger portion of total LCD's overall costs, it is critical for the LCD industry to attain supply chain integration with its component part suppliers. This chapter examines (1) the LCD industry structure from the perspective of product architecture and (2) the supply chain management (SCM) strategy of the Korean LCD industry. Korean firms possess a substantial competitive advantage in the large-scale LCD global TV market. We, with case illustrations, analyze how Korean firms have built their SCM system. We also present lessons of how product architecture affects the nature of global SCM and practical examples of how Korean LCD manufacturers implement supply chain integration with upstream component parts manufacturers.

1.3.7 Chapter 7, "Korean TV Industry: A Case Study of LG Electronics"

The global market demand for flat-panel display (FPD) TV has been rapidly growing for more than 10 years. However, very few studies are available in regard to the strategic or operational-level analysis of FPD TV and its global market dynamics. This case study explores how LG Electronics (LGE) has adopted modular product architecture to both FPD and LCD TV across both upstream and downstream of the supply chain. In addition, LGE has implemented unique operational management practices (LG Production System) applying the Toyota Production System. Such integration of product architecture and operational practices has secured its globally competitive market position. This case study suggests the importance of the integration of both the business model and operational practices for sustainable competitive advantages.

1.3.8 Chapter 8, "Korean Mobile Phone Industry: Product Architecture of Mobile Phones and Network Capability"

Increasingly, the product architecture of electronic products is rapidly moving toward modularity. Little has been examined about the product architecture of mobile phones from the standpoint of product development. The modularization trend in the mobile communication industry is examined first. A special focus is on network strategy of smart mobile phones and module design strategy of webstores that offer diverse applications. Both the new mobile phone businesses (e.g., Apple, Google) and the traditional global firms (e.g., Samsung and LG) emphasize leader-driven innovation revitalization in the areas of innovative contents development and rapid distribution through mobile operations system platform (MOSP), which is the key of the emerging Smartphone market expansion and applications. The dominant leaders of the mobile phone operation systems (OS) intensify their efforts to establish de facto standards like 4G communication standards for their competitiveness, just as Microsoft did in the PC market. It is then critical to create an open network environment (e.g., application webstore) through which lead users initiate and sustain innovation.

1.3.9 Chapter 9, "Suppliers Support for Supply Chain Integration: The Korean Automobile Industry and the Steel Industry"

Business organizations of the twenty-first century operate in the context of dynamic network relationships along with information flows, customers, suppliers, and competitors. It is essential for firms to implement supply chain management, fulfill multiple and rapidly changing customer requirements, and sustain their competitive advantage through internal and external collaborations. With an increasing level of globalization, firms are expected to construct an e-logistics infrastructure and service offerings that overcome the limits of time and space constraints. As one of four leading export-based growing industries (along with the semiconductor, electronics, and shipbuilding industries) in Korea, these auto manufacturers continue to expand their operations in the global market. Accordingly, effective uses of global supply chain management become more important than ever. In contrast to global multinational companies in Korea, small and medium-sized (SME) suppliers that support them are usually small and quite vulnerable to changes (Youn et al., 2008). Recently, the policy of the Korean government shows a noticeable shift to achieve equitable growth in the supply chain. As an illustration of this changing policy focus, this study shows how Hyundai-Kia Motor Company (HKMC) strengthens their supplier base through developing product development capabilities and the overall competency of their supply chain. Details of business practices and their implications are discussed.

1.3.10 Chapter 10, "Product Development of Japanese Electronics Industry"

Effective product development depends on how firms utilize their product architecture in achieving their comparative advantage. In this respect, the usage patterns of computer-aided design (CAD) have serious implications in the ways firms utilize their product architecture. In this study, we first present a research framework about product architecture in electronic products. Our inquiry is extended to compare the product architecture and CAD usage patterns of electronic products. We explore computer-aided design (CAD) usage patterns in Japanese firms. To analyze our research model, we applied an "integral architecture index," which has a dozen specific measures of architectural characteristics of each product. We also present our research methods and findings of survey questionnaires collected from selected Japanese electronics manufacturers. These integrative and comparative analyses suggest that product architecture and CAD usage patterns between two products (i.e., automobile products and electronic products) are quite different, and the product development of Japanese electronics manufacturers tends to be near integral architecture. In conclusion, we discuss over-spec problem of product development of Japanese firms through these findings.

1.3.11 Chapter 11, "IT Usage Strategy of Korean Firms: Case Studies of Mobile Display Manufacturers"

Many firms in today's business environment utilize diverse information systems to sustain their competitive advantages. However, too often the return of investment on information technologies is not as obvious as expected. This is particularly true with many small and medium enterprises (SMEs). This study presents a research model and examines how mobile display manufacturers implement their information systems for the enhancement of supply chain performance. For the purpose of this research, we involved two firms and considered critical success factors of their information integration practices. One successful firm links its existing database to new information systems and aligns its information system for the larger requirements of supply chains. Another firm possesses different organizational capabilities and accordingly shows poor outcomes. Our findings are based on extensive interviews with IT executives, supply chain professionals, and IT vendors within the supply chain network of these two firms.

1.3.12 Chapter 12, "IT Usage Strategy of Japanese Firms: Product Life Cycle Management for the Global Market"

In this rapidly changing business environment, Japanese firms have put much emphasis on effective product life cycle management (PLM) for sustainable competitive advantage in the global market. In this study, we present a research model of product life cycle management that depicts the essential elements of PLM in terms of processes and outcomes. Four case studies of large Japanese firms examine the business practices that support their global market strategy through specific PLM practices which include data exchanges, design knowledge management, supplier integration, and BOM (Bill of Materials) design. These case studies suggest that PLM practices are implemented differently according to strategic focus, product, and market characteristics. Lessons from the case studies are discussed as well.

1.3.13 Chapter 13, "Integrated Manufacturing and IT Strategy for Futuristic PLM: A Conceptual Framework from Japanese Firms"

Different from traditional IT systems, a futuristic IT system requires fast utilization of design information in new product development according to customer value requirements. This paper presents a conceptual framework of futuristic PLM from the standpoint of integrated manufacturing. This futuristic PLM model, in contrast to the traditional PLM model, translates customer values into product development and emphasizes the importance of integration of product design reflecting customer needs, design feedback, and management strategy. Three case studies illustrate the practical applications of this research framework. Managerial implications are discussed as well.

1.3.14 Chapter 14, "Conclusion"

The key differences between Korean and Japanese firms in terms of their competitiveness are explained. Japanese firms experienced catch-up in analog periods and thus utilized Japanese skilled workers for the enormous scope of process innovation. On the other hand, Korean firms engaged in catch-ups in the digital age and thus drastically shortened their learning cycle for product innovation and utilized IT system capability for their global market penetration. Both Japanese and Korean firms need to excel in ways that demonstrate their market leader capability to create and deliver products and services that meet the changing needs of customers in the ever-expanding global market. These customers continue to seek innovative, noble, and fantastic cultural and innovative values that fit their cultural, social, and technological norms and thus enhance what they define the outstanding quality of life.

2

Korean IT Industry and Network Leadership: A Comparative Study with Japanese Experiences

There has been substantial discussion in regard to the phenomenal growth of the Korean IT industry. Despite extensive studies on the Korean IT industry, little research has ever focused on the complex roles of the Korean government. This article presents the success factors of the Korean semiconductor and mobile communication industries that represent the Korean IT industry. These Korean examples are compared with those of Japanese counterparts. This article also examines the impact of Korean governmental policies on network leadership formation, the competitive environment of the industry, and global technological standardization. Management implications are presented as well.

2.1 INTRODUCTION

As of 2009, Korea has attained the global rank of fifteenth in terms of economic outputs. (In 2003, Korea attained the global rank of eleventh in terms of GDP.) Such rapid economic progress within 40 years is noticeable when considering that for a similar level of economic progress other industrial nations usually took more than a 100 years of historical processes. After experiencing dramatic successes in the heavy chemical, shipbuilding, automobile, and steel industries, recently high value-added and knowledge industry products such as semiconductors, liquid-crystal displays (LCDs), and mobile phones are leading Korea's economic growth. The IT industry in particular has been a driving force for Korea's economic growth since the 1997 Currency Crisis. IT is closely associated with the rapid productivity growth in the manufacturing and service sectors which focused on radical process improvement and efficient resource utilization. In 2004, 50% of the GDP growth was attributed to IT's contribution (Kim and Jung, 2005). Since 1999, the Korean IT industry's annual growth rate is 17.7%, which far exceeds the global average. In a sense, the Korean IT industry enabled Korea to overcome its economic crisis (November 27, 1997 to August 23, 2001) and is regarded as its core driving force for economic leaps. In brief, the Korean IT industry has positioned itself as the vital growth engine for the healthy growth of the Korean economy (ETNEWS, 2005.12.26).

Within the Korean IT industry, dynamic random access memory (DRAM), code division multiple access (CDMA) mobile phone, thin film transistor (TFT)-LCD, and digital TV are some of the world's best industrial goods (E. Lee, 2003). In 2009, semiconductors, mobile phones, and displays occupied the top second to fourth of the major export items of Korea. These three items in fact account for 25.5% of the total exports values.

And the mobile communication sector has shown an outstanding level of growth. Samsung Electronics (hereafter Samsung) and LG Electronics (hereafter LG), Korea's two top mobile phone leaders, are third and fourth in the rankings of global mobile communication companies. Samsung alone accounts for 15% of Korea's total exports (B. C. Lee, 2003).

The growth patterns of Korean global firms like Samsung and LG are better understood in the context of the rapid economic growth of Korea (Table 2.1). Since 1960, Korea has experienced vigorous economic growth through concerted government initiatives (Hattori, 1996). Certainly, the Korean government considered the diverse growth models of developed

TABLE 2.1

Changes of Top Five Major Industry-Level Export Items

Rank	1990	2000	2009
1	Clothing/textiles (11.7%)	Semiconductors (15.1%)	Shipbuilding (12.4%)
2	Semiconductors (7.0%)	Computers (8.5%)	Semiconductors (8.5%)
3	Shoes (6.6%)	Automobiles (7.7%)	Hand phones (8.5%)
4	Video equipment (5.6%)	Petrochemicals (5.3%)	Displays (8.5%)
5	Shipbuilding (4.4%)	Shipbuilding (4.9%)	Automobiles (7.0%)

Source: Institute for International Trade, 2010.

nations and adapted them to Korea's situation. Japan, in particular, provided useful models to follow in terms of economic development and business growth. The positive roles of the Korean government for the growth of the Korean economy are well documented (Kim, 2004).

Even in the early 1980s, the Korean IT industry had hardly any of its original technological capabilities. The macro and micro factors of its phenomenal growth are rarely well understood. Little research has ever examined the interactive roles of the government for the growth of the Korean IT industry. In this chapter we raise two general questions and subsequent specific questions: (1) In what way were the policies of the Korean government instrumental to the growth of the Korean IT industry? How did the Korean government establish a network environment as a way of securing Korean IT's competitive capabilities? (2) How different are the Korean experiences compared to those of Japan? What kinds of mechanisms are used to develop constructive competitive business environments for the semiconductor and mobile communication sectors?

To explore the above questions we first examine the theories of economic development, particularly the roles of government. The theory of development state is presented as the theoretical basis of our research framework. We focus on the semiconductor and mobile communication sectors as the basis of our comparison between Korean and Japanese experiences.

2.2 AN ANALYSIS OF ECONOMIC GROWTH MODELS OF EAST ASIA

2.2.1 Literature Review

Two opposing theories (i.e., market-based theory or government-role theory) in regard to the utility of government industrial policies have been debated over the years. Market-based theory focuses on market mechanisms and opposes any free market failure scenarios. On the other hand, government-role theory is derived from the principles of welfare economics that assume the positive roles of government policies and understate the probability of policy failures. These two views are strikingly different in regard to the economic growth of newly industrialized nations (NIEs). According to Amsden (1990), such governmental policies too often disrupt market mechanisms contrary to what government subsidies intend to achieve. Theories that support government industrial policies recognize the positive roles of government (e.g., nurturing strategic infant industries). Wolf (1988) asserts that the government can have a complementary role on free-market shortcomings. The theory of culture highlights the educational systems, quality labor force, and Confucian work ethics. The theory of neighboring impact discusses the geographical proximity and cultural similarity as the primary factor for economic growth (Chang, 2005).

Because Korean economic growth patterns are somewhat similar to those of Japan, we examine the economic development theory in regard to Japan first. Johnson (1982) suggested that Japanese economic miracles are based on Japanese comprehensive practices as a regulatory state which is characterized by respect to market rationalization, effective Japanese banking control, harmonious labor relations, economic bureaucrats' independence, balanced usage of social incentives and command-and-control measures, and the prevalent role of *zaibatsu* and foreign capital.

Utakawa and Abe (1995) list other factors such as careful selection of development priorities, economic and industrial policy implementations by proactive government entities such as the Ministry of International Trade and Industry (MITI), and cooperative relations between the government and private sectors. The Japanese example indicates that a national government may play legitimate roles in terms of the protective growth of infant industries, assisted termination of declining industries, countermeasures for market failures, and the correction of trade imbalances.

In their empirical research, Porter and Takeuchi (2002) argue that Japan's economic success was possible when the government supported free market competition instead of using artificial intervention and control policies. In their analysis of competitive factors, they conclude that banking control, reduction in income taxes, and bond issuances for regional development are temporary measures that have little prospect for success. After the War, Japan's MITI policy measures that were intended to correct the patterns of business competition through industry reconfigurations all proved to be failures except when MITI allowed more businesses to enter the market for intense competition. They recommend that Japanese policy makers and business leaders work toward the formation of effective competitive structures.

In a sense, MITI's selection of strategic industries, openly sharing its policy information, consistent application of its industrial policy, rules for fair opportunity for all, and limiting the time frame for protection of infant industries are all examples of built-in mechanisms by which fierce competition among businesses is promoted.

The theory of the developmental state (NIEs and Korea in particular) considers the positive impact of governmental leadership. Amsden (1989), who applied Johnson's model of the development state in Korea, suggested that the growth factors of Korea include government investment decisions on major industries, corresponding pricing distortion, and selective subsidy payments. This article focuses on network leadership derived from the integration of collaborative and competitive strategies as the basis for the success of the Korean IT industry. The Korean semiconductor and mobile communication sectors adopt a catch-up success model as followers of the United States, Europe, and Japan.

Shin (1996) cites 10 success factors of Korean firms as:

- Securing superior human resources based on human resource first policy
- Indigenousness of cutting-edge core technology through R & D investment
- Proactive business responses to government policies for necessary support
- Business–labor collaboration (cooperation)
- Responsible management with the utilization of professional expert know-how
- Top management foresight of business trends
- Continuous innovative new product development
- Business culture that emphasizes a unified effort for excellence
- Pursuit of a diversification policy
- Global market expansion to overcome the limit of the domestic market

Government-supported policy is again listed as one of five success factors of Korean global business firms (Han, 2002).

For the growth of Korean business, the leapfrogging strategy is also mentioned as an important way for emerging followers to catch up with top leading firms, particularly in the case of the Korean digital TV industry (Lee, 2004). Late starters use the leapfrogging strategy to quickly eliminate the technological gap by jumping over conventional technological development stages. Such leapfrogging entails risks associated with rapid technology development and global market expansion. Even so, such a strategy frequently results in fantastic success through the collaborative effort between the supportive Korean government and daring Korean businesses.

Two success factors for the Korean digital TV industry are government supportive policy and technological quality standardization (Lee, 2004). By 1997, Korean firms had already achieved the level of standardization required by the Federal Communications Commission (FCC) prior to their global market entry.

In spite of the above studies about the Korean economy and particular industries, little research has been attempted to examine the Korean IT industry from comprehensive viewpoints, especially in comparison with that of Japan. As of now, collaborative and competitive strategies are emphasized on the business level and not as a national industrial policy. In general, in the standard competition of strategic IT businesses, their competitive patterns are somewhat unique with a mixture of collaboration and competition.

In the presence of different standards, competitive firms strategically align as partners in the beginning. In the subsequent step, with the achievement of superior standards, firms compete for a greater market share (Ootaki, et al., 2003). In the Japanese video tape recorder (VTR) industry, it is well known how Sony with Betamax and Victor with VHS standards competed (Udagawa et al., 2000). We can also see the same thing in the DVD disc industry between Sony with Blu-ray and Toshiba with HD standards in the 2000s (Figure 2.1).

Analog Era
(Betamax vs. VHS)

Digital Era
(Blu-ray vs. HD)

FIGURE 2.1
Standard competition.

For standardization, two patterns are possible—either a de jure standard set by an official institution or a de facto standard set by network leadership. Without any public institution to control quality standards, a de facto standard is widely accepted in the market, as it was in the case of VHS and Blu-ray through a high level of market domination (Takahashi, 2000). Intel, Microsoft, and Cisco have established de facto standards through rapid technological development in the areas of computers, communications, and electronic equipment. Network (platform) leadership refers to the ability of firms that establish such de facto standards (Gawer and Cusumano, 2002). Practically, it is impossible for any firms (without original technology on their own) to establish such widely accepted network leadership in the rapidly changing digital industry. In this respect, the establishment processes of network leadership by the Korean digital industry are worthy of careful examination.

2.2.2 Research Framework

In our research framework (Figure 2.2), we analyze the success factors of the Korean IT industry based on three assumptions: (1) in the initial stage, private firms are more likely to make a high level of risky investment for innovative technological development if the government provides appropriate incentives of risk sharing; (2) in the commercialization stage, the desirable governmental policy is to encourage competition within the industry; (3) setting widely accepted industry standards is an important strategic goal in the digital industry. Our case analyses focus on two pillars of the Korean IT industry—semiconductors and mobile communication.

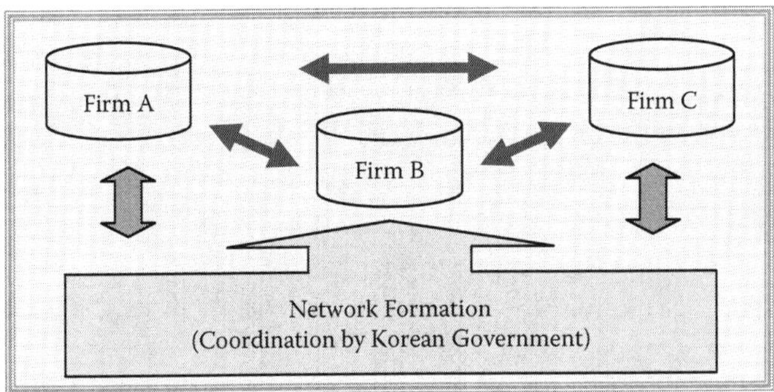

FIGURE 2.2
Research framework.

Since the 1990s, Samsung has positioned itself as a highly successful global firm that specializes in semiconductors, mobile phones, LCD, and digital home appliances. LG also occupies the number three spot in the global mobile phone market. Pantech Group, the third largest in Korea, is one of the top ten global mobile phone marketers. Thus, an examination of these firms provides insight about the success factors of the Korean IT industry as a whole. In Figure 2.2, our research framework shows the roles of the Korean government in the formation of a technological network and a competitive environment. The formation of a network business requires the presence of dominant leaders in the market. However, in the absence of such dominant leaders at the beginning, the government may coordinate industrial policy which is neither planned control nor laissez-faire indifference. Rather, the government works toward the fine balance between the needs for collaboration and competition. The contradictory nature is that partnership demands collaboration, and differentiation requires competition. Network leadership is possible in an environment of competitive collaboration (i.e., joint partnership and fierce competition by multiple key players). Here, we examine the Korean government's policies that strive toward the rapid catching up and continuous speeding up of the Korean IT industry.

2.3 CASE ANALYSIS

2.3.1 Comparison of Korean and Japanese Semiconductor Industry

Both the Korean and the Japanese semiconductor industries were successful in catching up to their counterparts in the United States (Table 2.2). In fewer than ten years (from the mid-1980s to the 1990s), there was a lot of jockeying for position among these three nations. In 1986, the Japanese semiconductor industry surpassed that of the United States; subsequently, in 1992, Korea surpassed Japan (Itami, 2000).

Japan's MITI leadership was based on the policy of arm's-length regulation, smooth policy implementation mechanisms, subsidy, diverse tax incentives, strategic loan programs, and the formation of research cooperatives (Udagawa and Abe, 1995). Building up the Japanese semiconductor industry was not exclusively the results of these government initiatives. As

TABLE 2.2

Success Factors of Korean and Japanese Semiconductor Industries

Category	Korea	Japan
Success model	Catch-up	Catch-up
Government industrial policy	Limitation of 51% ownership; investment on technology development	Various institutional support, subsidies, VLSI Research Cooperative
Research institutes	ETRI (Electronics and Communications Research Institute)	Japanese Telephone Telegraph Cooperation, Electrical Communication Research Institute
Competition for new product development and commercialization	Yes	Yes
Market	Export orientation	Competitive capabilities for domestic market

research institutes, such as ETRI (Electronics and Telecommunications Research Institute), played a significant coordination role among Korean firms, VLSI Research Cooperative, Japanese Telephone Telegraph Corporation, Electrical Communication Research Institute, and other research institutes under MITI also made substantial contributions to the new technology development in Japan (Song, 2005; Udagawa and Abe, 1995).

As of 2010, the Korean semiconductor industry (DRAM) had over a 50% share of the global semiconductor market (Figure 2.3). This occurred in fewer than 50 short years. In the 1960s, the Korean Department of Commerce took strategic initiatives to build up the Korean electronics industry and component parts suppliers. By the 1970s, the emphasis was to increase foreign direct investment for the growth of the Korean electronics industry (Hong, 2004a). During this period, the Korean government implemented supportive measures for domestic business ownership (i.e., foreign ownership is limited to 49% and domestic ownership must be at least 51%). The Korean government invested $400 million in the form of long-term, low-interest-rate loans to build up high-risk wafer manufacturing by large Korean manufacturers. Such an effort was similar to what the Japanese MITI did for the VLSI Research Cooperatives (Hong, 2004a). In reality, the Korean government supported 40% to 60% of R & D expenditures during this period (Song, 2005). It also provided necessary tax incentives for enhancing the technological capabilities

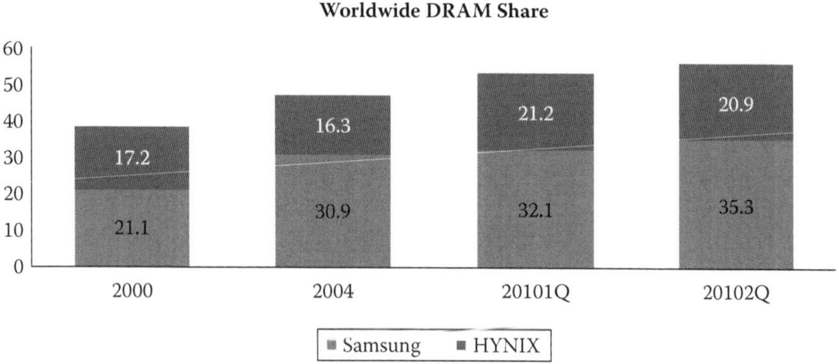

FIGURE 2.3
Worldwide DRAM share.

of Korean firms. In the 1980s, it worked as a coordinator and environment maker for the semiconductor industry (Matthew and Cho, 2000). Its effort focused on: (1) removing social and political factors that are detrimental to target business growth, (2) making massive investments for research and development, and (3) preparing the required human resources.

After firms acquired original technology and competitive capabilities, ensuring a competitive environment was the key for continuous growth. In Korea, firms and research institutes collaborated for network formation. However, as far as new product development and commercialization are concerned, each company worked on its own (Song, 2005). In Japan, basic research was a joint effort, but for new product development and commercialization, competitive relationships were maintained beyond collaborative work among themselves (Utagawa and Abe, 1995). In this way both Japan and Korea have had similar growth processes for their semiconductor industries. Yet the Japanese semiconductor industry experienced a prolonged recession after the 1990s, while Korean firms maintained a high level of growth. The difference is that Korean firms learned from Japanese experiences on what to do after catching up. Japanese firms engaged in a mutually destructive identical competition mode while Korean firms pursued differentiated competition patterns. After accomplishing the successful commercialization of their products, Japanese firms focused on domestic market development, while Korean firms focused on exporting their products (Porter and Takahiro, 2002; Chang, 2005). Samsung, for example, focused on memory specialization with an Asian market concentration, continuous investment, and a bold global strategy implementation (Itami, 2000). After 2000, Samsung expanded its market to nonmemory areas, and its strategic portfolios include semiconductor devices, LCDs, mobile phones, information communication, and digital media.

2.3.2 Korean and Japanese Second Generation Mobile Communication Industry

According to the Korean Ministry of Information and Communication (MIC) statistics, the total number of Korean mobile telephone subscribers is 38.34 million people, which are 81.1% of the total population (Digital Times, 2006.5.10). As of the third quarter of 2005, the percentage of Korean subscribers is 14% of 280 million global subscribers (Digital Times, 2006.5.10). Global System for Mobile Communications (GSM) technology has been the mainstream of the world mobile telephone market, and yet as Korea commercialized the Code Division Multiple Access (CDMA) technology, the world market now has two competing technologies—GSM and CDMA.

CDMA commercialization in Korea is a success case of new technology and industry development beyond Time Division Exchange (TDX) and semiconductor memory development. In this part, we present case studies of Japanese and Korean second-generation mobile communication development. Success factors of the Korean mobile communication industry and the importance of technology selection in the digital age are discussed here.

2.3.2.1 Success of the Korean CDMA Industry

According to the Electronic Technology Research Institute (ETRI, 2002), the Korean CDMA mobile communication industry achieved an annual 37.2% growth from 1996 to 2001, with a total accumulated production of $42 billion ($28.3 billion in domestic production and $13.7 billion in exports), and therefore it has become the major component sector of the Korean IT industry. Korea's phenomenal success in the mobile communication industry was possible with the development of CDMA technology. CDMA technology, since its successful commercialization in 1996, achieved an accumulated production impact of $12.5 billion by 2001 (for five years) and also had the effect of creating 1.42 million new jobs.

The CDMA mobile communication industry drastically improved the national foundation for mobile communication technology. Through a self-sufficiency program for its component parts, the domestic suppliers' portion is 70% of the total required parts, and therefore it substantially impacted the growth of the national industrial base. During this time, ETRI received from Qualcomm USA the royalty of $100.25 million. This is the largest technology-related revenue by any Korean research institute.

By 2005, the total export amount of Korean mobile phones was $20 billion. The global market share of Korean mobile phones is about 20%. Three Korean firms offer wireless Internet trade by mobile phone. In 2006, with High Speed Downlink Packet Access (HSDPA), it is going to realize the transportation card transaction function. In 2005, Korea commercialized satellite digital multimedia broadcasting (S-DMB) phones. In 2006, they commercialized terrestrial digital multimedia broadcasting (T-DMB) phones and wireless broadband (WiBro) which challenge European DVB-H, U.S. Qualcomm, and the next generation's mobile phone media market (Song, 2006). Korea is entering the online game contents market as well. In the near future, the integration of electronic radio frequency identification (RFID) and mobile communication may result in a ubiquitous environment.

2.3.2.2 Background of CDMA Industry Development

After the 1988 Seoul Olympics, customer demand for mobile communication drastically increased in Korea. In 1989, the Korean government started the next generation's digital mobile communication development projects (Song, 2006). In 1991, Korea adopted the standardization methods of mobile phones known as Code Division Multiple Access (CDMA). Prior to Korea's adoption of CDMA as a global standard, European nations had already chosen the GSM standard. In the United States and Japan, time division multiple access (TDMA) method digital mobile phones were advancing ahead of European nations. Korea has never developed any wireless communication technology before. Then why did Korea adopt its own CDMA mobile communication technology? An analogous mobile phone was introduced in Korea during the 1986 Asian games. At that time, the American Motorola hand phone sold for more than $1,000 (ETNEWS, 2006.4.20). At first, in the 1990s, the Korean mobile communication equipment market was dominated by American firms such as Motorola (D.H. Lee, 2005). In 1989, Korean analogous mobile phones reached 10 million subscribers. The sales figure for Motorola was about $500 million. Although Motorola improved various service features, the Korean government and research institute concluded that new technology development was needed to tackle fundamental issues. Instead, they considered (TDMA) methods as an alternative (ETNEWS, 2006.4.20).

MIC and researchers of ETRI visited the United States and European communication firms and asked for technology transfer, but firms responded to their requests by saying, "Korea has no capabilities for new technology development" (ETNEWS, 2006.4.20). They concluded that, by adopting European methods, Korean communication manufacturers would not be able to compete in the global market (Tukamoto, 2002). Therefore, in view of the drastic increase in customer demand and the TDMA technology transfer issue, Korea decided to choose CDMA instead.

2.3.2.3 Success Factors of the CDMA Industry

In this section we consider the formation of network leadership and a competitive environment.

2.3.2.3.1 Technology Resources and Management of Knowledge Capabilities through TDX Development Projects

Song (1999) cites critical success factors of the CDMA industry as (1) learning through the prior successful TDX technology development, (2) MIC's leadership as a national research development project, and (3) management capabilities of accumulated technology resources.

Other researchers such as Chung and Lee (1999), ETRI Report (2002), and Oh (2004) also indicate that the TDX technology development project was a critical success factor for CDMA. In1980, Korea enacted the "electronic industry growth act" and identified communication as a major strategic focus. The Korean pioneering effort in this area was through the "TDX Development project." Korea's ETRI poured $240 million into the project over five years for its successful development. Through TDX development, Korea became one of 10 nations in the world that developed digital exchange technology (ETNEWS, 2006.4.20). Such achievement was the basis of challenging CDMA technology development. Network leadership requires, therefore, prior technology development experiences.

2.3.2.3.2 Korean Government's Innovative CDMA Technology Selection and Development Management Capabilities

Oh (2004) appreciates the Korean government's innovative technology selection in the transition period between analogous technology and digital technology as another important success factor. At the beginning of CDMA technology development, because no nation had ever commercialized a digital system yet, a large number of risk factors existed. In 1990, USA Qualcomm, from which CDMA technology was imported, was nothing but a small venture business with no more than 15 employees (Song, 2006). However, compared to the European GSM methods, CDMA selection was based on the assumption that Korea might lead CDMA technology because of its high-frequency efficiency, low service cost, and super communication sound. Chung and Lee (1999) give credit to MIC's contribution on CDMA technology development. The ETRI report (2002) also recognizes MIC's utilization of the large system development capacity that was acquired through the successful TDX exchange development project. MIC recognized the potential value of CDMA as an emerging technology when analogous technology was still widely used. MIC's technology development commitment, mobile phone subsidy system, and technology selection process are important success factors (Song, 1999). The Korean MIC and its associates (i.e., component manufacturers, communication manufacturers) were developing CDMA while the Korean Ministry of Commerce, Industry, and Energy (MOCIE) and its associates (i.e., electronic research associations and other suppliers) were working on the GSM project. At that time, the efforts of MIC and its partners were more credible than those of MOCIE and its partners with their detailed technology development time reduction plans and their better sense of political priorities. Since ETRI had already invested $100 million of the development budget, all the stakeholders had no option but to move further and complete the project (ETNEWS, 2006.4.20).

In this way, the Korean government assisted the formation of network leadership by choosing CDMA for the mobile communication industry.

2.3.2.3.3 ETRI as National Research Institute

Chung and Lee (1999) cite that ETRI effectively used Qualcomm's technology performance. Song (1999) also refers to the outstanding efforts of ETRI's technology development team that coordinated complex research initiatives, fairly represented the interests of manufacturers, and promoted technology learning. They accelerated the development deadline to 1995—two years before 1997. Each firm made the equipment with the production responsibility for trial purposes during the whole development process. Their prototypes were delivered to ETRI. ETRI disclosed information for other firms that participated in the technology development process to be able to share information and knowledge by disclosing information on the product that had been delivered.

Moreover, to adjust ETRI with firms participating in the technological development activity, and to examine and evaluate the product that the firms had developed, the mobile communication technology development business management group was set up (D.H. Lee, 2005).

For CDMA network formation and commercialization, the project leader's leadership and the role of ETRI is never too exaggerated.

2.3.2.3.4 Manufacturers' Role in Technology Development and Demand Creation

Chung and Lee (1999) also suggest that, in addition to ETRI's research efforts, the sheer hard work of manufacturers and participants played a role in success. Chun (2000) also indicates the importance of component manufacturers' continuous new technology development, light and compact mobile phone development and manufacturing, the best service quality, and consistent and extensive service offerings. With ETRI, manufacturers such as Samsung, LG, Hyundai, and MAXON did their best for new technology development as well. In the development process, the firms produced hardware. The mobile phone was made by Samsung, LG, Hyundai, and MAXON, the control station by LG and Hyundai, the base station by Samsung and Hyundai, and the exchange bureau by Samsung and LG, and the prototype was delivered to ETRI. ETRI took charge of work to integrate it as a whole system (D.H. Lee, 2005).

In addition to Korean firms' innovative product development and global marketing efforts, all contributed to the rapid growth of the Korean domestic mobile communication market and the CDMA industry. Network (platform) formation is, in a sense, infrastructure development through global standardization efforts through mobile communication technology (Gawer and Cusumano, 2002).

2.3.2.3.5 Supplier Development for Mobile Communication Industry

It is to be noted that strengthening the base of component suppliers as the support infrastructure is strengthened is also critical for the Korean IT industry's competitiveness. The Korean government took serious steps of improvement in this area. In 1998, no more than 40% of component parts were made by Korean firms. By 2001, it was 70%. By 2004, the homemade percentage of component parts was almost 100% (Oh, 2004).

The Korean government worked toward building a sufficient domestic supplier network in Korea as a way for CDMA success through the continuous enhancement of technology capabilities, increasing the participation of mobile communication manufacturers and the commercialization of standardized technology.

2.3.2.3.6 Participation of Product Development by Customers

Young Koreans, a major user group, are sensitive to new trends and styles. They provided an adequate demand support basis for continuous new product introduction. Korean mobile communication manufacturers kept refining design and functional features to satisfy rapidly changing customer requirements (ETRI, 2002). A spokesperson for Korean manufacturers said, "Korea could become an IT powerhouse through building infrastructure, outstanding products and most of all demanding customers" (ETNEWS, 2006.4.20). Recently Samsung changed its design features in response to customer feedback that indicated that it was no more than a cheap design imitation. Samsung immediately recalled all the newly introduced mobile phones and modified the design features before full commercialization (Kukminilbo, 2006.5.5).

2.3.2.3.7 Formation of a Competitive Structure

As a way of competitive development, the Korean government adopted a system evaluation system. At the first system evaluation, Samsung was number one, LG was number three, while Hyundai was number two. LG, after losing its number two spot to Hyundai, regarded the day as the "Day of Shame." Ku, the CEO of LG, promised all necessary support to the development team and challenged them to have a better performance during the next round of evaluation (ETNEWS, 2006.4.20). Such promotion of fierce competition enhanced the product quality of mobile communication and service offerings (Chun, 2000; Oh, 2004). For example, as more firms joined in the market (e.g., in 1995 Sinseke Communication and in 1996 three more firms), SKT, the market leader, reduced user fees and offered additional services. As a result, the number of service centers drastically increased to 10,000 in 1999; it was merely a couple hundred at the beginning (ETNEWS, 2006.4.20). At present, an effective competition policy is being implemented in Korea. Such a competition policy was an official policy of MIC. In 1993, Dr. Suh, the chief project leader of the mobile communication team, implemented a competitive development strategy. He switched the mode of work from joint development to competitive development. Many leaders opposed his idea. Dr. Suh said, "Have you examined if your train has engines or your conductor is qualified? Are you aware of the destination, the time of departure and arrival and the cost," and insisted on the necessity of a competitive development structure (ETNEWS, 2006.4.20).

2.3.2.3.8 Other Success Factors

Other success factors are the standardization policy, consistency, and flexibility in the development policy (Oh, 2004). As joint development with Qualcomm was delayed, Korean firms engaged in their own development based on basic design (ETNEWS, 2006.4.20). As a result, in 1994 (after three years of development effort), KSC-1 was introduced to the market. Engineers that left large firms started their own businesses, and accordingly, the continuous expansion of mobile communication technology was possible.

2.3.2.4 CDMA Industry Spreading Effect

Success of CDMA has a tremendous impact on the Korean IT industry. Here, we consider its multiplier impact in a number of ways.

2.3.2.4.1 Achieving a Number 1 Position in the Global Wireless Mobile Communication Industry

CDMA technology development has a positive impact on the trade balances of Korea. As shown in Table 2.3, the growth between 1996 and 2001 was seven times in terms of sales. In a 2004 MIC report, CDMA mobile phones were $7.98 billion (34.5% of mobile phones), GSM $12.96 billion (63% of mobile phones), TDMA $46.1 million (a 64% reduction), and others $80.5 million (a 36% reduction). Therefore, CDMA technology development capabilities are being applied to GSM mobile phone development. Table 2.3 is a summary of performance results through CDMA technology development between 1996 and 2001.

Figure 2.4 shows the mobile phone production, export, and import differences. A 2002 ETRI Report identifies 14 performance measures of CDMA technology development—seven qualitative and seven quantitative industrial performance measures. After CDMA technology commercialization, Samsung, LG, and Pantech Group are positioned as three of the top 10 global firms. The combined global market share of these three firms is 30% of global sales. As of April 2006, these three big

TABLE 2.3

Performance Results through CDMA Technology Development (1996–2001)

Performance Measures	Performance Details
Commercialization of CDMA technology	First in the world
Securing cutting-edge radio communication technology in a short period	Motivational IMT-2000 (CDMA technology application); reduction in technology development time
New formation of CDMA industrial cluster	Mobile phone manufacturers (4); component parts manufacturers (11); suppliers (60)
Promotion of growth of the Korean mobile communication industry	Mobile telephone subscribers annual increase by 180%
Product innovativeness and diversity	World top class in terms of the product quality performance
Customer satisfaction	Quality competitiveness is superior to other top brands
Accumulation technology know-how	Brand image and after service: world top level
Production capacity	As of 2001, $10.9 billion (number one in the world)
Sales revenues	As of 2001, number one in the world (Samsung is number three in the world)
Major export items	Export: $4.1 billion (year of 2001)
Market share	Domestic market: 100% (2001), world market: over 69% (2001)
Rate of domestic production of components	Mobile phones: 100%; parts: 70% (2001)
Price competitiveness	Match to the level of the United States, Europe, and Japan
Multiplier effect on national economy	Production effect: $125.2 billion (1996–2001); value-added effect: $65.2 billion (1996–2001); employment effect: 1.425 million (1996–2001)

Korean marketers occupied the number one position in ten countries. In 30 countries these firms occupied either the number two or three positions. Samsung developed the CDMA phone in 1996 and in 1997 achieved the sale of one million phones (B. C. Lee, 2003). Using innovative designs for diverse new product development (e.g., folder, slide, horizontal display), Samsung is leading new product development in the camera phone and DMB satellite phone. Samsung's blue black phone (model D500 and model D600) achieved sales of 10 million. Samsung is gaining the number one position in hand phone sales in France and

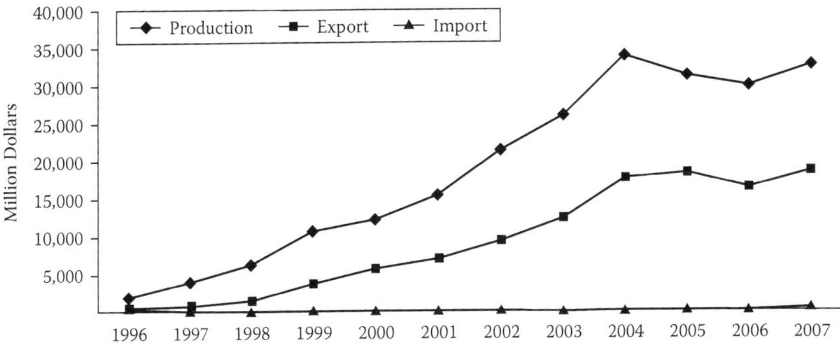

FIGURE 2.4
Mobile phone production and trade balances. From "Annual Information Communication Industry Statistics" by Korea Association Information and Telecommunication (KAIT): 1996–2007 (including CDMA, GSM, TDMA, W-CDMA, and other mobile phones).

Russia. In England, Samsung consistently shows a number one rating for customer satisfaction. Four years in a row they attained the top brand with a premium brand. LG also occupies number one or two in the United States, India, Brazil, and Mexico and is number one in the CDMA market. In the U.S. CDMA market, they have 30% of the market share. Pentech Group is doing well in South America and the Middle East. In Mexico, its brand is making a strong showing with outstanding customer satisfaction results (ETNEWS, 2006.4.20). Samsung and LG possess new product development capabilities that satisfy customer demands. They steadily introduce streams of new products with multiple functions and complex features. Samsung is leading in video communication, wideband CDMA (W-CDMA) mobile phones, HSDPA mobile (third generation), T-DMB, and S-DMB phones, DVB-H, and Medica Flow (ETNEWS, 2006.4.20). In terms of market research, product strategy execution, and marketing promotion, they are ahead of their global competitors, and accordingly they achieve global sales growth beyond the industry average (ICA, 2003).

2.3.2.4.2 Leading Technology Standardization

Mobile communication manufacturers and CEOs of major manufacturers around the world attend Samsung's 4G forum. As these Korean global firms lead in the information market, Korea's WiBro, the next generation's communication technology, is spreading to the global market. Samsung's DMB service mobile phone, WiBro phone, commercial HSDPA phone system, CDMA DVB-H phone, and Smartphone, along with LG's world first W-CDMA and Java-based smartphone, are examples of such an effort. For network leadership with the new technology (e.g., DMB and WiBro), ETRI, KT, Samsung, and LG jointly pursue global standardization (ISBI, 2006.3).

2.3.2.4.3 The Japanese and Korean Second-Generation Mobile Communication Industries

Japan achieved the national standard for the second generation (2G) mobile communication industry. Even with such a good start, Japanese manufacturers are not doing well in the global market. Japanese 2G development is done by NTT Docomo, who separated from NTT in 1992. With the need for a Japanese national standard, Japan adopted personal digital cellular (PDC) in 1993. In the late 2000s, Japan's PDC sustained 88% of the Japanese national market. From a global standpoint, it was one of many available technologies. In 1992 the number of Japanese PDC subscribers was 750,000, which is much larger than GSM users.

In Japan, the PDC standard 2G mobile phone is unique to the Japanese standard. Therefore, other national brands could not easily enter the Japanese market. At the same time, Japanese brands were not appealing in the global market which had adopted the GSM standard (Korea IT Research Report, 2001). Afterward, Docomo challenged Europe's GSM by adopting W-CDMA through a strategic alliance with Ericsson for world market domination. However, too many Japanese manufacturers competed for a smaller share of the available market. NTT Docomo's methods are not widely used in the global GSM market (Tsukamoto, 2002). By the end of 2002, Japanese Kyocera was number eight globally and Matsushita (Panasonic) was number nine in terms of sales. Kyocera became the top in Japan with its strength of CDMA, but with a lack of global acceptance its competitive position was drastically reduced (Tukamoto, 2002).

This Japanese 2G development strategy failure also impacts others in the mobile communication industry. In Japan, NTT Docomo has a NTT family communication device based on a cooperative relationship with NEC, Matsushita, and Fujitsu (Sugiyama et al., 2006). Therefore, NTT family communication manufacturers developed a hand phone with NTT's subsidy. As NTT's W-CDMA 3G and i-mode failed in global market penetration, such a subsidy was discontinued after a miserable financial performance in the market. Firms like Sharp and Sony Ericsson developed their own mobile phones without depending on NTT. These firms do not have an infrastructure-building business and are not involved in standard setting. Rather, they raise their competitive position with their focus on the contents area that uses applications and user suggestions (Sugiyama et al., 2006).

In 2006, the Korean mobile communication industry was also a carrier-dominated structure. It is fundamentally different from Japan in that 2G CDMA was developed through the support of the Korean government. Carrier and mobile phone manufacturers maintain a certain level of independence based on the Korean government's network formation strategy. Accordingly, after CDMA development, the 3G standard was divided into W-CDMA and CDMA 2000. In July of 2000, SK IMT and KT ICOM were selected to provide 3G service (Oh, 2004). These Korean mobile manufacturers consistently targeted the global market because their domestic market is relatively smaller than Japan's. However, NTT management practices and strategic execution are not necessarily the reason for Japanese IT's relatively weak performance in the global market. It is suggested that competitive conditions were less fierce in Japan because they had high levels of barriers for entry by new firms (Korea IT Research Report, 2001).

Here, the strategic importance of achieving a global standard through technology standardization in an increasingly networked economy is noted (Sugiyama et al., 2006). In our global age, Japanese manufacturers did not sustain network leadership with their primary focus on the Japanese national standard. In Korea, with CDMA commercialization, firms were successful in their standardization strategy beyond the Korean domestic market (Lee, 2004). Therefore, global standardization is an important success factor evidenced by the Korean and Japanese examples.

2.4 IMPLICATIONS OF KOREAN IT INDUSTRY SUCCESS FACTORS

2.4.1 Importance of Network Formation

Network leadership is very important as shown in Intel, Microsoft, and Qualcomm. Qualcomm, in horizontal specialization, has network as its strategic priority. While continuing license management, semiconductor, and OS development, it is selling off mobile phone–related businesses

(Sukiyama et al., 2006). In today's digital industry, for a late starter to establish network leadership is almost impossible. The Korean IT industry is an example of a late starter. Because a tremendous initial investment is required, government support for network leadership is a realistic option. For the formation of a mobile communication industry of the Korean catch-up type, network leadership formation was possible through the Korean government's investment strategy. The Korean government also played vital roles in ensuring a competitive environment for continuous innovation. Recently, network leadership for small and medium enterprises (SMEs) has been pursued in the areas of DMB and WIBRO as well as the Korean semiconductor (nonmemory) industry. MIC (Ministry of Information and Communication; Ministry of Knowledge and Economy in 2008) is working on a synergistic effect for supporting SMEs. As it expressed in its annual report, it will focus "on enhancing the competitive capabilities of IT component suppliers." MIC completed the reorganization process of transferring the Korea Institute of Public Administration (KIPA) IT-System-on-a-Chip (SoC) to ETRI. Through the establishment of the SoC Industry Promotion Center, all SoC enterprises could have access to ETRI's IP (semiconductor design asset) and other know-how. SMEs also receive innovative products testing, confirmation, and marketing and all industry support services. Securing core human resources is also possible through ETRI. In brief, establishing network leadership for SMEs was through a collaborative effort.

2.4.2 Standardization Issue

Standardization is an important issue for the digital industry. Korean mobile phone manufacturers are paying 5.25% of the sales price per phone in domestic use and 5.75% of the sales price per phone for exports as a royalty payment to Qualcomm (Digital Times, 2006.5.10). According to MIC, mobile phone manufacturers have paid $2.63 billion since 1995. There has been a vigorous debate whether or not such royalty payments are excessive. The Korean IT industry is working toward the development of new technologies on their own while lowering their dependence on Qualcomm.

Figure 2.5 shows the amount of royalty payments by Korean firms to Qualcomm based on the report of the Ministry of Information and Communication (MIC). 1,000 Korean won is translated per dollar. The Korean government recognized the importance of standardization based on the IT Industry Success Model. Recently, it has been planning the

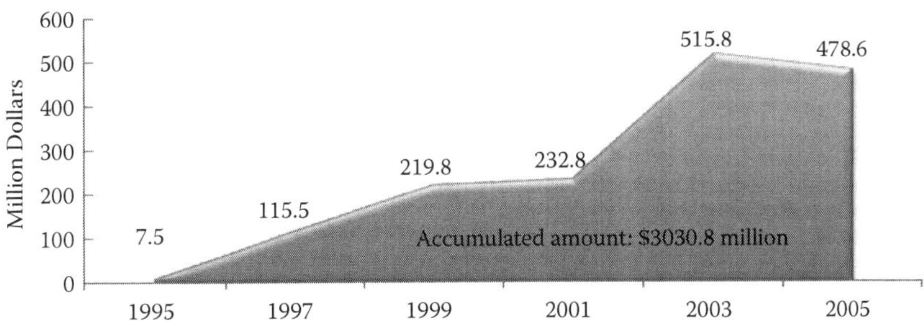

FIGURE 2.5
The amount of royalty payments by Korean firms to Qualcomm.

strategy that will lead the digital industry through the development of DMB and WIBRO. Services for DMB started in 2005, and services for WIBRO in 2006. They are going beyond Qualcomm's CDMA and leading technology standardization. Through the global standardization effort of DMB and WIBRO, the Korean mobile communication industry is moving toward further progress. Samsung has developed a mobile phone using DMB. Samsung is working on a WIBRO mobile phone export, HSDPA mobile phone development, and a CDMA type DVB-H mobile phone. Therefore, Samsung negotiated with Qualcomm in regard to WIBRO (Mobile WiMax; 3.5 generation new product) until August 2006. Samsung holds about 25% of the global mobile WiMax patent rights. Samsung's Information Communication CEO reported, "With acquisition of WIBRO patents Samsung has the key for royalty negotiation with Qualcomm" (Digital Times, 2006.5.10). LG also engaged in the development of W-CDMA T-DMB and DMB phone development, as well as a Java-based smartphone. In the IT industry, the key is how to achieve global standardization. Therefore, the fight for global standardization might be the real challenge for the coming years.

2.4.3 Summary of Korean IT Industry's Success Factors

We have examined Korean IT success factors through its semiconductor industry and mobile communication industry. Both of these industries did not possess their original technology at the beginning, and they adopted a catch-up model and experienced rapid growth. In order to develop a catch-up type industry, the issue is how to transfer the technology from an advanced country. As with the semiconductor industry, strategic alliances and the utilization of human resources of advanced nations were used. Or as in CDMA commercialization, it is possible to purchase precommercialization technology for a short period of time. Samsung has such capabilities. In the digital age, time is money, and any technology that can be purchased with money may be acquired by all means. Japanese firms have outstanding manufacturing technologies. However, they are somewhat behind in utilizing their technologies for commercialization purpose. The Korean IT success model might be useful to many developing countries and, at the same time, it also suggests a helpful insight for Japanese firms as well. In summary, the Korean IT success model is about building up network leadership through government initiative and support and having the necessary competitive environment. Furthermore, they were successful in increasing mobile communication industry subscribers, utilizing the service enterprise cooperation model, establishing global standardization, and effectively gathering and selecting information and developing technology.

2.5 DISCUSSION

The Korean IT industry has several outstanding firms (e.g., Samsung and LG) that have global competitiveness. It is pointed out that Samsung does not even possess its own original technology like Sony of Japan, or Intel, Microsoft, and Qualcomm of the United States. In the rapidly changing IT industry, in addition to innovative product development, global technology standardization is a must. For example, Japan developed the mobile communication standard PDC, and it was passed over by another mobile communication technology—GSM, CDMA (Yoon, 2006). Mobile Internet (WiBro), the fourth generation of the mobile communication axis, is in the process of standardization by the Telecommunications Technology Association (TTA), and ETRI and Samsung are working on a wireless connection standard and accordingly global standardization. Particularly, WiBro is regarded as a strategic new innovation. Korea has second and third generation mobile communication system know-how. Based on such merits, it has a vision to become a global IT leader through fourth generation mobile communication system development and global standardization. With such a vision, Korea's TTA is working toward global standardization (Yoon, 2006). In a ubiquitous age, the growth of the Korean IT industry depends on cooperation between government and business. Of course, the Korean government network leadership is not necessarily all successful. It is to be noted for the role of government's network leadership that has promoted the competitive growth of the Korean IT firms (Digital Times, 2006.3.28). However, in the digital industry, the real challenge is how to secure a competitive environment even after the establishment of market leadership by early participating firms.

3

Growth Mechanism and Management of Korean Firms: A Comparative Study with Japanese Experiences

This chapter shows a growth mechanism of the Korean economy—particularly through the case analysis of two Korean global firms—Samsung Electronics (SE) and Hyundai-Kia Motor Company (HKMC). This chapter presents a research model, case history, and the results of in-depth interviews of senior executives of these two firms. We examine the factors how SE and HKMC have grown as global firms in a relatively short period.

We pay special attention to the role of the Owner/CEO in the development of organizational capability in a Korean business context. We also discuss how two different firms translate "speedy Owner/CEO decision making and large scale of investment" into sustainable competitive advantage through the use of IT and organizational learning from a product architecture perspective.

3.1 INTRODUCTION

In the competitive business environment of the twenty-first century, firms increasingly expand their own resource base and integrate the diverse interorganizational capabilities to create new business opportunities. However, the resources that provided competitive advantage in the past might become either irrelevant or ineffective in response to the changing needs of market reality. For example, more than 60% of 43 firms declared bankruptcy just five years after Peters and Waterman

(1982) had cited them as excellent firms. Successful firms of today do not necessarily guarantee continuous growth and development in the future. Thus, it is critical for firms to build new organizational competencies and reconstruct value chain capabilities by (1) expanding the base of existing resources and (2) combining diverse resources base. In brief, innovative learning capabilities are essential for effective response to customer value transitions.

Japanese and Korean firms have been successful in catching up with the front-runners such as U.S. and European firms. In the past Korean firms learned much from Japanese, U.S., and European firms. In recent years Korean global firms are noted for their phenomenal growth. Samsung and LG Electronics in particular have demonstrated their noticeable progress, while Japanese firms, having once dominated in global electronic industry, are now somewhat stagnant.

A growing body of literature suggests differences in the management styles between Japanese and Korean firms. Japanese firms focus on (1) development and accumulation of hands-on knowledge and expertise deriving from real work settings and (2) utilize them through systematic coordination in product development and manufacturing processes. Japanese practices—such as heavyweight product development manager (Clark and Fujimoto, 1991; Rauniar et al., 2008a, 2008b), front loading (Tomke and Fujimoto, 2000; Fujimoto, 2003, 2006b; Fujimoto and Nobeoka, 2006; Park et al., 2007a; Park et al., 2010a), and Toyota Production System (Clark and Fujimoto, 1991; Tomino et al., 2009)—reflect the hands-on knowledge and multiskilled workers and complex process capabilities of Japanese firms. In contrast, Korean firms quickly respond to the demands of market reality, implement a large scale of investment, and achieve mass sales results through rapid learning curves. Korean firms practice iterative cycles of learning/unlearning through engineering/reengineering practices.

In this chapter we review the economic and business growth models. Our conceptual model suggests that two factors (i.e., the Owner/CEO's powerful role and organizational implementation capability) are related to "rapid decision making for effective large-scale investment." We further examine how Korean firms (e.g., Samsung Electronics and Hyundai-Kia Motor Company) have quickly attained their global competitive advantage. We also focus on strategic mechanisms that connect early learning of senior executives to the organizational learning process in the context of firms' making massive scale of investment decisions. Such organizational learning capabilities require information system communication capabilities that effectively process invisible resources (i.e., knowledge-intensive and technology-related learning) into critical resources for competitive advantage.

3.2 LITERATURE REVIEW

3.2.1 Firm Growth Model and Learning Theory

We use firm growth models because our aim is the analysis of growth factors of Korean firms. Penrose (1959), as a pioneer of the firm growth model, defines a firm as a collective unit of resources and firm growth as the actualization and accumulation processes of unutilized potential resources. Thus, this theory of firm growth is based on the accumulated resources within. A real source of a firm's growth is in the diversification of innovative resources (Karube, 2004b). Theories that extend her theory develop further into a resource-based view that regards firms as collections of resources and a competence (capability)-based view that coordinates and integrates diverse management resources toward the higher level of organizational capabilities.

In general, the weaknesses of the resource-based view and competence (capability)-based theory are in the static concept similar to Porter's competitive position-based theory. A firm's core competence cannot stand still. Without continuous processes of renewal, "core competence" may at some point become "competence trap" or "core rigidity" (March, 1991; Leonard-Barton, 1992; Helfat and Raubitschek, 2000; Danneels, 2002). Under the rapidly changing environment any resources that function as a source of core competence may become an obstacle to growth with the passing of time. As an economy is stable, then the strategy might be static. However, in this current dynamic competitive environment it is critical for firms to quickly respond to continually changing customer needs (Stalk et al., 1992). Successful firms are quite dynamic, in that they frequently and swiftly enter a new market with their new products, or they quickly withdraw from an unattractive market reality. In a sense, resource-based or competence-focused theory is more or less centered on the exploitation of existing resources, and thus, less research attention is paid on the exploration aspects (March, 1991; Levinthal and March, 1993).

However, firms may expand their system capability in horizontal fashion by applying organizational learning within strategic business units (SBU) and core competence as a coordinative and integrative ability (Prahalad and Hamel, 1990). A natural extension of knowledge-based theory and learning theory is dynamic capability theory. It is conceived that dynamic capability (in addition to core competence) is a real source of sustainable competitive advantage (Teece et al., 1990, 1997; Utterback and Suarez, 1993; Henderson and Cockburn, 1994; Teece and Pisano, 1994; Miller and Morris, 1999; Teece, 2007; Quinn and Dalton, 2009). The resource-based view focuses on the firm's internal utilization capability of its resources while dynamic capability theory emphasizes resource creating and expansion capability through integration of intra- and interorganizational resources.

Henderson and Clark (1990) and Henderson and Cockburn (1994) suggest architectural competence or dynamic capability which is characterized by a firm-specific resource (i.e., component competence) plus new resource creation and expansion through strategic integration of intra- and interorganizational resources in response to changing market reality. Such architectural competence and dynamic capability include both specific incremental changes (focusing on management of existing resources) and radical architectural changes (reconfiguring architectural change of the current level of resources). In this sense, dynamic capability theory by Henderson and Cockburn (1994) is related to knowledge-based and learning theory in that firms' organizational learning and strategic initiatives and actions may reconstruct resources and reconfigure capabilities. Based on such dynamic capability theory, Nonaka and Takeuchi (1995), leading proponents of knowledge-based theory, argue for more careful analysis of knowledge creation processes. Diverse functions of an organization certainly better interact and create unique new resources if additional investments are poured into a system. Thus, in the intensely competitive environment firms are required to develop innovative organizational learning and creative system capability in response to customer value transformations (Christensen, 1997, 2006; Christensen et al., 2002).

Learning theory is useful in understanding Japanese firms' catch-up process with U.S. firms (Aoshima and Kato, 2003). Some excellent examples are Honda's motorbikes growth in the U.S. market (Pascale 1984; Christensen, 1997; Mintzberg et al., 1998) and Toyota's development of its own production system after its unsuccessful joint venture effort with Ford Motor Company (Sakakibara, 1988; Fujimoto, 1997). Japanese firms adopted emergent strategy in the course of their steady and solid catch-up (Aoshima and Kato, 2003). Japanese firms have gradually developed their unique front-loading practices of new product development and complex manufacturing processes according to their organizational and cultural characteristics (Mintzberg and Waters, 1985). On the other hand, Korean firms have acted on rapid strategy implementation practices for their learning from U.S., European, and Japanese firms. The learning patterns of Korean firms show rapid and dynamic adjustments to changing environment. These quick learning practices are associated with enormous investments and impressive sales growth. Senior executives' effective investment decision making (i.e., "implement swift and massive investment") and organizational capability are quite obvious in achieving competitive advantage in a relatively short time period.

3.2.2 Research Framework

Figure 3.1 is the research framework of this chapter. It shows the growth processes of an organization from its early business to global business. It suggests that decision making capability of the CEO affects investment decisions of early businesses and prototypes of organizational capability system development. IT system capability is also instrumental in developing prototypes of organizational capability into large global organizational capability. In the following section, a brief discussion involves a comparison between Japanese and Korean firms. Then two conditions

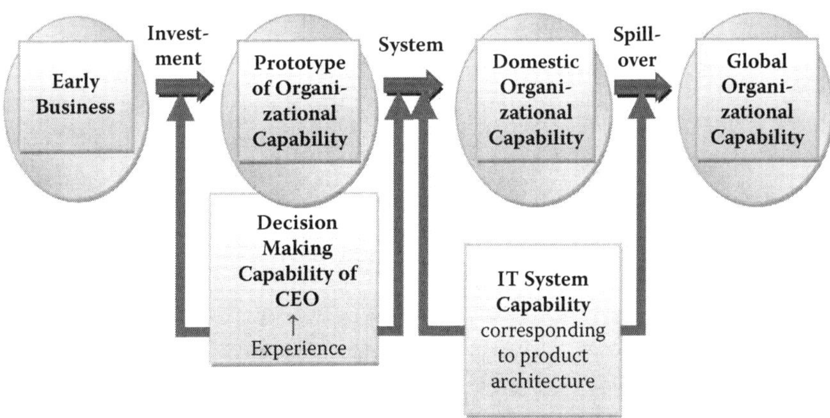

FIGURE 3.1
Research framework.

that make Korean firms (CEO decision making capability and IT system) are examined.

In a relatively short time, Korean firms have caught up with Japanese, U.S., and European firms. Particularly, many Korean executives have adopted Japanese firms as their initial role models because of geographical and cultural proximity in North East Asia. After World War II, Japanese firms, under scarce resource constraints, focused on knowledge accumulation and application to new product development and manufacturing processes through systematic coordination efforts (e.g., Kaizen activities). Practices such as heavyweight project managers, front loading, and Toyota Production System (TPS) are all based on the development of employees with multifunctional skills and innovative problem solving through business processes.

Of course, Korean firms from an early period, just like Japanese firms, grew through the active support of the Korean government in accordance with the domestic industry growth policy. Soon these firms successfully built their unique organizational capabilities that utilize advanced technologies and complicated knowledge systems. Their keen attention to the rapidly changing market environment motivated them to increase learning capability through the massive investment and large global scale of sales. Korean firms implemented the parallel cycles of learning/unlearning through engineering and reengineering practices. The power of owners/executives of Korean firms is particularly important in understanding their investment decision making. Korean business culture strongly supports the active roles of the Owner/CEO's power for the rapid firm growth. In this section we examine general business conditions that support "swift and massive investment decisions."

First, successful executives function well with an effective decision making mechanism. Making quick decisions on the precise timing and the methods of starting a new business are not necessarily easy even for the most powerful executives. Decision making about withdrawal from the existing market or entrance to a new market requires careful analysis and prudent judgment. Executives need appropriate decision making and implementation mechanisms. Some Korean firms, however, thrive on quick and effective investment and business decision making. Relevant research questions are, "How is it possible for the executive to make bold and risky decisions?" "What are the supporting mechanisms for such swift decision making?" "How do organizations achieve reliable outcomes repeatedly?" Highly effective firms require a broad range of organizational capability in terms of flexibility, decisiveness, and managerial insight—especially if they frequently make important decisions in an environment of abrupt and volatile changes (Weick et al., 2005).

Second, "swift and massive investment" for large scale of production is related to meaningful learning processes and outcomes. By executives' investment decision making, firms may implement a large scale of mass production facilities and acquire new learning. What if these learning outcomes are not applied to create new business opportunities? Would these investment decisions contribute to achieving the firm's competitive advantage? Product portfolio management may result in rapid learning curves in the short-term production and sales. However, other firms from emerging economies (e.g., India and China) might learn these practices and rapidly catch up with their low-cost production advantage. Then, such competitive advantage is short-lived. It is critical for firms to continue organizational learning, avoid rapid catch-up of other firms, and thus sustain their competitive advantage.

Successful firms connect learning outcomes (from large investment decisions in the form of expanded facilities) to spillover experiences or horizontal expansion. Horizontal expansion refers to the efficient system configurations through which learning outcomes are shared among the related business processes such as product development, production, and distribution network. Organizational learning should impact the performance measures of subsequent product development and production processes (i.e., production cost and product quality). Otherwise, product development and marketing efforts may require additional investments. Or firms experience massive profit reductions because of the catch-up effects of rival firms. Organizational learning is to be applied in all levels, so that headquarters or central organizations (not factory-level employees) try hard to involve plant-level employees and implement learning practices as widely as possible before making any new massive investment decisions. In brief, "swift and massive investments" require organizational learning capability that is essential for the sustainable competitive advantage.

In this chapter, we examine if the two conditions—(1) Owner/CEO decisions on "swift and massive investment" and (2) organizational capability that connects investment decision into competitive advantage—have contributed to the growth of Korean firms as global business leaders. Since an organizational learning capability requires systematic information sharing, we also examine the role of the IT system as an essential mechanism for sustainable competitive advantage. An effective IT implementation is based on strategic fit with the firm's product architectures and corresponding innovative organizational processes. Otherwise, the potential value of IT is not fully realized (Park et al., 2007a; Park et al., 2010a). In fact, many electronics firms do not necessarily use IT to achieve their product architecture effectiveness and organizational capabilities. Electronic products (with mostly modular type architectures) need to respond more quickly to market environment than automobile products (with mostly integral type architecture).

Our structured executive interviews explore in depth how Korean firms use their IT system to support massive investment decisions and extend the subsequent organizational learning outcomes into competitive advantage. We further study about how Korean firms upgrade their IT systems for new factory construction and production line support.

3.3 CASE STUDIES

This case study involves executive interviews of Samsung Electronics and Hyundai-Kia Motor Company. This study contains multiyear in-depth executive interviews of these two firms. Other data include strategic, operational, and statistical details and historical documents of these two firms (e.g., *50 Years History of Samsung Group*, *Samsung Electronics 40th Year Anniversary Issue*, and "30 Years History of Hyundai Mobis") and other published data. In the next section a brief overview of these two firms is introduced.

- *Samsung Electronics*

  The annual sales figure of Samsung Electronics amounts to 13% of the total exports of Korea, and the combined total sales including the overseas sales are 121 trillion Korean won (about $121 billion; currency is $1 = about 1000 Korean won). The total accumulated sales from 1969 to 2008 are 609 trillions 559.2 billion won, and the accumulated profits are 69 trillions 272.9 billion won. The accumulated sales from 2000 to 2008 are 460 trillions 251 billion (won), and the accumulated profits are 61 trillion and 266.6 billion (won)—Sales 136 trillion (profit 10.9 trillion) won in 2009.

  The total number of employees is 164,000. The ratio of employees outside of Korea is 47.8%. R & D personnel with masters or doctoral degrees are 21,200, and the total employees working in the areas of R & D are 42,100 (Samsung, 2009). Samsung Electronics are certainly committed to securing high-quality human resources.

Samsung Electronics (SE) has 87 overseas operational business units in 48 countries. Its 24 legal corporate entities also conduct production and marketing and other complex business activities in 15 branches. SE maintains diverse sets of research, development, and marketing services by regions. The number of U.S. government registered patents grew from 1,545 in 1999 to 3,515 in 2008. The brand value was $3.1 billion in 1999 and $17.51 billion in 2008. It was ranked 19th in the world in 2008. In July 2009 SE announced "Creating New Value through Eco Innovation." SE is committed to environmental management and sponsors diverse world sports events for its marketing effectiveness.

- *Hyundai-Kia Motor Company*

  In 1999, Hyundai Motor Company (HMC) merged with Kia Motor Company (KMC) and became Hyundai-Kia Motor Company (HKMC). Hyundai Motor Company (HMC), the mainline of HKMC, declared the year of 2005 as the first annual global management, and since then it is committed to innovation for customers. It is one of the top 100 brands of the world and the sixth largest auto-motor company in the world. The total brand values of HMC are 8 trillion (won). It is the number two ranked firm in Korea. Adding the brand value of Kia Motor Company, the other family brand, the total brand value of Hyundai-Kia Motor Company (HKMC) is 12 trillion (won). Its projected global sales for 2010 are 5.39 million vehicles. The details of these goals are being reviewed by region and model. HMC plans to produce and sell 3.45 million and KMC 1.94 million.

  Table 3.1 is a summary of HMC's performance between 1968 and 2007 in terms of capital, production volume, sales, number of employees, and brand value. This shows a phenomenal growth in all aspects.

TABLE 3.1

Hyundai Motor Company's Performance

	Capital (Billion Won)	Production (Vehicles)	Sales (Billion Won)	Employees	Brand Value (Billion Dollars)
Before (in 1968)	0.1	533	0.528	590	0
Now (in 2007)	1,485	2,602,322	31,134	55,501	4.45

Source: HKMC IR Report.

3.3.1 Electronics Industry

3.3.1.1 Growth Process of Samsung Electronics (SE)

We now start with memory semiconductors to see the nature of SE's organizational learning. In 1992 SE developed the 64M DRAM for the first time in the world, and since then it positioned itself as the number one firm in this area of business. Thus, we examine how SE engaged in organizational learning in semiconductors and how it further extended its business opportunities horizontally.

The semiconductor industry has some unique characteristics that are distinct from other industries (Hong, 2004a; Park et al., 2008a). (1) The semiconductor industry involves a huge scale of facilities which involve massive investment. The manufacturing sector of the memory semiconductor industry requires continuous massive investment in R & D, facilities, and equipment. (2) The semiconductor industry is a highly risky business because of rapid technological change. (3) Sustainable competitive advantage in the semiconductor industry requires rapid construction of a large scale of production system through massive, timely investment. (4) The semiconductor industry is a knowledge-intensive business with enormous multiplier effects and value-added potential opportunities. (5) The semiconductor industry is quite sensitive to changes in business cycles. Sunk cost is large and the price fluctuations are quite severe. Thus, the semiconductor industry fits to the "swift and large investment-driven" growth patterns of Korean firms, which show the characteristics of time-based competition, large dependence on social indirect capital, and complexity in strategic and operational details.

3.3.1.2 Technological Accumulation Stage through Organizational Learning

Samsung Electronics (SE) succeeded in catching up with U.S. and Japanese firms by specializing in the semiconductor industry with the help of the Korean government's strategic industry preference policy that provides flexible tax incentives and other policy support details (Park and Ogawa, 2008; Park et al., 2008a). The Owner/CEO's swift investment decision making was an important ingredient of the success of the semiconductor industry. In the course of accomplishing this catch-up strategy, SE also secured diverse resources including technological, financial, organizational, and managerial capabilities (The Korea Economic Daily, 2002; Shin and Jang, 2006; Chang, 2008). Through organizational learning practices, SE enhanced its capabilities and utilized these diverse resources for the growth into new business opportunities.

First, the Owner/CEO's experiences and effective decision making for fast advancement in the semiconductor industry. It was after Byungchul Lee, SE's founder, experienced the rejection of the technology transfer request to Japanese NEC that SE entered the semiconductor industry in the early 1980s with a huge investment (The Korea Economic Daily, 2002; Shin and Jang, 2006). He overcame strong internal opposition of the Korean government and other research institutions. His clear strategic goal statement was "Surpass NEC by all means!" This is what Toyota has also experienced in its pursuit of the technology exchange program with Ford. Toyota gave its utmost dedication to catch up with U.S. automakers since then. Similarly, SE's Lee met semiconductor engineers in Japan during each week with one goal in mind—first catch up with Japan's NEC. At weekends he came with Japanese engineers and consultants for the training purpose of Korean engineers, for example, in clean room technology. By such concerned efforts he upgraded production technologies and management structure (Lee, 1997; Chang, 2008).

In 1974, the SE executives pictured a bleak future for semiconductors; KunHee Lee (second SE owner) saw the vision for the semiconductor industry and recommended to his father Byungchul Lee and used his own assets to acquire Hankuk Semiconductor (the prior name of Samsung Semiconductor). He, known as a semiconductor mania/doctor, mastered the intricate details of semiconductor technologies and manufacturing processes (The Korea Economic Daily, 2002). He read all the relevant journals and documents and met prominent scholars and experts in the semiconductor business. He himself recruited the top-notch scientists and specialists for the business (Shin and Jang, 2006). In 1980 the operational income losses continued and the semiconductor business unit became the nuisance among the entire SE's group performance. Yet, the Owner/CEO's unswerving conviction and commitment continued to invest more than 50% of its sales for the expansion and upgrade of its organizational capabilities. The Owner/CEO played a critical role in selection of expensive technologies and major investment decisions (Cho et al., 2005; C. Y. Lee, 2005; Shin and Jang, 2006; Chang, 2008). For example, in choosing between trench and stack methods, it was Lee himself who made the final decision. In the later part of the 1980s, Lee again approved the investment decision for an 8-inch wafer facility in spite of huge technological risk with a clear vision to go ahead of its competitors. Through such bold and consistent investment decisions, SE could successfully catch up with Japanese firms developing 16M DRAM in October 1990. In August 1992, SE again developed DRAM ahead of Japanese firms and became the first mover among U.S. and Japanese rivals. Based on such successful experiences, Lee again initiated early investment for a 12-inch wafer facility, overcoming internal opposition.

For the competitive advantage in semiconductors, it is critical for mass production and speed in new product development (Cho et al., 2005; Shin and Jang, 2006; Chang, 2008). Professional managers rarely assume uncertain risks for the long term. It takes much time to persuade and overcome the internal opposition and external misunderstanding. However, the Owner/CEO is willing to personally bear the risks and power to make a huge investment decision. One of the reasons why Japanese firms fell behind SE is the professional management that focuses on consensus and risk management (Lee, 2005). Japanese firms somehow failed in the management essentials of selection and focus with their enormous advantage in high level of technologies and superior market share (Nagai, 2003).

Second, Lee's (SE's Chairman) flexibility in regard to technology development. Instead of insisting on internal development he values time-based competition. These unique characteristics of the semiconductor industry dictate SE to pursue a fast new product development cycle. Lee instructed both Korean R & D and U.S. Silicon Valley teams to develop new chip technology. The famous story is that the Korean team did beat the U.S. counterpart.

SE used concurrent development that integrates development and production, which is quite common in semi-industry (Cho et al., 2005; Shin and Jang, 2006; Chang, 2008; Park et al., 2008). In the semiconductor industry, time to market (i.e., the time that is required to develop and introduce a new product to market) and PLC (product life cycle) are different. Concurrent development is widely practiced. For example, it takes five years to develop a new generation of chip, while it requires no more than three to four years since the introduction of new products to the market until replacement by new products. So it is necessary to develop a new generation of chips before engaging in a large scale of production of previous generation chips. From its early period SE, therefore, emphasized concurrent product development and strengthened the integration of development and production. Some specific examples of current development are

(1) the early 64K DRAM and 256K DRAM and (2) the subsequent 16M DRAM, 64M DRAM, and 256M DRAM (Cho et al., 2005; Chang, 2005; Shin and Jang, 2006; Chang, 2008).

Multiple innovative practices from these integration efforts of development and production reduced the required time for new product development and commercialization. It further improved production costs, design engineering, manufacturing processes, and rapid mass production capacity. Intergenerational product development strengthened concurrent development and concurrent learning systems that achieve both multiple product and technology development. Through this concurrent development/improvement/high-functional product development (e.g., DDR SDRAM), SE achieved consistently higher average sales prices (ASP) compared to its rivals. After securing adequate profits, SE also implemented huge cost reductions and rapid sales growth through economies of scale production (Shin and Jang, 2006; Chang, 2008). Figure 3.2 shows that SE's prices in the market are 10% to 30% higher ASP than its rivals for all its DRAM products because of fast development and high-functionality products such as DDR SDRAM (Shin and Jang, 2006).

Third, organizational learning of complex manufacturing processes for building rapid mass production systems. Specifically, SE involved itself in strategic alignment with diverse global firms and acquired organizational learning capabilities (Chang, 2005; Chang, 2008). In 1969, at the

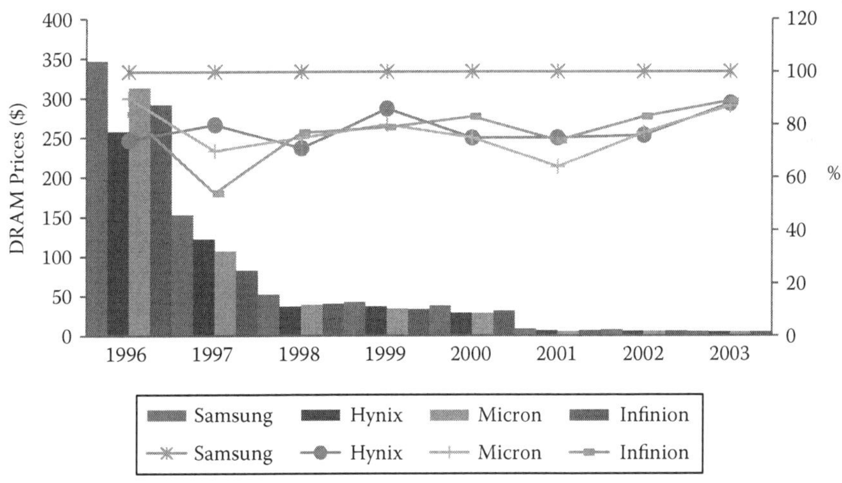

FIGURE 3.2
DRAM price (ASP) comparison between SE and rival firms (based on 256M DRAM) (Unit: $,%). From Shin and Jang (2006).

time of founding SE, SE Manufacturing Corporation was established as a joint venture with Japanese Sanyo and started manufacturing electronic component parts. Afterward, SE also aligned with Japanese firms such as Sharp, Toshiba, and Sony. SE extended its strategic partnership with U.S. IBM, Intel, Microsoft, Qualcomm, Corning, and Rambus as well. Consistent objectives of all these strategic alignments are reduction of technology development cost and time reduction through speed management through organizational learning.

For mastering construction know-how of the mass production facilities, SE imported semiconductor equipment. Until 16M generation SE acquired from Japanese firms, and from the further advanced 64M/256M generation the new equipment source became U.S. firms (Chang, 2005). Acquisition of this semiconductor manufacturing equipment was an important source of organizational learning in the 1980s. Semiconductor manufacturing firms and equipment firms worked together for the evaluation of manufacturing processes and joint research projects. In the middle of the 1990s, flexible moves of the process knowledge workers from one firm to the next was the important source of process technology transfers (Yoshioka, 2007; Shintaku et al., 2008). SE secured semiconductor equipment that provided specific process recipe, and thus it could quickly construct its own mass production capabilities.

Fourth, the specializing process of memory semiconductor and external learning practices. SE has to consider these factors: (1) the growth rate of the DRAM market is considerably high; (2) Japanese firms successfully achieve catch-up with U.S. front-runners; and (3) in the commodity stage, mass production is critical for competitive advantage (Chang, 2005). Strategic alignment made its reverse engineering for product development faster than before. SE sufficiently utilized external technologists. Actually, memory semiconductors were developed by technologists from America (16M DRAM by Daejae Jin, 64M DRAM by Ohyun Kwon, 256M DRAM by Changyu Hwang). In this way, SE could position as a front-runner through its continuous organizational learning practices that focus on developing its own semiconductor unique core competencies (Shin and Jang, 2006). All the successes in the key elements such as persistent investment capabilities, new technologies development, and production unit cost reduction are all possible through organizational learning and knowledge accumulation. Learning from successes in semiconductors also impacted on the rapid growth of other business areas (i.e., flash memory, liquid-crystal display [LCD], mobile phones).

3.3.1.3 Spillover Stage (Horizontal Extension)

3.3.1.3.1 Spillover Events

Now, let us see how Owner/CEO swift investment decisions and external learning effects are horizontally extended (spillover) to other organizational units.

First, a sense of crisis by the Owner/CEO. initiated large scale and risky investment decisions. The organization members in response share the risk of the Owner/CEO's strategic investment decision (Cho et al., 2005; C. Y. Lee, 2005; Shin and Jang, 2006; Chang, 2008). One senior executive said, "In the 1990s we all lived with the word, 'crisis.' Senior executives and field engineers all accept and work with this perpetual sense of crisis" (Shin and Jang, 2006). Another SE manager commented, "Every year SE conducted reorganization and shook the organization. Sometimes business units are separated and then recombined." President Jisung Choi (one of the senior executives of Samsung) affirmed that SE's sustainable growth is possible through its culture of enjoying and living with changes. SE infused a healthy sense of crisis to prevent a defensive mindset of its members after becoming the number one firm. Instead, its members need to remain dynamic and energetic as they dare to face the challenges and implement the Owner/CEO decision outcomes.

As a specific example, in August 1992, just after SE successfully developed the 64M DRAM, Lee gathered 1,800 senior managers in Frankfurt, Germany, announced New Management, and adopted it as the new management policy directive with a slogan, "Let's Change!" This has become the basis of SE's globalization initiatives. In 1996, Design Revolution Manifesto prepared SE for development of products to become the global market leader. In Korea's Financial Crisis of 1997–98, the motto was again, "Eliminate!" and removed 120 business units including the automobile unit. In the twenty-first century, SE is exerting its energy on Readiness Management for seeking future core technologies. In June 2007, Creative Management was announced (Shin and Jang, 2006; Itohisa et al., 2009; Samsung, 2009; Yunhap News, 2009). With this perpetual sense of crisis and change, such culture is naturally adopted and cultivated within the entire SE organization.

Second, organizational learning outcomes through Owner/CEO's initiated large-scale and risky investment decisions. In 1995, SE started mass production of 10.4-inch panels immediately after the construction of its first LCD line generation adopting semiconductor experiences. In the early period the quality failures were very high (up to 50%), and Japanese front-runners waged the price war against SE. With these internal failures and external obstacles, a prevailing argument was to withdraw from LCD business. However, Gunhee Lee included LCD as one of the top strategic priority businesses for the following 10 years' sustainable revenue sources. SE's investment decision patterns (e.g., memory semiconductor and LCD) show the essential aspects of its sustainable competitive strategy: (1) keep focusing on new innovative business development, (2) recover quickly the required level of justifiable profits for the investment, and (3) reap the continuous benefits of premium price advantage of its products over its competitors in the global market (Cho et al., 2005).

While SE was going through the internal debate about the second line, Sharp (a Japanese rival firm) expanded the panel size to 11.3 inches, and other competitors also followed its lead. Sangwan Lee, senior executive with long industry experiences in semiconductors, knew then that the real battle is with time, so he decided on 12.1-inch LCD process investment through investment experiences of 8-inch wafers in semiconductor (Samsung, 2009). In 1993, SE produced 8-inch wafers, not 6-inch (then its world standard), in spite of technical risks, and thus secured its position as the front-runner. In 1998, SE secured its position as the front-runner in the LCD industry. A follower cannot become the front-runner by doing what others do. Instead, it is critical to do something bold that others do not dare to do. Such "Surpass DNA" is a part of SE's executives' mindset in conducting business decisions (Samsung, 2009).

Third, quality management through the new management directive. After the 1982 Frankfurt meeting, SE also switched its management focus from "quantity" to "quality." Behind such policy change directive a few memorable incidents occurred. At the beginning of 1993 (February) Lee presided over the Evaluation and Assessment Conference on Electronic Products Section of the Export Products. He was quite shocked at seeing dusty "Bargain Sale" advertisements over Samsung products in the local Wal-Mart (Cho and Yoon, 2005). In the summer of 1993 he happened to give away mobile phones to every SE employee as his sincere expression of appreciation. He found that 25% of these mobile phones had quality defects. So he ordered the recall and destruction by burning of all the phones and the remaining inventory of mobile phones—total 150,000 (Lee, 2005). In June 1993 Lee also watched SBC's documentary which reported the poor quality of SE's washing machine. At that time, with the overwhelming number of customer orders of washing machines, SE marketed the washers with a hastily designed unfit plastic cover without taking an adequate time for solid design of the cover. Lee was furious about the fact that 6,000 out of 30,000 needed quality repairs. He further stressed quality, crisis, and change management (Lee, 2005). Through these unpleasant but real incidents, SE has pursued excellence in quality management in all other business lines beyond its successful transformation as the global number one manufacturer of semiconductors.

Fourth, the use of the functional system for the effective information delivery of the organization (The Korea Economic Daily, 2002; Chang, 2005; Cho et al., 2005; Lee, 2005; Shin and Jang, 2006; Chang, 2008). SE had the Group Executive Administrative Support Office (GEASO), which after 1998 became the Group Restructuring Center Office (GRCO) and Future Strategy Group (FSG). SE's successes are ascribed to an internal governance mechanism that connects Owner–GEASO(GRCO)–management functions–self-management system. It is the role of effective and powerful GEASO/GRCO that communicates the information from the CEO to all the employees of the organization and coordinates and manages the huge organizational system demands.

Fifth, exploration and application of new knowledge through regional experts system and global human resources network. With the implementation of global management initiatives from 1993 it has become obvious that SE's understanding of global customers is inadequate. From 1990 SE adopted a regional experts system (Cho et al., 2005; Lee, 2005; Chang, 2008). This is to send a pool of carefully selected managers to different countries of the world for one year. Each participant of these programs (1) learns the language of the country he/she visits; (2) familiarizes himself with the political economy, culture, and customs; (3) builds the basis of a future network of relationships with the people of the nation (Jun and Han, 1997). By 2006 3,319 of SE's employees enrolled in this program (Lee, 2005; Itohisa et al., 2009). In this way, SE secured rich information and knowledge on the diverse segments of the global market and translated them for new product development and marketing efforts. SE also stresses organizational learning through the non-Samsung-affiliated human resources. In catch-up stages SE's focus was to adopt advanced technologies and master the critical know-how of manufacturing processes and facilities. After SE becomes the first mover, the system focus is to develop new innovative technology. For example, SE increased the size of internal research and development from 5,000 in the year 2000 to 17,000 in the year 2004 and 42,100 in 2009 (Chang, 2005; Samsung, 2009). Korea's domestic production-based human resources are restricted to a few limited business areas such as LCD and semiconductor production. Most of the other employees work in core areas such as research and development (R & D), marketing, and design (Yunhap News, 2009). According to Samsung Business Reports, production positions are 24,100, which are only 28% of the total SE's employees in Korea. Instead, the proportion of SE's employees in the areas of R & D, marketing, and design are 61% which shows a sizable increase compared to 46% in 1998. SE's employee size is substantially larger than its rival LG, which produces most of its products outside of Korea (60%), and the number of its employees in Korea is 29,600. 20,700 people work in the areas of R & D and administrative functions, and more than half of its total employees is devoted to R & D areas. LG plans to redeploy about 20% of its workforce to the new product and business development for sustaining its growth engine (Yunhap News, 2009).

SE exerts its organizational learning efforts through quality human resources from countries outside of Korea for the sake of new product development and innovation for the global market (Chang, 2005). SE strives for the fast learning of applicable working knowledge for quality and trendy design, increasing focus on ever smaller and lighter products and fast responsiveness to global customer needs. In 1996 SE started Design Center, which has more than 600 designers (Itohisa et al., 2009). From Silicon Valley SE in 1999 recruited Eric Kim who helped J. Y. Yoon (Vice Chairman) to master brand marketing methodology (Katahira, 2005).

All these R & D systems are enabler mechanisms for SE in its catch-up processes. Park and Gil (2006) suggest that Samsung's Corporate R & D Center integrates R & D capabilities to business strategy and Design for Six Sigma (DFSS) to R & D processes in ways to leapfrog SE from technology follower to technology leader. They cite SE's success drivers as organizational transformation, including consensus on the need for organizational change, strong leadership from top management, close alignment of R & D and the business units, and actionable planning and performance management. Here again, Owner/CEO leadership is regarded as an important element of SE phenomenal successes.

Sixth, application of improved current concurrent development and learning systems to the development and learning for subsequent generations of new products (Cho et al., 2005; Lee, 2005; Shin and Jang, 2006; Chang, 2008; Park et al., 2008). The material costs of semiconductors are about 10% of the final price, which is drastically more advantageous than that of computers, household appliances, and communication industry products. With a large scale of purchase, the costs of component parts and facilities and equipment are all the more reduced (Shin and Jang, 2006).

In addition to DRAM, a similar system is applied for the reduction of development time for other new products (e.g., flash memory, TFT-LCD, mobile phones). Particularly, the thin film transistor liquid-crystal display (TFT-LCD) is regarded as an extension of memory semiconductor technology, and thus duplication of technological details is quite visible. Compared to cutting-edge memory technology TFT-LCD is rather less sophisticated, and in 1991 SE started R & D line 1, and in 1994 the line was in full operation. By 1998 (including the third business line), SE virtually was positioned as number one in terms of competitive capabilities and bottom line results. SE applied a concurrent development system (initially memory semiconductor was used) to TFT-LCD in a horizontal extension (Samsung, 2009). Particularly, SE experienced serious challenges at the early business period of TFT-LCD with their frequent quality problems and front-runner price-cutting initiatives. In 1994 the rate of quality failure was 4% to 50% higher than that of the front-runners for the 10.4-inch PC line. In 1995, to resolve these recurring quality issues SE heavily invested with the earnings from memory semiconductors. Different from Japanese firms, SE aggressively invested in 12.1-inch lines (Samsung, 2009). Similar to its experiences with the memory semiconductor, SE pursued large-scale production through its massive investment on the new 17-, 32-, and 46-inch product lines. In mobile phones SE was also able to sustain its new product design cycle time between 3 and 6 months, which for its rivals usually takes more than one year. Thus, SE acquired organizational capability to achieve a high profit rate through its rapid market penetration and expansion (Chang, 2008).

3.3.1.3.2 Spillover Process and the IT System

SE is known for swift and accurate information management. In fact, at the center of SE's organizational culture and operational process lies information mind. SE put strategic value of information in major functional initiatives including human resources management, infrasystem construction, and IT investment. With its high-quality management in IT, SE has succeeded in the memory semiconductor, LCD, and mobile phone businesses (The Korea Economic Daily, 2002). By 1991 SE implemented internal business announcement mechanisms and electronic e-mail systems two or three years earlier than the other Korean large firms. From 1995, SE has used SINGLE (a system that integrates electronic e-mail and other budget and management decision functions) and TOPIC (management and other vital business information-sharing mechanisms). From 1993 SE also started E-CIM (Engineering Computer Integrated Manufacturing) Center, which integrates new product development processes, and by 2001 (the project started from 1995) the completed Global ERP system included all other overseas business units. Besides, other integrated business process systems such as supply chain management system (SCMS), customer relationship management system (CRMS), global product data management system (GPDMS), and product life cycle management system (PLMS) are widely available. According to SE's CIO, these integrated business systems allow senior executives to have access to any relevant and vital information at any time for more effective decision making in any part of the world (The Korea Economic Daily, 2002). These organizational system capabilities are extended to its global business network. For example, it is now possible for SE's executives to check the inventory status of its 28 Chinese plants and to market the products made in China in Russia (Lee, 2005). This shows that SE utilizes the comprehensive IT system (e.g., SCM, ERP) through synchronizing product design, raw materials sourcing, and production–marketing integration and achieves synergy effects.

In the next section we focus on the E-CIM Center and the VIP (Value Innovation Project) Center to examine how the organizational learning practices of the memory semiconductor business are extended to other business areas. Note: In 1992 SE achieved the number one global market position in DRAM product development. From 1993 its learning practices have received much attention both within and without SE.

It is the IT system that supported organizational learning practices and their global extension through the E-CIM Center and VIP Center (Park et al., 2007). At SE, after the announcement of "New Management" in 1993, a 60-member task force established the E-CIM Master Plan based on its actual analysis of existing product development processes, benchmarking of other rivals, and forecast/prediction about changing trends of information technologies. From 1994, E-CIM (Engineering Computer Integrated Manufacturing) started its operation for continuous, innovative product development projects. A specific E-CIM's goal is to expand product development capability to three times the level of its inception. Samsung's four group firms including SE have worked on developing components/products/documents by a single technology standards system. Specifically, the new development process is established based on concurrent engineering (CE). The PDM (Product Database Management) system functions as a key organizational support mechanism that uses CAD infrastructure and systematically manages development information. Innovation initiatives called E-CIM (Engineering Computer Integrated Manufacturing) also contributed to reducing development time from two years to four months.

The mission of the E-CIM Center is to assist competitive advantage by (1) maintaining information on new development processes, (2) standardizing component parts design, (3) using 3Ds for CAD/CAM/CAD, and (4) managing design information by PDM. These series of specific supportive functions overcome the past development shortcomings, including tangible real objects–based product development, inadequate information infrastructure, work overload of designers, and lack of design data availability.

As a specific way to move away from Proto, EVT, and DVT which use actual product feature–based and serial process–focused designs, the new innovate design methodology, Rapid Prototype Interface (RPI), was adopted to enhance collaborative design and concurrent engineering. The results of such new product development at the E-CIM Center made PDM (Product Database Management) technology and component parts standardization and integration of the diverse data base possible. In that way, much wasteful overlap among organizations is greatly reduced.

Electronic products, different from automobiles, contain a wide variety of features, and thus interproduct independence tends to be quite obvious. Each business unit has its own Bill of Materials (BOM), and purchasing patterns of component parts are vastly complex. Business units of SE as a whole adopt numerous IT systems. Each business unit, not IS department, determines the scope of actual usage. Although the global market requires flexible and speedy responses, development engineers or individual functional staff members need to inquire about particular product issues to the appropriate business unit with a great deal of inconvenience and waste of time and resources. To deal with such serious system inefficiency SE built a horizontally and electronically connected product information management system which enabled SE business units to share BOM information of PDM according to the ever-changing global market needs. With such integrated data bases (PDM), all the functional units in SE now communicate with suppliers and other strategically aligned external organizations.

Through such technological standardization by PDM, all the codes of 30 different overseas plants are unified. From 1996 new standard body types were applied. All the overseas business units and plants all use identical codes for the same products. One-time authorization for particular component parts is now accepted for all other business units. Besides, global information sharing about a component's quality and functional characteristics drastically improved the procurement and operational efficiencies with group purchasing (*50 Years History of Samsung Group*, 1998). As SE's IT system is integrated with SAP (enterprise resource planning; ERP) and PDM from 1995, the lead time of color TV was reduced from 12.1 months to 6.2 months in 1997. Thus, E-CIM supported all types of engineering-related innovation and achieved total PDM integration until 2002. For example, SE has attained global number one market share in LCD TV starting with its huge success of Bordeaux TV. SE's supply chain management (SCM) is based on the innovative IT system which effectively supports the worldwide order fulfillment and inventory control processes. SE is able to respond within two to four weeks from the day of receiving an order from any country of the world. Its accurate forecasting is possible through IT systems that are designed to search for the optimum system solution based on the integration of SCM and SAP (ERP) which use comprehensive measures of fluctuating historical demand patterns, global market trends, and market share goals (Chang, 2008).

Yet, PDM's horizontal connectivity requires additional innovative VIP Center. SE uses VIP (Value Innovation Project) Center in which development personnel stay together for a few months and engage in Coliseum type of product development. SE then applies concurrent engineering and concurrent development methods to other product lines beyond the semiconductor business. SE started the VIP program with awareness that 80% of overall costs and quality dimensions are determined in the front-end of product development. In the case of Bordeaux TV, 11 development team members (including specialists from product planning, market research, design, marketing, and distribution) live and work together for three months. During this intensive period, they carefully examined design, product specifications, time-to-market, dealers' responses, and price premiums and then introduced it to the market. It is not so common that product designers and engineers work together. However, through VIP teamwork structure, both design and system engineers integrated a highly successful product concept with all the delicate features of a smooth wine cup and all customer-preferred functionalities, excellent visual quality, and $3,000 premium value of a large TV (Chang, 2008). As of 2005, 90 project teams and 2,000 new product developers participate in VIP programs each year.

3.3.2 Automotive Industry

3.3.2.1 Growth Processes of Hyundai-Kia Motor Company (HKMC)

The root of HMC is Hyundai Motor Maintenance Services Inc., which was mostly specialized in auto maintenance services. On December 1967 the name of the firm changed into Hyundai Motor Company in Seoul, Korea. The starting capital was 100 million (in Korean won). With technical support arrangements with Ford, it started producing Cortina, Ford 20M, and busses in larger volumes. HMC's goal was to make Hyundai as an independent automobile company. Thus, it sent Hyundai employees to U.S. Ford headquarters and plants to learn all the auto-manufacturing basics including design, engineering, and manufacturing. The immediate goal was to become an independent automaker on its own.

The first complete model that Hyundai made was the Cortina. In 1967 Hyundai, with Ford's technical assistance, introduced the 1,500-cc Cortina to the domestic market to compete against its rival Shinjin's Corona. Cortina's key performance indicators are (1) displacement of 1,598 cc, (2) inline 4-cylinder engine, (3) 75 horsepower, (4) maximum speed capacity of 160 km. Within one year Hyundai produced 5,000, and the total amount of sales was one billion (won). The price was 1.1 million (won)—200,000 won more than that of Corona—but it was very well received in the market. However, in September 1969 Korea's major flood caused the cars to be under water, and subsequent massive component parts failures resulted in huge returns of Cortina in the middle of 1970.

From 1971 Hyundai concentrated in quality improvement of the Cortina, and the new Cortina was introduced afterward. By regaining customers' confidence with the new model, by 1976 Hyundai successfully sold 23,141 Cortinas including other derivative product lines such as truck pickups, and van and wagon models. The total sales of Cortina models including prior to 1971 was 31,450. In 1972 Ford decided to discontinue the joint venture arrangement with Hyundai. This became a turning point for Hyundai's journey toward a truly independent auto manufacturer.

Under the leadership of the late S. Y. Chung (Brother of J. Y. Chung, the Founder of Hyundai Group), in January 1976 the Pony was introduced to the market after four years of development efforts. At that same year the export of the Pony started with the initial five cars to El Salvador, then large volumes of cars to countries in the Middle East, South America, and Africa. In 1983—seven years after the initial export to other countries—total export volume hit the mark of 100,000; in 1988 one million with the Hyundai brand; and at the end of 2007, 1,970,747; and at the end of 2007, Kia's sales volume (acquired in 1998) were 1,088,461, and thus HKMC's total sales were about 3 million. HMC, with the technical assistance from Ford and Mitsubishi, developed its own first engine, "Alpha," and in 2002, the "Theta" engine, and exported these to Daimler-Chrysler and Mitsubishi, which surprised all the world. Under M. G. Chung's leadership, Hyundai-Kia Motor Company (HKMC) renewed itself as an automobile global brand group and excelled in quality management. As of 2009, its global status as an exporter of cutting-edge technologies is being steadily established. For example, to other global auto makers including Benz and Mitsubishi, HKMC exports the cutting-edge technologies and receives royalties from these firms. And HMC's Genesis was named 2009 Car of the Year in the United States.

3.3.2.2 Technology Accumulation through Learning

HMC experienced Owner/CEO management leadership changes (i.e., J. Y. Chung, S. Y. Chung, and M. G. Chung). HMKC established itself as a global auto manufacturer under the leadership of M. G. Chung, who assumed the group leadership in 1999 after the 1998 Financial Crisis.

HMC entered the U.S. market in 1986 with its first global model, Excel, which was priced at $4,995 (Kim and Lee, 2005; Lee, 2008). U.S. consumers initially purchased the car with its low price advantage. Soon quality problems became quite apparent. With rampant customer dissatisfaction, its sales performance was contemptible. However, Hyundai's "10 year/100,000 miles" quality guarantee somehow stopped such downward sales trend. HMC's quality management with Owner/CEO leadership initiative is the very foundation of its becoming a global auto maker.

First, excellent quality management (based on organizational learning) infuses the organizational vitality. In 2001 M. G. Chung presented "Quality Management" as the top strategic priority. Since his tenure as the head of HMC in 1999 (just after the 1998 Financial Crisis) Chung's motto is, "Strive to make the best car in the world." Chung resolved to overcome the dishonorable reputation in the U.S. market, "Hyundai competes only by low prices." In March 1999, he presided over the first quality management conference and established the Quality Conference Room and the Quality Assurance Office. In 2001 Hyundai moved to the Yangjae-dong new headquarters in which Chung secured three rooms for global quality management. In March 2002 he again organized the Comprehensive Quality Management Center, and in February 2003 he instituted quality management organizations in the United States and other overseas markets. His strategic focus was to centrally manage quality and after services and therefore upgrade Hyundai's product and services performance to the first rate of the top global auto manufacturers. Quality management that has taken its room in HMC as its organizational philosophy and practices is primarily Chung's commitment and dedication to this organizational goal (Lee, 2008). "Quality" is not the word that Chung emphasized prior to assuming the chairmanship in Hyundai. Yet, Chung as the chairman was directly involved in quality management meetings with the executives of the suppliers. Certainly, learning has taken place. We analyze how such transformation occurred.

Chung's long resume includes his work experiences in Hyundai Construction, Hyundai Motor Company, Hyundai Motor After Services, and Hyundai Mobis. Particularly, Chung spent more than 20 years in Hyundai Mobis. His comments on the work experiences are:

> The establishment of Hyundai Mobis is based on the management experiences at Hyundai Services. At that time it was my conviction that Hyundai Group's success in automotive manufacturing depends on after services (AS) that support production and marketing. It was essential to expand service network and repairs and maintenance business units. Yet, the real need was in quality manufacturing. Therefore, in 1975 just after the establishment of Hyundai Services we all searched for a plant construction that handles military vehicles repairs and remanufacturing and at the same time produce key auto-component parts such as bumpers and mufflers. At that time it was risky to pursue two businesses for after services (AS) and component parts manufacturing. In February 1967, Hyundai just signed a technical assembly contract with Ford, and started producing new Cortinas in large volumes. From December 1975 Hyundai was producing its first model, Pony. Hyundai experienced tremendous delivery delays of component parts from Ford Motor Company. I traveled many corners of Korea with other senior executives carrying the component parts in the service trucks. In heavy rains the trucks frequently fell into the ditch or

> rivers. Yet, I visited all these fields and listened to the customer complaints and concerns. These were the very basis of my commitment to quality management. (Hyundai Mobis, 2007)

He continues,

> The years at Hyundai Mobis provided me with excellent opportunities for learning and growth. In the course of working on a variety of business projects I became familiar with complex management practices. I saw the critical value of actual reality-based management practices. In this way, field reality management and quality management have become the two pillars of my management philosophy. 3S (Seeing, sensing and solving) issues in the fields and then securing the results are the very essence of my management ideas. What matters is not merely speaking with words (i.e., management by words) but engaging in the real fields. There I must see, sense, solve and secure the field quality. From 1978 HMC supported quality circle activities, promoted various quality achievement certificates and licenses, distributed quality standards manuals and quality management documents to suppliers. (Hyundai Mobis, 2007)

Through his extensive experiences at Hyundai Mobis, he was convinced that quality is the most obvious obstacle for Hyundai's growth (Lee, 2008). Chung's quality management principle is that it takes $1 to fix a quality problem in the early development time, $10 at the time of mass production, and $100 after sales because of returns and recalls. He saw the critical need to integrate quality-production-design. He naturally emphasizes the essential role of R & D.

At present, according to Chung's instruction, the first floor of Hyundai-Kia's Yangjae-dong Headquarters has three quality-related spaces (i.e., Global Quality Status Office, Quality Conference Room, and Quality Assurance Office). Chung explained the reason for creating the Global Quality Status Office (GQSO) by saying, "Have you ever thought about a possibility that our car stands in the Sahara desert?" (Kim and Lee, 2005; Lee, 2008). GQSO operates 24 hours, 365 days and checks any Hyundai product failures in real time, and then the reports are sent to the R & D Office. The previous overnight reports are distributed to Chung and other senior executives the next day. In early 2000s Hyundai executives discussed the global market strategy. One idea was to pursue a luxury brand like Lexus and upgrade Hyundai's image. However, Chung insisted, "Without securing solid quality reputation, such luxury car would only make our reputation worse." He then reemphasized "first quality upgrade." Chung also stressed the innovation in production areas as well as R & D to enhance the quality performance to the level of the top rival performers. He announced specific management messages to realize various strategic initiatives in spite of strong internal opposition. Management directives such as "10 year, 100,000 miles" just after the 1998 Financial Crisis and massive investment decisions for the new emerging markets (i.e., China and India) all reflect the Owner/CEO management commitment. He stressed more investment in time of crisis. His message is that any crisis is a process for the greater level of growth.

Second, field-based management emphasizes implementation speed of strategic cutting-edge practices. His leadership style values action and implementation speed. His methods of instruction are not by words, but by example (Kim and Lee, 2005). It is to show himself as a man of action. In 2001 Chung's performance action direction had quite an impact in the organization. Since 2001, Chung visited all the HMC's plants including domestic, United States, India, and China.

Chung's instruction on quality management was decisive, and yet it was not quickly communicated to the employees in the field (Lee, 2008). The work habits of the employees were "fast and cheap." Chung therefore checked the fine quality details of the plant. In August 2002, he drove to test the Kia Opirus export model and discovered a little noise and recommended that the shipping be postponed for the next 40 days until the noise problem was fixed. At that time, the manager reported, "If we do that, the loss is too great." Chung responded, "If this is for quality, then such loss is OK." Such aggressive management leadership infused a real sense of urgency, and the employees worked for the high level of quality. Chung delegated people to work in a competitive environment. It was to make quality cars through proper delegation and performance accountability.

He came to work at 6:30 in the morning and discussed the topics with other senior executives (Kim and Lee, 2005). By his habits of field reality management Hyundai's global plants network was rapidly constructed. HMC has been expanding its global market base through actual presence of its plants in key locations—Alabama and Georgia, the United States, Slovakia, Eastern Europe, and other major countries including China and Russia. With such speed management in Beijing, China, a new word, "Hyundai Speed" was circulated among people. It reflects Hyundai's rapid rise in the Chinese market, although its entry was somewhat late.

Three S (Seeing, Sensing, and Solving) in the real field became Chung's personal management trademark (Kim and Lee, 2005). It is somewhat similar to Toyota's field-based management. In particular, his early experiences instilled in him through the after service business became his management motto based on quality management. Even in the 1998 Financial Crisis, he was able to acquire and turn Kia Motor Company (KMC) around through his field reality management. After acquisition of KMC, Chung visited Kia's plants and examined the situation of the field reality. He thoroughly saw the actual work status in every department including engine plant, foundry, and boiler piping room. KMC's employees responded to his frequent visits with a high level of morale, dedication, and loyalty.

3.3.2.3 Spillover (Horizontal Expansion) Stages

3.3.2.3.1 Spillover Events

Here we consider how Owner/CEO-initiated quality management practices are communicated and implemented through organizational learning processes.

First, the role of Global Quality Forum and Office of Global Quality Status. To take the critical rapid catch-up step is knowing about when, how, and why problems occur. To the extent that problems are quickly recognized, the time reduction for problem resolution is possible. According to Chairman Chung's instruction Hyundai-Kia's Office of Global Quality Status operates as a primary problem-detecting mechanism (Lee, 2008).

In 1999 Mr. MongGu Chung visited the United States. To his shocked disappointment, he learned by first-hand experience that the customers perceived Hyundai products as nothing but cheap and worthless in the market (Kim and Lee, 2005). With poor quality performance many consumers demanded overwhelming recall requests. Upon his return to Korea, he instructed that Hyundai receive consulting advice of J. D. Power and Associates, which suggested the following five critical problem areas: (1) not listening to customers and failure to reflect their voices in product planning/design/manufacturing; (2) ongoing quality issues are not resolved with the new models; (3) lack of specific problem-solving mechanisms and subsequent deterioration of market share; (4) number of problem areas per car are two to three times the industry average; (5) inadequate quality control management of the component parts suppliers.

In response to these assessments Chairman Chung initiated Hyundai-Kai Quality Central Office and instructed integration of all the quality functions (i.e., design, production, marketing, and after service). Simultaneously, he insisted that the Quality Conference Room be located in the first floor of Kia Motor Company (KMC) as well. Since then, he presided over monthly strategic quality sessions. Even in the newly built Hyundai Headquarters, three more quality-related rooms are reserved in the first floor. Since then, the Global Quality Status Office collected customer complaints in relation to quality from 5,000 dealerships and after service networks for 24 hours throughout the year. Twice a month quality-related meetings are held in the Quality Conference Room and in the Quality Assurance Office.

December 2, 1999, he visited the Office and found that the quality problem reported in the morning of the day by the overseas sales office was being handled in the evening of the day (Lee, 2008). He instructed to operate the Office for 24 hours to quickly respond to the global service requirements.

Without holidays or weekends, the Office accepted quality problem reports, and those reported problems are posted in the electronic Web sites (Kim and Lee, 2005; Lee, 2008). Within 24 hours the problem resolution action steps are communicated to the dealership that had initially reported the problems. The Global Quality Status Office (GQSO) started December 6—four days after Mr. Chung's instruction. Thus, any problem report is combined and prepared as a QIR (Quality Information Report), which is sent to the relevant functional department. Prior to instituting the GQSO, it took several days for any quality-related report to ever be delivered to the proper department head. But after utilizing GQSO, within a day all the relevant quality reports are properly prepared and delivered. Chairman Chung paid attention to specific quality problems and asked about the reasons for the problems, and urged specific problem resolution to the relevant department head. In this way, HMC has developed the effective problem resolution culture by following through any reported problems that involve senior executives and appropriate, responsible quality-related functions. In this way, the Global Quality Status Office (GQSO) monitors global quality issues. GQSO practically checks the status of quality problems of Hyundai cars from the reports of 200 countries. GQSO operates 24 hours/365 days. This GQSO demonstrated Mr. Chung's commitment to Hyundai quality excellence. In the past a quality problem report was available to only certain managers; however, with the use of GQSO, the quality issues are reported, communicated, and resolved by all the relevant managers. In this way, all Hyundai employees recognize quality problems as for all people.

Inside of the first floor of the Global Quality Status Office (GQSO), according to the Chairman's instruction, all types of auto component parts are displayed. This is to more effectively examine specific reported quality issues with the real tangible parts on hand in full visibility (Lee, 2008). The summary words of J. D. Power's critical reviews and recommendations are also a framed picture, for constant reminder until HMC actually surpasses Toyota in all quality standards. Such are the ways that strategic organizational learning priority is being implemented. To communicate the speed quality concept a technical hotline has been in operation from March 2003 after one year's preparation from 2002. The mission of this Technical Hotline Center (THC), being located just right side of GQSO, is to achieve immediate and effective responsiveness to the quality problem inquiries and complaints. An organizational restructuring allows THC to transfer all its specific functions under more comprehensive accountability of Total Quality Governance Command (TQGC), not to OGQC as was in the past.

A high level of difficult goals is constantly adopted and achieved through continual benchmarking of the world's most recent and best practices and subsequent organizational learning with a sense of real urgency (Kim and Lee, 2005). In 2003, after benchmarking Nissan's outstanding cost management through drastic human resources restructuring by the directives of Carlos Ghosn, Hyundai instead adopted more challenging goals, simultaneously achieving (1) no layoff policy, (2) drastic quality enhancement, and (3) total cost reductions. Chung's message is, "Whatever needs to learn, then do not worry about costs and learn and improve!" Thus, more non-Korean consultants and professionals are hired. Honda's lifelong customer management program is implemented in Hyundai as well. By setting a continually higher level of goals, he infused a healthy sense of crisis in Hyundai's business culture. His constant reminder to the senior executives was, "By 2010 let's surpass Toyota in quality. Then, let us work with specific action plans now." On June 2, 2004, he addressed the senior executives with the following message:

> Be ready to fight good fight with renewed spirit and resolution. Prepare for ever growing challenges of the future. Learn from Toyota that has been working toward higher and almost impossible goals all these years. For the increasingly uncertain future we must change. Toyota is already engaged in mass production of hybrid cars. We are far behind in this product development of future cars. We must strategically invest in research and development for innovative future cars. (Lee, 2008)

Second, Hyundai-Kia Motor Company (HKMC) uses a quality pass system for securing high-quality requirements for new models. All the models that HMC produces have specific quality goals in every step from new product concept planning to sales (Kim and Lee, 2005; Lee, 2008). Chung's demand is that any goals to be achieved be completed before moving to the next step. Starting from 2001, the quality pass system (i.e., line stop system) was instituted. The key processes are divided into five steps such as (1) product concept planning, (2) engineering design, (3) prototype, (4) R & D–based pilot test production, (5) large-scale production (Lee, 2008). Each step has a set of quality requirements which must be satisfied before going further into the subsequent steps.

Each step of quality evaluation is done according to new model quality requirements and standards (i.e., Hyundai's Process Bible). In the product concept planning stage, after careful analysis of market trends and benchmarking of rival automobiles, HMC determines specific quality goals in terms of engine power, functionality performance, and coordinative stability. In the design stage, the most fitting component parts suppliers that receive Quality Five Star Assessment (QFSA) are chosen according to the analysis results of the best compatible rival car's quality performance. This system was adopted in 2001. The trigger occurred between the end of 1999 and the beginning of 2000. At the meeting with the strategic partner suppliers, HMC announced (1) the intention to select component parts suppliers according to objective criteria and (2) Internet use for the purchase of component parts. Specifically, by the end of February 2000, the objective evaluation standards were adopted with the involvement and support of the Korean Standards Association and the Germany Technical Inspection Association. HMC, HKC, and HM's 446 suppliers all received the announcement in detail. By the end of June, the initiatives for comprehensive supplier evaluations were implemented. An example of supply-chain-wide adoption of these evaluations is Quality Five Star Assessment (QFSA). Three areas of evaluation are quality, technology, and productivity. All the evaluation results become openly available. Any suppliers that dispute the evaluation results may request reexamination. The evaluation team consists of a total of nine members—five from purchasing, and one each from quality, R & D, manufacturing, and auditing. Evaluation members from purchasing focus on cost competitiveness, quality on components quality, R & D on technological capability, and auditing on transactions transparency. Evaluation details include 0% to 30% on prices, 40% on quality, and 30% to 40% on R & D.

In the prototype stage, customers outside of Korea (e.g., United States, Europe, and China) are invited for honest and realistic evaluation. At the time when R & D designs a new model car, a real plant floor employee is involved for the multiple quality tests in terms of manufacturing fitness including system/electrical and electronic parts/driving requirements. Just before large-scale production, quality is reexamined and confirmed; 19 detailed items in six areas are again examined. After satisfying all these steps, the new model car is ready for mass production. To improve the quality performance, at the early period of sales, one more comprehensive examination is conducted.

Third, HMC built an organizational system that supports horizontal quality management. In 1999 HMC implemented Six Sigma, a scientific quality innovation movement, to manufacturing processes and administrative management system and process improvement efforts (Kim and Lee, 2005; Lee, 2008). In 2002 HMC also adopted DFSS (Design for Six Sigma) for examining design quality in advance and made the turning point for Six Sigma activities. It is by the pilot prototype and front-end quality innovations that enabled HMC to receive new model quality awards from J. D. Power (Lee, 2008). Real innovation occurs in the pilot prototype building (factory) by which test production/inspection/driving are conducted before large-scale production. In the new model testing process, quality issues are resolved prior to the mass production of new models. Problems that occur in the old models are resolved in a new model based on the learning experiences, and thus such concerted efforts make consistent enhancement of customer satisfaction possible.

New model cars that R & D Office has developed are transported to the pilot prototype room after design, engineering, test, and evaluation (Lee, 2008). In this pilot factory floor, the quality issues are resolved in the course of examining all the product features and manufacturing process details. In this way, the roles of the pilot factory detect and correct any potential quality concerns including the training of the employees in the factory floor.

Fourth, it is the components standardization/common platform sharing system. With the establishment of the component business unit after the merger with Kia Motor Company, component parts sharing system contributes to the overall quality improvement (Kim and Lee, 2005; Lee, 2008). The synergistic effects are possible through the common platform sharing between Hyundai and Kia. Specifically, the functional responsibilities are divided into five areas such as power train, electronics, design, chassis, and body. For each team 20 to 30 executives of R & D and the Purchasing Center participated (the total number of 150). Platform sharing of the component parts started from March, 1999. After two years' combined efforts, 3,566 different component parts were reduced to one-third the level of standardized component parts (1,258 parts). By using standard component parts, the overall unit production cost of suppliers is substantially reduced. Besides, HKMC is also assured of high-quality assembly processes.

Fifth, HMC nurtured the quality culture that values after service (AS) and design as essential components of quality. From September 2001 HKMC executives all attend at least once a year after service field (i.e., a training ground) (Kim and Lee, 2005). The main participants of this annual training are executives from R & D, quality, production, marketing, and general management functions. Because minor problems (not related to critical safety issues) are the reasons for major customer complaints in many places, Chung recommended all these executives actually acquire after service field experiences. The AS location is where customers and the firms actually meet. Therefore, HMC executives actually go to AS centers, observe and listen to the customers. Chung usually emphasizes AS, sales, and component parts as three pillars of business. Poor quality in component parts lead to AS failures, which further result in decline in sales. In March 2002 the time period for this intensive training was five days, and 3,400 executives had field service experiences. The newly hired R & D personnel were required for six months of field work training, but later it is reduced to two months. It was based on his quality awareness through the long experiences in diverse areas as the department director of component parts in 1970, the office of Seoul service operations in 1972, and president of an independent business unit in 1974.

Furthermore, E. S. Chung (son of Chung, Vice-Chairman of HKMC) pursues global competitiveness through unique design. In 2006 he invited Peter Schreyer as the VP of the Design Department to take charge of the comprehensive design strategy and education.

In addition to quality and design management, its aggressive global marketing campaigns support HKMC's continuous successes. From January 2009, the sales of HKMC drastically increased after the adoption of "Hyundai Assurance Program" in the U.S. market. This system allows any customer to receive back all the monthly payments made if he/she is out of a job within one year after the purchase of a Hyundai car. This marketing campaign is based on the reality that many consumers postpone the new car purchasing decisions with the fear of losing their jobs. With the extended recession and massive unemployment, this campaign might be quite risky for HKMC. In preparation of such possibility HKMC has insurance arrangements with WalkerWay, which will cover up to $7,500 in depreciation expenses (Joins, 2009).

Sixth, it is the modularized systems that support excellent quality management. Behind HKMC's quality improvement is the indispensable role of Hyundai Mobis (HM; renaming Hyundai Precision Industry "Hyundai Mobis" in November 2000). HM is the world-class core components supplier with a zero defects reputation and highly efficient modular production methods for HKMC's domestic and global markets. It is HM's modularization that allowed HKMC to assemble all major parts in modular fashion and to conduct advanced quality inspection as the very central element of HKMC's quality improvement.

HKMC has made huge progress in Vehicle Dependability Study (VDS), the most frequently pointed weakness areas, as well as Initial Quality Survey (IQS). In 2009 J. D. Power awarded HMC and KMC better evaluation than the other competitors such as Chrysler, Nissan, and Volkswagen in its Vehicle Dependability Study (VDS). Hyundai's rapid quality improvement efforts resulted in this duration quality survey as well. This reflects improving Hyundai's brand image in the global market with its aggressive marketing campaigns and Hyundai Mobis' consistent quality performance through modularization and its supportive roles (Edaily, 2009).

Hyundai Mobis (HM) is quite a unique business organization, with its successful integration of AS components business and module/component manufacturing business. In late 1998, JeongIn Park (then CEO of HM) proposed an initial idea about integration of the AS component business and the module/components manufacturing business.

Chung enthusiastically approved this new line of business. Such swift decision making is possible through his actual field work experiences of AS and manufacturing business through Hyundai Motor Service and Hyundai Mobis.

Modularization is to combine diverse components in particular system units according to relational proximity and directly supply them to the finished assembly production line. Hyundai Mobis (HM), as the initiator of modular production methods in Korea for Hyundai-Kia Motor Company (HKMC), goes beyond supplying simple modular component parts for finished assembly. In fact, Hyundai Mobis successfully implements highly complementary strategic alignment with HMC through dynamic collaborative relationships. Chung comments:

> As Hyundai Mobis assumes the front- and back-end of manufacturing requirements through AS segment details and components manufacturing, HKMC is able to totally devote to production and marketing areas. By modularization Hyundai Mobis assures all the quality standards of the complete processes from product design, development, test, and manufacturing. Thus, it makes HKMC to avoid the substantial R & D investment requirements and generates other tangible results including production line simplification and product development time reduction. In this way, HM has played an indispensable role for HKMC to become a global automaker. (Hyundai Mobis, 2007)

Seventh, building a model standard plant as the basis of global plant expansion efforts. Based on automated systems of the Asan Korea plant, in 2002 cutting-edge automated plant started operation within three months (Kim and Lee, 2005; Lee, 2008). In July 2002, HMC deployed production-related engineers to China. Starting from September 6, the existing plant facilities were discarded, and a new plant was constructed. On December 23 of that year, within three months, the first model EF Sonata was introduced. The India plant is also another success case. At the end of 1997, the India plant was completed. In early 2003 HMC sent Korean executives to learn about the secret of successful localization efforts. Other management members working on production planning and technology implementation for the Alabama plant also came to India to learn about the India plant's sources of competitive advantage. Through such concerted internal benchmarking, the U.S. Alabama plant was completed with the total investment of $1 billion. This plant is to supply high-premium-value brands such as Sonata and Santa Fe. This is not merely an assembly plant but a comprehensive auto manufacturing plant that is able to manage new product development projects, manufacturing processes, and complete technology and knowledge intensive tests and examinations. Furthermore, it is the new car assembly line that has been 100% automated with the one higher level upgrade beyond that of the current plant by applying cutting-edge technologies and processes. The plant competitiveness lies in easy production of diverse models with small investment. For this Alabama plant has become a standard model of all other global plants that continue to implement the available cutting-edge technologies and manufacturing processes. Real-time check of factory-level problems started from the Alabama plant.

Chung also considered the idea of supplying large volumes of Hyundai cars through mass production for the plant open ceremony (Lee, 2008). So he suggested that the plant open in May 2005, but that the production start from March. The reason is that at least 13,000 cars needed to be ready by May 2005 to cover 650 U.S. dealerships. By advancing production start day two months ahead of the plant opening, he initiated a new method by which the mass production volume meets the expected market demand of dealers. He visited the plant construction site in November 2004 and determined that 60 people are not adequate to ensure production and quality training plus mass production system, so he ordered a 150-member quality task force. In January 2005 the first 40 arrived, and then in February another 110 followed to secure quality standards. From several months before the start of production Chung received the progress report every morning and evening through video conferencing and supervised the plant construction and production details.

3.3.2.3.2 Spillover Process and the IT System

It is the IT system that supports all the quality-related functional systems. In the early part of 1999, R & D, manufacturing technologies, and production systems were not properly integrated. Master data needed to be copied, and production change plans then communicated one week later to other departments. For system integration HMC considered the SAP-based ERP system. However, as the precondition of IT system integration, HMC changed the BOM structure for the consolidation of the BOM Master. A 20-member team worked on this for five to six years. The first plant that applied the new BOM was the U.S. Alabama plant, which applied ERP best practices. Except for specialized areas for customization, this new system was almost entirely adopted. After construction of Integrated Global BOM, HMC initiated SCM(i2) from 2002. Based on the SCM system, monthly/weekly/daily plans are implemented according to system capabilities. SCM(i2) and ERP(SAP) were first adopted in overseas plants, and in January 2009 they were installed in the Asan plant, Korea, as well. By applying a standard template for minimizing customization constraints, the implementation timeline includes system construction in six months and then stabilization tests for the next six months. After its successful implementation in the Alabama plant, other plants in Slovakia, Czech Republic, and Georgia, U.S. adopted the standard templates.

In addition to such standard template application, HMC also integrated SAP to the GQMS (Global Quality Management System) and e-procurement. In the past all the quality-related reports were on paper, but with the IT upgrade they are electronically available now. GQSO can tell who and when particular reports are reviewed. All the managers even during their overseas trips prepare their reports online.

A new department called Computer Center (CC) is created to get in charge of component quality to resolve engine part failures. Since the start of his chairmanship in 1999, Chung was concerned about frequent engine failures. In June 2002 he instructed to investigate the root causes of engine problems. According to the investigation committee report, mechanical failures are fairly small, while sensor failures are 70%, and computer failures 5%. Afterward, the Complete Computer Inspection System (CCIS) was initiated so that all the computer systems for new cars go through a complete check-up before they are installed. To respond to global quality problems, starting from 1999, video conferencing was applied to check the problem components by video screen, and concerned people discussed the details face to face. Recently, online cameras were installed even in the factory floor level so that any problems that occur may get immediate feedback for problem resolution.

A Five Star System (FSS) is also implemented for all the component part purchase decisions. An electronic bidding system called VAATZ (Value-Added Automotive Trading Zone) is adopted as well. In the early years most purchasing decisions used prearranged contracts. However, the new system uses electronic competitive bidding instead. In this way, all the purchasing decisions of component parts are transparent, and thus the entire quality performance is naturally enhanced.

Since January 2008 all the above-mentioned systems are in operation in the name of Autoway M-channel Plus (AMP) that makes real-time information available online. In the past GQSO discussed quality issues through video conferencing. However, with the new system implementation all the critical data including overseas plant utilization rate, sales performance indicators, market share, and inventory level are all available in real time. The complete menu includes global management status information, domestic sales and global sales reports, production, quality, logistics/components, R & D, IT, reporting requirements, and other manager input sections. As of November 9, 2009, a new updated system version was upgraded. This comprehensive IT system allows the senior executives to assess the overall business status with sufficient details on each of the HMC's global operational units.

In the new plant global ERP/MES has been simultaneously applied to all the plants since 2005, the year when the Alabama facility was equipped with the cutting-edge automated system. New plant construction requires a complete setup of manufacturing technologies/mass production system including IT system construction within the next six months. Such a comprehensive plant system construction involves 50 professional experts, including a 20-member task force team and other consultants. A revenue center unit employs a 25-member diverse functional team instead. With such human resources configurations, the new plant support system is quickly constructed and completed. SAP is used for the global market to support their wholesale-based dealership, while in the domestic Korean market a custom-made retail-based system is used.

3.3.3 Spillover (Horizontal Expansion) Mechanism

The three research questions in this chapter are: (1) What is the organizational mechanism that allows senior executives to make large-scale investment decisions? (2) How does such investment decision making affect learning outcomes? (3) How are such learning processes and outcomes translated into competitive advantage?

We examined how the impact of swift investment decision and organizational learning outcomes are communicated to other organizational units. In this section, we discuss the spillover mechanism. Based on the former knowledge experiences of semiconductors, SE's Owner/CEO infuses a sense of crisis through aggressive investment decisions, facilitates new technology/product development and thus helps its managers not to settle in conservative and defensive posture after attaining number one position. Aggressive investment decisions too often disrupt the delicate organizational balance within the firm and instead create a new growth opportunity engine.

Hyundai-Kia Owner/Management also adopts a 10-year/100,000-mile service guarantee system and strives toward a high level of challenging goals with real sense of crisis. The organizational capability grows in the course of trying to achieve these goals one by one. In this way, the organization brings forth dynamic energy out of its hidden organizational resources (Aoshima and Kato, 2003). New business initiatives are planned and implemented beyond the current level; instead, the slack resources within the organizational system are mobilized for greater business opportunities (Karube, 2004b).

Penrose (1959) distinguished untapped potential productive resources (not yet utilized for current productive activities) and exploited productive resources (used for current productive activities) within a firm. Firm growth diversification or innovation is the actualization process of potential productive resources for current productive purposes. Such an exploration process is similar to the overextension and stretch logic of organizational capability (Itami, 1987; Hamel and Prahalad, 1994). The utilization of untapped productive resources is viewed as critical for firm growth, diversification, and source of innovation.

By assuming an organization as having a slack economy, management continuously seeks underutilized resources for dynamic new business opportunities in spite of internal organizational resistance. Naturally, the organizational members need to exert more effort to address the system disequilibrium with the implementation of more difficult organizational goals. Management also adopts aggressive and risky investment decisions to expand the resources required for the continuous growth of the organization. Through such interactive processes, organizational members are mobilized for a greater level of productive efforts, and new information and knowledge assets are created and accumulated within the organization, which then become another basis for the business growth engine (Hamel and Prahalad, 1994; Aoshima and Kato, 2003).

Here, SE members do live with a healthy sense of crisis with the presence of the strong rival LG Electronics. LG's outstanding performance challenges SE not to become complacent and rather continuously upgrade and move forward with new innovative products. Both SE and LG do not limit their competitive battlegrounds in the small domestic market; rather, their vision and goals are derived from the global markets. Japanese firms have also maintained global competitive advantage through the intense competition between Sony and Matsushita in their domestic market. In this sense, SE's dynamic learning mechanism is facilitated by an ongoing rivalry with LG Electronics (Chang, 2005).

For the effective control and management of business risks, it is essential to deploy external management resources. In a sense, SE has perpetuated the state of organizational disequilibrium that requires continuous utilization of regional expert systems for technology transfers and acquisition of external facilities, product development by external human resources, and development of internal human resources. Based on their success in semiconductor products, SE has kept pursuing diverse, horizontal business opportunities and secured IT systems for its global management requirements with timely support of critical information and knowledge resources.

HKMC has also constructed a systematic learning system and implemented organizational learning for all employees for the purpose of institutionalizing quality management. For the attainment of global quality management goals, HMC has adopted centralized collaborative governance system structures that include modularized component parts, after services by Hyundai Mobis, and integrated production/marketing efforts by Hyundai-Kia Motor Company (HKMC). HKMC utilized an IT system that effectively supports their global quality and brand management initiatives.

Figure 3.3 summarizes the ECIS (externalization, combination, internalization, and socialization) model of Korean firms' learning cycles that promotes fast and effective learning systems for rapid growth into global firms. Such growth patterns of Korean firms can be explained with the SECI (socialization, externalization, combination, and internalization) model (Nonaka and Takeuchi, 1995). In the early growth stage, Korean firms adopted fast learning system formalization. For effective learning the senior management of Samsung and Hyundai often stressed a sense of crisis and fast investment strategy to catch up with U.S., European, and Japanese practices. They use IT for the effective communication and implementation of formalized learning systems. At the same time, these system learning details are electronically stored and become internally available

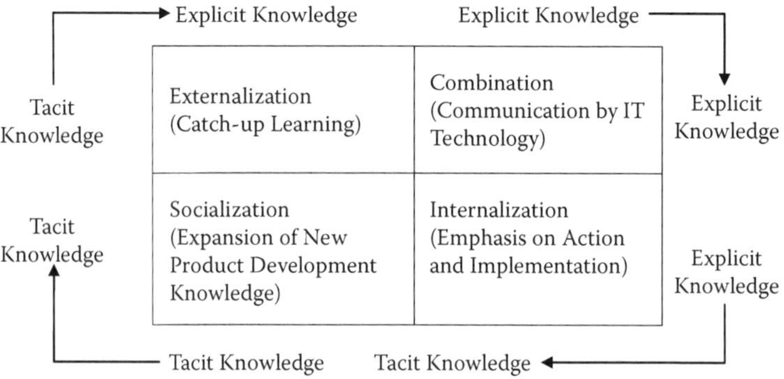

FIGURE 3.3
Learning process of Korean firms' growth (ECIS model).

to facilitate specific action plans and routine practices. In the course of transferring knowledge and experiences acquired from particular new product or business development projects, these firms have instituted systematic knowledge-sharing mechanisms for knowledge acquisition, absorptive capacity, and innovative exploration of more advanced levels of knowledge and technology development. In a sense, Korean firms have implemented ECIS (externalization, combination, internalization, and socialization) rather than Nonaka and Takeuchi's initial SECI (socialization, externalization, combination, and internalization) model for their unique growth patterns.

3.4 CONCLUSION

This chapter analyzed the cases of two Korean global firms of Samsung Electronics and Hyundai Motor Company that represent the growth mechanisms of the Korean economy.

First, swift decision making ability and organizational learning capability. These two cases suggest that senior executives' decision making ability (according to the motto of "speedy decision making and massive investment") and organizational learning and communication capabilities that connect executives' decisions into competitive advantage are critical success factors of these two global firms—Samsung Electronics and Hyundai-Kia Motor Company.

Second, decision support organizations. In terms of senior management decision making, success/failures of Korean Chaebols depend on the owner/senior executives' decision making; it is critical for the best possible decision making. These two firms are different from other global firms that are heavily governed by a professional managerial hierarchy. Instead, these owner/senior executives utilize Samsung's Office of Future Strategy (in the past Office of Administrative Executives and Office of Strategic Structure Coordination) and Hyundai's Comprehensive Quality Status Office for quality decision making support. Rapid new product development follows the swift and massive investment decisions. From a product architecture perspective, these two firms have advantages in terms of rapid product modularization and synergistic process capabilities. In the case of Samsung Electronics, their success in semiconductors is extended to synergistic product and process capabilities in the areas of flash memory,

LCD, mobile phones, and TV. In the case of HKMC, Hyundai Mobis supports HKMC's finished products through global simultaneous manufacturing by applying modularization of component parts. From a product architecture standpoint, the finished products of SE and HKMC are somewhat opposite. Yet similar modularization of component parts is applied in both SE and HKMC. These two firms adopt open integral product architecture and at the same time apply differentiation strategy through black box and design excellence.

Third, IT systemization and packaging capability are critical for Korean firms to connect a large-scale investment to competitive advantage. Different from Japanese firms that possess organizational learning capabilities within the employees in the plant level, Korean firms package diverse sets of business processes (e.g., production line management and purchasing management) by centralized management structures.

This centralized management is useful for coordinating various functions, including all product development efforts, global management, overseas production, and marketing systems, through highly integrated and synchronized IT systems. For example, any production line problems are handled through the know-how of production managers scattered in the global network and central management through online Internet visual applications. Problem solving and responding capabilities are excellent for these Korean firms. Since all important learning outcomes of key business processes are organized into useful packages, these management systems support any new rapid investment decisions and also lead firms with sustainable competitive advantage.

The past business strategy of two case firms is based on efficiency-driven/low-cost or value-added differentiation advantages. However, in the areas of consumer electronics (e.g., Sony, Microsoft) or digital cameras (e.g., Canon, HP, and Olympus), intense global competition requires more than the combinations of low cost and differentiation strategy (Ishikura, 2003). Pursuit of efficiency is a basic requirement for global competition. What is required is dynamic strategy that attains both efficiency and differentiation (Aoshima and Kato, 2003; Ishikura, 2003). In brief, these global Korean firms use IT systems to implement front-loading practices either for products with modular architecture (e.g., SE) or those with integral architecture (e.g., HKMC). In this way, they sustain their competitive advantage.

Thus, the growth of Korean global firms suggests the important roles of IT systems in building dynamic network capability as an important source of their sustainable competitiveness. The essence of the twenty-first century competitive advantage is the integration of both efficiency strategy through cost reduction and premium value creation and delivery to customers. Senior executives of Korean global firms first achieve low-cost efficiency during the early catch-up stage and then pursue dynamic strategy that combines low costs and differentiation through high premium value creation and delivery for their global customers. The continuous future successes depend on dynamic organizational capabilities that enable firms to quickly respond to rapid environmental changes through simultaneous attainment of efficiency and value added and thus achieve their sustainable competitive advantage.

4

Product Architecture and Technology Transfer: New Catch-Up Patterns in the Digital Era

This chapter shows relationships between product architecture and technology transfer: New catch-up patterns in the digital era. Rapid modularization of product architecture is in progress in semiconductor micro controller unit (MCU) that contains firmware (i.e., control software of all digital products). Thus, technological transfers rapidly occur from Japanese firms to NIE (Newly Industrialized Economy) firms including Korea. Such changes in product architecture in the course of transition from analog era to digital era make a huge impact on the speed of global technological transfer and technology catch-up patterns as well. From a product/process architectural standpoint, this chapter analyzes how these changes in product architecture impact the speed of technological transfer with the case illustrations of Japanese CD/DVD and TV industries. We also show the differences between Japanese catch-up patterns during the analog era and those of NIE countries in the digital era. Special focus is on Korean firms in particular.

4.1 INTRODUCTION

The twenty-first century business environment rapidly changes with the transition from the analog to the digital era. The open environment of the supply chain in the digital era transformed the business environment into a borderless world, because firmware controls the basic software functions of semiconductors that are embedded in all digital products. That is, such firmware functions impact the product architecture of these products to move away from integral to modular type. Such product architectural change allows traditional closed economic systems to move into more open international collaboration.

In the analog era, interorganizational specialization occurred. In the early stage, most manufacturing functions stayed with the advanced nations in the United States, Europe, and Japan. Semiconductor MCU with firmware software in all digital products influenced rapid modularization of product architecture in the form of turn-key solution. Advanced manufacturing nations accomplished international collaboration with firms from newly industrialized economies (NIEs) and Brazil, Russia, India, and China (BRICs). NIEs/BRICs specialize in assembly of modular types of products and technologies, while advanced manufacturing nations focus on integral type of products and technologies.

For modular type of products, barriers of entry are low, and thus it is fairly easy to enter the market, and the speed of technology dispersion is quite rapid. On the other hand, the speed of technology transfer of the integral type is relatively slow. From the perspective of product architecture, twenty-first century international specialization refers to the two and distinctly different architectural types of technology transfer (i.e., dispersion spectrum) in the global market. The global supply chain is an infrastructure that supports this new pattern of business structures.

Thus, product architectural change with the transition from analog to digital impacts the global technology transfer speed. In this chapter we focus on how so many NIEs firms participate in the global market as product architecture changes from integral to modular type. We particularly note that different technology catch-up patterns emerge between Japanese firms in the analog era and Korean firms in the digital era. We use case studies of Japanese firms to illustrate this point.

4.2 PRODUCT/PROCESS ARCHITECTURE AND GLOBAL COMPETITIVE ADVANTAGE

Behavioral practices of Asian multinational corporations strongly reflect the industry catch-up patterns and the business structures of Asian nations.

In general, many multinational corporations (MNCs) possess abundant management resources and successfully establish their international competitive advantage. However, the number of Asian MNCs (AMNCs) that occupy such global prominence is relatively small because the economic development of these Asian nations started somewhat late compared to that of the United States and European nations. AMNCs thus form strategic partnerships with firms from other advanced nations and pursue their technology strategy to build their manufacturing base through rapid technology transfers (Masuyama, 2002).

Much of the research has focused on the success factors of Japanese or Korean firms in their catch-up stages. Yet little research attention has been paid to explain how these success factors are related to sustainable competitive advantage of individual global firms from these nations. Korean IT industries include component parts (e.g., semiconductors), mobile communication, LCD, and digital TV industries. They have achieved a very successful catch-up with other advanced Western and Japanese firms. In spite of the relative competitive advantage of several Korean global firms, rapid modularization is occurring in all these industries. It is worthwhile to compare Japanese and Korean global competitiveness from a product/process architectural perspective, regarding recent digitalization of electronic products experience in (1) product minimization and intensity, (2) short product life cycle, (3) change in component parts formation, and (4) restructuring the value chain structure (Joo et al., 2003). In view of the very short product life cycle of electronic products, even an outstanding firm may quickly lose its competitive advantage as the market environment unexpectedly changes in a new direction. Thus, for their sustainable global competitiveness, in addition to the growth model of Korean IT industry, it is worth examining, from a product architectural perspective, how Korean firms implement their global strategy for their sustainable global competitiveness.

Architecture is about product design ideas (Fujimoto, 2001). It defines the relationship of a product with (1) its component parts and (2) related work processes. It maximizes a product's overall performance by presenting appropriate design methods by clarifying the functional requirements and thus coordinates the interfaces between component parts and work processes (Fujimoto, 2003). Traditional classification is modular/integral and open/closed (Ulrich, 1995; Fine, 1998; Baldwin and Clark, 2000; Fujimoto, 2003). The right product architecture provides firms with a desirable level of competitiveness through timely innovation corresponding to the changing market requirements (Henderson and Clark, 1990; Fujimoto, 2003; Park et al., 2007a).

Compatibility requirements between product architecture and national/industry capability suggest that Japanese firms in general fit to integral products, while Korean firms (broadly firms from emerging economies) do well with modular products (Fujimoto, 2006a). Korean firms (and other Asian firms) reduced the required catch-up periods with the increasing global demand of modular products. Shintaku (2006) observes that it is quite challenging for these firms to sustain their competitiveness, because stiff price competition and fast change speed characterize the modular type products (e.g., CD-ROM, mobile phones). Therefore, product architecture makes a huge impact for these Asian nations to achieve their rapid catch-up strategy (Shintaku et al., 2006). Samsung and LG, two representative Korean global firms, have very strong modular architectural orientation for their electronic products. Since manufacturing know-how of these modular products is easy to imitate, the value-added base and the source of competitive advantage of these electronic products naturally move away from manufacturing to research and development, marketing, and logistics (Joo et al., 2003). In addition to product architecture, it is important to pay attention to the corresponding process architecture as well. Process architecture is quite useful in explaining the competitiveness of the process industry.

Figure 4.1 shows the difference between integral and modular architecture in terms of relationship between function and structure. Fujimoto (2003) and Tomita et al. (2011) extended the architecture concept to the production process (i.e., process architecture) of the process industry (Figure 4.2). According to their research, "process" entails a system that is made up of a series of production equipment, tools, workers, process of

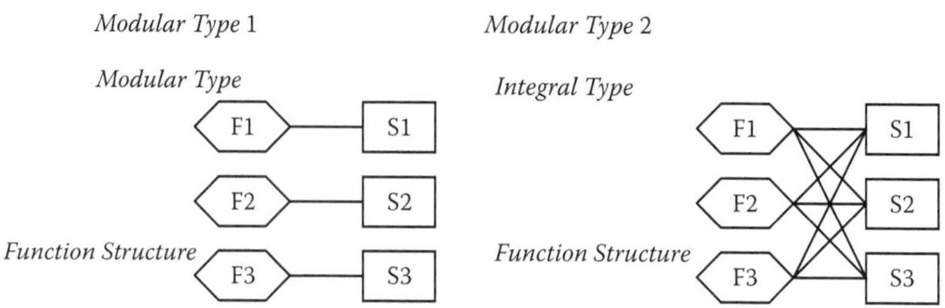

FIGURE 4.1
The basic type of product architecture. Adapted from Fujimoto (2003), Tomita et al. (2011).

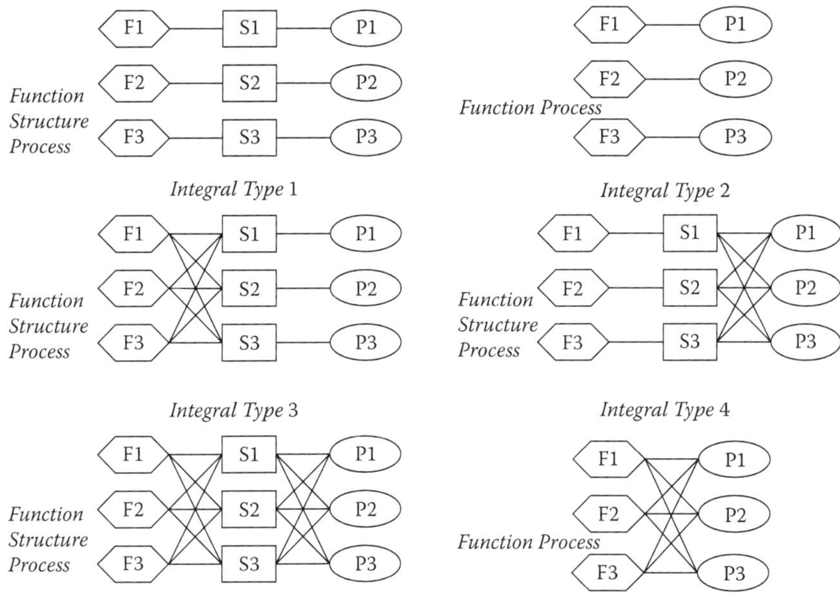

FIGURE 4.2
The basic type of process architecture. Adapted from Fujimoto (2003), Tomita et al. (2011).

working, and operations for commercialization. Production process functions by transforming raw materials into finished products under specified structures. Connecting series of complex processes requires effective design layouts. In a sense, process architecture might be defined just like product architecture. Its definition recognizes the following two essential relational aspects of a system. The structure of a system requires proper relationships with corresponding (1) function and (2) process. Process architecture is classified into the two types—modular or integral. The former resembles one-to-one relationships such as the relationships among the function, structure, and process of a system (Modular Type 1), while the latter is similar to the relationships between the function and process of a system.

The integral type indicates complex relationships between (1) the function and structure of a system (Integral Type 1), (2) the structure and process of a system (Integral Type 2), (3) the function, structure, and process of a system (Integral Type 3), and (4) the function and process of a system (Integral Type 4). Other types of architecture are the open or closed type (Fine, 1998; Baldwin and Clark, 2000). The former is of the modular type and is defined as "a system whose interfaces among elements are standardized at the industry level." Therefore, it enables the design of a functional product by combining several elements (modules) across firms. The latter is defined as "a system whose interfaces among elements are standardized within a certain firm." Therefore, it is only possible to combine several elements within a certain firm to efficiently develop a functional product (Tomita, et al., 2001).

Architecture is a relative concept. For example, if the process elements of a system are highly interrelated or the connection requirements between functions and processes are huge, then process architecture tends to become more complex and integral. On the other hand, the opposite is also true. Architecture is also a dynamic concept. Particular architecture is not fixed; rather it may change from once being integral to later modular or vice versa (Fine, 1998; Chesbrough and Kusunoki, 2001). Interestingly enough, the technology transfer depends on the type of architecture. For example, if architecture is modular and open, the speed of the transfer of technology from developed countries to developing countries is more rapid (Ogawa et al., 2009; Shintaku et al., 2006b).

4.3 PRODUCT ARCHITECTURE AND TECHNOLOGY TRANSFER

4.3.1 Growth of Japanese Firms and Technology Transfer

Technology transfer is an important concept for a study of international competition based on innovation. Recently, some Japanese innovation leader firms have not necessarily reaped the real competitive benefits because of their "too rapid innovation transfer" and thus find it difficult for them to maintain their international competitiveness (Shintaku et al., 2008). Such "too rapid technology transfer" is not merely an issue with Japanese firms. In the middle 1980s and the early 1990s U.S.–Japan trade conflicts occurred because of "too rapid innovation transfer" from U.S. firms to Japanese counterparts. Much research in the 1980s focused on such "too rapid technology transfer by U.S. firms" or "too swift catch-up by Japanese firms" (Abernathy and Clark, 1985; Teece, 1986). This particular issue stirred up American nationalism sentiment in the 1980s. In this context, a theory of strategic trade management is developed (Tyson, 1992).

Now, we consider the growth process of Japanese firms. After World War II, Japanese firms attained phenomenal growth through technology import from U.S. and European firms. The actual number of technological import cases from 1949 to 1966 is 4,135 (Yamazaki, 2004). 60% of these transfers (2,471 cases) are from U.S. firms, and 448 cases involve those from Germany. In this sense, after World War II Japanese firms depended for their technological innovation mostly on the assistance of U.S. firms. The number of cases, by industry, is electrical machinery (826), transportation equipment (158), and other manufacturing machinery (1,358), which account for 56.6% of total technology transfers. Japanese firms devoted themselves to independent research and development based on technology know-how that has been accumulated over the ten years of post-War technology transfer processes. Such R & D investment in growth industry contributed to overcome the technological gap between Japanese and other advanced nations. Particularly, it is these private firms that sustained R & D activities. 70% of R & D expenditures was from these private firms in the period from 1950 into the early part of the 1980s (Yamazaki, 2004). In this regard, the Japanese pattern is quite different from the United States, in which the government portion of R & D is fairly high.

Between the latter part of the 1950s and the early 1970s, R & D investment by the private sector had shown very high growth in the petrochemical, petro-process, steel, machinery, and electrical industries. Strong capability in heavy chemical industry supported vigorous R & D investment. After the first Oil Shock in the 1970s, more R & D investment poured in new cutting-edge industry as well as in the traditional assembly industry (e.g., electrical machinery and automobiles). Through this process, in the 1960s there was a noticeable boom in establishing and expanding centralized research centers initiated by electrical manufacturers. Nippon Electronic Company (NEC) established research headquarters in May 1965 and integrated its existing basic research units, communication technology research functions, and electronic machinery research center. Matsushita and Toshiba also reorganized and strengthened the functions of research headquarters. Matsushita Co. also started their Research Center at Katoma of Osaka in 1953 and expanded its functions with an additional research complex in 1962. Toshiba also established their Research Complex in 1942. From July 1961, basic research was further strengthened with the establishment of the Central Research Complex. In 1959 Toray was number four among Japanese firms in terms of its R & D expenditures (Yamazaki, 2004). By March 1965, 16% and 8% of total R & D personnel of Toray were employed in the Central and Basic Research Center, respectively. Thus, Japanese firms emphasized on developing basic technological capabilities through central research centers in the 1960s after they achieved early catch-up with U.S. and European firms. Strengths of Japanese firms are not in product innovation from R & D centers, but in process innovation (i.e., improvement and progress) in the field. According to the government statistics, the overall proportion of R & D on basic research is not very high. However, the role of central research centers is critical for developing cutting-edge technologies and new product development. As of 1963, a significant number of R & D results in Matshushita showed world-class quality. In Toray the specific outcomes of such basic research center in Toray are the development of an anti-cancer drug called Interferon and its participation in the carbon fiber.

Of course, the Japanese government's support for such development efforts was real. For example, LSI Technology Research Cooperation (lasted four years from 1976 to 1980) is a case of successfully developing cutting-edge technology by Japanese firms that effectively competed against the U.S. computer and semiconductor industry. Such development required a two-tier system—collaborative research (concentrated research) and business group research (decentralized research). This Research Cooperative (RC) challenges the basic research that is essential for future premium value creation which is too expensive for a single firm to handle. On the other hand, business group research—Computer Development Laboratory (CDL) of the Fujitsu-Hitachi-Mitsubishi group and NEC Toshiba Information Systems (NTIS) of the NEC-Toshiba group—focus on specific research related to particular product lines. This RC, five to ten years after its termination of operations, made it possible for the Japanese semiconductor industry to increase Japanese manufacturing competitiveness and thus dominate the global market in the area of 1M DRAM.

In brief, Japanese firms experienced high levels of growth after the 1950s through their rapid technology imported from the United States and European counterparts, their joint research with Japanese government, and independent centralized R & D centers. It was during the analog era, and Japanese firms achieved successful catch-up with Western firms by manufacturing field process innovation and thus kept their sustainable competitive advantage.

4.3.2 Product Architecture and Technology

In studying catch-up of newly industrialized nations, it is easy to think about the Japanese pattern of technology import from the United States and European countries. However, Japanese technology export in the 1990s is not so simple to explain. For example, the cutting-edge technologies of the steel and chemical industries remained with Japanese firms, while those of the semiconductor and LCD industries were fairly quickly introduced to Korean and Taiwanese firms (Fujimoto, 2006a). It is good to remember that the transition from analog to digital era involved product/process architectural change as well. Any industry with open modular product/process architecture for its products achieves relatively rapid catch-up, while closed integral architecture requires a much longer catch-up period. The Japanese material industry that is built on the Japanese chemical industry still maintains very strong global competitiveness. Toray (a Japanese chemical firm) accomplished its growth through technological import from U.S. DuPont. Its catch-up was not so easily attained. Rather, its independent technological development was possible through a few decades' accumulated investment on basic research from the 1950s. Reverse engineering is not quite feasible in material science or chemical industry, and thus technology transfers do not occur so readily. The technology transfer speed is different by industry. Product architecture has a certain hierarchical intensity. If a firm's product is more or less finished assembly goods, technology transfer is easy. However, if a firm's product is mostly component parts or materials that require basic technology know-how, then technology transfer is difficult with the requirements of process know-how and patent restrictions. The representative cases are CD/DVD players and LCD panels, and semiconductors with smooth technology transfer. However, little technology transfer occurs in the areas of light pickup, light film, filter, silicon wafer, and liquid panel. Besides these component parts, Japanese firms still maintain technological advantage in the areas of infra-equipment areas of semiconductors and LCD panels.

From a product architectural standpoint, Japanese firms hold technological know-how in the areas of integral products (i.e., having very strong interdependent relationships among component elements and infra-equipment), while technology know-how of modular products (e.g., DVD players and liquid panels) is mostly transferred to newly industrialized nations. What is important to Japanese industry is that classification of integral/modular product architecture is dynamic, not static. Product architecture, once determined, is not necessarily permanently fixed; instead, it changes over time. Such architectural changes make a huge impact on the international competitive advantage of Japanese firms.

4.4 CASE STUDIES

4.4.1 CD-ROM/DVD Industry

Prior to 1980, Japanese electrical products with analog technology contained multihierarchical structures among component parts. These multidimensional interdependent relationships were quite complex. Product functionalities for customers also had hierarchical multidimensions. Such complexity and multidimensionality among component parts and functional relationships characterize all integral types of product architecture for both passenger cars and digital still cameras (DSC).

Analog products that have complex interdependent relationships and multihierarchical relationships among their component parts do not fit to open environment. Firms from NIEs/BRICs could not overcome the high barriers of entry, and international specialization was not possible to attain. The global supply chain was quite closed and partially operating within an internal network of firms in the form of vertical integration.

It was Japanese firms that introduced CD-ROM drives in 1987 to the world market. At that time MCU capability was still low, using analog feedback control mechanisms. The market size was also fairly small in terms of sales—0.9 million units in 1991 and 1.8 million units in 1992. However, the digital integrated circuit (IC) chipset was distributed in an impressive volume—20 million units—in 1994 alone. Toshiba introduced CD-X and EX series, new kinds of IC chipsets for CD-ROM drives in an open environment in 1994. Figure 4.3 shows how the complex mechanisms in analog type of complex mechanisms are simplified in digital autonomous feedback mechanisms.

However, it was Korean and Taiwanese firms (not Japanese ones) that achieved massive distribution by applying digital feedback mechanisms. Figure 4.4 shows the details of miraculous market expansion with product architectural change. From the latter part of the 1990s Taiwanese Lite-on and Ben-Q and Korean Samsung and LG Electronics all used an IC chipset that uses digital feedback control mechanisms. Just five years after their impressive start in 1995-1995, each of these firms recorded more than $1 billion of sales as huge global business enterprises.

The number of emerging firms from Korea, Taiwan, and Singapore that participated in the CD-ROM drive market in 1995–1996 is more than 50 (each company had about 1.5 million customers). All of these firms

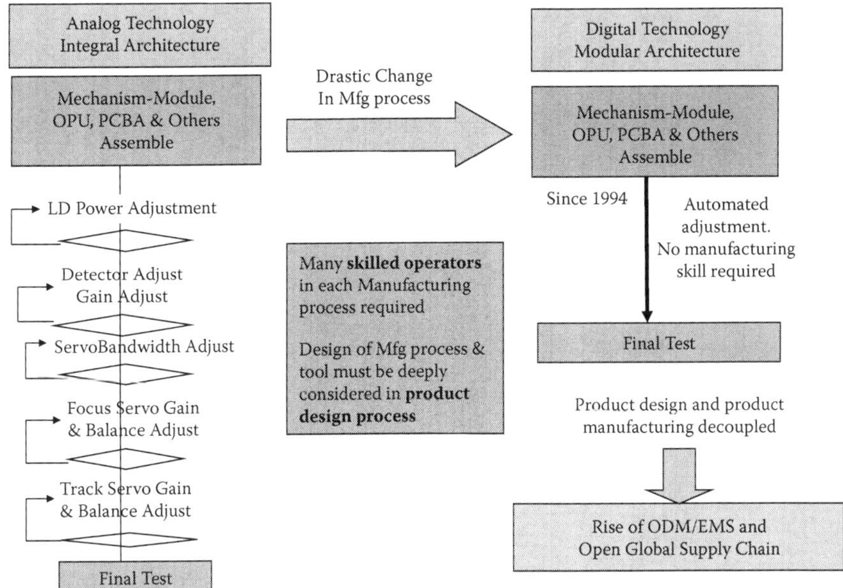

FIGURE 4.3
MCU has changed product architecture of the CD-ROM drive. From Ogawa et al. (2009).

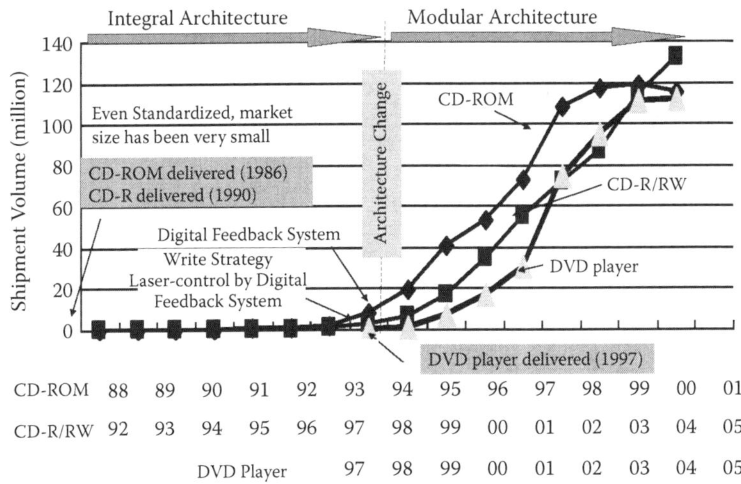

FIGURE 4.4
Miraculous growth market expansion by product architecture change. From Ogawa et al. (2009).

purchased digital IC chipsets made by Toshiba. In addition to CD-ROMs, other optic disc drives also adopted digital feedback control mechanisms. Product architecture was quickly switched to modular type. A few years after Japanese firms developed new products, Korean and Taiwanese firms dominated the global DVD-drive market. At the same time the process architecture of products also turned into modular type as well. Just as in analog VTR, the CD-DVD industry change in product architecture occurred in digital servo and digital control which has firmware embedded in MCU. With this modular type, a drastic export increase of Korean and Chinese firms was possible through mass production (Shintaku et al., 2008).

Even in this open environment, Japanese firms maintained their competitive position like Intel in their core component parts. It is Japanese firms that developed CD-ROM and DVD drives with their technological systems. Figure 4.5 shows the different types of global supply chain in the DVD industry based on the year 2006. Firms from NIEs/BRICs maintain key segments in the DVD player and record DVD drive market. Chinese firms hold more than 60% of the global DVD player market in which modular architecture is quite common. However, Korean and Chinese firms hold 80% of the integral type of global DVD market.

As shown in Figure 4.6, Japanese firms maintain their competitive advantage in the product segments (e.g., optic pick-up, micro-light component parts) for which the vast technology know-how details are hidden in a black box.

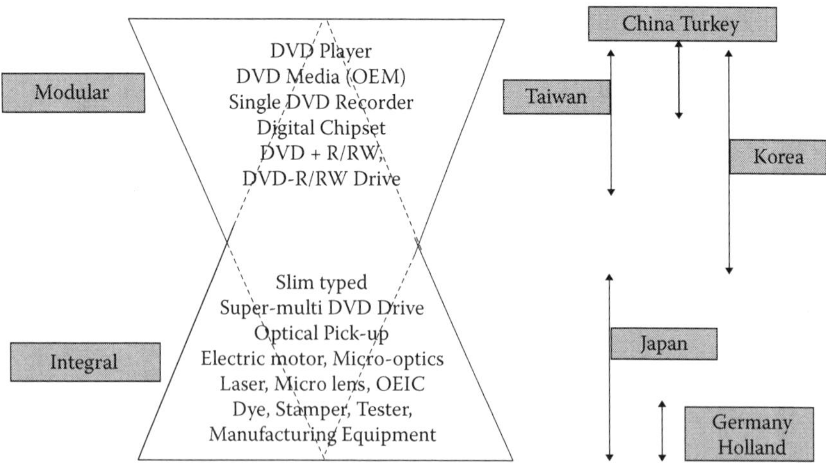

FIGURE 4.5
International division of labor in optical storage industry after product architecture change. From Ogawa et al. (2009).

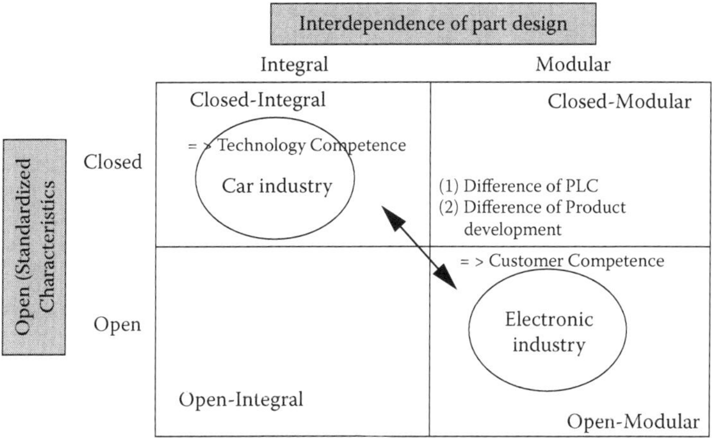

FIGURE 4.6
Comparison of Japanese and Korean firms from product architectural perspective.

International specialization like in the DVD industry is to utilize the comparative advantage of each nation and strengthen mutual interdependence in the global market. A similar pattern is also repeated in the PC industry of the 1990s as firms from advanced nations and NIEs/BRICs collaborated with the principles of international specialization and interdependence.

4.4.2 TV Industry

Another example of developing international competitiveness by such architectural change is the TV industry. The product architecture of the black and white screen TV was entirely modular. In fact, Matsushita Electronics Co. started TV assembly-based production from 1945 by importing brown tubes from U.S. Phillips. However, these black and white brown tubes too often failed to function (short product life) and needed quick replacement, like light bulbs. Brown tube sockets became generic with no particular distinction among manufacturers (Shintaku et al., 2008). Therefore, any manufacturers could produce finished black and white TV without any real difficulty of obtaining the core component parts (i.e., black and white brown tubes).

In the era of color brown tube TV, change took place in product architecture. The color brown tube generates electronic beams using three electronic guns. Different from the black and white brown tube, it is difficult to control the desirable level of beam, focus, and color. Color TV functionality requires very strong interference among deflection yoke and sash circuit that control the beam quality. Color brown TV thus switched its product architecture toward integral type. In the 1980s Japanese firms enjoyed the golden opportunity when color TV was developed and produced by integral product architecture. Japanese firms manufactured color TVs as finished goods and supplied color brown tubes as well. Their sales were excellent with little worry about potential competitors.

In the late 1990s the situation was completely changed. Korean firms (i.e., LG and Samsung) started producing color brown tubes. The target market was the emerging economies in Asia. Color brown tubes and TV's sash circuit are quite interdependent. It is critical for these firms to produce both color brown tube and sash circuit together using their internal design and manufacturing capabilities. Color TVs for advanced nations require high-quality control. Yet, in these Asian nations it was quite possible to produce both of these components in ways to satisfy competitive requirements. For color brown tubes these firms used the ITC brown tube which has a standardized deflection yoke and the desirable level of purity for customer requirements. Initially, these color TVs were assembled. By deploying the ITC brown tube, it was quite possible to control heat elements and quality requirements in the screen of the color TV (Yoshimoto, 2007; Shintaku et al., 2008). With the advancement of semiconductor technologies, simple assembly production methods of color TV are adapted as well. MCU has absorbed all differentiation elements of the color brown TV by assuming the functions of sash circuit and generic parameter control functions. In the early stage it was Japanese firms that supplied such MCUs. For color TV products, highly skilled workers in Japan used analog controls, but with modular product architecture, color TV production no longer needed such skilled workers. Instead, digital control by using MCU eliminated interference needs among processes.

Transition from color brown tube TV to LCD TV is quite dramatic from a product architecture perspective. Product architecture of LCD TV is much more modular than color brown tube TV. Process modularization was also intensified as well. As a consequence in the LCD TV era, focused manufacturers for core component parts in other emerging manufacturing powers (e.g., Korea and Taiwan) rapidly acquired relevant technologies. In the brown TV era, key TV makers handled all the production of core component parts and MCU chips. In this way, these TV manufacturers maintained their competitive advantage in the market.

However, in the LCD TV era, collaboration occurred involving Korean and Taiwanese LCD panel makers, U.S.-based LSI suppliers, and

Taiwanese semiconductor design firms. Korean TV manufacturers made huge investments for LCD panels and accelerated LCD panel sales worldwide. It is now feasible for Chinese firms to produce LCD TV by procuring core components. The suppliers of LCD core components are Korean and Taiwanese firms, LSI from Japan, or U.S. firms. With the appearance of contract manufacturing firms, it is no longer possible for Japanese firms to claim any distinct competitive advantage of core components. Complete modularization of products created a new pattern of international specialization—costly component parts from Korea and Taiwan, LSI requiring specialized know-how from semiconductor firms of Japan and the United States, and assembly functions are by Chinese firms. In brief, change in product architecture allowed a new type of international specialization.

4.5 DISCUSSION

The product design core of almost all electronic products contains the MCU/LSI system which has experienced drastic change from integral to modular architecture. Rapid technology transfer occurs in Korean and NIEs firms from Japanese firms. In this chapter we examined how such architectural change impacts the technology transfer speed based on case illustrations of Japanese CD/DVD firms. It shows that Japanese firms have taken different catch-up patterns in the analog era compared to what Korean and NIEs firms do in the digital era.

It is worth noting the similarity and difference in these catch-up patterns. Table 4.1 summarizes the details occurring in the automobile and electronic industries. The critical difference is in the catch-up objects and timing. Japanese firms achieved their catch-up in the analog era utilizing highly skilled workers through process innovation over several decades, while Korean firms in the digital era accomplished rapid catch-up in a relatively very short time period and utilized IT capability for their global business management.

From a product architectural perspective, Japanese firms grew in the analog era and focused on closed integral industries. Even the electronics industry (now all modular) used to be integral in the analog era. With the changing product architecture, Korean firms have achieved rapid catch-up in electronics industry by taking advantage of open modular architecture. The point is that the product cycle in closed integral product architecture

TABLE 4.1

Comparison of Growth and Catch-Up Patterns of Japanese and Korean Firms

	Japanese Firms	Korean Firms
Before 1980	World factory→high growth	Massive investment→rapid growth
1990s	Bubble economy→business restructuring	IMF Crisis→business reorganization
2000s	Globalization→Focus on U.S. and European market	Globalization→export to global market (90%) vs. domestic market (10%)
2010 and beyond	Global Financial Crisis (2008)→global market expansion effort (high yen—Japanese currency)	Global Financial Crisis (2008)→emerging market (low Won—Korean currency)
Catch-up pattern	(Analog era)(catch-up with U.S. and European firms)	(Digital era) (U.S., European, and Japanese firms)

is long, and product development emphasizes the analog elements. In contrast, open modular architecture adopts a short product life cycle, and it demands speed in product development. Korean firms pursued appropriate organizational systems and management decision making styles that fit the open modular types of business environments. This is what made Korean firms very successful in achieving competitive advantage in the global market.

Section II

Case Studies of the Korean IT Industry

5

Korean Semiconductor Industry: A Comparative Study with Japanese Counterparts

The Korean semiconductor industry has grown with an active industrial policy of the Korean government and aggressive investment of Korean semiconductor firms. However, the global market share of Korean firms in the memory semiconductor industry is no more than 20%. In this context, it is noteworthy to examine the whole picture of the Korean semiconductor industry from the standpoint both of the memory and nonmemory sectors. Particularly, the price drop of memory semiconductors is closely related to product/business architecture. For this reason, it is meaningful to compare the Korean and Japanese semiconductor industries from the product/business architecture perspective.

In the 1990s, Korean semiconductor firms displayed their superior performance over their Japanese counterparts with their competitive strengths; however, in the 2000s, with the specialization of business architecture (i.e., separation of design and manufacturing), Korean firms are drastically losing their competitiveness. Instead, American venture firms that specialize in semiconductor design and Taiwanese foundry firms dominate the global market. In this respect, it is critical for Korean and Japanese firms to know how to implement their long-term strategy. In brief, this study compares and contrasts the Korean and Japanese semiconductor industries and provides an insight on how Korean and Japanese firms compete in the evolving semiconductor industry.

5.1 INTRODUCTION

Over the years, heavy industries such as automotive, steel, and shipbuilding have been the primary leaders in the continuous growth of the Korean economy. At present, IT industries (e.g., semiconductors, cellular phones, TFT-LCD [thin-film transistor–liquid-crystal display]) are the leading economic power sectors (Ko et al., 2006). The evolution patterns are from textile to automotive and then to the IT industry. From 1970 to the early 1980s, light industries (e.g., textile/clothing and food processing) contributed to the economic growth of Korea. From the latter part of the 1980s, heavy and chemical industries (e.g., automotive, steel, and oil refinery) have received the baton of industrial leadership. The Korean IT industry has assumed the leading role of economic expansion since the 1997 monetary crisis. Productivity growth through the IT industry plays a huge part in changing the growth patterns of the Korean economy from the expansion of production factors to efficiency enhancement of the productive capabilities. For example, after the monetary crisis more than one-third of the actual GDP was through the growth of the IT industry, and IT's contribution was about two-thirds of the net export growth (Kim and Jung, 2005).

From the latter years of the 1990s, the semiconductor industry in particular (among all the players of the IT industry) has led the economic growth, and its overall contribution to the growing economy is steadily growing. The contribution of semiconductors and electronic components to the GDP growth rate was 14.4% in 1996–2000, 19.4% in 2001–2005, and is currently about 20% (Ko et al., 2006).

The Korean semiconductor industry—both the pioneers and the followers (e.g., LG and Hyundai Semiconductors)—have experienced growth in their technological capabilities through the combined effects of the unique Korean style of fierce competition among large Korean firms and an active policy support of the Korean government. By 1995, Samsung, LG and Hyundai became three of the top seven players in the global semiconductor industry, and they therefore achieved the name of the "Korean Silicon Yellow Wind Storm" (B. C. Lee, 2003).

Such successes in the semiconductor business have impacted the outstanding performance of Korean cellular phones and the thin-film transistor–liquid-crystal display (TFT-LCD) market as well. Samsung Electronics, as a global firm, shows excellent market records with semiconductors, cellular phones, LCDs, and digital household goods. Samsung applied its technological and organizational capabilities (acquired through its experiences in the semiconductor industry) to other competitive areas as well (Shin and Jang, 2006). Therefore, it is quite relevant to examine the effective mechanisms of the semiconductor industry in reviewing the success factors of the Korean electronics industry. Just as Korean firms grew with the active investment and the vigorous support of the Korean government, Japanese industries, the memory semiconductor industry in particular, also started well with the active support of the Japanese government but gradually lost their competitiveness as product architecture of semiconductor design changed.

On the other hand, the global market share of the Korean semiconductor industry, a strong symbol of Korean firms, is no more than 20%. As of 2010, the total global semiconductor market was $304 billion. The memory portion was no more than 22%, and the nonmemory portion was 78% of this overall figure. In this respect, it is important to compare Japanese and Korean firms, not only in the memory sector, but also in the nonmemory area as well. The price drop in memory semiconductors is closely related to changes in product/business architecture. In this respect, the focus of this study is the analysis of the Japanese and Korean semiconductor industries from the perspective of product/business architecture.

5.2 AN ANALYSIS OF THE SEMICONDUCTOR INDUSTRY FROM AN ARCHITECTURE-BASED PERSPECTIVE

5.2.1 Structure and Characteristics of the Semiconductor Industry

The diverse families of semiconductors include discrete semiconductors (i.e., nuts and bolts such as diodes and transistors), memory (i.e., combined data using nuts and bolts), logic that calculates digital signals, light-emitting diodes (LEDs, producing white and red light), sensors that recognize the temperature and pressures, and amplifiers that magnify sound (Akira, 2006). The further classification of semiconductors by function and structure includes the following six kinds: (1) discrete individual semiconductor, (2) light device, (3) microwave device, (4) sensor, (5) IC (integrated circuit), and (6) hybrid IC. System LSI (large-scale integration), a kind of IC, is widely used recently and is called system on a chip (SoC).

This is comprehensive semiconductor technology (e.g., digital appliances, cellular phones, electronic equipment for automobiles). Integrated circuits (IC), which occupy about 80% of the total semiconductor market, are divided into memory and logical branches. Memory is again divided into volatile/involatile memory, and it includes DRAM, SRAM, NOR flash memory, NAND flash memory, mask ROM, and EPROM. The logical branch has microcomponents (MPU, MCU, MPR, DSP), logic IC (ASIC, ASSP etc.), and analog IC.

Figure 5.1 shows the structure of the semiconductor industry. As of 2007, the total export values of Korean semiconductor industries are about $40 billion with $30 billion in import amounts and so the net value added is about $10 billion. A total of 64,000 people work in the memory device branch of Korean semiconductors, and fabless (not fabricating silicon wafers) is only 4,000.

The major players of the semiconductor industry are IDM (Integrated Device Manufacturers), design specialty fabless firms (design house), entire process manufacturing specialty foundry firms, back-end processing assembly firms, and package-centered assembly firms. IDM are the comprehensive semiconductor firms that cover all aspects—from semiconductor design, wafer manufacturing, assembling, and testing, all the way to packaging the produced chips in the state of a lead frame. In Korea, Samsung and Hynix are examples of such firms. Broadly speaking, the back-end portion of the semiconductor industry includes various equipment, elements,

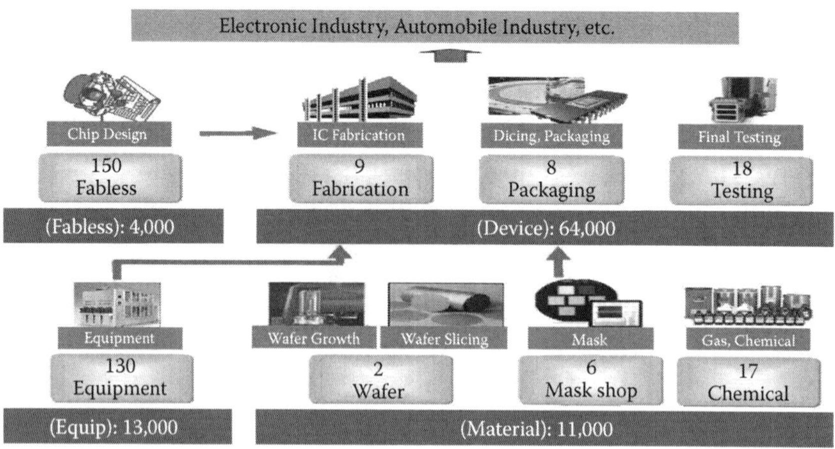

FIGURE 5.1
The structure of the semiconductor industry. From Park et al., 2008.

and infrastructures (clean room, automated facilities). The typical industries that use semiconductors are electronics, information communication, automotive, and machinery industries. Now we consider the characteristics of the semiconductor industry. We focus primarily on comprehensive semiconductor firms that lead the Korean semiconductor industry. The semiconductor industry has a few distinct characteristics which are quite different from other industries (Hong, 2004a; Park et al., 2008a).

First, the semiconductor industry requires a massive investment for large-scale facility capacity. Particularly, the memory semiconductor sector demands a huge investment for continuous research and development as well as equipment and infrastructure development. Samsung, which entered the semiconductor business in 1982, made a consistent investment, although no real profit was realized until 1987. Hyundai Electronics (now Hynix) also received some profit in 1993—almost 10 years after its initial investment in 1983.

Second, the semiconductor industry is a high-risk business in that the speed of technology development is very fast. In the early stage, new products were introduced every three or four years. In 2000, the new product cycle was reduced to two to three years. Therefore, both mass production and research development need to be simultaneously implemented.

Third, successful semiconductor firms should determine the precise timing of investment and use mass production systems at the earliest possible time, earlier than their rivals. For example, by the 1980s Japanese firms maintained absolute superiority in memory semiconductors (e.g., DRAM). However, from the 1990s, it was Korean Samsung that claimed competitive advantage because of its early implementation of mass production for new products.

Fourth, the semiconductor business provides a strong foundation for the knowledge society because its high-value-added industry characteristics have huge relational impacts on both front- and back-end businesses. The cost ratio of its raw materials is less than 10%, and therefore its business advantages are absolutely greater than computers, household electronics, and communication industries. If the raw materials are purchased in large volumes, the cost of raw materials and manufacturing equipment is further reduced (Jang and Kim, 2001; Shin and Jang, 2006).

Fifth, the semiconductor industry is quite sensitive to market fluctuations. It requires a huge investment. The range of price changes is quite large and volatile. The price of memory semiconductors (which claims Korea's major competitive strengths) is being drastically reduced, and

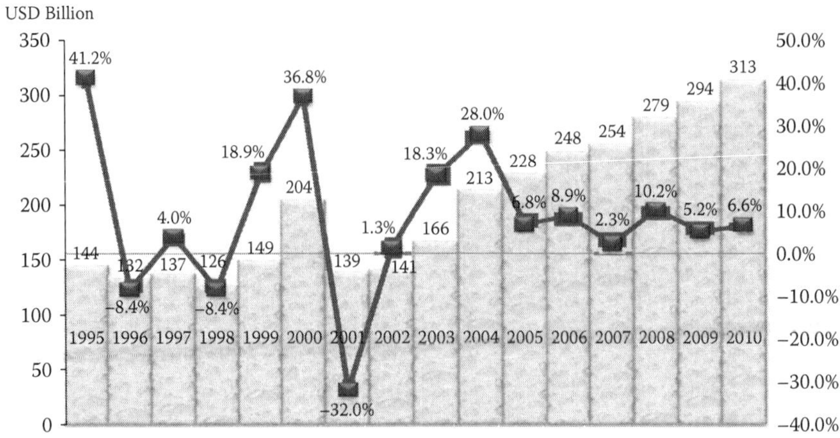

FIGURE 5.2
Four-year silicon cycle of the semiconductor industry. From Park et al., 2008a.

its profitability has seriously worsened in the 2000s. Besides, the semiconductor industry has time-based competition and heavily depends on social indirect investment and carries too many aspects that are kept in secret. Figure 5.2 is the four-year silicon cycle of the semiconductor industry which shows overall sales trends.

5.2.2 A History of the Semiconductor Industry from an Architecture-Based Perspective

A brief review of the history of the world semiconductor industry suggests three catch-up stories. Until the 1970s, when Japanese firms showed their substantial presence, the semiconductor industry was led by American enterprises. It was in the United States that the semiconductor industry was born, and the formation of basic technologies, the product development of major semiconductor products and basic concepts (e.g., microprocessor), were all started with American businesses. The Japanese semiconductor industry rapidly caught up with American firms in terms of production volumes in a relatively short time period. By the early 1970s, Japanese firms quickly produced about 60% of U.S. volumes (Itami, 2000). From the middle of the 1980s, demand for DRAM (memory semiconductors) increased drastically. By 1986, the Japanese semiconductor industry had the largest market share in the world, far exceeding that of U.S. firms. However, Intel determined the design details, and Japanese firms had to bear the huge cost of new development of DRAM and massive investment of production facilities (Miwa, 2001; Ogawa et al., 2009).

In this circumstance, the U.S. semiconductor industry focused on the development of high-value-added items such as the MPU of PCs, surrounding equipment and video processing mechanisms. By 1993, U.S. firms regained their top market position (Itami, 2000; Park and Hong, 2006). On the other hand, Korean makers such as Samsung, which grew from the latter part of the 1980s, surpassed Japanese firms in 1992 in terms of sales volume of DRAM. After the 1990s, Japanese firms experienced serious competitive challenges from Korean firms. But Itami (2000) comments that Samsung Electronics' number one position in the world is merely a firm-level victory; it does not necessarily suggest the Korean industry's overall superior performance over their Japanese counterpart. Taiwanese firms also demonstrate their unique position in the global semiconductor industry through their success in the foundry business in the 1990s (Park et al., 2008).

Figure 5.3 shows a semiconductor's Makimoto waves. Depending on the focus on either standardization or customization, the business waves take turns over the years. Rapid standardization is followed by customization, which in turn pushes standardization for mass production. In other words, standardization is mostly to support massive market demand, while customization is to differentiate the products from those of competitors by offering unique values.

Table 5.1 shows the changing patterns of the semiconductor industry by decade from 1960 to 2000. The five periods show distinct differences in terms of major industry, the kind of semiconductor products, and business models.

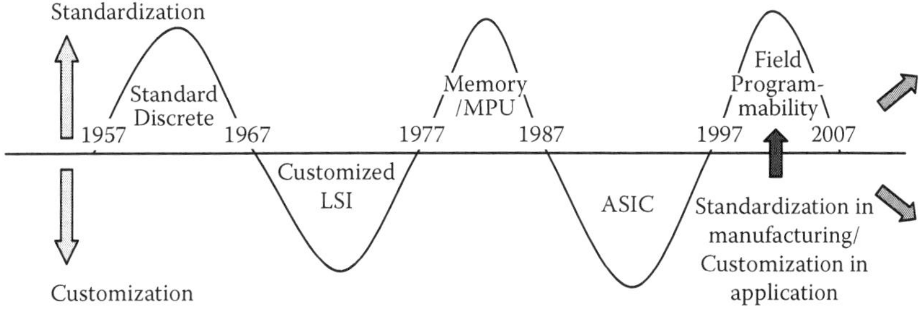

FIGURE 5.3
Semiconductor's Makimoto waves. Adapted from Nikkei Electronics (2004.2.6); Wang and Banta (2004.9).

TABLE 5.1

Changing Patterns of Semiconductor Industry by Decade (1960–2000)

Decade	1960	1970	1980	1990	2000
Major industry	Large computer, defense industry	Large and mini computer	Work stations and PC	PC + communication	Internet, digital house electronics
Products	Transistor TTL	Integrated circuit component parts	MPU, memory	ASIC	SoC, IP + program software
Business model characteristics	Low integration	High integration	ASIC business model	System LSI	Reuse of IP, SoC platform, programmable processor

Source: Miwa (2001).

5.3 CHANGING KOREAN SEMICONDUCTOR PATTERNS (FROM MEMORY TO LOGIC SEMICONDUCTORS)

In this section, we examine changing patterns of the Korean semiconductor, particularly the memory semiconductor. Figure 5.4 shows that Korean semiconductors successfully dominated the memory semiconductor market with a global market share of up to 50%. With this, Korean firms have sustained their competitive advantage in memory-related products (e.g., mobile phones). However, in nonmemory areas, their market share is very minimal.

Figure 5.5 is the summary of the ratio of the memory and nonmemory markets. Korea has relatively larger market share (41.2%) in memory market share, while the United States is the leader in system IC market share.

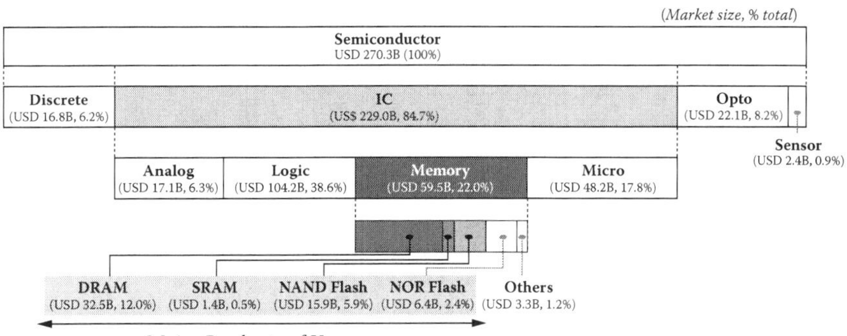

FIGURE 5.4
The Korean Semiconductor Industry and its contribution. From Korean Semiconductor Industry Association (2007); Gartner (2007); NECST (2008.2).

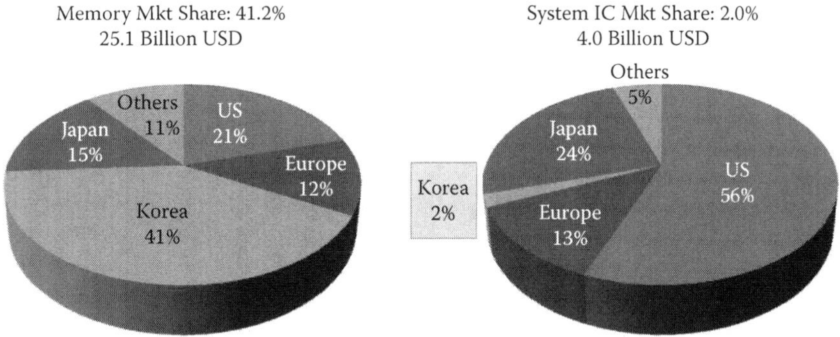

FIGURE 5.5
The ratio of memory and nonmemory sectors in the Korean semiconductor industry. From Korean Semiconductor Industry Association (2007); NECST (2008.2).

Figure 5.6 shows the Korean fabless industry situation. Different from the memory semiconductor, the market share of Korean firms is noticeably low.

Figure 5.7 shows the status of the Korean equipment industry in the global market. It suggests that Korean firms make slow progress in the world market. One noticeable fact is that Korean firms depend on key component parts from Japan and the United States, and therefore their value added from the equipment market is fairly low.

The status of the Korean raw materials industry is also somewhat minimal (Figure 5.8). Raw materials of semiconductor products are mostly imported from Japan. Therefore, their profit level is somewhat limited as well.

(USD Billion)

	2003	2004	2005	2006	2007(E)
World	21.3	28.8	32.8	35.7	37.9
Korea	0.6	0.9	1.2	1.3	1.4
Market Share	2.8%	3.3%	3.5%	3.7%	3.7%

FIGURE 5.6
The status of Korean fabless industry in the global market. From Korean Semiconductor Industry Association (2007); NECST (2008.2).

(USD Billion)

	2004	2005	2006	2007(E)	2008(F)
World	30.1	32.9	40.5	41.7	41.0
Korea	5.2	5.8	7.0	7.4	7.3
Market Share	17.2%	17.6%	17.3%	17.7%	17.8%

FIGURE 5.7
The status of the Korean equipment industry in the global market. From Park et al., 2008a.

(USD Billion)

	2004	2005	2006	2007(E)	2008(F)
World	27.9	31.0	35.6	42.2	46.9
Korea	3.6	4.2	5.0	6.0	6.6
Market Share	12.9	13.5	14.0	14.2	14.1

FIGURE 5.8
The status of the Korean raw materials industry in the global market. From Korean Semiconductor Industry Association (2007); NECST (2008.2).

5.4 KOREAN AND JAPANESE SEMICONDUCTOR INDUSTRIES AND FUTURE PROSPECTS

In this section, we compare the success factors of the Korean and Japanese memory semiconductor industries. The Korean semiconductor industry is heavily focused on the memory business. In the application specific standard produce (ASSP) market, Japanese firms are inferior to American firms. But Japanese firms have a competitive advantage in the application specific integrated circuit (ASIC) market. Yet, as mentioned before, Korean firms hardly have a market share even in the level of ASIC, without mentioning ASSP. At present, the market share of Korean SoC and foundry is about 5% (Park et al., 2008). According to the 2007 comparative data among the United States, Japan, and Taiwan, Korean semiconductor size is clearly shown. Semiconductor-advanced nations have focused on developing system semiconductor industries. Major investment started in the United States in the 1970s, in Japan in 1975, in Taiwan in 1980, and in Korea in 1990. Korea started late in their investment in SoC, equipment, and raw materials. The Korean semiconductor industry is fairly weak primarily because of their lack of original technologies, inadequate establishment of trust, and limited investment in facilities. It would be challenging for Korean firms to grow as global leaders in this respect. For example, no Korean firm is ranked within the top 50 global equipment firms, and Korean raw material firms are ranked around 20 to 30. Table 5.2 is a summary of semiconductor sales volume by country as of 2007.

Therefore, our comparison focus is on the memory semiconductor industry in which Korean firms maintain global competitiveness. Success factors of the Korean and Japanese semiconductor industries include their

TABLE 5.2

Semiconductor Sales Volumes by Country (2007) (Unit: $100 Million,%)

	Memory	Nonmemory	Equipment/ Raw Materials	Total
United States	125 (20.6)	1,435 (57.9)	285 (35.1)	1,845 (47.3)
Japan	93 (15.3)	501 (20.2)	335 (41.2)	929 (23.8)
European Union	75 (12.3)	259 (10.5)	93 (11.4)	427 (10.9)
Korea	251 (41.2)	36 (1.5)	78 (9.6)	365 (9.4)

Source: Korean Semiconductor Industry Association (2008.3.25).

effective catch-up strategies with the active support of their government. Both countries are examples of successful catch-up models in the world (Park and Hong, 2006).

The role of government is quite obvious in both countries. The Korean government's major policy support was intended to develop component part suppliers at the beginning. However, the government policies of both countries do not merely dominate the overall patterns of industry growth. Rather, both governments encouraged private initiatives through governmental and firm research collaborations (e.g., ETRI for Korea and VLSI Research Cooperatives for Japan).

Japanese firms failed to differentiate their competitive advantage as Porter and Takeuchi (2002) pointed out. Another factor is that Japanese firms focused on the domestic market, while Korean firms concentrated on export orientation from the beginning. In this way, Korean firms acquired the necessary capabilities to compete in the global market. Figure 5.9 shows how the export-oriented Korean semiconductor industry rapidly grew from 1983 to 2008.

However, the deeper reasons for their successes might be found in the transition of product architecture in the 1990s. As digital technology is deeply applied in the design of finished products, the product architecture was rapidly changed into a modular type (Ogawa, 2008a, 2008b; Park et al., 2008; Ogawa et al., 2009). Table 5.3 is the summary of comparison of the Korean and Japanese semiconductor industries.

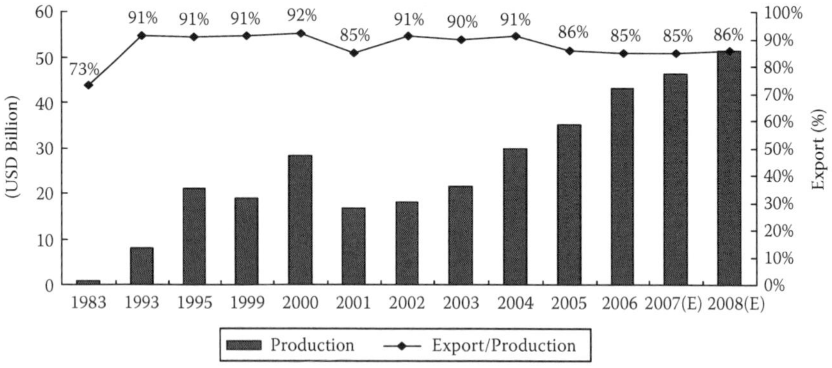

FIGURE 5.9
The export-oriented Korean semiconductor industry. From Park et al., 2008a.

TABLE 5.3

Comparison of Korean and Japanese Semiconductor Industries

Classification	Korea	Japan
Success model	Catch-up model	Catch-up model
Moment of catch-up	1986 U.S./Japan Semiconductor Conflict	1976 formation of VLSI Research Cooperatives
Government's industrial policy	51% ownership limitation, investment on technology development	Subsidy of various systems and VLSI Research Cooperatives
Leading institution of research and development	Korean Electronic and Telegraph Research Institute (ETRI)	Japanese Electrical Telegraph, Electrical Research Institute, and other Electrical Manufacturing Research Institute
Industrial and competitive policy	Yes	Yes
Domestic market condition	Export orientation	Domestic market competitiveness
Industrial focus	Specialize in memory semiconductor	ASIC business trap

5.5 DISCUSSION

In this study, we compared the Japanese and Korean semiconductor industries from the perspective of product/business architecture. The Japanese and Korean semiconductor industries did not start with their original technologies, but successfully pursued catch-up growth. The critical success factor for successful catch-up is the speed of importing the technologies from developed countries. Rapid technology development of the semiconductor industry may also require securing and utilizing of critical human resources from developed nations (e.g., United States and Japan).

On the other hand, just like Korea's code division multiple access (CDMA) development, it is possible to acquire and market precommercialization technology. Samsung Electronics is quite proficient in this way of technology development. Its principle is, "In the digital age, time is money. Any valuable technology is worth spending money on for acquisition." Japanese firms possess outstanding monozukuri technologies that American and European firms may not imitate so easily. However, they are not so outstanding in utilizing their technologies and business development. The growth pattern of the Korean IT industry may certainly be a good model for follower nations, but also useful to Japanese firms and the Japanese government.

British ARM's IP business has a great reputation for its ability to use both integration and specialization cycles for its business development. Any firm may have a better chance of success, even in the semiconductor industry, if they use the proper product/business architecture. In this sense, Korean firms are successful with their memory-focused business strategy. On the other hand, Japanese IDM tried to strengthen its competitiveness through realigning or integrating its business areas. Sony specialized in horizontal specialization, while Matsushita and Toshiba remain as IDMs. It is unclear who will survive in the long run. Realistically, many Japanese firms pursue the IDM strategy. In view of IDM's characteristics, the SoC integration and optimization strategy might be more fitting than the divide and conquer strategy. Kayama (2006), for example, argues that fabless and foundry business models use vertical integration, not horizontal specialization. Therefore, IDM, which seeks total solution, is expected to pursue a vertical integration model for future cutting-edge technologies and their markets. Future research may consider a comparative study between the vertical integration model of IDM and the horizontal specialization of the fabless and foundry models. It would be worthy to explore the success factors of each business model in light of product/business architecture.

6

Korean LCD Industry: Product Architecture and Global Supply Chain Management of LCD

In the liquid-crystal display (LCD) industry, LCD panel makers operate in between upstream component suppliers and downstream LCD TV. Because component parts carry a larger percentage of the total LCD's overall costs, it is critical for the LCD industry to attain supply chain integration with its component part suppliers. This chapter examines (1) the LCD industry structure from the product architecture perspective and (2) the supply chain management (SCM) strategy of the Korean LCD industry. Korean firms possess substantial competitive advantage in the large-scale LCD global TV market. This chapter, with case illustrations, analyzes how Korean firms have built the SCM system and are implementing supply chain integration with upstream component parts manufacturers.

6.1 INTRODUCTION

In the early 2000s digital household electronic products such as liquid-crystal display (LCD) TV, mobile phones, and DVD players/recorders contributed to the recovery of the Japanese economy. In a similar way, the semiconductor and mobile phone industry have aided in the expansion of the Korean economy (Shintaku et al., 2006b). Particularly, Korean LCD panel makers have functioned as a critical link for bringing multiplier growth effects on the downstream LCD manufacturers (LG Economic

Research Institute, 2006a). With the recent introduction of digital broadcasting and broadband Internet, customers increasingly expect diverse and high-density video presentations. Main display players are switching from traditional brown tube to flat-panel display (FPD) (Park, 2009).

The LCD is used in a variety of applications that require high-quality display—from mobile technologies to large TVs (LG Economic Institute, 2007a). After 40 years of experience with the CRT (cathode ray tube), TV customers are now rapidly switching to LCD. Although early display technologies started in the United States and Europe, Japanese firms such as Sharp have attained its commercialization success. Korean firms, with their relatively late entry, adopted an aggressive investment strategy and successfully caught up with Japanese front-runners. The Korean LCD industry, represented by Samsung Electronics Co., Ltd., and LG Display, began their production in 1995. Within four short years, Korean LCD panel makers lead the global market (Samsung Economic Research Institute, 1999). By 1998, Samsung's global market share was number one, and by 1999 LG followed as a close number two. In this way Korean firms have positioned themselves as global market leaders with sustainable competitive advantage over Japanese rivals (Hong, 2004b).

Recently, the Taiwanese thin film transistor (TFT) LCD industry, with huge technological support from Japanese firms, has challenged Korean firms in the global market. By 2004, the Taiwanese LCD industry occupied 40% of the global market share, and price competition between Taiwanese and Korean firms was intensifying (Shintaku et al., 2006a). Prior to 2000, Japanese and Korean LCD firms competed for the notebook PC market. After 2000, Taiwanese and Korean manufacturers have vigorously competed in the monitor LCD panel market (Samsung Economic Research Institute, 2005). With such a changing competitive landscape from 2005, LCD panel prices have been drastically cut. The average profit rate of the LCD panel industry (e.g., the top four firms) also dropped from 19% in 2004 to 7% in 2005. They are expected to be lower than 5% in 2006 (LG Economic Research Institute, 2006b). In the LCD industry, competitive panel manufacturers must achieve overall cost and lead time reduction through supplier collaboration. Changing customer requirements dictate that firms must design and implement supply chain management.

Size requirements for LCD panels become more demanding because mobile phones, notebooks, monitors, and TVs are rapidly adopting more complex features. For example, a 40-inch TV is 5.5 times (and a 52-inch

TV is 9.4 times) of the size of a 17-inch monitor TV. As panel size becomes larger, supply chain costs drastically increase and without supply chain innovation, the short-term competitive advantage of the LCD industry is quickly lost (Samsung Economic Research Institute, 2006).

In the large-sized LCD industry, two supply chain structures are component parts suppliers in the upstream and LCD TV in the downstream. The Korean LCD industry focuses on design, mass production, and marketing of LCD TV by using component parts from upstream suppliers. With limited options for cost reduction and technological differentiation in downstream TV assembly and marketing, competitive risks for market obsolescence are relatively high (LG Economic Research Institute, 2007b).

The Korean LCD TV industry has positioned itself as number one in its global market; yet its competitive capabilities are not so solid in that many of their component parts are imported from Japanese suppliers. In 2005 the average profit rate of LCD panel firms fell below 10%—even down to 7%. Over the years the average profit rate of Japanese component parts firms has not substantially dropped in view of their comparative advantages. Major component parts firms like Nitto Denko have sustained their target profit rate of a little over 10% (Samsung Economic Research Institute, 2006).

In view of the Korean LCD TV industry's competitive strengths in widescreen LCD TV and their competitive challenges with component suppliers, this study examines: (1) the LCD industry structure from the standpoint of LCD product architecture; (2) supply chain strategies of the Korean LCD industry; and (3) supply chain management (SCM) system formation and SCM integration strategies of Korean firms.

6.2 PRODUCT ARCHITECTURE AND SCM (SUPPLY CHAIN MANAGEMENT) OF LCD

6.2.1 Product Architecture of LCD

Product architecture is the basic process structure of connecting core components of products (Fujimoto, 2001a). The choice of product architecture governs the essential rules of analyzing product requirement functions, dividing products into component parts, and designing the interfaces of components (Fujimoto, 2004). Two usual classifications of product architecture are modular/integral and open/closed (Ulrich, 1995; Baldwin and

Clark, 2000; Fujimoto, 2001). Strategic application of product architecture influences the degree of a firm's competitiveness in the ways it facilitates innovation according to changes in market reality (Henderson and Clark, 1990; Fujimoto, 2004).

Alignment patterns between product architecture and organizational capabilities are different. Japanese firms do better with integral products, while Korean firms, with their relatively late entry in the market, focus on modular products. Korean firms have caught up with Japanese firms in a relatively short time and have shown their increasing prominence in modular products. Yet LCD displays (even as they are regarded as modular products) have component parts in which control elements are complex and rapid catch-up is not so readily attainable, because Japanese component suppliers keep their technological know-how for their own advantages (Shintaku et al., 2006b).

LCD products have both modular and integral components. In general, LCD product architecture of upstream (component suppliers) is close to an integral pattern, while downstream architecture (LCD TV) adopts a modular one. No firm has all aspects of competitive strengths. Instead, competitive advantage in the supply chain depends on the extent of network leadership by which a firm controls the overall process. In many industries, because diverse product components are interdependently connected and innovative capabilities are scattered across firms, no firm, regardless of its size, can make independent decisions without considering other collaborators within the supply chain networks (Gawer and Cusumano, 2002). With continuous market change requirements, core and complementary product makers redefine their relationships in terms of a hierarchical power structure. Periodically firms reexamine their contractual commitment because they constantly acquire their own innovative capabilities in managing complex system modules (Song, 2006; Y. W. Park, 2006).

Figure 6.1 shows the three-layer structure and SCM flows of the LCD industry. The top layer is component part suppliers (upstream); panel makers are in the middle, and the downstream is for large and small LCD manufacturers. Increasingly larger widescreen LCD TVs require the formation of win–win relationships with upstream suppliers and downstream LCD makers. Except for Sony, which receives panels from S-LCD, the joint-venture firm with Samsung Electronics, the majority of LCD TV makers have completed vertical integration in downstream (LCD panelmakers and large and small LCD manufacturers). The struggle is what to do with the upstream component suppliers.

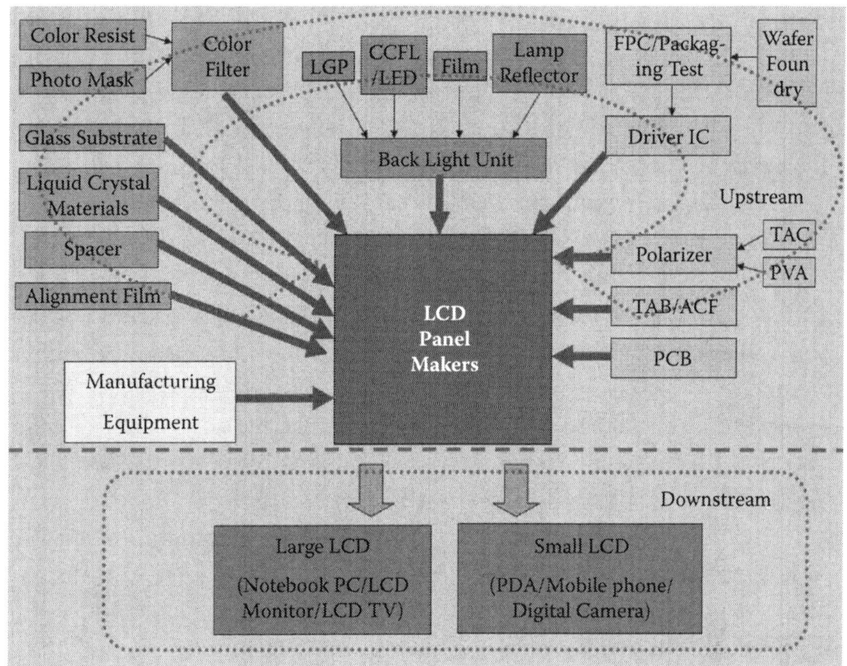

FIGURE 6.1
Three-layer structure of the LCD industry and SCM flows.

Korean Samsung and LG have been market leaders in the global LCD market. Recently, they have been leading the global market in LCD TV. A major portion of the value added of their products is concentrated in component part makers in the upstream. Therefore, it is critical for LCD TV makers to forge stable relationships between LCD panel makers and its component suppliers. As far as LCD component parts are concerned, Japanese firms possess the major competitive advantages. Japanese component parts suppliers possess their own unique black-box processes and original technologies with legal protection of their patent rights. Vertical integration in the upstream with these component parts suppliers is not easily realized.

6.2.2 LCD and SCM (Supply Chain Management)

The supply chain includes business processes within and outside a company that enable the value chain to make products and provide services to the customers (Lummus and Vokurka, 1999; Lambert and Cooper,

2000). The International Center for Competitive Excellence defined supply chain as integration of key business processes from end user through original suppliers that provide products, services, and information that add value for customers and other stakeholders (Changchien and Shen, 2002). Supply chain management (SCM) is the twenty-first century global operations strategy for achieving organizational competitiveness (Gunasekaran and Ngai, 2004). Levary (2000) suggests that the benefits of a supply chain include: (1) minimizing the bullwhip effect, (2) maximizing the efficiency of activities, (3) minimizing the inventories, (4) minimizing cycle times, and (5) achieving a high level of quality outcomes.

Integrating the effort of diverse players across the supply chain is an important theme of supply chain management (Zhang et al., 2006; Park et al., 2007b). Suppliers and customers work as partners for the common objective of enhancing competitiveness and profitability for the whole supply chain network (Patterson et al., 2003). Effective information flows is critical for value creation and delivery in the supply chain. Therefore, interorganizational IS requires more accurate demand forecasting, inventory management, and other transactional activities and procurement processes (Whipple and Frankel, 2000; Gunasekaran and Ngai, 2004).

Increasingly, full participation in e-marketplaces requires firms to integrate their internal and external supply chain activities through strategic and operational information sharing. Construction of an appropriate IT system is indispensable in the design and implementation of a SCM strategy. Besides, the supply chain is about product flows. Product life cycle management (PLM) is useful in that it provides a framework to examine how Korean firms approach their value creation through managing flows of multiple generations of products (Chiang and Trappey, 2007). Specifically, this research identifies the functions of product life cycle management (PLM) that integrates different organizations in supply chains. The liquid-crystal display (LCD) industry is used as a case study to explain the value system framework and its PLM adoption.

This study examines supply chain management practices of Korean LCD manufacturers. This study is organized in the following order: (1) an examination of the context of the Korean LCD industry; (2) supply chain management systems of Samsung and LG, particularly information integration for their value creation; and (3) product life cycle management for their multiple generations of LCD.

6.3 STRUCTURE OF THE LCD INDUSTRY AND INVESTMENT OF KOREAN LCD FIRMS

6.3.1 Changing Structure of the Value Chain System of the LCD Industry

Japanese firms first commercialized LCD products in the world, and from its early years of development, component suppliers, equipment manufacturers, and final assemblers have collaborated in new product development. The Japanese LCD industry practiced supply chain management to make LCD panels in collaborative relationships between panel makers (e.g., Sharp) and related material suppliers that produce color filters (e.g., Dai Nippon Printing and Toppan Print) and polarizers (e.g., Nitto Denko). With the gradual deterioration of Japanese competitiveness in finished products, particularly device makers, Korean firms (e.g., Samsung and LG) have engaged in aggressive R & D investment, and have acquired manufacturing process technologies and raw materials from Japanese process and component manufacturers. Soon they became the leaders in the global market (Shintaku, 2006).

Japanese semiconductor manufacturing firms have tried to keep technologies that govern design and manufacturing processes of semiconductors and LCD panels secret. Korean LCD makers achieved rapid catch-up in a very short period through their collaboration with Japanese firms and continued to develop new generation technologies. Then, what did Korean firms do exactly, and what are their current and emerging issues? We will first pay attention to supply chain integration strategies of LCD panel makers with component parts suppliers.

6.3.2 Korean Firms' Position in the LCD TV Market and Investment Status

Korean LCD TV makers now occupy leading positions (Samsung and LG being the first and the second) in the global market (Table 6.1). In terms of market share of FPD TV including LCD TV, Samsung has been ranked as number one since 2006. As of the 3Q in 2010, LG was ranked number two, but the global competitiveness of Korean LCD TV remains very high.

Since the late 1990s, Korean LCD makers have made a wide range of aggressive investments. Samsung and LG-Phillips have adopted somewhat different strategies. Samsung's investment focused on the fourth generation

TABLE 6.1

Global Flat Panel TV Market Share (Based on Sales)

	1Q 2010	2Q 2010	1–3Q 2010
Classification	**TV Market Share**	**TV Market Share**	**TV Market Share**
Samsung	22.3%	24.4%	22.8%
LGE	14.1%	14.1%	13.9%
Sony	10.1%	12.8%	11.6%
Panasonic	7.3%	9.0%	8.5%
Sharp	6.5%	6.4%	7.0%

Source: Display Search.

development immediately after their successful launching of 3.5 generation products. LG instead bypassed the fourth generation and implemented the fifth generation project, and since May 2002, LG has successfully marketed the new products. Samsung invested for the fifth generation facilities since September 2002. Samsung and LG accelerated their competitive battles from the fifth generation production lines. Samsung applied the fifth generation 17-inch production line for 1100×1250 mm, while LG implemented an 18.1-inch panel production line for 1000×1200 mm (Park et al., 2007b).

By 2002, 15-inch products were discontinued. Intense competitive battles were fought between Samsung's 17-inch and LG's 18.1-inch products. Their fight was for securing industry standards for the succeeding generation's products—sixth and seventh. In the first half of 2005, Samsung began producing the 7-1 line through S-LCD (partnership with Sony) and invested an additional $2.9 billion in expanding clean room facilities and equipment for the 7-2 line (Nikkei Microdevices, 2006). Samsung also set the glass substrate standard as 1870×2200 mm, which was quite similar to that of the 7-1 line (Samsung Economic Research Institute, 2006). In this way, Samsung went a few steps ahead in the competitive battles of the LCD panel supply and LCD TV standard war.

Table 6.2 shows Korean TFT-LCD makers' investment status. The 7-2 line facilities of Tanjeong of Choongnam, South Korea are capable of mass production of 32-inch, 40-inch, and 46-inch TV panels while simultaneously processing 12 pieces of 32-inch standard, 8 pieces of 40-inch standard, and 6-pieces of 46 inch by one glass sheet. The production volume of its 7-1 line increased from 45,000 sheets in April 2005 to 60,000 sheets by October 2005, and its current target is 75,000 sheets. As of January 2006, the production target of its 7-2 line, for which Samsung alone invested,

TABLE 6.2

Korean TFT-LCD Makers' Investment Status

Classification		Production Line	Generation	Production Year	Production Capacity (Glasses/Month)
Samsung	Gihung	370×470	2	1995.3	45,000
		550×650	3	1996.9	40,000
		370×470 (low-temperature Poly S)	2	—	—
	Chunan	600×720	3.5	1997.10	80,000 [17″ (4 pieces), 24″ (2 pieces)]
		730×920	4	2000.9	80,000 [15″ (8 pieces), 17″ (6 pieces), 21″ (4 pieces)]
		1100×1250	5	2002.9	30,000
		1100×1250	5	2003.6	30,000
		1100×1250	5	2003.10	60,000
		1100×1300	6	2004.2Q	120,000 [26″ (6 pieces), 32″ (3 pieces), 40″ (2 pieces)]
	Tanjeong (S-LCD) Samsung	1870×2200	7-1 (S-LCD)	2005.4	Starting 45,000→90,000 [32″ (12 pieces), 40″ (8 pieces), 46″ (6 pieces)]
			7-2	2006.1	Starting 45,000→90,000
		2200×2500	8-1-1	2008.6	50,000 [46″ (8 pieces), 52″(6 pieces)]
		2200×2500	8-1-2	2009	60,000
		2200×2500	8-2 (S-LCD)	2009	60,000
		3000×3320	11	2011 (?)	30,000

(Continued)

TABLE 6.2 (Continued)

Korean TFT-LCD Makers Investment Status

Classification		Production Line	Generation	Production Year	Production Capacity (Glasses/Month)
LPL	Gumi	370×470	2	1995.8	110,000
		590×670	3.5	1998.2	115,000
		680×880	3.5–4	2000.5	124,000
		1000×1200	4.5	2002.5	154,000
		1100×1250	5	2003.3	170,000
		1500×1850	6	2004.8	195,000 [32″ (8 pieces), 37″ (6 pieces)]
		370×470 (low temperature)	2	—	5000
	Paju	1950×2250	7 (7.5)	2006.1	172,000 [42″ (8 pieces), 47″ (6 pieces)]
		2200×2500	8	2009	83,000 [47″, 52″]
Hydis	Ichun	370×470	2	1996.10	20,000
		550×650	3	1997.9	8000
		620×720	3.5	2000.3	50,000

Source: Korean Semiconductor Industry Association (2010).

is 90,000 sheets per month, far beyond the current 45,000 monthly production volume (Nikkei Microdevices, 2006).

In addition to the rapidly increasing demand for 32-inch LCD TVs, Samsung has taken strategic initiatives in setting industry standards for 40-inch and 46-inch wide-screen LCDs. Recently, as the industry leader, Samsung also suggested the size of the eighth generation as 2200×2500 mm and the eleventh generation as 3000×3320 mm.

LG, on the other hand, started the sixth generation production line in 2004. Their standard size is 1500×1850 mm, and the glass substrate of one sheet contains six pieces of 37-inch and eight pieces of 32-inch. Its productivity is about four times the fifth generation production line (1100×1250 mm) that produces two pieces of 37-inch and 32-inch, respectively. LG's strategy was to lead industry standards by offering its sixth generation production line of 32-inch and 37-inch LCD TV and seventh generation production line of 42-inch LCD as its strategic products (Electronic Components, 2006). Initial planned production volume by the end of 2004 was 30,000 sheets and 90,000 sheets by the third quarter of 2005 (Nikkei Microdevices, 2006). In the fall of 2006, it intended to increase the production volume up to 112,000 sheets. In this way, LG intended to continue its global number one position in the LCD TV panel market in 2005 and market leadership for the wide-screen TV market. From January of 2006, LG began the seventh generation (1950×2250 mm) production lines and achieved a monthly production volume of 172,000 sheets (Park et al., 2007b). In 2009, LG began the eighth generation (2200×2500 mm) production lines.

6.4 SCM STRATEGIES OF KOREAN LCD MAKERS

6.4.1 Building SCM System by LCD Firms

6.4.1.1 SCM System Building Effort by Samsung

Samsung's LCD business has four product lines in Korea (Kiheung, Chunan, and Tanjeong) and China (Suzou) and produces LCD panels all year round, 24 hours a day for 365 days. Their Tanjeong facilities (located in Asan, South Korea) handle the seventh generation TV panels. With $30 billion additional investment by 2015, it will be transformed into the Crystal Valley of the LCD Cluster.

The LCD panel has evolved its usage from initial PC notebook monitors to TV panels. The global TV panel market is rapidly expanding, and the trend is moving toward wider screens. Compared to 17-inch computer monitors, 40- and 52-inch TV panels are 5.5 and 9.4 times as large in terms of screen size. As the screen becomes wider, the cost of logistics also increases drastically. According to Samsung's internal review, by 2007 even one day's production volume may cause substantial traffic bottlenecks from Chunan to Tanjeong. In this context, the LCD industry has taken supply chain management as one of its core strategic initiatives in improving the speed throughout the supply chain. For example, Samsung has initiated logistics innovation projects since 2004 to improve its supply chain performance (Park et al., 2007b).

With its global supply chain management, Samsung has secured its global market position by successfully marketing Bordeaux TV by 2006. Samsung's global SCM system integrates the worldwide networks of all the marketing entities, operations facilities, and its Seoul headquarters. Daily, weekly, and monthly sales data are available, including all performance details by product lines (e.g., volume sales by inch models and production origin). One Samsung senior executive said, "By SCM system, we now manage the sales volume, inventory details, production planning, and demand forecast of Bordeaux TV much more effectively and the market appeal of this product has been substantially improved. Besides, by drastically reducing the requirements of inventory level of products, we have enhanced customer satisfaction through timely and consistent order fulfillment."

Since 2004, Samsung has enlarged SCM implementation to both domestic and global operations and therefore secured more accurate and timely information. In 2006, its SCM system was applied to HighMart and EMart in the Korean market, and therefore real-time information updates and checks of daily sales became a reality (Park et al., 2007b). In 2007, Samsung had implemented SCM strategies to sustain its position as a global market leader (Park et al., 2007b). The President of Samsung Digital Media Business announced its 2007 focus on LCD TV and its marketing campaign on moving beyond 40-inch TV. Samsung's competitive advantage lies in their capabilities of reducing inventory levels and keeping loyal customers through timely and reliable delivery (Park et al., 2007b).

As the logistics costs increase with the trend toward bigger and wider screens, logistical innovative solutions in the LCD business are critical for its global competitiveness. With its strategic decision to build the SCM

System for logistical innovation, Samsung achieved the goal of SCM system build-up by the end of 2006.

In December of 2006, Samsung LCD business announced three planning aspects of its SCM system that focuses on inbound logistical innovation activities for securing upstream raw materials: (1) logistical delivery process mechanisms and corresponding system standardization; (2) an integrated transportation and information system; and (3) import and export routes between China and Korea. Suppliers that collaborate with Samsung's inbound logistical supply management were allowed to gain access to its direct delivery system, and even its second tier suppliers were then integrated into its logistical information system.

A senior executive of Samsung LCD Business said, "We have standardized all the tools of inbound logistics (i.e., supplier logistics). Our SCM system ('Clean Room to Clean Room') connects our entire supplier network—not only the first but also the second tier suppliers. In this way, quality of supplier products steadily moves through production lines throughout the year—365 days. In Samsung LCD Business, in 2006 alone, more than $110 millions have been saved through logistical innovation that streamlined its vital raw material flows" (Park et al., 2007b). In March of 2007, Samsung announced "Simultaneous Global Launching" (SGL) to maintain its number one global market position.

In the past, Japanese TV firms such as Panasonic and Sony have implemented SGL to one single TV model in particular regions. Currently, Samsung utilizes its "Self-Sufficient Production System" in Mexico, Slovakia, and Hungary. Its global marketing network also helps make SGL initiatives possible. It became possible to extensively implement global supply chain management through a cutting-edge IT system that monitors worldwide inventory levels and facilitates rapid responses to the ever-changing global market (Park et al., 2007b). Samsung's SCM system has secured technological system and internal organizational processes that are applicable even after 2010. In this sense, Samsung has succeeded in laying the groundwork for win–win relationships with suppliers.

6.4.1.2 SCM System of LG Display

LG Display (LG Philips LCD until February of 2008) (from its suppliers to vendors and customers) needs to satisfy increasing production volume requirements while simultaneously meeting other complex challenges (i.e., short product life cycle, long product development lead time, and facility expansion needs). The needs for global SCM become more obvious with the addition of production facilities in Paju, Korea, and Nanjing, China. In this context, LG Display has adopted systematic global supply chains to enhance its competitiveness and production efficiencies.

Integration of the supply chain starts with identifying its supplier network, building prototyping, and stabilizing demand. In the initial stage, cross-functional teams clarify the scope and structure of the supplier network and carefully explore future direction for effective implementation of supply chain management. In the pilot stage, teams experiment with supply chain design models in specific business processes. In the actual implementation stage, teams refine and upgrade the supply network modeling system and work out the details. These vital planning processes ensure effective design and implementation of global supply chain management and continuous change management.

Supplier management of LG Display includes planning details of monthly capacity allocation, weekly supplier production requirements, and daily production schedules which utilize advanced planning and scheduling (APS), SCM monitoring system (response mechanisms to the real-time plan/outcomes/ key performance indicator (KPI) information), and the i-MELT system (accuracy enhancement between Manufacturing Execution System (MES) and ERP data). Marketing and operations collaborate with other functions close to suppliers to create SCM organization under the CEO. Redesign of the business's process, system, and organization support integration efforts. Examples of tangible performance outcomes are (1) reduction of monthly planning cycle time up to a weekly unit, (2) master planning lead time reduction of up to 20 days (3 days shorter than the previous plans), and (3) improvement of customer response time from 10 days to 3 days. Through such noticeable improvement in lead time initiatives, customer responsiveness is substantially enhanced. Performance of suppliers is also visible through real-time information sharing about sales, production, purchasing, and other operational plans.

6.4.2 Vertical Integration Strategy of LCD Architecture

LCD panels have quite complex product structures with diverse component parts. The quality of component parts determines the clarity of the screen image. In LCD product development these component parts (e.g., digital film, glass substrate) determine raw materials mix, line manufacturing process complexity, and cost competitiveness. The barrier of entry is quite high in these component parts (Samsung Economic Research Institute, 2006). Naturally, LCD panels assume the high cost of component raw materials—quite different from other products (e.g., semiconductors and cellular phones).

Figure 6.2 shows a TFT-LCD panel: Cost of its component parts in terms of percent of sales (in $ billions). In 2005, the total sales of LCD panels were $39.4 billion, and the sales figure of component parts was $30.7 billion. The value of components in an LCD panel is about 78% of total sales. In 2006, through radical process redesign and integration, the cost of component parts was reduced down to 60% of sales, and yet this is still very high. Therefore, LCD panel firms need strategic alliances and collaboration with their suppliers for better management of cost and innovation.

The rapid enlargement trend of LCD panels has widened the gap between technological and investment capabilities, and many small and medium firms simply fail and disappear from the competitive market. Prior to the fifth generation of glass substrate, five or six firms (e.g., Corning, Asahi Glass, Nippon Electric Glass, Schott) were operating in Japan. After the sixth generation, only two suppliers survived (i.e., Corning and Asahi Glass). Seven or more firms participated in the flat panel market for 40-inch TVs. Yet, the active suppliers are now only three—Nitto Denko, Sumitomo Chemical, and LG Chemical (Samsung Economic Research Institute, 2006). In such an intense competitive environment, LCD panel firms concentrate their efforts to strengthen relationships with upstream suppliers through technological collaboration and vertical integration. In

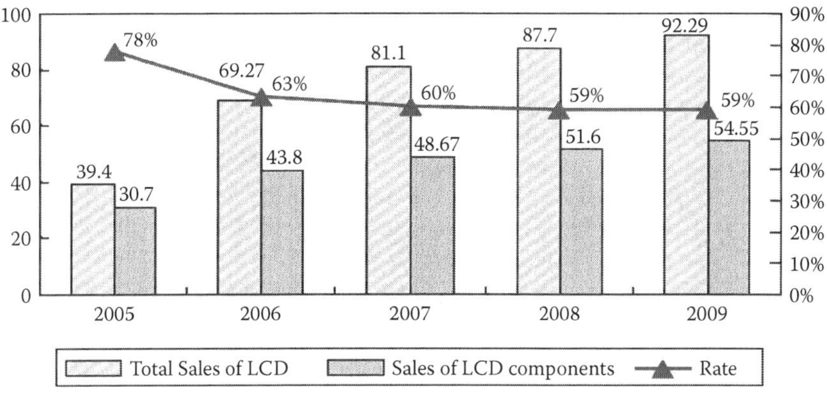

FIGURE 6.2
TFT-LCD panel: Cost of its component parts in terms of percent of sales (in $ billions).

this way, they try to achieve a stable supply of component parts and cost competitiveness.

For example, Samsung has technological exchange arrangements with Sumitomo Chemical for flat panel development, and LG established Paju Electric Glass through its partnership with Nippon Electric Glass. Table 6.3 is a list of firms operating in Korea through various strategic alliance and integration strategies.

These firms locate their facilities particularly near LG and Samsung clusters (Samsung Economic Research Institute, 2006). Samsung has been building

TABLE 6.3

Foreign LCD Component Parts Manufacturers Operating in Korea

	Firms in Korea	Firms (National Origin)	Market Share	Location (Time of Investment)
Glass substrate	Asahi Glass Fine Techno Korea (AFK)	Asahi Glass (Japan)	25%	Gumi (2005.8)
	Paju Electric Glass	Nippon Electric. Glass (NEG; Japan)	20%	Paju (2006.6)
	Schott Kuramoto Processing Korea Ltd.	Schott (Germany) Kuramoto Processing (Japan)	NA	Ochang (2005.11)
Polarizing plate/ polarizing film	Dongwoo Fine-Chem Co., Ltd.	Sumitomo Chemical Co., Ltd. (Japan)	20%	Pyungtaeck (1991)
	Korea Nitto Denko Co., Ltd. (KND)	Nitto Denko Corporation (Japan)	48%	Pyungtaeck (2005.1Q)
	Korea 3M	3M (America)	70%	Hwasung (2006.5)
Color filter	Dongwoo STI	Sumitomo Chemical Co., Ltd. (Japan)	NA	Pyungtaeck (2005 Dongwoo Fine-Chem Co., Ltd. to merge)
Back light units	Harison Toshiba Lighting Korea	Harison Toshiba Lighting Corp. (Japan)		Ochang (2004.5)
Liquid crystal materials	Merck Advanced Technology	Merck Ltd. (Germany)	55%	Posung (2002.8)
	Chisso Korea	Chisso Corp (Japan)	40%	Pyungtaeck (2005.11)

TABLE 6.4

Status of Vertical Integration of Panel Component Parts

Category	Glass Substrate	Color Filter	Polarizing Plate	Driver IC	BLU (Back Light Units)
Samsung	Samsung Corning Precision Glass	Internal sourcing	—	Internal sourcing	Cheil Industries Inc. LGP (light guiding panel)
LG (LG Display)	Paju Electric Glass	—	LG Chem, Ltd.	—	LG Electronics (prism sheet)

up LCD clusters for small TVs and PCs in Kiheung and Chunan, and has large TV clusters in Tanjeong. LG has also built its strategic clusters in Gumi and Paju for producing large-panel TVs (Samsung Economic Institutive, 2005). Korean LCD firms (i.e., Samsung and LG) have adopted SCM strategy that reflects LCD product and market characteristics that move toward bigger screens and three-layer product architectures (i.e., upstream suppliers, LCD panel makers, and downstream LCD manufacturers).

For some component parts that cannot be internally developed, Samsung and LG have invited other foreign firms near their cluster-proximity areas and achieved vertical integration for the internal production of LCD panels. For example, LG and Samsung produce 90% and 70% of LCD panels within their production network, respectively (Table 6.4). Vertical integration is also in progress for other major component parts such as glass substrate, polarizing plates, driver ICs, and back light units. For glass substrate, which requires a huge investment, Korean firms, Samsung and LG in particular, have created a network of their own affiliated suppliers through vertical integration (Samsung Economic Research Institute, 2006). In view of increasing logistic costs, SCM integration strategies invite other external firms into their clusters and form strategic partnership under their umbrella and achieve stable supplier integration.

6.5 FUTURE CHALLENGES FOR THE KOREAN UPSTREAM COMPONENT PARTS INDUSTRY

Thus, we have examined LCD product architecture and Korean LCD's business strategies from the SCM perspective. Samsung and LG adopted LCD TV as their strategic products, made huge capital investments, built

SCM systems, and achieved cost reduction and competitive advantage through vertical integration with their upstream firms.

Japanese component suppliers have long enjoyed the competitive advantage of maintaining high profit rates through relatively high-value-added component parts in LCD product architecture. To further protect their strategic interests, they have built up complex entry barriers through securing their original technologies and patent protection. In view of intense struggles between Korean LCD panel firms and Japanese-based component suppliers, the prospect of failing in this competitive war among small Korean component suppliers is growing. For LCD panels, Korean firms (even Samsung and LG) still depend on component parts mostly through imports. Particular weaknesses of Korean small component suppliers are a serious SCM strategic concern for Korean LCD firms. According to the Ministry of Industry Resources of Korea, the rate of import of these component parts is about 60% (LG Economic Institute, 2007b). Other global firms that operate in Korea import their components from Japan (about 70%), and the extent of knowledge sharing with Korean suppliers is quite minimal (Samsung Economic Research Institute, 2006).

The Korean display industry is mostly focusing on the assembling of final finished products. Except for continuous cost reduction, their potential for technological differentiation is fairly limited, and accordingly the risk of the product commoditization is serious (LG Economic Institute, 2006b). The recent price war between display LCD and PDP is a visible sign of such a competitive risk. In spite of the small range of cost reduction by panel firms through their independent process improvement, the pressures for continuous cost reduction are intensifying (Park et al., 2007b). Recently, many Korean LCD panel firms have taken steps to purchase component parts from Chinese and Taiwanese firms, and therefore, Korean small component suppliers face further serious competitive challenges. As LCD panel firms work on the formation of cluster strategy with other outstanding foreign component suppliers, Korean component suppliers experience greater risk that threatens their very survival.

Though Japanese firms, while holding a monopolistic position in component parts, maintain competitive advantage through upstream integration strategies, Korean component suppliers do not possess original technologies and therefore inevitably suffer competitive disadvantages in the value chain. For example, Nitto Denko goes beyond assembling component parts, inventing and patenting technological know-how of wide-viewing–angle film and reflection-prevention film and is expanding its businesses in the upstream value chains. Such a move is justified because the extent of value added is far greater in the upstream than in the downstream value chains. In the case of JSR which produces LCD core component parts such as color resists, overcoats, and photo spacers that transform the particles from the light source into color, the profit margin is about 30%. Kuraray, which dominates the PVA (polyvinyl alcohol) market, also maintains more than a 15% profit margin. 3M, which has monopolized the blue prism film market for more than 10 years, also achieves a 30% profit rate (LG Economic Research Institute, 2007b). Japanese firms, with their high barriers of entry through original technologies and patent protection, sustain a desirable profit rate regardless of LCD panel price fluctuations. On the contrary, Korean component suppliers that have little capability for technological innovation are at a high risk of business failure.

Although recently LCD panel architecture is being modularized, Korean LCD firms aim to gain competitive advantage through building SCM systems, and through integration with upstream suppliers that provide high-value-added potentials and corresponding cost reduction measures. Since Japanese firms mostly keep their competitive advantage through their original technologies and patent protection, the balance of power would be maintained for a while. It is not clear whether Korean LCD firms would maintain their competitive advantage through vertical integration with Japanese component suppliers and not with Korean component suppliers that have weak competitive strengths. In case of disappearance of Korean component suppliers, other foreign component suppliers may focus on vertical integration with Taiwanese firms that receive partial technology transfers from Sharp and other Japanese firms. In doing so, would they be able to sustain their competitive advantages? In this sense, it would be worthwhile to continuously observe Korean LCD firms and how they engage in vertical integration and survive in global competitive battles.

7

Korean TV Industry: A Case Study of LG Electronics

With the rapidly growing global market demand for flat-panel display (FPD) TV, the research interest on such products is receiving increasing attention. However, very few studies (in English, in particular) are available in regard to the strategic or operational-level analysis of FPD TV.

This case study explores how LG Electronics (LGE) has adopted modular product architecture to both plasma display panel (PDP) and liquid-crystal display (LCD) TV across both upstream and downstream supply chains. Besides, LGE has implemented unique operational management practices (the LG Production System) applying the Toyota Production System. Such integration of product architecture and operational practices has secured its globally competitive market position. This case study suggests the importance of integration of both the business model and operational practices for sustainable competitive advantages.

7.1 INTRODUCTION

With the increasing use of digital broadcasting and Internet broadband, more customers expect content-rich and high-density video expression in media. In this context, the mainstream of display is moving away from the traditional CRT (cathode ray tube) to flat-panel display (FPD) (Park, 2005). For a long time it seemed that the commercialization prospect of organic light-emitting diode (OLED) technologies was remote, though the FPD TV industry bloomed, utilizing liquid-crystal display (LCD) and plasma display panel (PDP) technologies. By the end of 2007, Sony was successful in developing OLED TV and testing it in the market by utilizing the OLED technology. The display TV market competition will intensify with products using combinations of the LCD, PDP, and OLED technologies.

Although the marketing effort of OLED TV started at the end of 2007, its commercialization success for the large-screen market requires overcoming major technological limitations. On the other hand, the competitive boundaries of LCD and PDP have almost disappeared. Prior to 2000, LCD technology was fitting to smaller screens instead of the larger screens. However, through successful applications of thin film transistor liquid-crystal display (TFT-LCD) technologies from the middle of the 2000s, rapid price competition among large-screen LCD TV manufacturers is in progress.

TV assembly manufacturers (quite different from their color TV days) are experiencing continuous deterioration of their financial performance (Ogasawara and Matsumoto, 2006). For example, this trend is quite obvious in the price change of LCD panels that are used for LCD TV. After 2005, a continuous LCD panel price reduction caused the drastic drop in the firm's operating income (top four firms) from 19% (in 2004) to 7% (in 2005) (LG Economic Institute, 2006a). Such a downward profit spiral of LCD panel firms has impacted the performance of FPD TV firms that produce LCD TV.

In a sense, the above changes are explained by the disappearance of the market boundary between LCD and PDP. More importantly, they are in response to the element of product architecture. Product architecture is an essential concept that explains the patterns of relationships among functional and structural requirements that satisfy core components of a product. In terms of interdependence of part design, two classification methods are either modular or integral. In terms of the extent of standardization characteristics, the organizational system is grouped either open or closed (Fujimoto, 2003). Particularly, the key word that signifies today's firm characteristics is modularity (Baldwin and Clark, 2000; Aoki and Ando, 2002). With the widespread use of the Internet in the middle of the 1990s, interfirm relationships have evolved to be more open, and therefore, even the products that had been characterized as closed integral product architecture are leaning more toward open modular product architecture. Such environmental changes have impacted the FPD industry. In general,

LCD product architecture of upstream (component suppliers) is close to an integral pattern, while downstream architecture (LCD TV) adopts a modular one (Park et al., 2007b). As a result, the FPD TV prices, charged ultimately to the customers, have significantly dropped over the years, and naturally the downward pressures to panel prices have been intensifying. Although the upstream component manufacturers certainly feel the heat of such sustained cost reductions, the extent of price pressures are most obvious in the prices of final TV products.

However, such modularized products must focus on cost reduction through efficient operations management unless innovation occurs in the fundamental business model level. This case study focuses on LG Electronics (LGE), which produces both FPD TV and FPD panels that are heavily affected by modularity trends. Quite different from venture firms that do not maintain any production factories, LG Electronics has difficulty in quickly implementing an innovative business model throughout its supply chains. This study, therefore, examines how LG Electronics (with both production of FPD TVs and panels) has implemented effective operations management practices. Particularly, this study presents how LG successfully adopted (1) supply chain management (SCM) in preparation for global dispersion of the components manufacturing plants in response to the modularity demand and (2) LGPS (LG Production System) in manufacturing assembly of electronic products.

7.2 PRODUCT ARCHITECTURE AND OPERATION MANAGEMENT

7.2.1 Integral Product Architecture and Modular Product Architecture

Product architecture is an essential concept that explains the patterns of relationships among functional and structural requirements that satisfy core components of a product. In terms of interdependence of part design, two classification methods are modular and integral (Figure 7.1). In terms of the extent of standardization characteristics, the organizational system is grouped as either open or closed (Fujimoto, 2003; Park et al., 2007b). Automobiles take closed integral architecture with the complex product functions and process structures, and naturally they are not so open with outside firms.

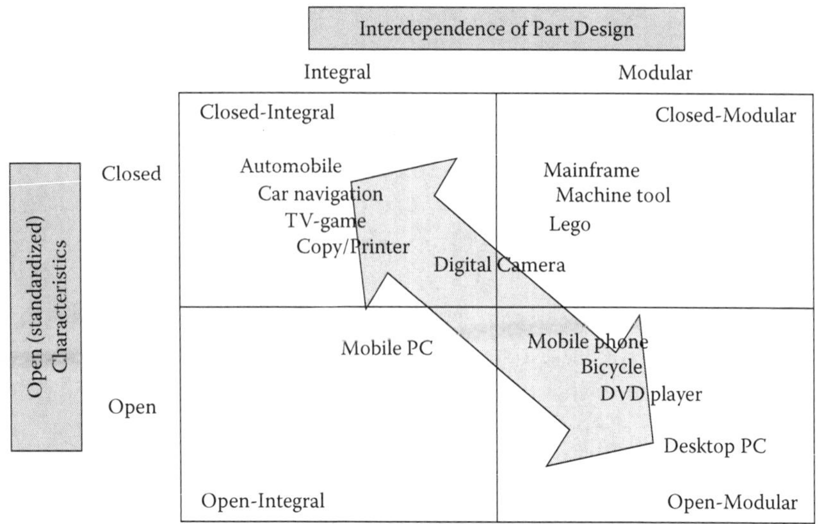

FIGURE 7.1
Types of product architecture. From Park et al. (2007a).

On the other hand, electronic products (e.g., personal computers) are close to open modular architecture with clear-cut one-to-one relationships among product functions and process structures. They tend to be more open in their relationships among firms (Fujimoto, 2003; Nobeoka et al., 2006; Park et al., 2007a).

With the widespread use of the Internet from the middle of the 1990s, interfirm relationships have evolved to be more open, and therefore, even the products that had been characterized as closed integral product architecture are becoming more open modular product architecture. Nobeoka (2006) argues that one factor for strong modularity is in the case of customer needs for the product's function reaching a limitation. Although firms with their continuous product development efforts introduce new products with higher functions, customer needs do not necessarily reach beyond a certain level, and therefore the process of modularity is accelerated through product standardization-specialization. For example, five million pixels are adequate for customer demands for pixels of a digital camera. Firms may introduce new products beyond five million pixels with heavy investment on R & D, but few customers are willing to pay higher prices for such new products. The so-called excessive product quality phenomena in Japanese electronic product manufacturers shows that product purchasing power no longer expands if customer needs do not respond beyond a certain price level. Therefore, firms focus more on cost reduction rather than on new innovative products with excessive functionality beyond the required level of customer needs. Naturally, modularity trends are accelerated through the application of standardization and specialization. Such modularity phenomena impact market segments, not only in local markets, but also in the global market. For example, global mobile phone markets have two market segments—a high-end market for advanced nations and a low-end market focusing on Brazil, Russia, India, China (BRIC). There are the integral markets for the customer needs that require high-value-added functionality and the modular markets for customers that prefer low-priced functional mobile phones (Park et al., 2008b).

In some cases, firms may deliberately accelerate the modularity process. Firms that have developed core technology may standardize assembly of the product and interfaces using their own technologies and therefore speed up the modularity process. For example, Intel has standardized its products based on MPU, and Cisco did the same for its external network and interfaces based on Router (Ogawa, 2007b). As many players acquire their own innovation capabilities through system modules, the relationships between producers of core products and suppliers of complementary products rapidly change, and accordingly, modularity tendency becomes more visible (Y. W. Park, 2006; Song, 2006). Besides, network technology development like the Internet has caused product architecture to become more open modular, and yet even for personal computers that are regarded as modular products, the core CPU is integral product architecture that other firms may not easily imitate. Even for modular products, too often many internal components of the subsystem adopt integral architecture (Nobeoka, 2006). The subsequent section is devoted to explaining the product architecture hierarchy in electronic products that are close to modular architecture and in particular examines the product architecture of FPD.

7.2.2 Hierarchy of Product Architecture in FPD TV

Product architecture is hierarchical, and even modular products contain integral product architecture in their subsystem level (Clark, 1985; Fujimoto, 2003; Nobeoka, 2006). The representative study of product architecture of a subsystem is on a DVD player (Shintaku et al., 2006). In the case of a DVD player, which is regarded as a modular product, integral product architecture is used for a subsystem which centralized some control elements. LCD products (one type of FPD display) also show such

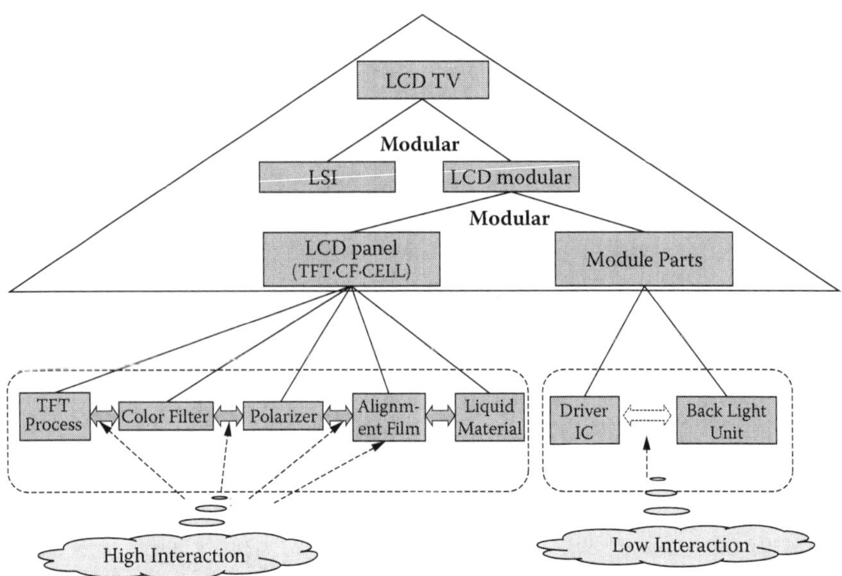

FIGURE 7.2
Product architecture of LCD TV. Adapted from Shintaku et al. (2007a).

patterns. The closer to the upstream component parts, the more integral product architecture is applied; the closer to the downstream areas, the more modular product architecture is common (Park et al., 2007b). The product architecture of LCD TV is described in Figure 7.2. LCD TV of downstream includes a LCD TV module which is the assembly of the three core components (i.e., LCD panel, driver integrated circuit [IC], and back light unit) and the final additions of image processing large-scale integration (LSI). As seen from the upper structure, it appears that the manufacturing process is simple assembly of modularized component parts. In reality, it is close to integral architecture in that the LCD panel requires complex interrelationships among component parts (Shintaku et al., 2007a).

Because of the above characteristics, firms that produce modularized products pursue a price-competitive strategy through production cost reduction. On the other hand, firms that produce core components in modular elements tend to exercise network leadership. In today's numerous industries, mutual interdependency of diverse products and widely dispersed innovation capabilities dictate that firms (regardless of their size) must consider the activities of other firms for their basic business decision making (Gawer and Cusumano, 2002).

As mentioned above, there are three kinds of FPD TV—LCD, PDP, and OLED. LG Electronics produces both LCD TV and PDP TV in its Factory A. This is possible because of the architecture characteristics of FPD TV. PDP TV is similar to LCD TV in terms of structures. In the next section, the characteristics of LCD TV and PDP TV are compared, and their differences are explained.

7.2.3 LCD and PDP

CRT TV has dominated the TV market for a long period. With the rapid expansion of the FPD TV market, the market share of FPD TV is noticeably increasing. Figure 7.3 shows the FPD market share trend since 2005. It is predicted that its market share would be more than 80% after 2010.

Technological characteristics of LCD and PDP are somewhat different, although they both belong to the FPD display family. PDP technology became popular in 1997 as firms commercialized 102-cm (40-inch) size TV for the purpose of public viewing by hanging on the wall (inews24, Dec 18, 2007). At the beginning of 2000, mass production systems for its production were already established in Korea and Japan. At that time, LCD technology, having been successfully applied in small digital technologies (e.g., mobile phones), was being considered for the TV market. By 2005 the serious competition between LCD TV and PDP TV became quite real in the market. At first, PDP TV was acknowledged for its cost advantage,

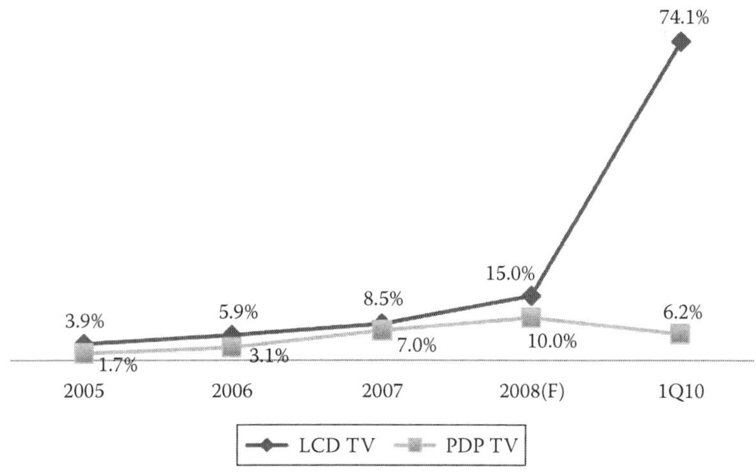

FIGURE 7.3
FPD market share trend. From Park et al., 2007b, DisplaySearch (2010).

smooth video image presentation, and wide viewing screen capacity. In contrast, LCD was not so appealing to the market because of its high cost and the poor viewing quality—particularly at the time of reproduction of video images. With the successful resolution of such LCD technological problems, the competitive boundaries between LCD TV and PDP TV soon disappeared.

Since PDP technology was developed for the purpose of wide screen product characteristics, it is difficult to achieve size minimization. In the area of DID (digital information display), LCD (with the introduction of new technologies) is positioning itself to replace both interior and exterior advertising billboards. LCD (although started for small-size display) accelerated its move toward the larger screen through a series of technological breakthroughs, and therefore by the late 1990s, the competitive boundaries between LCD and PDP no longer existed. LCD is used in a wide range of products, from small and medium equipment (e.g., mobile phones, notebooks, and monitors) to various IT technological products which include medium and large TVs. Although the 2008 market prospect is that LCD fits up to 40-inch TVs, and PDP is for beyond 50-inch TVs, LCD TV has already surpassed PDP TV for all sizes. Figure 7.4 shows that both LCD and PDP technologies have reached somewhat similar performance standards, except that PDP has a relative price and size advantage while LCD maintains its comparative superiority in terms of weight and bright room contrast ratio.

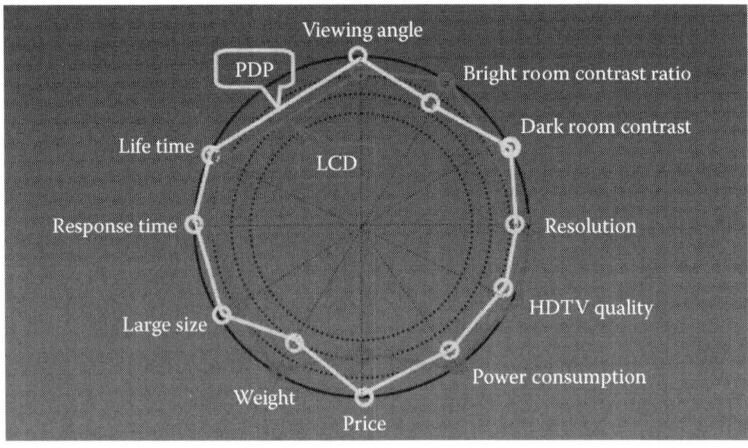

FIGURE 7.4
Comparison of LCD and PDP. From Park et al., 2007b.

From the product architecture standpoint, the product architecture of a LCD/PCD module (located in upstream of LCD TV and PDP TV) has noticeable differences. Compared to a LCD module, a PDP module is closer to integral architecture in view of its strong mutual interdependence of manufacturing processes. PDP is quite effective in reproducing smooth and quality video images because PDP uses the principles of analog phenomena that transform ultraviolet rays made by high-voltage electricity into fluorescent elements. However, if troubles in the manufacturing processes of a PDP panel occur, it is much more difficult to respond to them because of the analog technical constraints (e.g., electric discharge) of PDP (Ogawa, 2007a, 2007b). On the other hand, LCD module assembly is close to modular structure in that the key component parts (e.g., driver IC and back light unit) of the highly mutually interdependent LCD panel can be independently assembled without having any serious problems. Therefore, entire front-end manufacturing processes of the LCD module are done domestically, while back-end assembly processes are done in overseas plants. In this way, the differences occur in LCD/PDP (placed in between LCD TV and PDP TV) module architecture.

However, in the final TV assembly processes, complete open modularity is possible if LCD/PDP modules and other component parts (e.g., image processing LSI chip and cases) are purchased separately (see Table 7.1). Because of these characteristics, Chinese firms and American venture firms (e.g., Vizio) without any LCD/PDP module manufacturing facilities can compete in the U.S. FPD market against major brands such as Samsung, Sony, LG, and Sharp. Entry to the area of component parts that are close to integral architecture and to entire panel manufacturing is not easy. However, by purchasing all modules and TV component parts, firms

TABLE 7.1

Modularity and Comparison of LCD and PDP

	LCD	PDP	Focus
TV	Modularity	Modularity	Productivity/cost competitiveness
Module	Modularity	Intermediate integral (panel-module integration)	Productivity/cost competitiveness
Panel	Intermediate integral		Process/cost competitiveness
Parts	High integral	High integral	Quality competitiveness

can easily supply cost-competitive TVs without having any prior TV assembly technologies. Therefore, in the final TV assembly stage, brand power and cost performance determine the firm's competitive advantages.

In this context, operations management is becoming more important in recent FPD TV manufacturing processes for the purpose of productivity enhancement and cost reduction. As most TV manufacturers show losses in their financial statements, it is critical to maximize the production efficiencies and minimize assembly costs for profitable FPD TV production. This case study therefore focuses on changes in the manufacturing processes in the final assembly line of LCD/PDP TV among FPD TVs.

7.3 CASE STUDY

7.3.1 Case Background

Korean FPD TV makers occupy the top positions in terms of global market share. In all TV global markets, Samsung and LG maintain first and third place, respectively, and accordingly, the global competitiveness of Korean firms is fairly high. LG Electronics, the firm that is the focus of this particular case, has four business units—DA (Digital Appliance), DD (Digital Display), DM (Digital Media), and MC (Mobile Communication) (Figure 7.5). Flat panel TV belongs to DD (Digital Display), and it produces both LCD and PDP TV. The panel module that is the core TV module is produced by LGE's PDP Unit and its subsidiary LG Display (changed from LG Philips LCD in 2008). As of 2008, DD

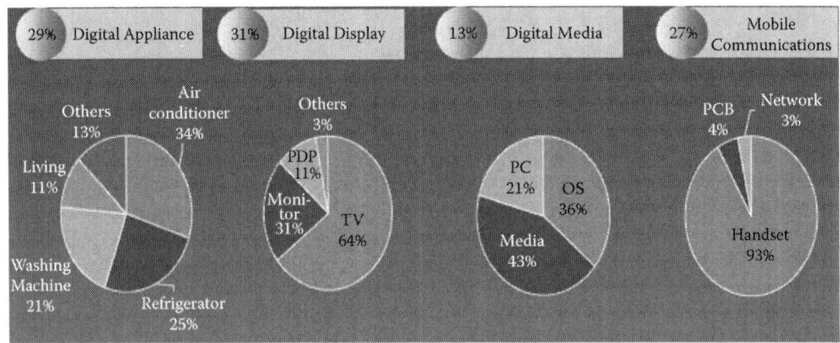

FIGURE 7.5
Business areas of LGE. From IR document of LG Electronics (2008.2).

TABLE 7.2

PDP Market Share (3rd and 4th Quarters, 2007) (Based on Market Volume)

Firms	3rd Quarter	4th Quarter	Growth Rate (Compared to 4th quarter of 2006)
Matsushita	32.7%	36.8%	48%
LG Electronics	27.3%	28.4%	113%
Samsung SDI	28.8%	25.1%	95%
Hitachi	6.8%	6.4%	17%
Pioneer	4.2%	3.2%	−39%
Orion	0.2%	0.1%	80%
Total	100%	100%	62%

Source: DisplaySearch.

(Digital Display) Business Unit is 31% of LG businesses, and therefore its significance is well-noticed.

In the global market, the FPD market share of LGE is rapidly increasing (Table 7.2). As of the end of 2007, its rank is third in all TV markets and fourth in the FPD market. LGE sold 6.5 million LCD TVs and 2.5 million PDP TVs and maintained 9% of the market share (fourth) in the world. For PDP (with its own manufacturing facilities) in the fourth quarter of 2007, LG surpassed Samsung's SDI and ranked second in the world market (inews24, 2008. 2.1).

In 2008, LGE's goal is to attain 10% of the market share and therefore catch up with Sharp by developing innovative strategic products and concentrating marketing capabilities (ETNEWS, 2008.1.8). In the 2000s, with the drastic reduction in panel price, in addition to effective marketing and product development strategies, improvement in profit rate through productivity enhancement is becoming an important strategic priority.

7.3.2 Case Analysis

7.3.2.1 Integration of Panels and SCM System

This case examines integration details of supply chain with LG Display, the producer of LCD panels of LG Electronics (LGE). Specifically, it is about integration of panel modules (i.e., the core of TV products) in view of their short product life cycle and long lead time from component parts suppliers to the finished products. With the continuous TV price decline (i.e., value-added reduction in supply chain), substantial production cost reduction requires integration of manufacturing processes of component parts and assembly processes of finished products. Since assembly costs of all products in Korea are relatively expensive, LGE established 17 manufacturing facilities worldwide for back-end manufacturing of LCD/PDP modules and other TV component parts. Different from the PDP panel, which belongs to the family of internal digital displays, LCD requires final TV assembly of panels (which are manufactured by LG Display) in the Gumi and Paju facilities in Korea, Nanjing in China, and other facilities around the world. This is the background of how LGE has built global supply chain management by which integration of panel firms and SCM resulted in overall logistical cost reductions.

This SCM system of LGE is integrated with the enterprise resource planning (ERP) system of LG Group. LGE built an ERP system so that various management information (accounts, production, marketing, product development, customer service) which becomes business resources can be spread to the post of whole group strategically from 1996. LGE introduced the Oracle ERP system in seven sections (financial accounting process, production schedule, shipment process, business process, product development process, customer management process, and logistics process) over three years and six months.

At first, in 2001, LGE and LG Display (changed from LG Philips LCD in 2008), LG Innotech, and LG Communications successively introduced the ERP system (Park et al., 2007b). LGE and affiliation companies of LGE came to have GSCM (global supply chain management) and CRM (customer relationship management) at the same time through integrated ERP construction. In addition, other business management practices like supply chain management (SCM), business process management (BPM), and services relationships management (SRM) have become more available to LGE. And advancement work was done in all fields of supply chain planning (SCP) and supply chain execution (SCE) of SCM. The result of part number redesign work to standardize parts information of LGE was reflected in the SRM system, and this system was inaugurated in March of 2005. LGE built a global unified supply network planner for the unified production schedule establishment of whole-world production and sales departments. The Transport Management System (TMS) was completed in their domestic division in 2005, and the Warehouse Management System (WMS), which was already built, was spread into the service and parts departments of America.

On the other hand, LGE carried out SCM integration with its affiliated suppliers through internal system unification in 2001. LGE developed an electronic document system (XML-EDI) which could process all duties to occur at the time of business with business partners on the Internet and has begun to apply it to all areas of purchasing since August of 2001. LGE with Korea Trade NET (KT-NET) developed the XML-EDI system, investing 1,300,000,000 won from 2000, to improve inefficient procedures to secure global competitive advantage through the reinforcement of subcontractors. As more than 2,500 subcontractors of LGE were connected to an XML-EDI system through the Internet network, a broad range of business processes (e.g., order form dispatch, L/C establishment, an article receipt, tax calculation) enabled rapid price settlement in material purchase negotiations. In this way, LGE's cost reduction was more than 5,000,000,000 won in a year, which does not even include an additional 30% of work productivity with the online transactions (Park et al., 2007b). In 2001 LGE installed the ERP system in the Web environment, through which real-time market analysis and information access for diverse business processes are achieved. Such IS system facilitated further cross-functional collaboration (e.g., operation, marketing, and services) with subcontractors in the interorganizational level as well.

In 2005, LGE began a project to improve their existing ERP system by 2010, and to build global unification systems (Oracle News). In the first stage, LGE introduced a unified GHRS (global human resource system) for early decision making from June 2005 to April 2006. In the second stage, global standard ERP was built through introducing domestic production ERP unification and a global standard system of marketing/accounts from October 2005 to December 2006. In the third and fourth stages, LGE planned to integrate all 11 of the offshore production divisions using Oracle ERP and would also include an in-house system of 65 divisions abroad through synchronization between domestic and overseas practice process by 2010 (Park et al., 2007b). Through the global ERP (G-ERP) unification project to unify overseas systems in the entire company, LGE expected that global visibility and cooperation would be increased. In addition, LGE says that the ability in performing an entire company business plan improves by building a global SCP (supply chain plan).

The ordering and supplying of parts was enabled through a SCM system which linked such global ERP with a cooperation part company by real time, so that it makes LGPS efficient. There are around 250 cooperation firms for TV parts, and LGE adopted the electronic Kanban system of Toyota. As mentioned, LGE introduced an SCM system connected with all its cooperation firms in 2001, and through G-ERP, information exchange in real time is possible between LGE and subcontractors. LGE now fixes the quantity of ordering before the 15th day and notifies it to parts companies in real time. Parts companies enter their production of parts with established part delivery information before the third day. Finally, component parts manufacturers complete delivery of each TV module to the LGE factory four hours before LGPS module injection and production on any particular appointed date of delivery. By using such an integrated SCM system, LGE maintains a high degree of collaboration relationships in the global scale.

7.3.2.2 Efficient Mass Production through Implementation of LGPS (LG Production System)

One manufacturing facility of LGE produces more than 10,000 FPD TVs daily (monthly production is about 200,000). In general, an average firm's facility produces about 500 TVs per shift. Japanese Sharp produces 800 TVs in the same time. Besides its facilities in the Gumi area, LGE maintains both its assembly lines and manufacturing facilities that produce panel modules. LGE assembles them as final products in the Gumi area and in 17 other foreign factories including Mexico (2), Brazil (2), Poland (2), Karzarkstan (1), Russia (1), Thailand, Indonesia, Egypt, and China (2), etc. Such a mass global production system is possible through the implementation of LGPS (LG Production System), which applied the TPS (Toyota Production System) method in their TV manufacturing processes. Five TV assembly facilities adopted TPS from 2004. It is being implemented both in Korean facilities and in other facilities located in Poland, Indonesia, and China.

As shown in Table 7.3, the case factory which adopted TPS involves seven lines that assemble PDP TVs, LCD TVs, and monitors—one stream conveyor line (with slat method), four pallet conveyor lines, and two mini lines that use cell methodologies which are all quite unique in LGE.

The specifics of the slat TV line configurations apply TPS in the following ways. First, PDP modules, the core of the assembly processes, are completed in manufacturing facilities nearby. Second, LCD modules supplied from LG Display and all other component parts are also delivered in modular forms.

TABLE 7.3

Case Plant Line Organization

Slat Method	Pallet Method			Cell Method
1st line	**2nd and 3rd lines**	**4th line**	**5th line**	**6th and 7th lines**
LCD TV, PDP TV	LCD TV, PDP TV	Monitor	Big monitor, LCD TV	Small lot, Cell assembly beyond 60 inch

Source: Interview results.

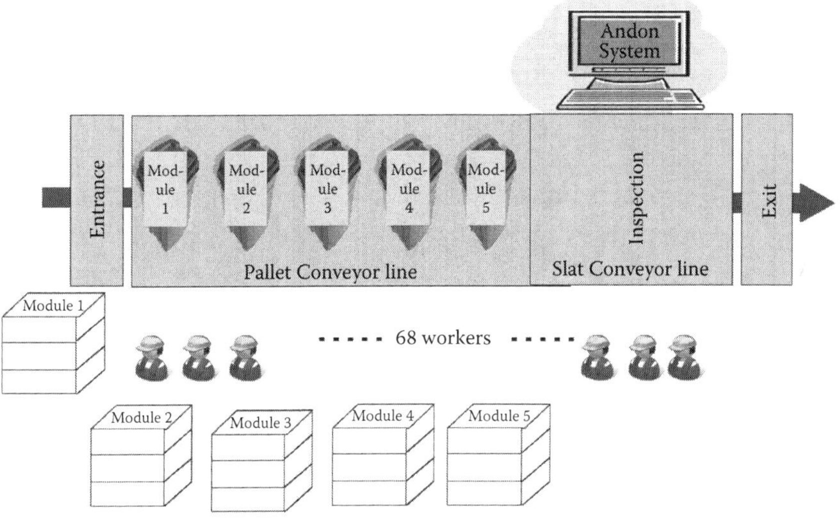

FIGURE 7.6
Conveyor line process.

Figure 7.6 shows the modular assembly processes (i.e., front modules → PDP/LCD modules → chassis modules (TV board) → back covers → stand). Different from automobile assembly that includes pallets, TV conveyors include the functions of pallets as well. Because the Andon System is programmed, the entire work processes are available through video monitors in real time.

Sixty-eight workers assigned to each line continue the assembly processes in a seamless fashion. By streamlining the module assembly lines into five modules and conveying the pallet, the overall assembly time is substantially reduced. LGE's assembly rate per hour is a maximum of 400, so that the maximum takt time is 7.8 seconds. Normally they operate at a production rate of 330 per hour (11 seconds takt time). (Note: Takt time can be defined as the maximum time allowed to produce a product in order to meet demand. It is derived from the German word *taktzeit*, which translates to clock cycle.)

LGE's operational performance is outstanding compared to that of other TV assembly lines. This is primarily because the number of module processes is reduced to five. Besides, such a level of performance requires solid collaborative relationships with external suppliers and strategic partners. Although core PDP and LCD panels are a part of this LGPS, the remaining four modules are all delivered as completely assembled parts, and therefore, LGPS as a whole achieves a very high level of production efficiencies.

The defect rate of the entire manufacturing processes is reduced to 0.7%. The ratio of inspection among module assembly lines is relatively high. Twenty-three workers are allocated to manage the sizable number of inspection items. The inspection processes are according to strict material standard requirements (RF/ AV 1,2,3 / Component 1,2,3 / HDMI 1,2,3,4 / DTV) and checking TV viewing quality. Pattern adjustments are not applied except the white balancing adjustment.

One group leader is placed by each line, and the length of each line is 130 m, so that one TV is produced for every 11 minutes normally. By the way, productivity rises when its distance is made shorter, because the frequency of pushing the Andon button reduces. To maximize this effect, LGE is going to have conveyer distance shortened. Their TV productivity target is 15,000,000 sets in 2008, and the ratio of Korean domestic production is now 8% to 10%. LGE has a plan to raise the Polish and Mexican production ratio.

Of course, although LGPS applies TPS of Toyota, it is fundamentally different from the principle of TPS in its delivery method of parts (Table 7.4). TPS is a production method for minimizing inventory level, but LGPS is the system that is useful for adjusting output requirements while fixing input factors.

7.4 DISCUSSION

This case study illustrates how LGE applied effective operations management practices in the context of product architecture characterized with intense modularity. As shown in LGE, FPD TV/panel manufacturing facilities (with the constant downward pressures of their product prices) are required to implement efficient operations management for cost

TABLE 7.4

Comparison of TPS and LGPS

TPS	LGPS
• A Pull production system (production as to be sold)	• Deciding production volume of each TV size setting TV standard time to make a TV (for example, set normal production time per one 32-inch TV in 10 minutes, decide production volume of one day, put it together with other TV size, and produce that amount.)
• JIT, Kanban system	• Kanban system
TPS = Output fixed/input variable	LGPS = Output variable/input fixed

Source: Interview results.

reduction. Just like many other modularized electronic products, production facilities are moving into China, India, and other nations that offer low labor costs. LGE has attained efficient cost reduction and productivity enhancement by implementing a global supply chain strategy and adopting LGPS that applied the TPS (Toyota Production System).

However, such operation management practices do not provide fundamental answers to the growing business challenges in view of the recent financial results of FPD TV firms. Although LGE is one of five big global TV makers, its profit rate is not very good. Long-term struggles with low profit-generating products exhaust both the senior management and the participating workers. Increasingly, businesses look for a new strategy model that creates substantial value-added products that contribute to a high level of profits.

Figure 7.7 shows that firms create value through product or process innovation. U.S. firms are relatively strong in production innovation, while Japanese firms (represented by Toyota) show their advantages in process innovation. The question is whether the value added is actually connected to the firm's profit performance.

Most FPD TV assembly makers show deterioration of their profit level. In contrast, small and medium component suppliers show higher profit levels. In a simple comparison of the profit rates of component suppliers and LCD panel firms, component suppliers do better. When we compare LCD panel firms with LCD TV assemblers, LCD panel and component firms show a higher profit rate (Sakakibara, 2006). Among suppliers, Japanese component suppliers (that have original technology know-how) are doing better than non-Japanese component suppliers. In general, the profit level

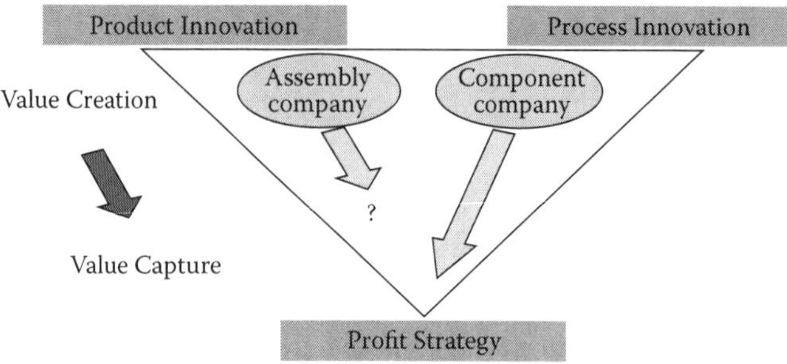

FIGURE 7.7
Dilemma of value creation. Adapted from Nobeoka et al. (2006).

of all firms is becoming smaller, and in fact, many firms reported losses in 2006–2007 (LG Economic Institute, Dec 13, 2006).

On the other hand, Vizio (Note: this firm appeared a few years ago like a comet and occupied the number one market position in the LCD market in 2007) does not have any FPD TV/panel manufacturing facilities. Vizio outsources almost all functions. It buys Korean-made panels, and assembly is conducted in Taiwan. It also sells its products mostly through discount chains to take advantage of a low distribution margin (Maeil Economy, Dec 25, 2007).

From the second quarter of 2008, LGE will supply a 32-inch PDP module (which is closer to integral than the LCD module) to Vizio (inews24, 2008.1.25). From August of 2007, LGE started selling 81-cm (32-inch) TV when many asserted that minimized TV is regarded as not so feasible. In a sense, Vizio utilized a better business model rather than better operations management. Even after achieving the best product innovation in the world, if it is not related to the firm's profit level, it is not so meaningful from the firm's strategic standpoint.

From the second half of 2007, LGE is strengthening vertical integration and innovation activities. The leader of the digital display business strives for innovative results through vertical integration among LGE (TV sets, PDP modules, core chips), LG Display (LCD module), LG Innotech (tuners), LG Micron (PDP back panels), LG Chemical (electronics components), and the domestic supply of component parts. Other value-adding efforts are the bold adoption of advanced business practices in the areas of purchasing and manufacturing technologies and the utilization of integrative module design with LG Display (inews24, 2007.9.2).

The first matter to be considered is profit strategy through product modularity. According to the comparative data of prices by inch for the

TABLE 7.5

Price Comparison of FPD TV Products (Unit: Inch)

Engine		**Image Engine(LSI)**		
	Panel	**Dependent**	**Independent**	**Total**
Panel	Purchase	(1) 4010.4 Yen (n = 64)	(3) 6780.2 Yen (n = 95)	5665.3 Yen (n = 159)
	Internal Production	(2) 4012.3 Yen (n = 32)	(4) 8356.9 Yen (n = 82)	7137.4 Yen (n = 114)
Total		4011.0 Yen (n = 96)	7510.7 Yen (n = 177)	6280.0 Yen (n = 273)

Source: Sakakibara (2006).

Japanese FPD TV product architecture, the prices drastically change depending on whether the image engine is independently developed or routine chips are used (Table 7.5). In the case of the highly priced type 4, the manufacturer develops the image engine and produces their panel by using its own internal capabilities. By the end of 2005, Matsushita PDP TV (bigger than 32 inch) and Sharp (maximum size of 65 inch) are included as well (Sakakibara, 2006). For the large-screen TV, the range of price reduction is relatively small; however, the development cost is also very high. However, with the purchase of panels, the final price of a TV set is somewhat lower than when they are produced internally. In a sense, this shows the commoditization of FPD TV, and yet, it also demonstrates the price competitiveness of the small and medium-size TVs (smaller than 30 inch).

In 2007, LGE made outsourcing contracts with Taiwanese firms at the volume level of 500,000 30- to 40-inch LCD TVs annually (Maeil Economics, 2007.12.25). LGE is also strengthening marketing campaigns in North America, Latin America, Europe, China, and Asia by regions with the budget of $1 billion. Internal product development is restricted to premium TVs larger than 40 inches, and all other smaller TV distribution (less than 30 inches) will be handled by outsourcing (ETNEWS, Jan 18, 2008). With the careful consideration of value added of each product, internal production and outsourcing decisions should be made beyond the implementation of effective operations management practices.

8

Korean Mobile Phone Industry: Product Architecture of Mobile Phones and Network Capability

Increasingly, the product architecture of electronic products is rapidly moving toward modularity. Little has been examined about the product architecture of mobile phones from the standpoint of product development. In this chapter we examine modular trends in the mobile communication industry and then study the network strategy (i.e., module design strategy of webstores that offer applications to the increasingly popular smartphone) of the mobile phone manufacturers. In addition to newly participating mobile phone makers (e.g., Apple, Google), traditional global mobile phone manufacturers (e.g., Samsung and LG) direct their strategic focus on emerging their user-initiated innovation capability by simultaneously pursuing mobile operation system (OS) platform (i.e., the emerging core competence in the mobile phone market with sales increase of smartphone, applications, contents development, and distribution) and application software (SW) market.

Furthermore, the real winner in the future mobile OS market should secure de facto standard for the future mobile phone OS market just as Microsoft has attained the dominant position as the OS firm in the traditional PC market. In the future mobile communication market vigorous discussions on 4G communication standards will lead toward intensive competition for mobile OS de facto standards. For this strategic competitive advantage it is critical for leading firms to build an open network environment that allows user-initiated innovation (e.g., application webstore).

8.1 INTRODUCTION

With the commercial use of CDMA (code division multiple access), the semiconductor, mobile communication, liquid-crystal display (LCD), and digital TV industries are regarded as the representative successful ones among Korean IT industries. Since 1996, the Korean mobile communication industry has shown rapid growth. As of 2010, two Korean giants, Samsung Electronics Inc., and LG Electronics Inc., occupied the number two and number three positions in the global mobile communication equipment market.

Park and Hong (2006) analyzed the success factors of Korean IT industries with the specific focus on the semiconductor and mobile communication industries. Its analysis focused mostly on the role of the Korean government in network building. In contrast, the emphasis of this chapter is on the product development strategies of individual firms. Shintaku (2006) concludes that electronic products (e.g., handset phones), with increasing modularization and fast change speed, experience severe price competition, and therefore, sustainable competitive advantage is hard to maintain. Such modularization is becoming more intensified as the product technology base is changing from analog to digital (Ito, 2005; Nobeoka, 2006; Shintaku, 2006). Yet, little is known on how these product technology base changes impact overall product development practices. This case study intends to address this important research question.

Korean firms, since January 1996, were successful in the commercialization of CDMA technology and established their strong competitive position in the global market against GSM (global system for mobile communications) mainstream technology (Park, 2008). In the age of analog mobile communication, these Korean firms had no wireless communication technologies. However, in the course of commercializing CDMA, they have acquired digital communication technologies (e.g., handset technology development) and have shown phenomenal growth as global firms in North American and European markets with their successful development of handsets using both CDMA and GSM applications. They have also developed 3G (CDMA2000, WCDMA) mobile communication technologies and WiBro (wireless broadband) which is regarded as a 4G mobile communication technology. Besides, with their successful global technology standard initiatives they now have a very strong prospect of leading the future global mobile communication market.

The issues of original technologies that utilize CDMA, GSM, and WCDMA (wideband code division multiple access) are important in these handset product developments. In 1996, Korean firms, for example, successfully developed handset products according to CDMA communication methods, yet they still have to pay a huge amount of royalty payments to Qualcomm which owns the critical original patents on air interface technologies. Likewise, Korean firms must purchase chipsets from their suppliers even when they develop their own GSM-oriented handsets in the global market. With this reason, the issue of original technologies (e.g., Chipset) is very important for their handset product development.

The recent focus of competition in the mobile phone market is in smartphones which allow diverse applications and services based on the mobile operation system (OS). In the global mobile handset sales of smartphones are growing rapidly by major developers of mobile OS (e.g., Nokia, Apple, RIM) and Web services and search engine providers (e.g., Google). In addition to newly participating mobile phone makers (e.g., Apple, Google), traditional global mobile phone manufacturers (e.g., Samsung and LG) direct their strategic focus on emerging their user-initiated innovation capability by simultaneously pursuing the mobile OS platform (i.e., the emerging core competence in the mobile phone market with sales increase of smartphone, applications, contents development, and distribution) and application software (SW) market. Furthermore, the real winner in the future mobile OS market should secure the de facto standard for the future mobile phone OS market just as Microsoft has attained the dominant position as the OS firm in the traditional PC market. In the future mobile communication market vigorous discussions on 4G communication standards will lead toward intensive competition for the mobile OS de facto standard. For this strategic competitive advantage it is critical for leading firms to build an open network environment that allows user-initiated innovation (e.g., application webstore). In this chapter we examine modular trends in the mobile communication industry and then study the network strategy (i.e., module design strategy of webstores that offer applications to the increasingly popular smartphone) of the mobile phone manufacturers.

8.2 PRODUCT ARCHITECTURE OF MOBILE PHONES

8.2.1 Product Architecture of Mobile Phones and Product Development

For the purpose of this study we define product architecture as "design philosophy in regard to the distribution of functions to diverse components of a product and interfaces." The most common method is modular/integral classification. Modular architecture is appropriate to a personal computer that shows 1:1 relationships between functionality and structure, and integral architecture is used when 1:1 relationships are not clearly established, as seen in automobiles (Ulrich, 1995; Fine, 1998; Baldwin and Clark, 2000; Fujimoto, 2003). Figure 8.1 shows the pictorial differences between modular and integral architecture.

Another parameter used is external environment, which is expressed as either open or closed. This product architecture impacts competitive capabilities of a firm through innovation in response to architecture changes and directly to product development practices (Henderson and Clark, 1990; Fujimoto, 2003; Park et al., 2007a, 2008b).

From the standpoint of product architecture, during the first generation (1G) analog period, a focal firm conducted all product development projects in a vertical integration structure. In the digital era, product development projects are organized into a horizontal specialization form instead. Prior to 1995, the set phone maker vertically integrated all of its research units in developing applications, operating systems, processors, and main devices. From the second generation (2G) after 1995, functional

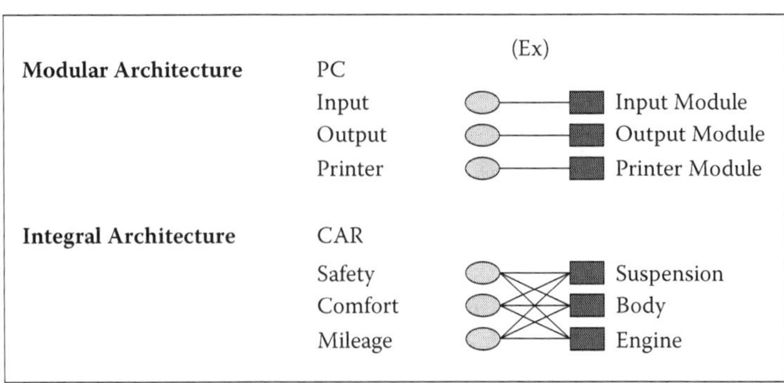

FIGURE 8.1
Modular and integral architecture. Source: Fujimoto (2003).

specialization started, and specialization is applied to all development efforts in the present third generation (Ito, 2005).

In the early stage of the handset market, the world's leading manufacturers (e.g., Nokia, Motorola, Ericsson) dominated the market with their superior technologies and brand power. Since 2000, the modularization in the handset market was intensified, and accordingly, original technology holders could no longer maintain their competitive market position (Kim, 2003; Park et al., 2008b). It is predicted that handset products will soon follow the path of commoditization as the products increasingly show less differentiation and fail to sustain integrative product family relationships. In the 2000s, many new manufacturers have been producing their products by buying main technologies in the form of licensing agreements, applications of modularization of hardware development, and software platform standardization (Kim, 2003; Park, 2008b; Nobeoka, 2006). A recent convergence trend of mobile equipment shows the one-chipization and modularization (KETI, 2007.8b). For example, the 7200 base band model (developed by Qualcomm in 2007) integrates diverse functions in one chip and then separates GPS, MP3, and QBGA across diverse chips. Samsung has successfully packaged MPU, NOR, NAND flash memory and leads the MCP (multi-chip package) market. As more functions are added to mobile communication equipment, the module trend will be all the more accelerated. Shintaku (2006) even asserts that it is becoming more difficult to sustain a market leader position in the environment of stiff price competition and fast changes.

Besides, handset markets are separated into two types—premium value and low cost. In the case of the premium market (e.g., slim phone), the consumer purchasing patterns are moving toward a focus on design features rather than on functionalities (KETI, 2007.8a). The noticeable trend is that diverse slim designs and the style of the products are becoming important in new products. Accordingly, with the support of a strong CEO, firms emphasize more on developing premium products with innovative designs (Park et al., 2008b).

With explosive growth in the mobile communication industry, the demand increase for handsets requires securing cost competitiveness through mass production and cost reduction. As numbers of producers increase with the easy entry into this market, price competition among the major manufacturers is quite intense. The time to market is also continually reduced, and customer loyalty is less common as more firms achieve technology evolution and service development (Kim, 2002). In this way, the

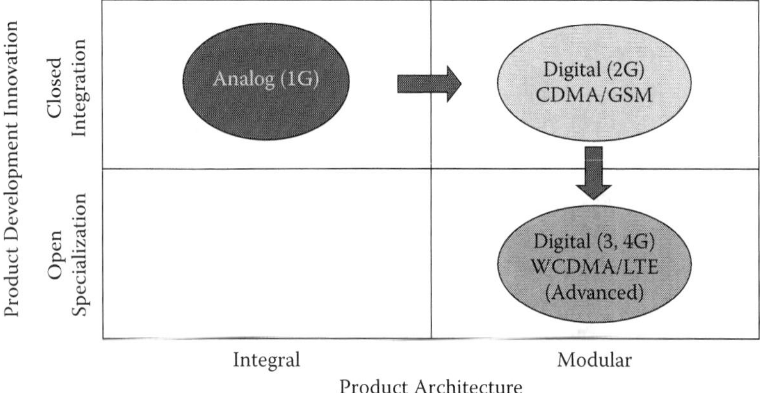

FIGURE 8.2
Product architecture and product development of mobile phones. Adapted from Park et al. (2008b).

handset market requires a new business model in light of a short product life cycle, slow growth of the premium market, and accelerating modularization (e.g., one-chipization) (Park et al., 2008b). Park et al. (2008b) show that high-premium electronic products with a short time to market adopt integral product architecture. Recently, the mobile communication industry also experienced greater openness with the modularization and communication methods standardization (Park et al., 2008b). Figure 8.2 shows the product architecture and product development of mobile phones.

Product architecture that is close to modular has a short product life cycle, and therefore fast time to market is an important competitive factor. Products that experience rapid modularization naturally require a faster product development cycle for a desirable firm profit level (Park et al., 2008b). Samsung as a global firm is quite aggressive in its marketing of diverse product lines, including semiconductors, mobile phones, LCDs, and digital household electronics. Among them, the relative importance of mobile phones on total corporate sales is quite substantial (Park, 2008b). As of the end of 2007, its mobile phone business line was number two globally in terms of sales. The case analysis concerning changing product development practices of Korean firms in response to increasing modularization is worthy of examination and has both theoretical and managerial implications.

Samsung and LG in particular introduced CDMA handset products in 1996 when CDMA methods were being commercialized. But at the present, the CDMA market is less than 20% of the global market in which GSM is still the mainstream method. With this market reality in mind, Samsung and LG simultaneously developed GSM mobile phones. Korean firms' market success of mobile phones reflects their experiences with semiconductors in the global market. Its strategic focus is on the rapid market introduction of innovative products with outstanding design features.

In keeping with digital technology, product modularization of mobile phones occurs at an amazingly fast speed. Each successive generation of products (2G vs. 3G) shows a greater extent of modular components and a continuous reduction of the product development cycle.

8.2.2 Smartphone and Innovation

A smartphone is a mobile phone that offers unique capabilities quite different from a traditional mobile phone. A smartphone usually allows the user to install and run more advanced applications, Internet functions, and run standardized dedicated operating system software providing a platform for application developers. The smartphone has a huge potential to provide innovative values to Web/information service providers and mobile phone manufacturers. Behind the phenomenal sales growth of smartphones, there has been sustained progress in mobile phone–related technology, network technology evolution, and increasing user demands. We now examine the reasons for rapid market growth of smartphones and innovation potential in the future.

First, in technological aspects the smartphone vastly improved the simple basic voice mobile phone with (1) wireless Internet service features using SMS (short messaging service) and WAP (wireless application protocol) and (2) other independent functions including color LCD, camera, MPs, GPS, and TV. In a sense, the smartphone has changed the previous vertical integration business model into a horizontal specialization business model. With the worldwide distribution of mobile phones the short product life cycle of mobile phones has pushed toward rapid market maturity, which in turn created increasing demand for innovative new product development.

Second, in the network aspect the development of mobile communication technology has enabled the smartphone to provide diverse service offerings based on data and vast improvement in communication speed.

Third, from a user perspective, compared to the traditional mobile phone, the smartphone is much faster in processing data, has stronger multimedia functions, and supports convenient applications with innovative UI and

GPOS (general purpose OS), more sophisticated wireless network usages (e.g., Wi-Fi, WiMAX, Bluetooth). This is possible through integration of huge data communication functions by the utilization of 3.9G (LTE and WiMAX) and emerging 4G (LTE Advanced, WiMAX Advanced) network environment from 2010.

However, the innovation background of such smartphone includes other important factors (i.e., open innovation potential) that goes much beyond the internal innovation within a specific organization. As discussed in the previous chapters, initial design of products/services may start with integral type, and with the passing of time it evolves into modular type. However, rapid modularization requires (1) system architecture that understands the total structure of the product and service features through precise and complete detail designs and (2) division of one complex process into numerous modular components by many module providers (Baldwin and Clark, 2000). Thus, establishing mobile communication standards and specifications and having product and service platforms allow numerous mobile communication industry players to both compete and collaborate for the growth of the mobile communication industry.

Figure 8.3 shows the transition of product development in the mobile phone industry—from vertical integration innovation in the analog era to open modular innovation in the digital era. In this evolution process, new innovation leaders in the mobile phone industry also have emerged. In the next section we will examine modular trends in the mobile

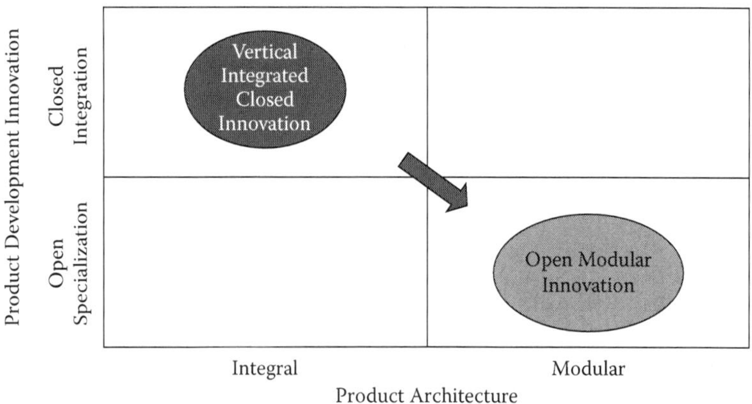

FIGURE 8.3
Vertical integration innovation and open modular innovation.

communication industry from a product architecture perspective and analyze the modular design strategy of mobile phone manufacturers and applications providers. Our particular research attention focuses on the cases of Korean firms that, as late followers, have achieved competitive positions among the global top five leaders.

8.3 NEW PRODUCT DEVELOPMENT OF KOREAN HANDSET FIRMS

8.3.1 Global Competitiveness of Korean Mobile Phone Makers

As of the end of 2007, the scope of the Korean mobile communication industry included mobile communication services (e.g., CDMA2000, 1X EVDO, and WCDMA), wireless mobile communication (e.g., TRS wireless data communication), and diverse patterns of communication network services. Other related industries operate in the forms of handset, platform, solution, and contents areas (WISEINFO, 2007.10). Samsung and LG, two of the top five global firms, are the leaders of the handset industry in Korea (Park et al., 2008b). Figure 8.4 shows the performance trends of the top five global firms.

The mobile communication industry, using 3G mobile communication of synchronization and asynchronous types, has expanded its broadband

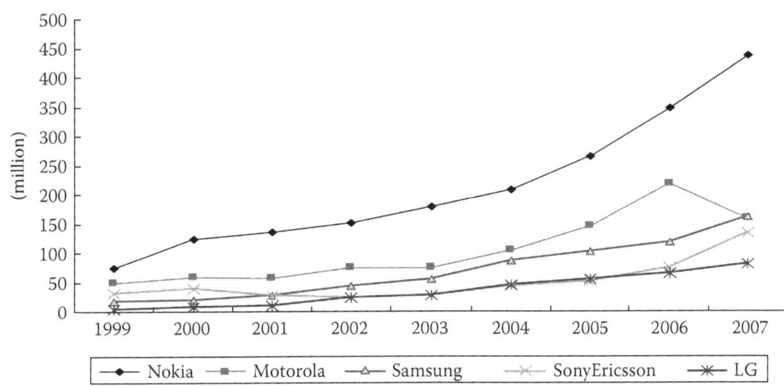

FIGURE 8.4
Global top five—production volumes of handset makers (in millions). From Park et al., 2008b.

services like a mobile Internet wireless broadband (WiBro) (International Standard: Mobile WiMAX) in Korea and North America. By 2012, fourth generation (4G) mobile communication will be available (Park et al., 2008b). According to the Ministry of Information Communication, as of 2008, Korean firms are expected to earn more than $31 billion a year for the next five years with the exports of new products and related communication equipment, and the royalty fees alone are expected to be more than $68 million. As of now, Korea has been an exporting nation of mobile phones with the commercialization of second generation (2G) CDMA. They paid $3.4 billion to Qualcomm in royalty fees and for the purchase of chipsets for every mobile phone. However, in the case of WiBro and mobile WiMAX (integrated with Intel's WiMAX), Samsung and Intel own 22% and 15% of these document patent rights, respectively, and therefore they expect to receive relatively large sums of royalty revenues (Park et al., 2008b). As a specific step toward such strategic changes, as of March 2008, Samsung has been designated as the sole supplier of WiBro equipment to U.S. Sprint Nextel and Japanese UQ Communication (Park et al., 2008b).

8.3.2 Product Development Strategy of Korean Handset Makers

Korean handset makers have made continuous growth in terms of quality and quantity in step with the mobile communication industry—particularly three mobile communication firms that started offering personal communication services (PCS) in 1997. At present, more than 100 firms support the mobile communication industry. Samsung's market share in the domestic market is about 50%. LG Electronics and Pentech & Affiliates struggled after the number two position. In December of 2005, Pentech & Affiliates merged with SKY Teletech and showed improvement in their market share. In 2007, Pentech & Affiliates showed less than 10% of market share due to recent labor disputes (e.g., walk-out in 2007) (Woo and Yoo, 2004). Manufacturers of Korean handsets experienced rapid restructuring and walk-out strikes, and many were discontinued. As of the end of 2007, most of these firms were either merged or out of business (Park et al., 2008b). Figure 8.5 is the comparative statistics of Korean handset manufacturers. Samsung's market position, as of 2007, was number one in the Korean market and number two in the global market in terms of sales.

This chapter focuses on Samsung's product development. Samsung's product development of mobile phones started with its benchmark analysis

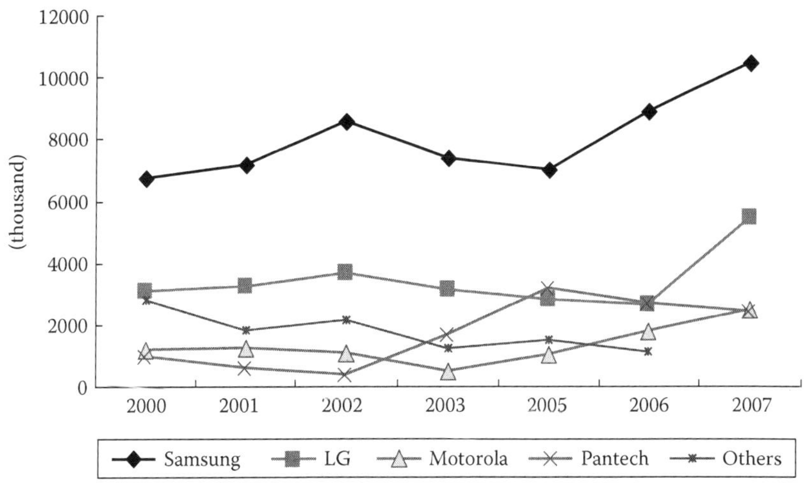

FIGURE 8.5
Market share of Korean handsets by sales. From Park et al., 2008b.

of the car-phone of the Japanese firm Toshiba and the introduction of the SC-100 in the market by 1984. In the year of the Seoul Olympics (1988), Samsung marketed the first analog mobile phone (SH-100) for VIPs, and quality issues were embarrassingly not yet resolved. In spite of continuous trial and error in its product development efforts, Samsung continued reverse engineering of Motorola products and succeeded in acquiring its own analog product development capabilities. In October of 1994, Samsung introduced the SH-770 with the brand name "Anycall." By the end of 1995, Samsung successfully caught up with Motorola that had captured over 40% of the Korean market (Song, 2005). By January of 1996, with the commercialization of digital CDMA methods, Samsung was positioned as the number one seller in the Korean market based on its analog handset technologies (Park et al., 2008). In the late 1990s, Samsung engaged in the global market with its mobile phones. By 2000, it showed noticeable progress in the global handset market. The profit rate in 2001, for example, was 15%, its market share was 7% (in the European market it was 4.7%), and its market position was number four (Kim, 2002). Samsung also strengthened its marketing efforts in the North American CDMA market and showed a high level of growth in GSM areas as well. With its emphasis on the high premium market, Samsung secured competitive profit rates in the global market without having large economies of scale production facilities like Nokia. Figure 8.5 shows the performance comparisons of global players in the handset market.

By July of 2002 (the fourteenth year of business since its first-year marketing effort in 1988), Samsung's total production volume reached 100 million. As a rare exception, Samsung effectively implemented its product strategy including continuous introduction of high premium products. Since 2002, it has attained a number three position in the global market. In 2006, with a sales volume of 118 million, it still occupied number three, and yet with the increase in marketing costs, deterioration of its profit level, and failure to introduce any market-leading products (e.g., blue black phones), the performance gap between Motorola (number two) and Samsung (number three) was temporarily widened (KETI, 2007a). Under the new leadership of CEO Jisung Choi, Samsung successfully targeted the low-cost mobile phone market. By the end of 2007, it surpassed Motorola and became the number two global marketer (Park et al., 2008). Samsung is number one in CDMA methods (exceeding Nokia; see Figure 8.6). Beyond its low-cost products, Samsung's marketing strategy is on producing and delivering premium handsets in the global market. Based on its successful marketing experiences with household electronic products, Samsung applies its integration capabilities of diverse product components (e.g., display, camera, and memory functions) (Sohn, 2006.4).

Besides CDMA and GSM, Samsung secured its growth in high premium products by TDMA methods of combining color and digital camera features (Sohn, 2006.4). For example, Samsung's premium mobile phones carry complex product features including high-density clarity thin-film transistor–liquid-crystal display (TFT-LCD) screens, embedded cameras, voice/video communication, and high-speed date connection. Samsung is successful in introducing handsets in the market by all different methods (GSM, CDMA, and TDMA) with 3G service offerings before any of its competitors. At the end of 2002, in addition to EVDO supportive 1X handsets (with CDMA

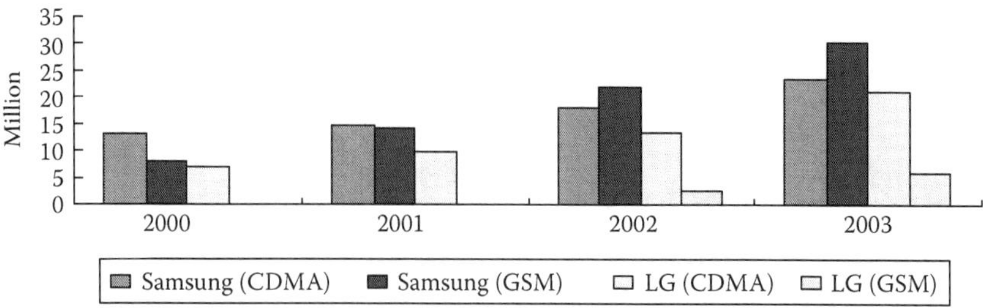

FIGURE 8.6
Production volumes of Samsung and LG handsets (CDMA and GSM communication type). From Samsung and LG investment documents.

2000 methods), Samsung offered comparable handsets for GSM and GPRS. From 2005, Samsung developed and commercialized the DMB phone, the HSDPA phone, and the WiBro phone. From 2006, Samsung's strategic goals included products with global super variety features. In 2007, Samsung started with "Ultra Edition 2" as a strategic showcase and continued its marketing campaigns with the other Ultra series such as "Ultra Edition 5.9" (i.e., the thinnest ultraslim bar, 5.9 mm with GSM methods), "Ultra Edition 9.6," and "Ultra Edition 10.9" (KETI, 2007a).

8.4 PRODUCT DEVELOPMENT STRATEGY OF KOREAN FIRMS AND SMARTPHONE RESPONSIVE STRATEGY

8.4.1 Comparison of Samsung and LG Product Development

Samsung has consistently pursued premium strategy with superb quality and outstanding design. As the mobile phone market becomes mature, such strategic focus is quite important. In 2007 Samsung temporarily adopted low-price strategy to increase the sales volume. In 2008 it again targeted the high-end market (ETNEWS, 2008). However, as Samsung successfully penetrates into BRICs (Brazil, Russia, India, and China) markets, the average sales price (ASP) has been falling since 2008. Over the years LG has somewhat adopted Samsung's strategic patterns. Gradually, it went beyond the middle- or low-end market in the early 2000s, and after 2006 it appealed to premium design with products like the Chocolate phone. Competitiveness of these two Korean firms is based on the early development of technological capability through the Korean government's CDMA commercialization, the utilization of Korean market as a test base of their products, and consistent adoption of design strategy.

Products with modular product architecture have a short product life cycle (PLC), and thus rapid product development is critical for competitive advantage (Figure 8.7). Samsung and LG have sustained rapid product development and thus have maintained a desirable level of profits. Samsung's strategy in particular reflects the lessons of its success in the semiconductor market (Shin and Jang, 2006). The differentiation strategy of Korean firms includes rapid new product introductions and superb design. On the other hand, Japanese firms have outstanding technological capability and a bigger domestic market than Korean firms. Their

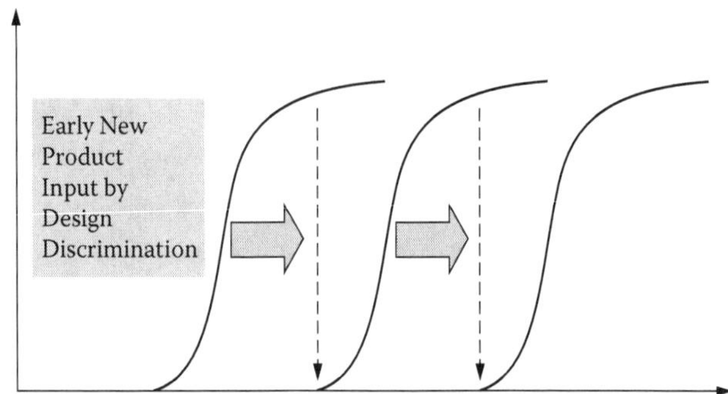

FIGURE 8.7
Fast product development responding to short PLC.

product development is not fast enough to meet the changing demands of the global market, and thus their competitive position has been weakened over the years.

Samsung and LG, both from Korea, have pursued somewhat different pricing strategies. Their average sales price (ASP) of mobile phones suggests dissimilar strategic patterns. By 2004 Samsung has focused on building its premium brand image in the North American and European markets. Samsung's tested technological capability has satisfied the sophisticated tastes of Korean customers. Yet, its strategy was not adequate to become one of the top global leaders. Samsung could not overcome the high competitive wall of Nokia and Motorola for years (Park et al., 2008b). In 2006 Samsung experienced tough competitive challenges in the high-end market, and in 2007 it temporarily targeted the low-end market by offering a $50 range of mobile phones in the emerging BRICs markets (e.g., Brazil, Russia, India, and China).

From 2007 Samsung has poured low-priced mobile phones in the emerging markets and yet set higher average sales prices (ASP) compared to Nokia and Motorola. By 2008 Samsung has already secured 40% of the low-end market and thus focused on the premium market (Park et al., 2008b). For competitive market share Samsung temporarily offered low-priced phones in the low-end market, and yet its core market strategy remains consistently targeting the high-end (premium) market.

On the other hand, LG raised average sale prices (ASP) as it switched from low-middle-end market focus to premium design models by upgrading its brand image after the middle 2000s. With its relatively low brand image compared to Samsung's, LG entered the European market with the

Chocolate phone, not as LG Electronics brand image. In the middle of the 2000s, LG's competitiveness suffered after giving up its number four global market position to Sony Ericsson. However, after 2006, LG experienced market share recovery through its hit model strategy with design excellence. For example, the Chocolate phone made a big hit in the global market with sales of 15 million units, the subsequent model, Sign phone (with 5.7 million units), Prada phone (700,000 units), and recent premium-level phone (Beauty phone in European market records more than 10,000 units per day) (Park et al., 2008b). The hit model strategy accomplished both brand awareness upgrade and profitability enhancement in such ways that by 2007 LG's profit level increased to more than 12 times of that of 2006. Based on such successful records, LG also targets the high-end phone market. Interestingly, Samsung's strategy is moving slowly from the high-end market (while keeping its market share) to the low-end market (increase market penetration in emerging markets), while LG is moving up from the low-end to the high-end market.

8.4.2 Smartphone and Business Model of the Mobile Communication Industry

The global mobile communication market (its current size is more than 120 million units per year) has temporarily slowed down in 2009 (Figure 8.8). The market leader of this huge market is traditional mobile phone manufacturers (e.g., Nokia, Samsung, and LG). It is Apple's smartphone that made a huge impact in this market. In 2009 the total market growth of the global mobile phone was –7.9% (negative growth), and yet smartphone's explosive growth captured 15% of the total global mobile phone market (Figure 8.9). New smartphone makers (i.e., Apple, RIM, HTC) have relatively small market share, and yet its high profitability lets them maintain premium price strategy.

As mentioned above, after 3G, the mobile phone OS is becoming increasingly critical in the competitive landscape. Figure 8.10 shows mobile phone OS structures by firm. It suggests four types: T-Mobile OS by traditional mobile phone manufacturers (Type A—Nokia; Type B—Samsung and LG) and new mobile OS by new business leaders (Type C—Apple; Type D—Google).

Nokia's OS is Symbian, which has a reasonable presence in the smartphone market. Samsung and LG (second and third in the market) have not developed their own mobile OS and instead use the Windows Mobile OS that Microsoft developed, and recently they offered products that are

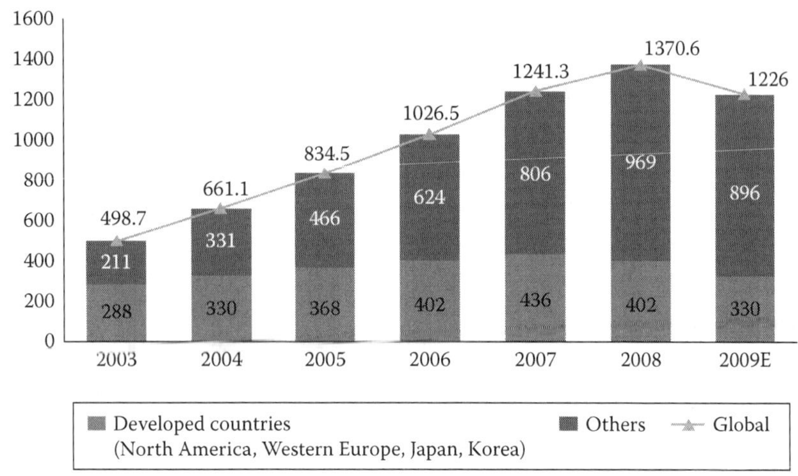

FIGURE 8.8
Global mobile phone market.

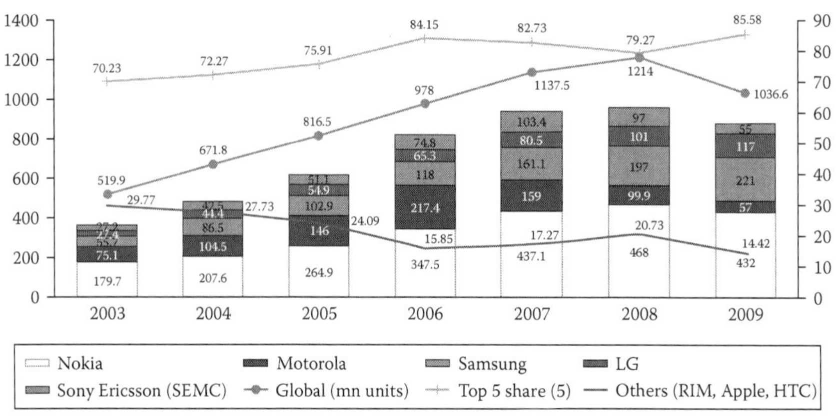

FIGURE 8.9
Market share of global firms in the smartphone market. From Yasumoto (2010).

equipped with Google's Android for free access. In 2009, Samsung offered its own OS called Bada, which is slowly gaining market attention. Samsung extended the Bada smartphone lineup with the launch of the high-end Samsung Wave II in January 2011.

In a challenge to the traditional global players in the mobile phone industry, these new service providers (e.g., Apple, Google, and RIM) slowly built their own market position in the global mobile phone market. As Apple continues to introduce the iPhone series in the market, it developed its unique iPhone-related mobile OS based on diverse applications services.

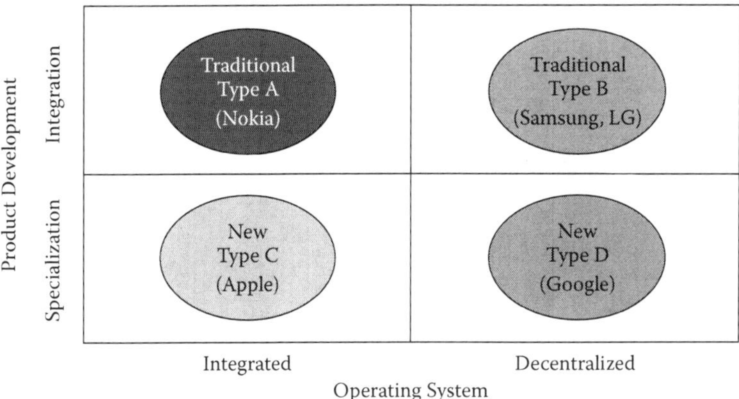

FIGURE 8.10
Mobile OS types by firm.

To support their service features Apple also offers App Store Services (i.e., application on-line Market Plus). Google produced Android with its strategic alliance with HTC, a Taiwanese mobile phone maker. The differentiation point of the Google phone is to build an Android market for which any users may freely register or download beyond its traditional service features (e.g., Gmail, Google Map, Google Calendar) to compete with Apple. Figure 8.11 shows mobile phone OS popularity by firm.

A strategic difference between Apple and Google is in OS openness. Apple users need their own OS-based diverse applications for iPhone. Thus, the App Store is closed to Apple's monopolistic OS. The distribution of profits from Market Plus registered contents is 70% for users (developers) and 30% for Apple. In contrast, Google's business model is open because of Google's business model that builds on the strengths of the huge advertising revenues. Since Google's OS is open, thus many existing mobile phone makers adopt the Google OS instead.

Google's Market Plus profit model is market friendly in that it allows 70% for users (developers) and 30% for communication service providers. However, smartphone requires sufficient service features for customers, just as rich application programs are so essential for the computer market. Figure 8.12 shows the importance of the user-initiated innovation environment. The competitive battle of future mobile phone market is not in the areas of hardware but in software contents. Therefore, the real winners are those that build a user-initiated open innovation environment and possess network capability. The future competition is about

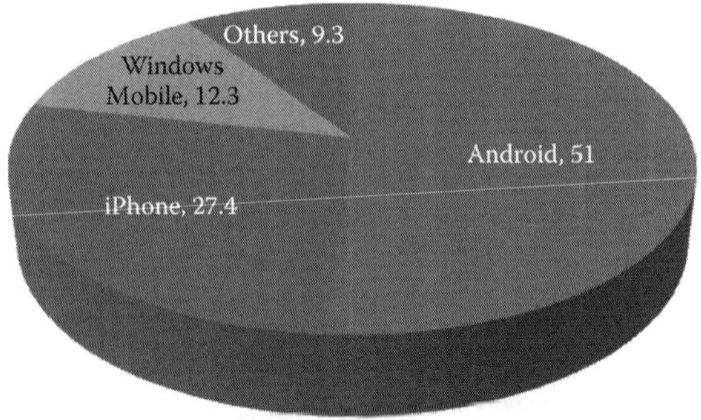

FIGURE 8.11
Mobile phone OS by firm. From Marketing Inside.

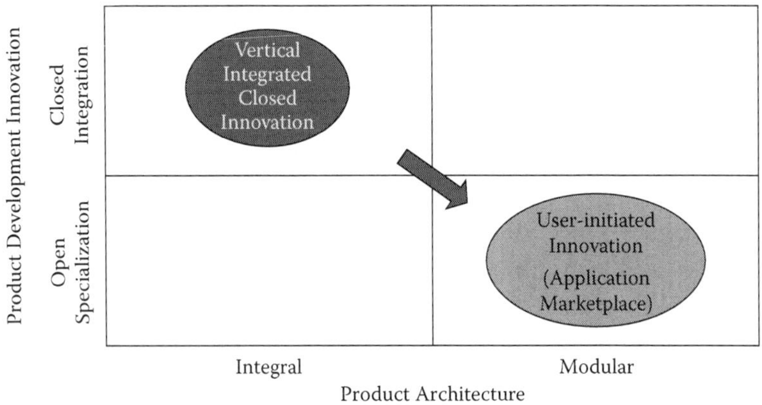

FIGURE 8.12
Strategy to build user-initiated open modular innovation environment.

standardization strategy. In fact, in DVD disc standard competition, the Blu-ray Disc (BD) standard defeated Toshiba-initiated HD DVD not only because of disc record volume but also because of contents supply aspects. For example, Toshiba introduced the HD DVD player in March 2006, ahead of Blu-ray in the U.S. market. The low-end model "HD-A1" was priced at $499. Toshiba captured the low-end market with a tremendous sales surge as it offered a $99 model which was less than half of what Blu-ray was offering. However, Blu-ray did not focus on hardware-based price competition. Instead, Blu-ray improved video quality and multimedia functions and offered new models of products that stimulated analog VHS manias. With its low-price strategy Toshiba sold more DVD players. By 2007 the annual sales ratio of software between Toshiba's HD DVD and Blu-ray's BD remained 1:2. Hardware low-cost strategy did not contribute to the HD DVD software sales. DVD player customers preferred a high-functionality DVD player. The users that purchased $99 low-end DVD player were not willing to purchase $35 worth of HD DVD software. Likewise, in the future mobile phone strategy, the differentiation strategy should not be restricted to hardware alone. Rather, the real value is in software that provides the appropriate values of hardware.

The key for competitive advantage in the future market is diverse user-based innovation in the open environment. For this reason traditional mobile phone manufacturers (e.g., Nokia, Samsung, and LG) focus on the applications market in response to the new players that penetrate the global market with their own OS and applications contents. Recently, Nokia offered a "Come with music" site and integrative OVI store services for the Touch phone (5800 Express music) customers to compete against Apple's iTunes and Apple Store.

As Apple's App Store received phenomenal success in the global market, Korean mobile communication firms and mobile communication manufacturers (e.g., KT, Samsung, and SK Telecom) opened their respective markets. Applications that are being offered in Korea's application stores are follower models, and they are not yet widely accepted (Park et al., 2011). For example, as of February 2010, KT's Show offered 21 applications, and no content is ever free. Samsung's application store had no more than 640 registered applications. SK Telecom's T-Store did much better with registered applications contents of 32,000. It is a positive step that communication providers (e.g., KT) and mobile phone manufacturers (Samsung, LG) are building open market plus for smartphone-based applications development and distribution.

There are several reasons why the Korean domestic application store market is developing not so well: (1) the Korean smartphone market started late with iPhone shock in 2007; (2) closed distribution environment; (3) as developers separately develop applications, one source–multi-user is not quite feasible yet. For this reason, the number of useful contents is small, and no free contents are being offered. For Apple's App store, the ratio of free contents is about 30%, and the users who are happy with free versions tend to purchase regular paid versions. Thus, experience marketing requires offering free versions first.

The hardware preference mindset of Korean mobile phone manufacturers keeps them from building an open contents environment. In February 2010 Samsung introduced Bada Phone Wave based on Bada (internally developed OS) at Mobile World Congress (MWC). However, display innovation called super AMOLED was noticeable, but there was no real competitive advantage in either OS or contents. In 2010 Samsung launched the Galaxy smartphone into the global market and made a serious effort to build an application store. Samsung therefore focuses on building a mobile phone platform that allows users to get access to popular applications rather than following Apple's App Store distribution model (Park et al., 2011a).

Mr. Kang, Samsung's senior executive, said,

> Apple's iPhone covers the world as a single smartphone. Some aspects of the smartphone may need to consider domestic preferences. Developers seek a store that can be sold in the global market. Too much focus on Korean customer tastes may not be good for positioning any product for the global market. The time (when the sales of mobile phones are based on functionality and design) is now over. Building platform like BADA and Samsung Apps is to encourage participation of the global applications developers and allow more users to use them.

LG was somewhat slow in responding to the market surge of smartphones, and thus 2010 was a tough year for its business. The communication ecosystem that is dominated by global firms weakens mobile contents competitiveness. As mobile manufacturers and mobile service providers compete in the market, mid-sized software or small- and medium-sized mobile service providers have no real room for survival. LG could not successfully position itself in the already crowded smartphone market in 2009. Mr. Ahn, President of LG Electronics, said, "Customer values are moving away from hardware based to software solutions. Future success depends on how to make effective mobile ecosystem which integrates mobile phones, platform, contents and services" (Park et al., 2011a). It is now almost impossible for any large global firms to dominate in the entire ecosystem. The key for competitiveness is in network collaboration ability. In light of its failure to respond to the smartphone market, LG has taken massive reorganization and replaced its CEO and most of its wireless communication leaders in 2010 and established a new smartphone department. In this way, Korean firms are slowly evolving from closed mobile applications development and distribution environment toward a marketplace that is characterized by more open environment.

At the center of such drastic change there are network portal providers (makers of mobile OS for SW platform) and major mobile phone manufacturers. Major mobile phone manufacturers and portal providers utilize their mobile OS technological capability (i.e., SW platform) and market influence for the goal of building more open innovation environment by inviting SW developers and integrating development and distribution network. Increasingly, sustainable mobile phone business success requires building a hardware applications environment rather than focusing on hardware functionality and design-based management.

8.5 DISCUSSION

The Korean IT industry (with Samsung and LG as its leaders) has acquired global competitiveness. In the memory semiconductor and mobile phone handset market, Samsung's performance received more research attention. The emerging challenges for Samsung and LG are how to develop and apply 4G technologies with innovative new product development practices. In this sense, Samsung's global leadership is to be tested all the more seriously (Park et al., 2008b). Our case study suggests that the continuous global competitiveness of Samsung and LG requires ownership of original technologies. Particularly, user-based open modular innovation environment (not vertical closed innovation) is important for smartphones, which integrate both hardware and software just like the PC market.

Korean firms (Samsung and LG) have been successfully benchmarking market leaders. Their organizational culture is not conducive to developing creative products with high levels of risk. Samsung has mobilized the entire organization for the set annual targets. In such environments, what matters is not creativity but conformance to the target date of market introduction. In this sense, Samsung has been successful in hardware aspects including design strategy for market needs, rapid product development through CE (concurrent engineering), and a low-cost strategy through SCM. One Samsung researcher said, "In the course of product development we come up with some outstanding ideas. However, the typical management responses to such innovative ideas are, 'Don't try to catch the clouds in the sky. Rather, focus on rapid product introduction ideas' (Park et al., 2011a). However, Samsung is benchmarking U.S. global IT firms (i.e., Google and Apple) to overcome such rigid organizational culture. With the restoration of Mr. Lee as Owner-CEO, Samsung makes massive investments on software, biotech, and nanotech beyond its hardware-focused market strategy.

In the smartphone market, new mobile phone players (e.g., Apple, Google) and traditional global mobile phone manufacturers (Nokia, Samsung, and LG) will compete on multiple fronts: (1) sales of mobile phones, (2) mobile OS platform building, and (3) applications software market. The competitive edge may depend on the successful development and utilization of user-initiated innovation environments. Whoever secures the de facto standard in the OS market, just as Microsoft did for the PC market, will be the final winner of twenty-first century business. In the future communication market, vigorous debate would be on 4G communication standard specifications, and intense competition is to secure an OS de facto standard. For this it is quite critical to build an open innovation environment like the application webstore which is based on user-initiated innovation.

Section III

Infrastructure of IT Capability

9

Suppliers Support for Supply Chain Integration: The Korean Automobile Industry and the Steel Industry

Business organizations of the twenty-first century operate in the context of dynamic network relationships along with information flows, customers, suppliers, and competitors. It is essential to implement supply chain management through which firms enhance internal and external collaboration, fulfill multiple and rapidly changing customer requirements, and sustain their competitive advantages. With increasing levels of globalization, firms are expected to construct e-logistics infrastructures and service offerings that overcome time and space constraints. Korean auto manufacturers and the steel industry are one of the big four leading exporters (i.e., semiconductors, electronics, automobiles, and shipbuilding) in Korea. In particular, Korean auto manufacturers will continue to expand their global market in view of their limited domestic market. The Korean steel industry plays an important role in the growth of the Korean economy. And POSCO, a representative firm of the Korean steel industry, pursued globalization by building production plants and also by making direct investment in the countries of Asia and America.

Accordingly, effective uses of global supply chain management become more important than ever. In spite of the noticeable presence of many global multinational companies in Korea, small and medium-sized (SME) suppliers that support them are usually small and vulnerable to changes. The Korean government has tended to focus excessively on large enterprises to attain their rapid industrialization and fast economic growth. Recently, the policy shows a shift toward more emphasis on the equitable growth in the supply chain. As a result of such changing policy priorities, large Korean enterprises sustain their growth through healthy support of their supplier base. As an illustration of this changing policy focus, this study shows how the Hyundai-Kia Automotive Group (HKAG) and POSCO strengthen their supplier base through developing product development capabilities and overall competency of their supply chain. Details of business practices and their implications are discussed.

9.1 INTRODUCTION

Increasingly, the embedded knowledge, combined skill capabilities of the work force, and innovative capabilities are critical in fulfilling customer needs. Accordingly, developing these organizational capabilities is an important strategic priority of firms. The creation and diffusion of an innovative knowledge base is possible through cooperation between large manufacturers and component parts suppliers by means of effective information sharing and active communication practices. Final products manufactured by large original equipment manufacturers (OEMs) require an accurate understanding of customer requirements, which are translated through the cross-functional processes of product planning, product design, logistics, production, delivery to ultimate customers, and reliable after services. These processes show that larger manufacturers (OEM) and SME (suppliers) should manage information flows concurrently to effectively design, produce, and deliver their products (Schilli and Dai, 2006). In other words, a supplier's PLM (product life cycle management) needs to keep up with the OEM's PLM practices (Che, 2009).

Creating new knowledge through effective communication among cross-functions (e.g., manufacturing, marketing, management, research and development) within the OEM and across supply chains is essential to sustain the required level of competitiveness. In particular, it is important to enhance opportunities of knowledge creation, storage, and diffusion across supply chain participants. In this sense, collaborative work patterns between OEMs and their suppliers are critical for sustainable supply chain performance. From this perspective, this chapter focuses on how effectively the Korean OEM and its suppliers (mostly SMEs) manage this vital information network flow.

One noticeable aspect of Korean manufacturing is the need for expanding supplier capabilities. Among South Korea's component suppliers, six out of ten business enterprises (59.2%) make and deliver products receiving orders from other companies, and 62.9% trade with mostly SMEs. SMEs which do business with both OEM and other SMEs are 23.9%. SMEs which deal only with large corporations are a smaller percentage—13.2%. As such, among South Korea's SMEs, 13.2% are in the first tier of suppliers, and the rest (86.8%) belong to the second and third tiers of suppliers. A strong supply chain base, therefore, requires close cooperation between OEM and SMEs in Korea. In this aspect, the Korean government's role is critical in promoting effective collaboration patterns between OEMs and SMEs. If SMEs generate very small profit margins, they cannot afford to invest in research and development, and accordingly, their innovative capabilities remain weak. Therefore, OEMs increase the extent of global outsourcing. This weak capability of Korean SMEs is the primary reason why Korea's huge export performance does not necessarily translate into the growth of its national wealth; instead, much of the export values are transferred to the innovative Japanese suppliers who provide premium-value high-tech component parts to Korean SMEs (Government Authorization Briefing Special Project Team, 2008).

In this context, this chapter examines how the Korean government promotes a closer level of collaboration between Korean OEMs and SMEs to increase innovative capabilities and their global competitiveness. This study presents a model that considers the role of the government that influences the cooperative relationship building between OEM and SMEs. Then, we analyze the specific cases of collaborative experiences between OEM and its suppliers. In response to the government policy that promotes collaboration between OEM and SMEs, the Hyundai-Kia Automotive Group (HKAG), which is South Korea's major global automotive manufacturer, supports various programs such as cooperative suppliers' management development, development of core competencies, and global management training programs (Park et al., 2011b). POSCO also supports various programs for collaboration with suppliers. Among these program initiatives, this study focuses on IT support practices for the information integration between OEM and suppliers.

9.2 LITERATURE REVIEW

9.2.1 Collaboration and Information Integration between OEM and Its Suppliers

The competitive climate of the twenty-first century is quite intensive. In this environment, no OEM may survive with its own capabilities alone. Collaboration between an OEM and its suppliers is essential for their survival. Japanese automotive OEMs have been successful in the global competitive war through their effective collaborative system with their suppliers (Asanuma, 1998). Increasingly, collaboration between OEM and suppliers is becoming more important in the midst of stiff global competition. Suo et al. (2004) state that, if market demand remains fixed, OEM and suppliers would engage in a zero-sum game. In the rapidly changing technology environment, it is critical to build cooperative relationships rather than engage in a zero-sum game. A win–win relationship requires close collaboration between OEM and suppliers (Che, 2009). In this sense, the close collaboration between OEM and suppliers is an essential element of effective supply chain management. At the same time, a small failure in the supply chain may also have a huge impact in the supply chain. For example, in 1997 the Toyota production line stopped for two whole weeks because a supplier of key component parts had a fire in their plant. In 1999, an earthquake temporarily stopped the production of Taiwanese suppliers, and their OEM experienced substantial business losses (Reitman, 1997; Sheffi, 2005). In 2008, the Sichuan earthquake of China destroyed the supplier base in that region, which affected the manufacturing production and economic growth as well. The spread of the global financial crisis that started with the failures in the U.S. mortgage market has affected the financial condition and business environment around the world. In view of the above mentioned tight interdependent relationships in the global supply chain, the quality of collaboration between OEM and suppliers is becoming an important strategic imperative of outstanding firms. Huge natural disasters and drastic changes in the global business environment might be beyond what one firm can handle. Yet, even in such extraordinary circumstances, it is enormously helpful to deal with the common challenges through real-time information sharing between OEM and suppliers.

In 2000, a sudden fire accident in a Philips microchip plant could have damaged Nokia and Ericsson, but Nokia could contain the damage through its quick responses to inventory shortages (Latour, 2001; Yu et al., 2009). Such real-time information sharing between OEM and SME is also beneficial to other strategic elements. Building such a collaborative information sharing system in ordinary time is quite important. Because a large majority of product development adopts rapid digital design, effective information sharing (with reliability and speed) is increasingly critical. Therefore, business-to-business information sharing is extremely important for supply chain management (Tomino et al., 2009). Through survey analysis based on data collected from over 200 firms, the importance of information sharing was also found. Monczka et al. (1998) showed that the following attributes including information sharing of supplier alliances were significantly related to the partnership between OEM and suppliers: trust and coordination, interdependence, information quality and participation, joint problem solving, avoiding the use of severe conflict resolution tactics, and the existence of a formal supplier/commodity alliance selection process. In addition, direct involvement activities of OEMs play a critical role in improving supplier performance (Krause et al., 2000).

Schilli and Dai (2006) extend the cooperation patterns between OEM and suppliers to the entire product life cycle. They list linking an OEM's product life cycle with that of suppliers as an important building block of the cooperative relationship. From the product life cycle perspective, the use of computer-aided design (CAD) data in product development is essential for the integration between the upstream and downstream IT system—particularly by enhancing the overall product development capabilities. In recent years, more companies focus on PDM (product data management) and PLM (product life cycle management). PDM refers to managing the various product data (product planning, development, and design) throughout cross-functional teams for effective utilization of information for value creation. PLM is a somewhat broader concept of PDM. It refers to managing comprehensive life cycle information across functional and organizational boundaries of marketing of products, planning, and manufacturing to the sales, maintenance, and disposal and external information such as manufacturing/sales cost or parts suppliers (Park et al., 2007a).

Effective PLM, therefore, requires involvement beyond the OEM. Because most of the component parts are sourced from suppliers, the PLM linkages cover throughout the value chain that involves the OEM and all its suppliers. In this sense, the OEM's investment on suppliers is for the effective PLM. Kogana and Tapiero (2009) argue that investment for effective information flows requires integration efforts between OEM and suppliers. They take Electronic Data Interchange (EDI) as an example of (1) the enhanced data exchange quality between OEM and supplier and (2) improvement of their profitability. A geographically dispersed global supply chain network needs to integrate and accelerate the information flows in the supply chain through information technology such as an enterprise resource planning (ERP) system (Lee et al., 2009).

Increasingly more firms construct shared information portal sites for intra- and intercollaboration and utilize social network services (SNS). Different from the previous traditional cooperative system, the new network-based cooperatives system (i.e., with Internet) shows an explosive level of growth. With the increasing popularity of mobile office systems, firms implement SNS for efficiency of business processes. Firm SNS not only maximize the rate of regular business system utilization but also create diverse collaborative systems. The location of many U.S. firms (e.g., Microsoft, Google) in the Silicon Valley is referred to as a campus, not an office. Communication style among employees reflects the work environment that is quite comfortable and convenient. With active usage of communication tools (e.g., SNS), firms generate better work results, which existing IT systems might not be able to produce. With the adoption of SNS, the broad scope of collaboration is possible through better sharing of internal firm information and by enhancing collaboration among project teams, functional units, the entire organization, suppliers, and across supply chains. Through SNS, firms process timely and relevant information (e.g., slow sales status and local order processing details) very quickly for overseas sales offices and affiliated firms. Therefore, it is important to use SNS and build the platform and connect other functional applications systems for effective supply chain communication.

In this study, the first research question is, "Does an investment for information integration between OEM and supplier contribute to the product development outcomes of both OEM and suppliers?" The second research question is, "Which variables affect the integration of OEM and supplier the most?" We then present a research model that defines key elements of information integration between OEM and suppliers. We then examine the role of the government to facilitate the integration of the OEM and suppliers in the context of South Korea.

9.2.2 South Korean Government's Policy to Support SMEs

Compared to Japanese suppliers, Korean suppliers have had a somewhat relatively weak position. Korean manufacturing SMEs (mostly suppliers) occupy 99% of Korean firms in terms of numbers; however, its overall contribution is weak compared to the large Korean corporations in that their portion of total employment is 61% while they contribute no more than 38% of value-added and export volumes (Lim, 2007). To overcome these problems, the Korean government has worked on the systematic development of SMEs, along with assembly of large companies and component parts suppliers, in the course of pursuing heavy-chemical industrialization from the middle of the 1970s. Specific enacted laws such as "SME Development and Diversification Act" (1975), "Credit Guarantee Fund Establishment Act" (1976), "SMEs' Facility Modernization and Investment Enhancement Act" (1976), and "Small Business Administration and Medium Industry Promotion Corporation Act" (1978) enabled establishment of necessary governance systems and organizational structures for ongoing support for small and medium enterprises. In the 1980s, additional laws were enacted (to support SMEs that were not vital parts of the 1970s' high-focused growth). They include "Group Free Contract System Act" (1981), "SME Priority Policy Act" (1982) and "Fair Subcontracting Business Process Act" (1984) (SMEs-Venture Study Group, 2006).

At the same time, from the mid-1990s the government policies have moved toward encouraging independence and flexibility of SMEs from the perspective of strengthening the overall industrial competitiveness. Additional initiatives such as "Balanced Regional Development and SMEs Support Act" (1994) and the establishment of "Small and Medium Business Administration" (1996) strengthened the central administrative structures. In the late 1990s "Special Development of Venture Firm Act" (1997) and the operation of "Special Committee for SMEs" (1998) enhanced the coordinative roles of government policies for SMEs (SMEs-Venture Study Group, 2006). All these consistent government efforts gradually bore fruit in promoting collaborative relationships between large global corporations and SMEs. For example, 124 large firms and 500 SMEs organized a coordinative association in 1993 through which more than 2,090 billion (Korean wons) for SMEs support fund was established and utilized. Large corporations transferred their technological know-how to the SMEs in an effort to enhance SMEs' R & D capabilities. In 1993, 39 large corporations transferred 1,337 technological product items to 572 SMEs. In keeping with these collaborative moves, building interactive information infrastructures between large firms and SMEs has become an industry-wide strategic priority, and therefore 50 large firms and 1,000 SMEs have completed an online information system through which large global firms shared up-to-date business information with SMEs (Lim, 2007).

In the 2000s, more drastic steps of collaborative efforts between large global firms and SMEs have been taken. In the period of 2003–2007, the Korean government set its policy to facilitate and promote the more cooperative relationships between OEM and SMEs. In 2005, the first year of this policy implementation, the South Korean government defined the three specific goals of collaboration: (1) building fair and mutually beneficial partnerships, (2) enhancing SME's independent capability, and (3) establishing a continuous coexistence cooperation implementation system. In 2006, the government expanded the scope of collaboration that involves multiple government entities and organizes specific implementation plans for this goal of greater cooperation between an OEM and its small suppliers (i.e., SMEs). It also legislated the law and prepared a system of governance, which promote the mutual collaboration between OEM and SMEs (March 2006). On May 16, 2005, South Korea's President Moo-hyun Roh presided at an industry-wide meeting that encouraged mutual cooperation, inviting executives from large OEMs and their suppliers (SMEs).

During that time, chairmen of Korea's global giants such as Hyundai-Kia Motors Company, Samsung, and SK Group affirmed that the cooperation with SMEs is the heart of global competitiveness (Government Authorization Briefing Special Project Team, 2008). For example, MongGu Chung, Hyundai-Kia Motors Company chairman, pointed out that, in the course of the globalization efforts in the world, the automotive industry needs to practice a high level of collaboration in all levels—domestic suppliers, overseas suppliers, and other strategic partners. Kun-hee Lee, chairman of Samsung, explained the industry such as automotive and electronics cannot produce quality products if parts are not good, and consequently OEM's success depends on the help of SMEs. He emphasized that, behind successful global firms with world-class products, SMEs play a vital partnership (Government Authorization Briefing Special Project Team, 2008).

In 2005 government initiatives also directed to promote the overall collaborative projects between large global firms (LGC) and SMEs. Special emphasis was placed on developing 10 core new product components and building critical innovative capabilities through technological cooperation and various patent consortiums (Digital Times, 2005.2.3). In 2005 the Ministry of Industry and Resources budgeted 14 billion wons for SMEs' IT system construction and proposed collaborative IT system structures between LGCs and SMEs (Inews24, 2005.2.2).

Specific policy directive details included component parts purchasing information portals for LGCs and SMEs and component products exhibitions in which LGCs actively participate. Key technological resources from LGCs were sent to SMEs for critical training and education projects as well (Digital Times, 2005.2.3). The Small Business Administration (SBA) coordinated diverse collaborative business opportunities between LGCs and SMEs through both public and private cooperative intermediaries, which facilitated the rapid introduction of innovative new products and expanded market opportunities for SMEs. The Small Business Administration and the Medium Industry Promotion Corporation (SBA and MIPC) actively supported upgrading information infrastructures for supply chains between LGCs and SMEs, including budgetary supports, education, and training. Other key private organizations such as the National Business Executives Association (NBEA) and SMEs Central Cooperatives supported various project initiatives such as sharing LGCs' patent rights, collaborative logistics systems construction, and consulting services for SMEs. In this environment, Samsung Electronics offered necessary funds, education and training, technological exchanges, and benchmarking projects to its 300 suppliers (Inews24, 2005.2.2). In this time period other collaborative activities between LGCs and SMEs have become quite noticeably obvious. Most notable examples are Electronic Technological Training Centers (ETTC) by Samsung Electronics, Electronics Manufacturing System (EMS) by LG Electronics, and Supplier Support Programs by Hyundai-Kia Corporation, and Tooling Center by GM Daewoo, which all directed to enhance SMEs' overall global competitiveness (Kim, 2006).

From 2004 to 2007, six meetings were held with the South Korean government related to OEM/SME coexistence. As a result of the South Korean government's efforts, the OEM's investment for coexistence management increased by 1,040 billion wons in 2005, 1,430.7 billion wons in 2006, and 2,782 billion wons in 2007. Organizations dedicated and organized for mutual cooperation have been spread to 4 companies in 2005, 15 companies in 2006, and 19 companies in 2007. Furthermore, in 2005, only 5 companies introduced "performance share system," but in 2006 the number increased by 20 companies, and in 2007 by 47 companies.

Starting from 2006, an unfair business activity survey was conducted not only between OEM and SME but also among SMEs. The content and scope of the investigation is now broadened to reflect the delivery price changes in raw materials. In particular, the South Korean government amended the law (May 2007) which promotes coexistence cooperation to prevent unfair trade-related technology. It also introduced the technology data depositing system (ESCROW) by which suppliers deposit their technology data in the bank vault instead of giving them to the OEM directly, and the OEM can see the data when schedule conditions are met. As a result of these initiatives, unfair business practices also decreased. According to a survey for SME's delivery failure and difficulties to OEM conducted by the Korea Federation of SME in 2007, the unfair subcontracting deals were 31.2% in 2004, but were 24.9% in 2005 when coexistence cooperation promotion was actively promoted. In 2006 it was further decreased to 21.5% (Government Authorization Briefing Special Project Team, 2008).

In 2009, the MyungBak Lee Administration (from 2008) allocated 10 billion wons for Cooperative IT System Development between LGCs and SMEs to overcome SMEs' passive roles in the utilization of LGC-dominated IT systems in the areas of purchasing, procurement, and design engineering and innovation. Such IT infrastructure intends to facilitate industrial and network competitiveness in terms of design engineering, production, and logistical processes between LGCs and SMEs (Ministry of Knowledge Economy, 2009).

This study argues that the cooperation between OEM and supplier is essential to secure a competitive advantage for product development and that the OEM's investment for SME suppliers which do not have the ability to invest in infrastructure is important. Particularly, in Korea where SMEs are weak and vulnerable, suppliers cannot develop outstanding new products without an OEM's active investment and support, and eventually, it affects the OEM's new product development. However, in a situation where the cooperation between an OEM and suppliers is not well established, the South Korean government supports the establishment of coexistence cooperation between an OEM and its SME suppliers. This study analyzes the case in regard to the cooperation between OEM and SME suppliers coordinated by the government and, furthermore, information integration in product development (Figure 9.1).

9.3 CASE STUDIES

9.3.1 Hyundai-Kia Automotive Group (HKAG)

9.3.1.1 Description of the Firm

First, we introduce the case of the Hyundai-Kia Automotive Group (HKAG), South Korea's leading automotive company (Park et al., 2009a,

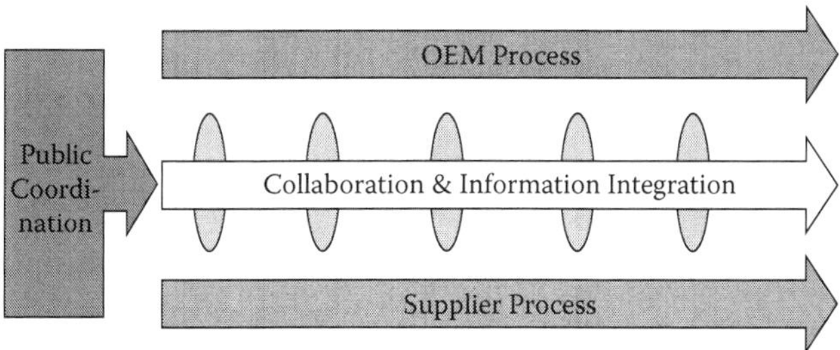

FIGURE 9.1
Research model. From Park et al. (2009a, 2011b).

2011b). A case analysis is conducted based on data from the IT president of the HKAG and from other published materials (Figure 9.2).

Hyundai Motors Company, the main company of HKAG, has the goal to produce/sell 3,050,000 cars in the domestic and overseas markets in 2009. In the beginning of 2008, Hyundai Motors Company's global sales target was set at 3,110,000 cars, but due to the global financial crisis in 2008, it estimated that it would sell about 2,800,000 cars instead (Edaily, 2008.12.4). Hyundai Motors Company also achieved 83.6% of the domestic market share in November of 2008. The overseas production capacity of the Hyundai Motors Company is expected to exceed 1,750,000 cars including production in the United States (300,000), China (600,000), India (600,000), Turkey (100,000), and the Czech Republic (300,000).

9.3.1.2 Coexistence Cooperation with Suppliers

9.3.1.2.1 Promoting Coexistence Cooperation

Influenced by the government's policy to promote the cooperation between OEMs and SMEs, HKAG actively expanded the support for its suppliers. HKAG supports various supporting programs such as developing a foundation for partners' management stabilization, strengthening core capabilities, and developing a foundation for global management. As a management stabilization program, it implements a cash payment for delivery, financial support (research and development, etc.), and a joint purchase of general materials and raw materials. As a program to strengthen core competencies, HKAG has evaluation systems such as five-star quality, five-star technology, the guest engineer system, the advanced technology benchmark system, auto parts operations, quality, production

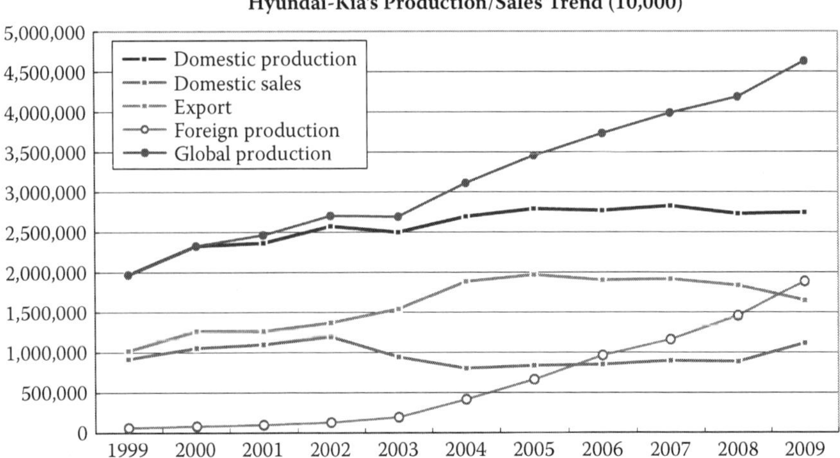

FIGURE 9.2
Sales trends of Hyundai-Kia's global production and sales. From Shintaku et al., (2010); Park et al. (2012); compiled with statistical information from Korean Automotive.

technology, and IT support. As a global management base development program, it has global human resources training/support, support for overseas plants, and system support for the global environment.

Hyundai-Kia Automotive Group (HKAG) is continuously promoting the "parts suppliers emergency assistance and mutual cooperation plan," which was implemented from May 2006 and strengthens the coexistence cooperation with second and third tier suppliers (AP, 2006.12 0.29). Due to the performance results of 2007, HKAG decided to fund $15 billion to their partners from 2006 to 2010, and in 2007, it strengthened the management stability foundation through supplying $2.5 billion for partners' raw material purchasing, research and development, and investment. In addition, HKAG supports SME suppliers' domestic components delivery payment with full cash payment and expands the joint purchase which is executed for cost savings in the purchases of partners. HKAG increased joint purchasing costs from $60.9 million for 296 companies in 2006, to $120 million for 421 companies in 2007. HKAG make joint purchases of $9 million with joint development partners.

9.3.1.2.2 IT Support for Suppliers

An OEM increases the role of partners in the process of product development through information technology, which is known as a core capability strengthen/support program. There are some goals of IT support for increasing the role and integration with partners in the process of production development: (1) collaboration and information exchange between HKAG-partners, (2) expanding the design area of partners, and (3) support for accelerating the product development process digitalization, information sharing as concrete information technology support, infrastructure support for product development, technology training for digital design, and information sharing for new IT technology. Below, the investment for suppliers and the results in 2005–2006 are presented.

1. Information sharing for product development
   - OEM enhances the collaboration system through implementing/managing a system for shortening partners' development information delivery and providing convenience (Table 9.1).
   - Practical information sharing for product development shares design information and production technology information. First, for information sharing for the design, it developed the system which shares bill of materials (BOM) information, car/PT design CAD models, electronic circuit diagrams, wiring design models, and parts spec information. It also built an information system for car frame design/molding information to share production technology information. The development cost of the system is $7 million, and the system operating expenses is $1 million every year, but it reduces the information passing time from seven days to one day and reduces the cost of system use by $1.5 million every year. In this way, 2,300 people from 370 companies are participating in the development of a new car through collaboration.
2. Support for digital design technology training
   - Education and diagnosis by digital-based design technology and productivity enhancement of suppliers support the digital development process in a number of ways. Practical technical training programs for digital design include: (1) education support, (2) technical information supply for digital design, and (3) diagnosis of digital design techniques. First of all, there are education supports using programs such as CATIA V5 training (offline), Guest Engineer CV5 design support, and cyber education Site guest engineer (G/E) provision. Second, as a provision of digital design technology information, the 3D modeling, making, and product quality standard data supply and CAx-related

TABLE 9.1

Data of the Information System Use

Support Information	Information System	Affiliated Firms	Suppliers (Tier 1)	Suppliers (Tier 2)	Total	Registered (persons)
BOM/design change/drawing information	BOM information system	3	—	—	3	2,030
	Design information system	13	628	392	1,020	7,635
	Component parts spec information system	13	389	346	748	1,390
Electronic information	Electronic information system		6	—	6	200
Automotive frame equipment production information	Automation production management system		65	13	78	137

technology data supply are included. Third, as a digital design technical-level diagnosis, HKAG holds a partner's CAD management meeting every year and supports a program which diagnoses Guest Engineer CAD capabilities level. The investment cost was $400,000 per year for the development of online education, training instructors and related costs, but as a result of education, $900,000 is being saved in the education and diagnosis area and in design techniques. The CATIA V5 design modeling for intermediate education supported fast product development through enhancing suppliers' design capabilities. In 2005, 243 people in 114 companies participated; in 2006, 316 people in 130 companies; in 2007, 1,159 people in 130 companies (Table 9.2).

3. Supply and digital design, infrastructure support
   - HKAG supports its suppliers' digital development infrastructure through providing them with digital design infrastructure and low-cost supply. The specific digital design infrastructure supports are (1) G/E design equipment and solution support, (2) the improving and building of data communications cable, and (3) low-cost digital design infrastructure for suppliers.
   - First, for G/E design equipment and solution support, HKAG supports its suppliers with 54 units of engineering workstation (EWS) equipment, 38 units of personal work station (PWS) equipment, and 255 units of server based computing (SBC) equipment. And for solution support, it supports its suppliers with the CATIA V4/V5 system and an electronic circuit design system. Second, for the improvement and building of data communications cable, HKAG built Auto-VPN. It strengthened the security and reliability of the data and reduced communication and operating expenses as well. Third, HKAG supplied the CAx/PDM licenses with low cost, and expanded the low-cost supplies through the joint purchasing of PWS equipment. It helped suppliers to build

TABLE 9.2

Education and Training Participants for CATIA Design Modeling

Year 2005	Year 2006	Year 2007	Year 2008
114 companies 243 people	130 companies 316 people	130 companies 1159 people	56 companies 151 people

Source : Interview document.

the low-cost digital design infrastructure. Thus, HKAG's introduction/investment cost is $11.5 million for the equipment and solution supply, but HKAG cut down $24.7 million of suppliers' equipment and solution introduction costs and $1.7 million in communication expenses per year.

4. Implementation of supplier development support system
   - HKAG enhanced suppliers' information processing capability by providing the know-how and new information technologies for the implementation of a component parts development support system. HKAG holds the Forum on Information Technology intended for parts suppliers once or twice a year and conducted CAx/PDM workshops for 24 companies in 2006. The investment costs reach $100,000 a year for the promotion, but the results of this specific effort is to help the suppliers to be aware of the industry trends (e.g., fast acquiring and sharing of technology information).

9.3.1.2.3 The Ongoing Support for Suppliers after 2007

For the ongoing support for suppliers, HKAG implements the system to reflect and support the needs of parts suppliers. HKAG examines the way to support suppliers because they demand (1) expanding training and technical support, (2) infrastructure support for digital design, (3) improving cable stabilization, and (4) the sharing and introduction of new IT information.

In particular, HKAG endeavors to gain competitive advantage through enhancing its suppliers' product development capabilities and through sharing real-time information. It promotes and strengthens the digital collaboration with suppliers for product life cycle through IT utilization. Specifically, HKAG supports suppliers for the improvement of digital design and digital video collaboration. It also builds up the digital development capability, improves the new IT integration infrastructure and technology security/maintenance system, and provides computer technical support. For example, HKAG supports rapid development and troubleshooting in digital collaboration with suppliers through applying and expanding video conferencing (M-channel) for the greater integration of its supply chain systems. In addition, in 2009 HKAG supported 796 domestic companies and 732 overseas companies (including KD) for installation and application of the security system.

9.3.2 POSCO

9.3.2.1 Company History

The Pohang Iron and Steel Company (POSCO), based in Pohang, South Korea, is the world's second-largest steelmaker by market value and Asia's most profitable steelmaker. Its headquarter office is located in Seoul, Korea. POSCO has two steel mills in the country, one in Pohang (handling a diverse scope of customized products in small volumes) and the other in Gwangyang (focusing economies of scale production for a narrow scope of products). USS-POSCO, a joint venture with U.S. Steel, operates in Pittsburg, California. POSCO supplies diverse steel products for the Korean shipbuilding and automobile industries. After its establishment in 1968 as Pohang Iron and Steel Company, it grew as a world-class company. By October 2000, ownership and management were formally separated. Its annual volume is about 30 million tons (Mt) of steel outputs. Based on its 42 years of manufacturing know-how, Pohang Steel (together with Gwangyang Mill that has outstanding modern facilities with superb technological capabilities) serves the global demand for steel and iron products. Seoul POSCO's main office operates the worldwide network of offices for its global marketing, customer services, and collaborative management. In 2009 most of the global steelmakers reduced their production volumes, but POSCO achieved cost reduction of more than 1 billion (US $) and strengthened the domestic and global market base and accomplished fast recovery. POSCO's production volume in 2009 is 29.53 million tons, sales 26,954 billion (Korean won) and 26 billion (US $) and net profit of 3,148 billion (Korean won) and 3 billion (US $) (Table 9.3). POSCO increased its R & D spending up to 5,000 billion (Korean won) and 500 million (US $), which reflects changes from 1.5% (2009) to 1.7% (2010). (Note: For convenience the exchange rate of 1000 (Korean won) to 1 (US $) is used.) More than 30% of its production volume (i.e., 33 million tons) is exported to more than 60 countries of the world, including the United States and Japan. Its global production network is being extended to India (2005), China (2006), Mexico (2009), and Vietnam (2009) with continuous galvanizing line (CGL) facilities.

- Overseas integrated steel mill projects are:
    1. India central government approved on forest diversion of plant site in Orissa (2,900 acres)

TABLE 9.3

Production Records

Units: 1,000 ton, 1million Korean Won	2006	2007	2008	2009
Production (crude steel)	30,053	31,064	33,136	29,530
Production (finished products)	28,904	29,727	31,837	28,243
Production (products for sale)	28,904	29,727	31,837	28,243
Sales volume (finished production)	28,542	29,581	31,166	28,437
Sales volume (products for sale)	28,542	29,581	31,166	28,437
Sales	20,043,409	22,206,685	30,642,409	26,953,945
Operating profit	3,892,307	4,308,275	6,540,059	3,147,998

2. MOA Signed to build integrated steel mill in Indonesia: first stage of 3 Mt/yr (~2013), total 6 Mt

- Downstream facilities in Asia and America are:
  1. Vietnam CR Mill completed: 1.2 Mt/yr
  2. Mexico CGL completed: 400 Kt/yr
  3. U.S. API Pipe Plant completed: 270 Kt/yr
  4. Vietnam ASC (Asia Stainless Corporation) acquired: STS CR 30 Kt/yr
  5. Global SCM base expanded: China, S.E.A (2), Japan (2), India, Mexico (2009/E Total 42)
- Raw material mine development investments are:
  1. Participated in Australian mine development, Roy Hill (first 3.75% equity, total 15% planned)
  2. Acquired 16.7% equity in Jupiter Mines (Australian iron-ore development company)
  3. Plan of acquiring 7.8% stake in Mozambique coal mine development project, Revuboe

POSCO plans to build a stainless steel cold-rolling mill with annual capacity of 200,000 tons in Turkey in 2010. Construction will commence in 2011 and is scheduled for completion by 2013. The new plant will enable POSCO to gain a foothold in Turkey's STS domestic market, which has been entirely dependent on imports. POSCO also seeks to exploit Turkey's geographic advantage to take advantage of new demand in the Middle East, Eastern Europe, and CIS regions.

9.3.2.2 POCSO's 3.0 Innovation Projects

POSCO has been implementing POSCO 3.0 Innovation Projects as its organization-wide effort to achieve sustainable competitive advantage as a top global firm. "Creative Innovation" is to break the traditional rules and adopt "creative and disruptive innovation" in its organizational culture and business processes. POSCO's creative innovation has three key pillars: (1) "Creativity and Challenge," (2) Family Values, and (3) Smart Work. The goal for all innovative efforts is to establish itself as the global leader beyond its fast follower status. The scope of innovation includes the entire family network within POSCO supply chains. The operational principles are to encourage participation and process focus is set for performance outcomes based on initiation and creativity.

9.3.2.2.1 Creativity and Challenge

This starts with creative destruction. Organizational members reinterpret from the very beginning for even the successful initiatives/production methods/products by creative destruction through which the goal of becoming the global top is being pursued and achieved. First, in each segment of business processes, all the key leaders strive for at least one project of "world best and world first" and implement innovative problem solving (i.e., trees utilization and idea creation) through participation and information sharing).

Second, the scope of innovation is extended to strategy and planning. It is important to secure organization capability to capture innovative trends in strategy, planning, and analysis of customer insight and to adopt big thinking methods for new idea development through involving the customers/external experts.

Third, develop POSCO's unique POSCO Production System (PPS). By upgrading Quick Six Sigma (QSS) activities for one stage further, the goal is to achieve optimization of the waste improvement processes (e.g., in the production/functionality/quality aspects) and zero maintenance, quality, and accident failures. In business areas, the goal is connectivity of work diet and value processes (VP), and daily routine waste discovery/redeploying slack workforce (saved through improvement efforts) into priority projects.

Fourth, develop innovative human resources that possess an open, challenging, imaginative, and creative mindset.

9.3.2.2.2 Innovation through Collaborative Families

POSCO's competitiveness resides in its supply chain. POSCO emphasizes two particular aspects.

First, seek collaboration among POSCO's domestic and global supply chain partners. All the POSCO's affiliated partners (i.e., families) participate in innovation sessions. Thus, the patterns of innovation strategy and behavioral practices are consistent across POSCO's supply chains.

Second, innovation performance is maximized between POSCO and its affiliated families. D+ activities within POSCO are applied in its affiliated families. Joint workshops between POSCO and its affiliated families enable them to discover Mega Y projects together, and the performance outcomes are shared through joint benefit-sharing programs.

9.3.2.2.3 Smart Work

Continuous evolution and development of IT technologies also impact on work processes. Thus, POSCO pursues 3A (Anywhere, Anytime, and Anyone) work communication methods through new communication and IT technologies that overcome the barriers of time and distance. Through 3A, POSCO anticipates synergy effects in broad aspects of business.

First, by automation much of the human work process is replaced by machines and thus improves the quality of work life of employees. For example, personal digital assistant (PDA) is used for the facilities and safety management. Inventory control for raw/component materials and finished products is automated through the adoption of RFID (radio frequency identification).

Second, mobile technology allows office workers to achieve "work by moving" very soon. By using smartphones, much of the office work (e.g., check and process order information, e-mail communications, order verification and payment) is conducted outside of regular offices (e.g., during sales calls, commuting time, or at home).

Third, provide systematic support for the effective collaboration among diverse cross-functional members. Any communication between POSCO and its affiliated families can be handled just like one company including integration of EP/mail and video conferencing with any PC. Thus, unnecessary transportation and waiting times are eliminated.

9.3.2.3 POSCO Innovation and Collaboration with Suppliers

Since 2005 strategic collaboration between POSCO and its affiliated family firms has been implemented as a part of leadership initiatives of the

Korean government. At present, its scope includes second and third tier suppliers beyond POSCO and its first tier suppliers. Such strategic collaboration started with IT system consulting support in 2005.

After 2009 POSCO Innovation Program (PIP) is extended to POSCO Supplier Collaboration Projects as well. The goal of PIP is to transfer innovation know-how and performance improvement details (i.e., POSCO's projects since 1999) to its suppliers. POSCO's innovative know-how has been accumulated through (1) first stage of electronic process innovation through Enterprise Resource Planning (ERP); (2) second stage of business process reengineering with Six Sigma program; (3) third stage of Quick Six Sigma (QSS) and Centralized Document Management Innovation Projects; (4) fourth stage is to share this accumulated know-how and performance improvement expertise with POSCO's suppliers.

POSCO's supplier development program since 2009 includes more than 50 different projects. Such projects encompass all aspects of business processes including financial support, technological support (consulting support program), innovation activities, education and training, purchasing, and sales collaboration. The financial support program is to strengthen the financial basis of these small and medium-sized suppliers. This includes low-interest-rate financing in the form of joint financial guarantee programs, collaborative special funds, and affiliated firm development funds for which second and third tier suppliers are also eligible for such special financing arrangements. As of September 2009, more than 699 affiliated firms received US $469.1 million (Sung, 2009).

Such financing support programs are for short-term collaboration projects, while technological support, education, and training are long-term collaboration initiatives. Customized technological support activities (i.e., techno-partnership) involve R & D projects with its suppliers as well. Many SMEs applauded the Korean government's program that supports R & D expenditures of large firms with the condition that these large firms commit to purchasing a specific amount of products from SMEs.

Recently, POSCO also strengthened the consulting support programs for its suppliers. POSCO routinized SME consulting support programs by connecting them as a part of its employees volunteer service programs in which all POSCO employees are encouraged to participate each month. The scope of consulting includes challenging IT areas for SMEs, innovation projects, safety management, and information security for which many of POSCO's experts visit these SMEs and offer their services.

POSCO's Collaboration Implementation Office (CIO) under the direction of the CEO establishes specific plans for collaboration and evaluates the results. From 2009 POSCO Global CIO has been organized as well. Its 34 plus members are Mr. Jung (POSCO CEO), Purchasing and Sales Executive VP, 17 presidents of affiliated firms, and 17 representatives of small and medium-sized suppliers. Twice a year CIO organizes performance evaluation and report meetings on the status and outcomes of such collaboration among POSCO and its affiliated firms and suppliers.

After 2010, POSCO's new motto is 3T (Trust, Together, and Tomorrow) and thus enhances the extent of collaboration in depth and width. In September 2010 POSCO announced that its Collaboration Innovation Program is expanded to all firms within its supply chain. POSCO has established collaboration contracts with its 15,150 affiliated firms first. Among them, there are 298 first tier collaboration firms and 11,783 second tier collaboration firms. By and large, the total number of firms that participate in collaboration innovation programs is 26,933. POSCO also increases the amount of financing support up to 730 million (US $), which is available not only for the first tier suppliers but also for the entire supplier network. Direct cash payment methods for first tier suppliers are applied to other suppliers. Any cost information and system improvement discussions can be made online through the second to fourth tier supplier network.

With its Patent Technology Pool System, POSCO allows its suppliers to use POSCO's patent technologies of green growth areas, and some of the new technologies are even transferred to its customers, too. Besides, POSCO applies the best optimal pricing (not lowest pricing) for order pricing decisions. Any SMEs that enter new facilities contracts also receive additional facilities fund support from POSCO.

9.3.2.3.1 POSCO's Information Sharing Portal and Collaboration through POSCO Daily

POSCO's fourth stage projects focus on transferring know-how and performance improvement details of Stages 1 through 3 to its affiliated suppliers. For this purpose, POSCO utilizes POSCO Daily as a communication network medium for POSCO's supply chain participants. For information sharing POSCO builds and operates its own portal (www.poscoway.net). For effective communication POSCO also standardizes its communication rules. POSCO's information sharing portal is available from June 2009. POSCO also opened POSCO Daily for promoting more communication among POSCO employees and its affiliated firms. This is to share essential information of POSCO to all POSCO's global network participants. The main contexts of POSCO Daily include various news and social services projects in the form of photos and hot news items. It has a variety of sections such as "hot news," "hot clicks," and "share together" for valuable intra- and interorganizational information and news. It also utilizes Twitter for free and fast communication. Twitter is a new social network service (SNS) which enhances the extent of communication among POSCO family members. With mobile features, it is available anytime, anywhere. Thus, POSCO Daily (as a common forum for any POSCO employees and global families) promotes a sense of shared identity and seeks a synergy effect through collaboration. POSCO Daily is available for both POSCO employees and its affiliated family firms (i.e., suppliers in POSCO's supply chain).

9.3.2.3.2 Expansion of Innovation Activities

POSCO plans to expand POSCO-initiated innovation activities to its affiliated suppliers.

- First, the operations of Session I included suppliers outside of Korea. From March 2010 Session Review (SR), POSCO shared its innovation plans with its suppliers. Through Session Follow-Up (SF) in July and August the innovation performance outcomes were examined. From December 2010, the performance outcomes were shared with firms in its supply chain with Session Innovation Festival (IF).
- Second, discover joint collaborative projects between POSCO and affiliated family firms for synergy effects.
- Third, conduct regular audits of innovativeness of its affiliated family firms and offer customized consulting, collaborate for innovative human resources development, and share best business case results.

9.3.2.3.3 Management Doctor System

POSCO uses Management Doctor System (MDS) for its management consulting for small and medium enterprises (SMEs). In 2010, POSCO's affiliated SMEs that participated in MDS are Shinil Intech and Seoul Engineering. POSCO offered diverse management consulting by management experts from the Korea Chamber of Commerce to these two firms for six months from May 2010. Shinil Intech raised the efficiency of the welding processes by 5% through this MDS, and improved nondestructive inspection failure rate by 30% and annual plant utilization rate by 26.9% as well. Seoul Engineering also adopted a more rational human resources reward system as well as more effective financial system analysis for organization performance improvement. POSCO intends to strengthen its entire supply chain competitiveness through offering customized consulting to any of its affiliated family firms.

9.3.2.3.4 POSCO's Global R & D Center

In 2010 POSCO completed its Global R & D Center in Inchon, Korea. This center offers total solutions for customers who use POSCO's products and services by strengthening EVI (Early Vendor Involvement). This R & D Center also extends its research network beyond POSCO and includes POSTECH, Pohang Research Institute of Science and Technology (PRIST), global firms in Seoul, Korea, and other global universities. Such extended global research network allows POSCO to develop new growth engines (e.g., complex and innovative product development and commercialization) for sustainable competitive advantage. Such research network also allows POSCO to secure innovative human resources for its global leadership.

9.4 DISCUSSION

Korea has quite a few large, prominent global firms. However, the SMEs that support them are somewhat weak and vulnerable. Historically, the policy priority of the Korean government was to build a few large global firms for the purpose of rapid national economic growth. Over the years, many global Korean firms (e.g., Samsung, Hyundai, and LG) have successfully built their brand names and a wide variety of product lines through vertical integration. However, as the global supply chain operates on a much greater scale and effectiveness, increasingly the Korean government and the large global Korean firms both recognize the limits of such an emphasis in policy. It is becoming increasingly clear that without the healthy and sound state of their suppliers, which are mostly small and medium enterprises, there is very little chance for the continuous and steady growth of these global firms. Besides, the poor power dynamics between the large global firms and their small suppliers received much media attention as well. Samsung's excessive demand for SME suppliers to reduce costs was reported to the Korea Fair Trade Commission in 2008 and serves as a good example.

As a proponent of SMEs and a powerful mediator on behalf of SMEs, the Korean government has played a significant role in facilitating cooperation between OEMs and SMEs. Through such active government involvement, the competitive capabilities of Korean SMEs gradually increased, and accordingly the patterns of relationships between OEMs and their suppliers have also improved.

Recently, Hyundai-Kia Automotive Group accelerated the coexistence cooperation program started in 2005. HKAG plans to expand the support for its suppliers to overcome the global financial crisis of 2008 together with its suppliers. HKAG is committed to supporting research and development of environment-friendly green cars ($20 million) and to purchase bonds issued by suppliers by creating a coexistence cooperation fund ($30 million). Such efforts may have a multiplier effect on the growth of its component parts suppliers which eventually impact other industries as well.

In September of 2008, Hyundai-Kia Automotive Group made an agreement with its SME suppliers for fair trade for their coexistence. The number of companies participating in the agreement pact is about 2,400, including its affiliated firms and 2,368 SMEs who are first tier and second tier suppliers. They have more suppliers than any other company in South Korea. Specifically, four guidelines for mutual cooperation have been presented as well (Park et al., 2009a). These four guidelines are: (1) fair subcontracting decisions reflecting raw material prices and the market environment, (2) exchanges of the written contract after the contract is issued, (3) objectivity and transparency regarding vendor selection and cancellation, and (4) installation and operation of the internal review committee for subcontracting transactions. These are not yet legally binding, because the companies voluntarily participated. HKAG, however, experienced practical results from government-initiated cooperation with suppliers. It accepts that the cooperation with its component parts suppliers is essential for future competitive advantage.

Such recognition is widely held among top management. For example, the vice president of Kia Motors said, “A car is made of 20,000 components. The success of this quality is due to the help of our partners. We will be world-class companies through coexistence cooperation with our suppliers.”

Since 2005 POSCO has also made serious efforts to collaborative strategic alliances with its suppliers. Instead of direct IT system support, POSCO offers consulting and builds common information portals for information sharing. POSCO Daily also facilitates the cooperative system with its suppliers and extends innovative activities and works toward synergy effects throughout its supply chain by applying Session I projects. As the user-initiated IT system becomes more important than the vendor-based IT system, the value of SNS as an intracollaborative system will increase even more within the extended network contexts.

In this study, we argue that IT support to share essential product development information for integrated product development is one aspect of the overall support for the suppliers. Thus, it is important to integrate the supply chain network system through the information system. In the unique Korean contexts, the Korean government has played a major role for building such network infrastructures. For their sustainable competitive advantage, global leader firms should all the more develop their rich ecosystem through the supply chain network.

10

Product Development of the Japanese Electronics Industry

Increasingly, the effectiveness of product development depends on how firms utilize their product architecture in achieving their comparative advantage. Besides, the usage patterns of computer-aided design (CAD) have serious implications in the ways firms utilize their product architecture. Very few studies have ever examined the diverse issues in these areas.

In this chapter, we first present a research framework about product architecture in electronic products. Furthermore, we extend our inquiry by comparing the product architecture and CAD usage patterns of electronic products. We then explore computer-aided design (CAD) usage patterns. To analyze our research model, we apply "integral architecture index," which has a dozen specific measures of architectural characteristics for each product.

We then present our research methods and findings of survey questionnaires collected from selected Japanese electronics manufacturers. These integrative and comparative analyses suggest that product architecture and CAD usage patterns between two products (i.e., automobile products and electronic products) are quite different, and the product development of Japanese electronic manufacturers tends to be near integral architecture. In conclusion, we discuss the practical implications of these findings.

10.1 INTRODUCTION

Increasingly, using an information system is essential for new product development. Because products delivered to customers are regarded as "design information embedded in media" (Fujimoto, 2005), IT systems such as computer-aided design (CAD) have a very important function as design information transformation media in new product development (Ueno et al., 2007). Over the years, design tools have evolved from hand drawing, to 2D (second dimension) CAD, and then to 3D CAD. In Japan, 2D CAD was widely available in the 1980s. By the middle of the 1990s, most large equipment manufacturers adopted it, and during the same time period more firms also accelerated their adoption of 3D CAD (Nobeoka, 2006).

Although 3D CAD adoption time and its implementation speed is somewhat slower than those of 2D CAD, the implementation impact is quite substantial. Various researchers have reported the effects of 3D CAD implementation (Fitzgerald, 1987; Velocci and Childs, 1990; Robertson and Allen, 1993; Baba and Nobeoka, 1998; Kappel and Rubenstein, 1999; Aoshima et al., 2001; Ku, 2003; Tan and Vonderembse, 2006). Their findings suggest that, if the electronic information transformation process is simplified and concurrent development is done, engineering design steps and development time are drastically reduced. The enhancement of product quality is possible through substantial reductions of transformation loss. By sharing 3D images, product development teams engage in new product development from diverse perspectives, and accordingly they experience rich product innovation. In the early stage of product development, product development teams adequately consider key concerns of back-end design engineering and therefore reduce the scope of design changes that can occur in the later stages (Aoshima et al., 2001).

3D CAD and computer-aided engineering (CAE) contribute to both front loading (i.e., early problem solving efforts) and decline of development time through shortening design changes (Fujimoto, 1997; Thomke and Fujimoto, 2000). Particularly, 3D CAD facilitates concurrent engineering activities and links product design and process design electronically. Concurrent usage of 3D CAD also enhances the design processes (Koufteros et al., 2001). Product information flexibility with 3D CAD usage also promotes the integration of mechanical design, electrical design, and detail design analysis to a greater extent and therefore promotes the simultaneous and concurrent interpretation of product concepts.

Despite adoption of this outstanding functionality, not all firms utilize its capabilities in the same way. It is important to consider differences in firm capabilities that use IT systems (Fujimoto et al., 2002; Fujimoto, 2006b). A study of 240 U.S. firms suggests that CAD usage has a greater effect on cross-functional information sharing and therefore indirectly affects product development performance more than it directly affects product development performance (Tan and Vonderembse, 2006). In other words, unless firms utilize CAD for greater sharing of cross-functional information, CAD usage itself may not directly impact product development success. In this sense, the integration of a CAD-related database is critical for a wider application of CAD-generated information (Park et al., 2007a). Organizational capabilities are unique competencies that have been developed for a long period of time. Building a cross-functional database is regarded as one way of expanding organizational capabilities.

Another factor that determines the extent of CAD utilization is product architecture. Compared to automotive products, electronic products are closer to modular architecture (Fujimoto, 2001a). Differences in product architecture impact the degree of CAD usage in product design. Even among the same electronic products, product architecture is not necessarily the same (Fujimoto, 2003; Nobeoka et al., 2006; Park et al., 2007a).

This study examines the relationships between the product architecture of electronic products (close to modular architecture) and CAD usage. This research is based on our survey results using product architecture questionnaire items initially developed by Oshika and Fujimoto (2006). Based on the theory of comparative advantage of product architecture, Oshika and Fujimoto (2006) empirically validated that products that are close to integral architecture tend to have more comparative advantage in the Japanese industry. Yet, they did not clearly explain why electronic products close to modular architecture show declining competitive advantages. Compared to the auto industry, the Japanese electronics industry shows weak competitiveness in new product development performance, and the reasons have not yet been explored. This study intends to fill this research gap by focusing on the CAD usage in electronic products and further explores the relationships between CAD usage and electronic product architecture.

10.2 PRODUCT ARCHITECTURE AND CAD USAGE

10.2.1 Design Idea and Product Architecture Measure

Product architecture may be classified into multiple patterns. Two important types of classification are (1) modular and integral and (2) open and closed (Ulrich, 1995; Fine, 1998; Baldwin and Clark, 2000; Fujimoto, 2001a, 2001b). In reality, the larger issues may be too complex to understand through such a simple method of classification. Even for the same products, different characteristics of product architecture are noticeable, depending on their product position and the extent of product complexity (Fujimoto, 2003). Product architecture can be classified on a continuum between two extremes—integral and modular.

Oshika and Fujimoto (2006) evaluated a few characteristics of architecture by using the Likert scale and derived integrality index. The results indicate that the automobile and its component parts showed the highest integrality index, while the lowest index was for electronic products. Other researchers also conclude that digital household goods are close to modular architecture (Ueno et al., 2007).

In general, integral products are consistent in structural and functional design options. For example, with given market demands, analog types of products require the consistent expression of structural design and functional design of small-sized mechanical products in terms of weight, intensity, and volume, and therefore, they usually show a strong integral tendency (Nishimura, 2004).

Besides, such integral products are not predetermined from the beginning; rather, modular products may become integral products, depending on changes in the market, technology, and the competitive environment. According to the analysis of integral processes, the degree of integrality of products is determined by the extent of interdependency among design elements (e.g., components, unit, and parts) in terms of product attribute elements and other external factors (e.g., market, technology, and competitive characteristics) (Fujitsu, 2007). The product attributes that affect product architecture are:

- Products that do not have a one-to-one relationship between functionality and component parts
- Compact and high-functionality products
- Newly devised component parts during design processes

- Critical characteristics of products rely on total products
- Interdependency between electrical design and mechanical design
- Reduction in design margin
- Products emphasizing design aspects

The factors from the market, technology, and a competitive environment that affect product architecture are:

- Reduction in time-to-market
- New model from reused designs
- Pursuit of design for users
- Technological progress and rapid changes
- Product development from a new concept
- New product development through technological integration

Therefore, integral assembly products tend to show a high ratio of specially customized design components, analog products, and mechanical components (Ueno et al., 2007). Modular products, in contrast, are manufactured from industry standard commodity parts, internally used common parts, digital parts, and electrical and electronic products. The cost proportion of electrical and electronic components is about 50% in PCs and digital household goods, 30% in premium automobiles, and 10% in low-cost automobiles. The cost proportion of commodity products is 50% in PCs, 30% in white household electronics (refrigerators and washers/dryers), and less than 10% for premium automobiles.

Classification (as either integral or modular) requires in-depth interviews and analysis of the internal product structure; however, access to firms' private databases is not realistically feasible. Therefore, it is reasonable to use survey methods to compare the product architecture of firms.

In general, three approaches are available in assessing product architecture. First, the "functionality structure relationship approach" examines the extent of integral architecture (or its opposite on the continuum, modular architecture) based on the technological interrelationship between functionality elements and structural elements for each product. Second, by focusing on the structural elements (component parts) and connective elements (interface) of component parts, the interface approach measures the degree of product particularity or the standardization/commonality of component parts (Fujimoto, 2002). These two approaches require a tremendous amount of time, because they involve interviewing specialists for each product for the purpose of validating the functionality structure relationship or interface characteristics in the case of multiple functionality elements and component part processes. These two approaches are appropriate for in-depth case studies but not for large sample data gathering or statistical empirical studies (Oshika and Fujimoto, 2006).

The third approach is the subjective evaluation approach that Oshika and Fujimoto (2006) used. This involves subjective judgment on the visible patterns of product process architecture that is close to integral (or modular). This method evaluates if specialists for particular products demonstrate the adoption of such design mindsets.

We measure the questionnaire items of Oshika and Fujimoto (2006) in order to quantify the degree of architecture.

10.2.2 Product Architecture and CAD Usage

This section explains the relationships between product architecture and CAD. Studies show that CAD system usage patterns differ between the automobile industry and the electronics industry in Japan (Park et al., 2007a). Because Japanese auto manufacturers have adopted integrated manufacturing, suppliers of component parts are required to use the same CAD systems as their OEMs (original equipment manufacturers) use. On the other hand, since more than 70% of household electrical and electronic products use common parts, the CAD systems of suppliers and their assemblers are not necessarily the same.

For a better understanding of product architecture differences, we compare the product design patterns of automotive and electronic products in terms of their CAD usage (Ueno et al., 2007). Let us first consider the integral architecture of automobile products. During initial product design, structure design is subject to total functional design. Because design aspects are so important in determining the value of automobile products, functional design and structural design are implemented through sequential processes. The functionality of products is too often determined in the structural design stage, which is in somewhat reverse order.

Traditionally, automobiles emphasized mechanical component parts, and therefore electronic parts and their embedded software have been usually subordinate to the design processes of mechanical components. With rapid electronicalization, the scope of electronic components in automobiles (e.g., addition of ECU and other electronic component parts) has expanded, and naturally, electronic design and software design are becoming more important. For example, the source code requirement for car navigation exceeds 5 million lines, which is beyond the source code length that other electronic components are allowed. In automobile manufacturing, the importance of software increases to the extent that diverse electronic component parts are used.

For electronic products, electronic components are more important than mechanical parts. With the increasingly short product life cycle in electronic products, reduction in time to market is becoming an expected norm. For example, as of May 2006, the life span of a Casio handset (mobile phone) and digital camera was four to six months (Toriya, 2006). By applying typical modular architecture, the electronics industry has not used CAD for the design of products with a short product life cycle (PLC). As requirements for product innovation become more complicated, the focus is becoming more on information control, not on actual prototype completion. In this environment, 3D CAD is more widely applied (Ueno, 2005; Park et al., 2007a).

In contrast to the analog age, electronic components are becoming more important in the digital age. Many other global firms, using a low-cost strategy, have successfully challenged Japanese competitive advantage in the market segments of DVD players and low-pixel digital cameras. With the commoditization of electronic products, any firm could produce electronic products with the appropriate assembly of component parts (Shintaku et al., 2004; Nobeoka, 2006; Ueno et al., 2007).

Recently, electronic products (with their market maturity) show strong pressures for differentiation and display a trend toward minimization, energy efficiency, and feature/image design. Naturally, mechanical design in electronic products regains its importance. Because mechanical design matters in the environment of integrating all of the complex components parts in a very small space, a high degree of image minimization and energy efficiency is required. With the accelerating expectations of fast design upgrades and appearance appeal, component materials are switched from plastics to magnesium alloy and from aluminum to titan alloy. Accordingly, rule changes in existing mechanical design are required (Fujitsu, 2007).

Such a trend is quite noticeable in products where minimization is the key differentiation strategy for premium values. Design has been an important competitive factor, not in electronic products but in automobiles, for a long time. In view of the fact that there is little room for differentiation in the technological performance of most consumer electronic products, design is becoming an important competitive factor.

For example, as design in mobile products (such as handsets, MP3 players, and digital cameras) impacts the sales volume, the actual design is not finalized even at the last stage. Because design is related to the minimization and flat tendency of products, space layout design is more challenging for design components (mostly external) and functional components (mostly printed circuit board [PCB] assembly and electronic components). In this environment, CAD for external design is becoming more seriously important (Ueno et al., 2007).

This study intends to examine the relationships between product architecture and CAD usage and to assess product architecture measures and mechanical CAD usage in the context of the mechanical design in product development. Particularly, we first examine the product architecture of mobile products (e.g., mobile PCs, handsets, and digital cameras), and then we further analyze the product development practices of Japanese electronics manufacturers and their CAD usage patterns.

10.3 RESEARCH MODEL AND FRAMEWORK

10.3.1 Research Framework

A previous case study compared the product development practices of electronics firms with those of automobile manufacturers in terms of product architecture (Park et al., 2007a). This study reported that integral product development patterns also exist in electronic products.

This study, as an extension of the previous one, focuses primarily on the product development practices of electronic products that follow integral product architecture patterns. In the previous study, we presented two parameters (i.e., integral/modular and open/closed). For the purpose of this study, we will focus on the integral/modular axis, and not the open/closed one. Figure 10.1 shows that automobile products are on the top of the integral side, and desktop computers are on the opposite, modular side. In between these two extremes, car navigation units, printers, digital cameras, mobile PCs, and mobile phones (handsets) are positioned.

Figure 10.2 shows that, in the case of derivative product development, common parts are used more and interfaces among component parts are highly standardized. They adopt modular product architecture.

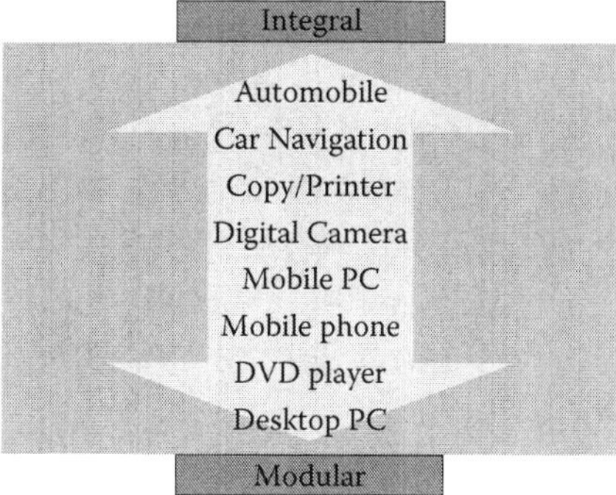

FIGURE 10.1
Product classification by product architecture. Adapted from Park et al. (2009b), Nobeoka et al. (2006).

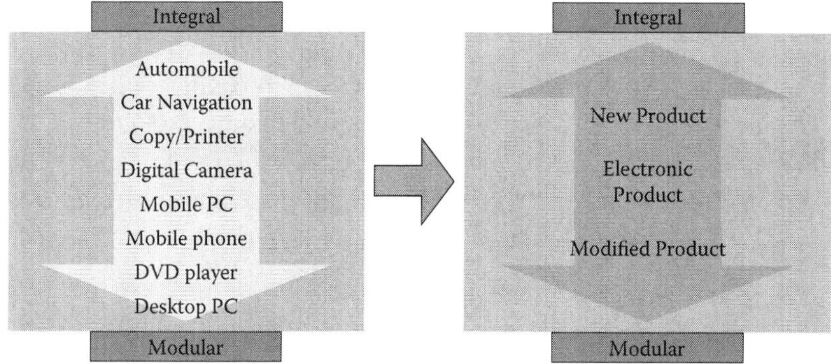

FIGURE 10.2
A research framework.

10.3.2 Research Methods

The Manufacturing Management Research Center (MMRC) of the University of Tokyo has conducted interviews in the areas of product development and CAD usage in the Japanese electronics industry. From the latter part of 2007, the research team conducted questionnaire surveys on the product development practices and CAD usage of electronic products that are classified as part of the assembly product family (Oshika and Fujimoto, 2006; Fujimoto and Oshika, 2006). This is the first study of CAD usage in the electronics industry in Japan.

We have adopted the instruments developed by Oshika and Fujimoto (2006) for the analysis of the content of product architecture. These measures examine (1) component parts design in terms of product specificity (four items), (2) connective parts in terms of internally restricted standards (four items), (3) design parameters in terms of mutual modifications (four items), and (4) a comprehensive five-step subject evaluation by product leaders (one item). Oshika and Fujimoto (2006) assessed the degree of integral architecture by adding the scores of all variables based on principal analysis. On the other hand, our focus was on small numbers of products, and therefore, for the purpose of this analysis, we have used the total score of only the 13th item. More details about this comprehensive instrument are available in Oshika and Fujimoto (2006).

10.4 RESULTS

10.4.1 Component Parts Statistics of Investigated Products

We investigated 20 products for 10 Japanese manufacturing firms. This study analyzes seven types of electronic products (i.e., mobile PCs, liquid crystal projectors, digital cameras, liquid-crystal display (LCD) TVs, walkmans, and handsets). The average score of component parts statistics of products is shown in Table 10.1.

TABLE 10.1

Basic Statistics of 20 Products

	# of Component Parts		Expected Manufacturing Lead Time (months)		Percentage of Component Parts Designed for the First Time		Percentage of Component Parts Produced Internally	
	Mean	**SD**	**Mean**	**SD**	**Mean**	**SD**	**Mean**	**SD**
Total	967	1117	7.3	6.21	66.3	30.39	21.5	17.90
Digital camera	750	250	8	2	45	35	36.5	33.5
Handset (derivative)	475	325	3	1	50	40	30	0
Handset (new)	618	297	4.3	1.16	69.3	29.69	13.6	13.57
Mobile PC	225	25	6	1	87.5	2.5	25	5
Projector	3650	150	24	0	87.5	2.5	*	*
LCD TV	1525	1225	7.5	1.50	50	25	27.5	2.5
Walkman	225	0	5	0	67.5	17.5	20	0

10.4.2 Product Architecture and Measurement Results

We show the results of the classification of product architecture. The simple average score of product architecture of these products is 4.1. This suggests that, even though they are electronic products, they are quite close to integral architecture. However, as we classify them in terms of high-performance product development and derivative models, the results are somewhat different.

Table 10.2 shows that the products reported as integral architecture are high-pixel digital cameras and new handsets with complex functionality. Product development for mobile PCs and LCD TVs is also reported as close to integral architecture. On the other hand, liquid crystal projectors and derivative models of handsets are somewhat close to modular architecture. These conflicting results reveal different product architecture between high-performance and derivative product models.

These differences in product architecture reflect the impact of differentiation by the minimization of mobile products. It shows that for consumer electronic products the primary way of differentiation is in design features (Park et al., 2008b). Particularly, the sales volume of all mobile products, such as handsets, digital cameras, and mobile PCs, depends on outstanding design expression, which includes the minimization and flatness of products. As a lot more complex component parts are squeezed into a smaller available space, the degree of integral architecture increases in electronic product designs.

Of course, product differences among mobile PCs, digital cameras, handsets, and liquid crystal projectors need to be carefully considered as well. In our study, multiple evaluators participate, and therefore, with the presence of perceptive biases, it is not quite possible to compare the

TABLE 10.2

Classification of Product Architecture by Seven Products

Product Architecture	Mean	SD
Total	4.1	1.18
Digital camera	5	0
Handset (derivative model)	2	0
Handset (new model)	4.6	1.05
Mobile PC	4.5	0.50
Projector	2.5	0.50
LCD TV	4.7	0.47
Walkman	4	0

absolute differences in product architecture. Yet, differences in product architecture are observed among high-performance products and their derivative products.

The implications of these results are useful for engineers involved in product development, in that (1) effective product development requires careful examination of each product's architecture; (2) the impact of product architecture on the CAD usage patterns needs to be examined; and (3) in view of excessive product quality issues, the extent of premium functionality is to be carefully considered.

10.4.3 Electronic Product Development and CAD Usage

This section examines CAD, CAM (computer-aided manufacturing), and CAE usage patterns for electronic products. The types of CAD systems used for component parts design are 2D, 3D Wire Frame, 3D Surface, and 3D Solid. Our study shows different characteristics between case design (mechanical design focus) and PCB base design (electrical circuit design focus).

Table 10.3 shows that case (housing) design uses mostly 3D Solid, while PCB base design is limited to 2D. 3D Solid is used for core components (e.g., digital camera lenses). In other words, besides PCB base design, it is not surprising to see that almost all component part designs use 3D CAD, CAM, and CAE.

Table 10.4 measures the ratio between CAD operators and CAD experts. The number of CAD operators in relation to the number of design engineers suggests that in most cases (except for a few cases of CAD operators) design engineers themselves input the CAD data. The percentage of CAE experts in the process is a little higher than that of design engineers (65.0% vs. 35.0%).

Since the middle of the 1990s, changes have occurred from 2D CAD to 3D CAD usage. We have examined the processes in greater detail in terms

TABLE 10.3

Types of CAD According to Component Parts Design

	Type of CAD in Design of Component Parts (%)				
Component Parts	**2D**	**3D Wire Frame**	**3D Surface**	**3D Solid**	**CAD No Use**
Case (housing)	11.6	0.0	0.2	88.3	1.0
PCB board	79.5	0.0	0.0	20.5	0.5

TABLE 10.4

Ratio between CAD Operators and CAD Experts

Number of CAD Operators That Support Design Engineers (Unit: Number of People)	% of Total Processes In Terms of CAE	
	CAE Experts	**Design Engineers**
0.5	65.0	35.0

TABLE 10.5

Ratio of 2D CAD and 3D CAD Usage in Design Processes

Design Process	2D CAD	3D CAD	CAD no use
1. Product planning	4.3	15.5	80.3
2. Design	10.5	81.0	8.5
3. Mechanical design	12.8	87.3	0.0
4. Electrical design (PCB design)	94.5	5.5	0.0
5. Equipment design	24.8	62.3	13.0
6. Interpretative design	2.5	94.8	2.8
7. Production preparation	7.5	82.5	10.0

of (1) product planning, (2) design, (3) mechanical design, (4) electrical design (PCB design), (5) equipment design, (6) interpretative design, and (7) production preparation. Table 10.5 shows the usage percentage of 2D CAD and 3D CAD in terms of seven different processes.

For product planning, 3D CAD is used 15.5% of the time, which means that for the majority of the time (80.3%) CAD is not used for product planning. In design, 3D usage is definitely large (81%), and then the 3D usage portion increases in mechanical design (87.3%), equipment design (62.3%), and interpretative design (94.8%). In view of the continuity from equipment design to interpretative design, 3D usage probably enhances the concurrent aspects of process management. However, 2D usage is heavy in electrical design (PCB design). Although some electronics firms try 3Dization in electrical design, 2D CAD usage still is more common. Increasingly, the effectiveness of 3D usage will be more obvious in all aspects of design processes in years to come.

Table 10.6 shows the effect of 3D CAD implementation in terms of (1) number of development processes, (2) number of design changes, (3) development time, and (4) total cost changes. The base line is 100% prior to the usage of CAD, and the ratio after CAD usage is assessed.

TABLE 10.6

The Effect of CAD Implementation

Development Process (%)	Design Process (%)	Development Time (%)	Total Cost (%)
100→102.0	100→74.7	100→60.0	100→92.9

Although some firms reported a decrease in their development processes, most of the firms reported an increase from 100 to 102.0 in the number of development processes after 3D CAD usage. The impact of 3D CAD usage is shown in the increased number of processes through (1) realization of front loading, (2) effect of division of labor by concurrent engineering, and (3) development process changes. In the 2000s, many firms effectively use 3D, and yet some firms (with a lack of organizational capabilities) instead increase the number of processes with 3D usage.

Increase in the actual number of processes suggests that, although the simplification of processes through 3D usage is attained, many firms still use 2D drawings as well (Park et al., 2007a). Some firms experienced a double work volume increase for design engineers with the adoption of 3D CAD when they did not change their organizational process capabilities (e.g., routines, functional roles, work processes, and design rules). However, when they improved the above mentioned organizational capabilities, they were able to reduce the number of work processes. Even so, many firms still use 2D drawings after their adoption of 3D CAD because of a lack of check measures for acceptance evaluation and other relevant measures for prototypes. This might be the reason for an increase in the number of processes with the adoption of 3D CAD.

With the adoption of 3D CAD, the number of design changes and development time is substantially reduced. The average reduction in design changes is more than 30%, and development time is also reduced by 40%. These reductions are mainly due to the time reduction in prototype preparation. However, this progress in design changes and the improvement of development time have not resulted in a substantial total cost reduction. This indicates that maximization of the effect of 3D CAD requires an overall reduction in the number of total processes through process redesign and internal organizational capability enhancement. Firms (with or without their improvement of organizational process capabilities) make huge differences based on the extent that they can reap the benefits of 3D CAD usage. This suggests that successful implementation of new technologies (e.g., 3D) must include a corresponding improvement of organizational capabilities.

10.5 CONCLUSION

Our research findings suggest interesting managerial implications. First, the high level of product development capabilities of Japanese electronics firms needs a better strategic business orientation. The integral architecture of high-functional digital cameras and handsets indicates that Japanese firms make significant efforts in applying innovative product development. Their commitment to outstanding product development (notice that they used to sustain competitive advantage in the 1990s) is clear and strong. The problem is that their high level of product development capabilities is not necessarily translated into global competitiveness. A critical issue is their pursuit of excessive product quality in the 2000s without responding to the global market requirements.

Compared to Korean handset (mobile phone) manufacturing firms, their Japanese counterparts are not inferior in terms of technologies (Park et al., 2008b). In fact, Japanese technologies in camera modules and component parts are much superior. Yet, except for Sony Ericsson, no Japanese electronics firms are global market players. Instead, Japanese firms pursue excessive product quality for their domestic market needs without resolving global communication methods and standardization issues. They have narrowly focused on the Japanese domestic market with the slogan "one model for 500,000." In the meantime, they have somehow failed to adapt to the changing global market reality. For example, in the European global system for mobile communications (GSM) segment that covers 80% of its global market, most customers do not demand high-functional handsets; rather they expect appropriate functionality for business. In reality, Nokia and Samsung have successfully focused on rapid product development and design-based product strategy. However, Japanese firms have been slow to respond to global market demands while directing their attention to domestic customer requirements in terms of diverse entertainment and leisure features. Their longer product development time and high cost somehow have not been so appealing to global customers.

Second, a firm's organizational process capabilities affect the extent to which the benefits of 3D implementation are experienced. 3D usage may improve front loading and concurrent engineering and therefore enhance product development capabilities. Full realization of 3D technologies requires a corresponding application of organizational process capabilities. This should include process innovation of the entire organization (Park et al., 2007a). 3D technologies are related to all organizational processes. Without an organizational structure that integrates all product development processes, 3D technologies become merely a process tool. Without proper organizational process innovation, the net results of heavy IT investment and CAD technology adoption are no more than the mere increase of work processes.

In this sense, building organizational process capabilities is becoming more important for sustainable competitive advantage in the context of strategic fit and IT system implementation (e.g., adoption of 3D CAD technologies). This study also addresses the current state of Japanese electronics firms and the realistic possibility for their competitive advantages. This requires their adoption of strategic product development priorities that tend toward design excellence through integral product architecture and organizational process capabilities. In this context, the successful adoption of 3D technologies is a realistic option for the enhancement of design excellence and organizational process capabilities leading them toward long-term global prominence again.

11

IT Usage Strategy of Korean Firms: Case Studies of Mobile Display Manufacturers

Many firms in today's business environment utilize diverse information systems to sustain their competitive advantages. However, too often the return on investment for information technologies is not as obvious as expected. This is particularly true with many small and medium enterprises. This chapter presents a research model and examines how mobile display manufacturers implement their information systems for the enhancement of supply chain performance. For the purpose of this research, we involve two firms and consider critical success factors of their information integration practices. One successful firm links its existing database to new information systems and aligns its information system for the larger requirements of supply chains. Another firm possesses different organizational capabilities and accordingly shows poor outcomes. Based on extensive interviews with the IT executives, supply chain professionals, and IT vendors within the supply chain network of these two firms, we present our findings. Lessons and implications are discussed.

11.1 INTRODUCTION

Modern manufacturing firms operate in very challenging circumstances. Sustainable competitive advantage requires more than applying efficient mass production methods or securing an adequate market share. The global competitive landscape continues to force firms to devise faster responses to the changing market demands. In this context, increasingly firms adopt product life cycle management (PLM) and supply chain management (SCM). With the application of PLM, firms try to meet comprehensive customer requirements with complex product features through flexible innovative capabilities (Garwood, 2006). Through PLM, firms aim to achieve business successes from the standpoint of the entire product life cycle (i.e., birth, growth, maturity, and termination). On the other hand, through SCM, firms deal with continuous value flows (i.e., information, product, and cash) from the perspective of the supply chain value network. In this sense, supply chain management (SCM) shares a real similarity with PLM in terms of goals, processes, and outcomes. For both PLM and SCM, it is critical to maintain an integrative database with component parts suppliers, production facilities, distribution, and customers.

An example of a complex manufacturing database is the bill of materials (BOM). The BOM is essential for manufacturing management. The BOM is the information chain pathways for assembling the components of a certain product, which defines the fine details of fulfilling customer orders and design specifications that involve the functions of sourcing, manufacturing, and maintenance. Deploying the right products that meet changing customer needs is a key for the firm's competitiveness. Thus, it is critical for firms to manage demand chain through the use of a well-designed product database that facilitates effective information flows about changing customer needs (de Treville et al., 2004; Walters, 2008). A successful fulfillment of complex customer requirements at the right time requires the design and use of an integrative database. The real challenge is how to integrate manufacturing-related BOM with management-oriented databases.

In fact, many firms fail to meet the changing customer requirements because of the inadequate integration between manufacturing databases and other functional databases. Product database management (PDM) may involve a huge investment, and yet its effect is too often disappointing. One global firm successfully implemented PDM by integrating the diverse IT systems including marketing information (product development information), concept information (functional information), design information (technology information), and production information (supplier production network information). Such complex information system integration allows the firm to achieve faster product development and sustain global competitiveness (Park et al., 2007a). In response to global SCM requirements, firms build global ERP (enterprise resource planning) along with diverse SCM systems. As a way of meeting changing customer requirements, firms choose APS (advanced planning and scheduling system), which is more advanced than the past MRP system. Such an innovative IT system will work only if an effective integration with other functional system databases occurs. In fact, massive IT investment does not necessarily generate tangible business results. In view of these findings, the key assumptions of this study are (1) effective IT system integration is critical for desirable business outcomes, and (2) IT integration effectiveness indicates the firm's organizational capabilities. For the examination of the above assumptions, this study presents a comparative analysis of mobile display manufacturers in respect to their IT organizational utilization capabilities.

11.2 LITERATURE REVIEW

11.2.1 SCM and Database Integration Capability

Integrating the efforts of diverse players across the supply chain is an important research focus of supply chain management (Zhang et al., 2006; Park et al., 2007b). Suppliers and customers work as partners for the common objective of enhancing competitiveness and profitability for the whole supply chain network (Patterson et al., 2003). Because value creation in the supply chain depends on effective information flows, key success factors for a supply chain require strategically aligned interorganizational IS that achieves accurate demand forecasting and cost effective inventory management, transactional activities, and procurement processes (Whipple and Frankel, 2000; Gunasekaran and Ngai, 2004). Successful participation in e-marketplaces assumes that firms must integrate their internal and external supply chain activities through strategic and operational information sharing. Therefore, construction of an appropriate IT system is indispensable in the design and implementation of a SCM strategy (Park et al., 2007b). In particular, integrating databases is a prerequisite to the successful adoption of a new IT system. Without integration of all existing databases, a huge investment for a new IT system would be in vain. For example, the mere adoption of a 3D computer-aided design (CAD) system without the corresponding organizational innovation may not achieve desirable outcomes (Robertson and Allen, 1993; Tan and Vonderembse, 2006). The widening gap between the intended goals of the 3D CAD system investment and actual outcomes of its use is quite real in many organizations (Beatty, 1992; Park et al., 2007a). The underutilization or ineffective use of CAD is suggested as the primary reasons for such an undesirable performance gap (Buxey, 1990; Twigg et al., 1992; Robertson and Allen, 1993; Liker et al., 1995; Park et al., 2007a).

3D CAD-CAE also promises reduction in development time through front loading and smaller design changes with appropriate organizational capabilities (Thomke and Fujimoto, 2000; Fujimoto, 2004; Fujimoto and Nobeoka, 2006). Yet differences in organizational capabilities account for the huge outcome variations in IT system utilization. With the implementation of the same types of IT systems, the average product development time of Japanese auto manufacturers is no more than 18 months, while U.S. firms report the time for average new product development projects is more than 30 months (Fujimoto, 2006). In another study, the U.S. (Chrysler as an example) and European firms adopted 3D CAD three years earlier than Japanese firms, and the actual results show that Japanese firms are ahead in regard to virtual digital mockup (Fujimoto and Nobeoka, 2006). In the late 1990s, most U.S. firms adopted 3D CAD for the full design draft (100%) of component parts, while their Japanese counterparts did only 49% of component parts. Japanese firms were lagging behind U.S. firms in terms of IT technology adoption, yet their better operational performance suggests that it is critical for functional specialists to master organizational routines for innovative problem solutions (Park et al., 2007a). These findings indicate that the organizational capabilities matter in determining the outcomes of IT system implementation (e.g., CAD, ERP).

On the firm level we now consider a BOM database which covers all business processes (i.e., design, manufacturing, purchasing, and after services). The foundational database for product BOM consists of master BOM, design BOM (E-BOM), manufacturing BOM (M-BOM), purchasing BOM, and service BOM. Master BOM controls other functional BOM (i.e., E-BOM, M-BOM, purchasing BOM, service BOM). However, these BOMs and other related data may be stored in the form of local files. Therefore, they may not be standardized. In this case, even the most outstanding new IT system might not produce any desirable system outcomes. On the other hand, any firm that has built an integrative database may secure a better competitive position. For example, in Bentley, the scientific experiment tool maker, almost all production design was done by the cutting-edge technology veteran during 1960–1970. However, in the process of introducing new products, the firm processes more than 1,000 types of engineering change orders (ECOs) each year. Once, it experienced the loss of all of their data in a fire. Afterward, Bentley adopted an ERP system. For the implementation of this integrative system, all the key stakeholders within the firm gathered in a meeting room. Their implementation planning covered all business processes with the use of a unified BOM database. As a result, it achieved a rapid rate of business growth with the support of an integrative and unified database that is linked to marketing, sales, cataloguing, technological documents, design pattern files, and product databases (Garwood, 2006). A case like this suggests the strategic importance of integrative databases. This study explores the value of having an integrative database among diverse IT systems. Case studies illustrate that IT integrative effectiveness depends on organizational capabilities as well.

11.2.2 Research Model

For the purpose of this study we adopt the perspective of supply chain management. Figure 11.1 shows database integration capability. It describes the interrelationships that involve existing systems (ERP, MES [manufacturing execution system], and other systems), Meta Database, and advanced planning and scheduling (APS).

A new IT system (e.g., APS) utilizes the existing ERP, manufacturing execution system (MES), and other database systems and therefore enhances the total integrative data capabilities, which in turn expand the firm's organizational capabilities. In this study, we assume that the level

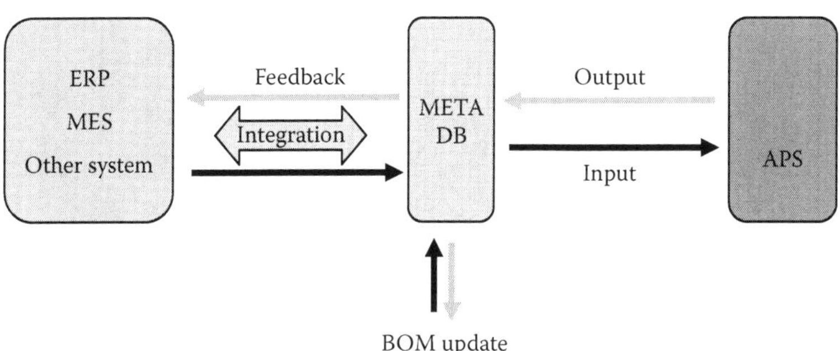

FIGURE 11.1
Research model.

of integration with the existing database (e.g., ERP, MES) may impact the outcomes of the newly adopted IT system.

11.3 CASE STUDIES

This study examines the cases of the adoption of an advanced planning and scheduling (APS) system by Mobile Display Manufacturers. We compare the experiences of two organizations (Firm A and Firm B) in terms of their database integration capabilities.

11.3.1 Case A

Firm A had the following management goals in the environment of a fluctuating market demand, intense display production, and price competition: (1) immediate response to customer orders, (2) strength of automation of production planning, (3) optimization of production schedules, (4) efficient utilization of resources, (5) reduction in lead time, (6) cycle time reduction, (7) improvement of delivery reliability, and (8) inventory reduction. For the accomplishment of the above goals, it was important to link their MES system and production scheduling. By adopting these systems, the management anticipated the systemization of production planning, productive utilization of limited resources, flexible responses to changes, and cost minimization.

TABLE 11.1

Adopted Plant

Factory	Shop	# of Product Lines	# of Production Processes (MES based)	# of Work Groups (ERP based)	Comments
• Domestic factory	• Array • Cell • Module	• 3 line • 3 line • 6 line	• Around 100	• 25 • 10 • 10	Sacrifice of process that becomes basis of production
Overseas factory	Module Array, cell→building plan				

Table 11.1 shows two kinds of factories: domestic and overseas. It also shows the different types of shops (array, cell, and module), number of production lines, production processes, work units, and comments. Specifically, the firm planned to adopt an APS system in its Array Process 3 Line (AP3L), Cell Process 3 Line (CP3L), and Module Process 6 Line (MP6L) in its domestic plants.

In this section, we first introduce the mobile display production process, which is a critical component for the successful IT adoption of Firm A. The basic production processes include the array process, cell process, and module process. The array process includes the transistor board and CF board. In the cell process, panels are made using a combination of transistor boards and CF boards. In the module process, other supportive component parts are added. Figures 11.2, 11.3, and 11.4 show the details of all of these processes.

Figure 11.2 is the array process. It is the process of depositing transistors on glass substrate. It includes a deposition process, a photolithography process, and an etching process. Through these serial processes, transistors are arrayed in the right sequence on a glass substrate. It is a unique process and different from semiconductor processes, which use wafers instead of glass.

Figure 11.3 shows the cell process. A transistor is placed in the bottom layer, and a color filter is on the upper layer. As these two are attached in order, a spacer is used, and then these particular liquid-crystal display

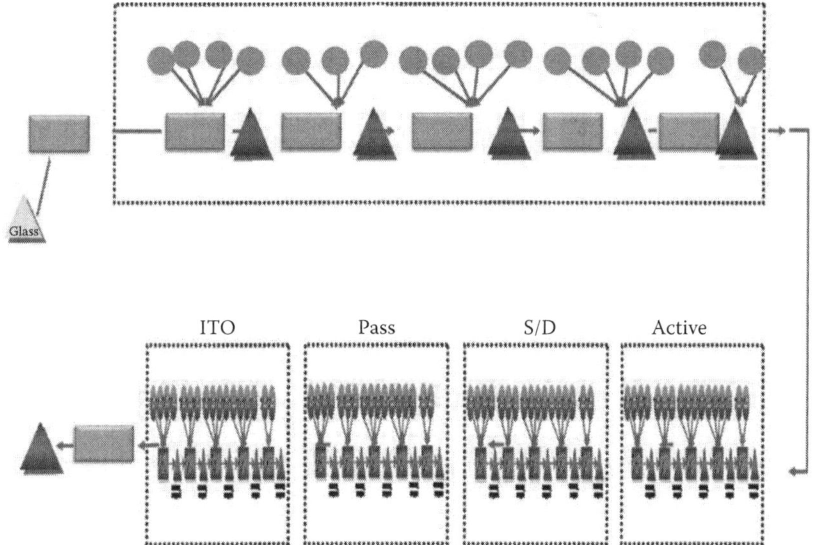

FIGURE 11.2
Array process.

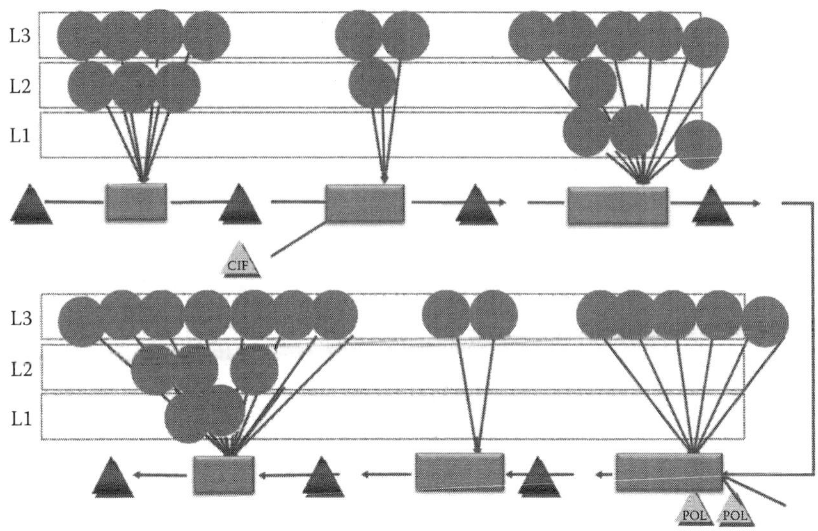

FIGURE 11.3
Cell processes.

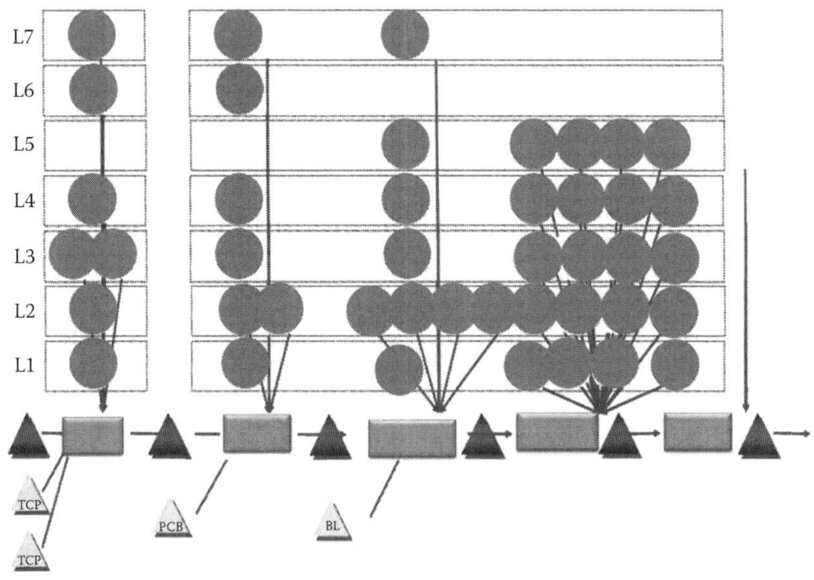

FIGURE 11.4
Module process.

(LCD) processes are completed with seal printing that requires liquid injection through the fine tunnels in between the two layers.

Figure 11.4 is the module process which determines the quality of products that are delivered to the customers. It is the process of attaching a polarizer to the panel which has passed through the cell process, and then including the driver-IC, assembling the printed circuit board (PCB), and finally completing the module process with the addition of the backlight unit.

The time frame of this IT introduction project is six months. The first step is to make production plans on a product line/shop level/daily basis. These are used in an automated pilot system that generates the production plans for two months within a few minutes. Then it provides the system proof-of-concept according to daily and process level in-out planning requirements. In this way, realistic plans for LCD production are prepared that reflect diverse facility and parts constraints (Figure 11.5).

However, the newly introduced APS system produced scheduling by using a Meta database from an existing enterprise system. In the course of the system's introduction, the master database failed to integrate the core of all systems within the planned time frame of six months according to the vendor's requirement. The existing database (e.g., SAP, MES) was assumed to be reliable. In reality, the database was not integrated. The new system failed to generate credible production schedules with the use of inaccurate old data outputs. Later, it was discovered that the heart of these problems was the failure of the manufacturing director. With continuous interfunctional conflicts and political pressures, the manufacturing director was unable to involve other functional directors to integrate other specialized databases (e.g., product design information, purchasing, marketing, accounting, and finance information). Thus, this wonderful project did

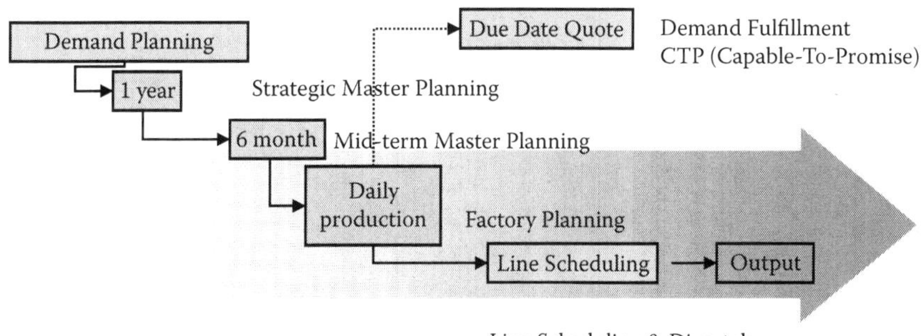

FIGURE 11.5
Building project according to SCM processes.

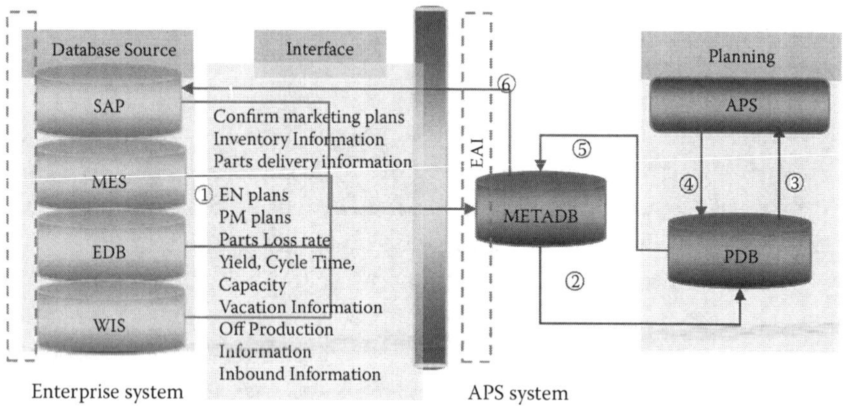

FIGURE 11.6
Integration issues with ERP database.

not produce the intended desirable results in spite of the vendors' serious launching efforts (Figure 11.6).

11.3.2 Case B

Firm B is also a mobile display manufacturer. It implemented the assembly of display products in its overseas plant in China. Just like Firm A, Firm B also experienced frequent changes in production plans because of the fluid market environment.

To overcome these problems, Firm B adopted an APS system for six months, starting from February of 2008 (Figure 11.7). However, it successfully completed the project two months earlier than planned. Firm B built flexible production methods by implementing daily deadline checks, daily production orders, and efficient production schedules and by reducing the number of changes in planning and its ratio. The outcomes of this system introduction showed drastic improvement in production planning.

Figure 11.8 indicates a vast improvement in terms of the firm's fixed plan ratio. In regard to the 80% target for fixed plan ratio (FPL), the actual performance outcomes are, on average, 68.8% just after the introduction of the above mentioned project. The plan adjust ratio (PAR) is currently at 19.2% (average) compared to the target ratio of 10%. In view of the past planning ratio changes (more than up to 80% of planning adjustment), it is certainly an outstanding success.

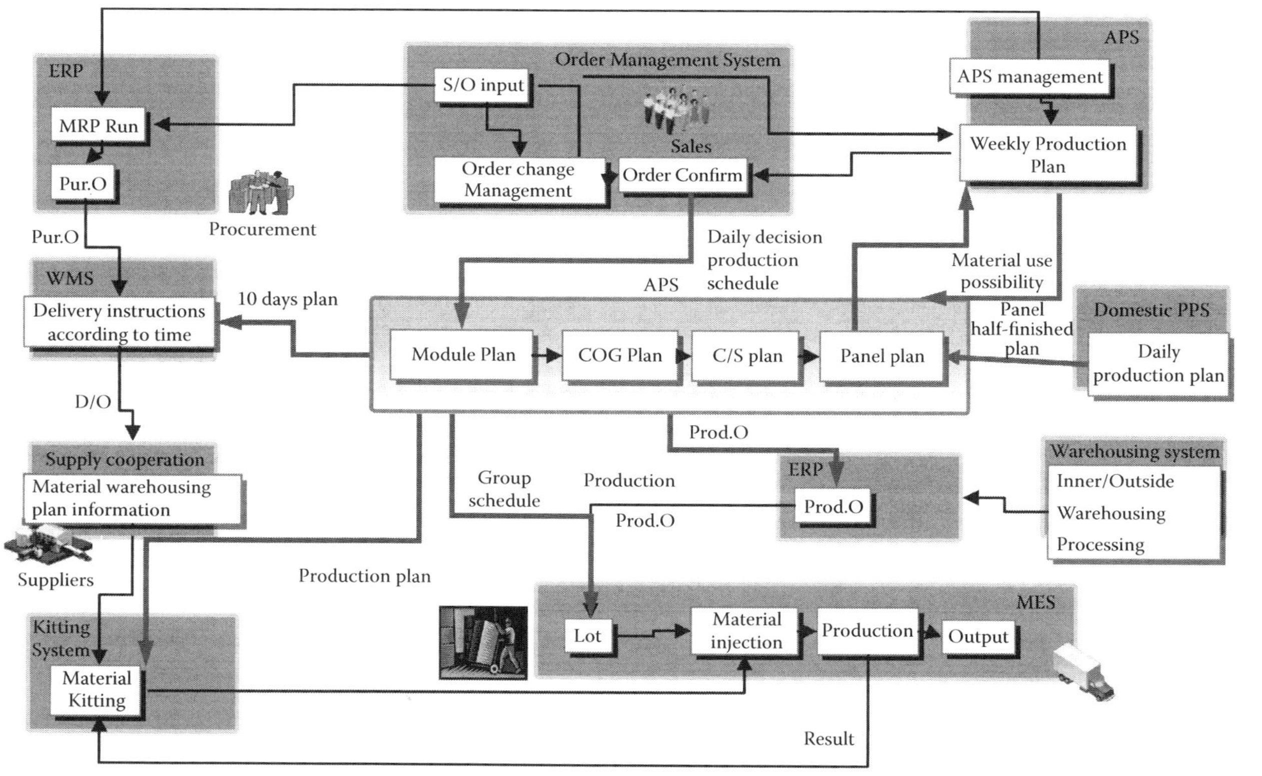

FIGURE 11.7
Basic database system and newly adapted APS system.

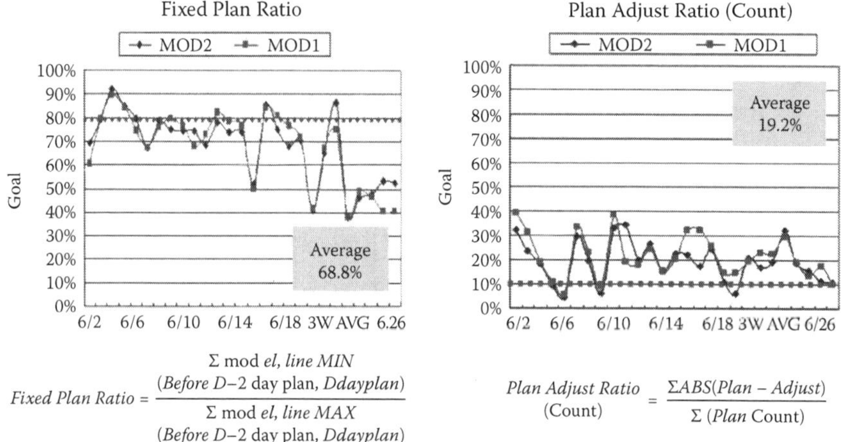

FIGURE 11.8
Outcome of IT system introduction.

11.4 DISCUSSION

The above comparative analysis of two mobile display firms suggests how an existing database is integrated with a new IT system. Firms can achieve greater IT utilization outcomes through integrating diverse system databases. Then why is it so challenging for many firms to integrate their database systems? Our case studies show that many firms fail to integrate their database for a few obvious reasons.

First, successful database integration requires a corresponding level of IT investment. The cases discussed in this study report the integration effects of the old IT systems on new APS system introduction. Our recommendation to Firm A (in view of its failure to produce desirable results) is, "Complete the efforts of integrating the existing database systems." This requires additional IT investment for the construction of a unified database system. Such a high level of investment requires substantial resources of the firm. The successful data integration of Samsung Electronics, a Korean global firm, is possible with its huge investment capabilities.

Second, organizational capabilities are essential for effective database integration. In addition to an appropriate level of IT investment, the management leadership needs to exercise a strong decision making influence. For example, Korean and Japanese organizational structures and management leadership show noticeable differences. Compared to Korean firms, many Japanese firms lack strong management leadership.

Besides, the walls between diverse business units are too high to achieve cross-functional integration. Korean firms accomplish database integration of their IT systems through effective top-down decision making. On the other hand, Japanese firms that focus on the efficiency of users do not accomplish the integration across organizational units. It is possible to attain IT system and database integration if firms are willing to exercise serious disciplined leadership to achieve the effectiveness of the entire organization. This organizational leadership challenge is what Japanese firms need to meet in order to accomplish desirable IT utilization outcomes and global competitive advantages.

12

IT Usage Strategy of Japanese Firms: Product Life Cycle Management for the Global Market

In this rapidly changing business environment, Japanese firms have put much emphasis on effective product life cycle management (PLM) for sustainable competitive advantage in the global market. In this chapter we present a research model of product life cycle management that depicts the essential elements of PLM in terms of processes and outcomes. Four selected case studies of large Japanese firms examine the business practices that support their global market strategy through specific PLM practices, which include data exchanges, design knowledge management, supplier integration, and BOM (bill of materials) design. These case studies suggest that PLM practices are differently implemented according to strategic focus, product, and market characteristics. Lessons from the case studies are discussed as well.

12.1 INTRODUCTION

With the advancement of information technology and the expansion of the global market, firms experience intense competition along with growing business opportunities. Rapid product development is a critical strategic priority for outstanding firms to sustain their competitive advantages. In this global business context, a drastic reduction in product life cycles is expected. For example, CIM Data shows the growing trend of shorter product life cycles. Recently more than 90% of all products are being developed and introduced to the market within a five-year period, compared to 55% of all products in 1986 and 74% of all products in 1998. A survey of Japanese electronics firms also indicates that the development time for most electronic products is less than one year. The product cycles of mobile phones and digital cameras are no more than six months, due to the wide application of modular product architecture.

In this rapidly changing business environment, Japanese firms have put much emphasis on effective product life cycle management (PLM). In fact, many large Japanese firms have adopted a PLM system to manage in both strategic and systematic ways. Japanese firms increasingly integrate PLM in their *monozukuri* (i.e., Japanese unique manufacturing system advantages). It is essential for leading Japanese firms to coordinate their domestic R & D and product development functions with their overseas counterparts in the form of globally integrated PLM.

In view of the coordination needs for global product development and commercialization, we explore three specific research questions: (1) What are the effective ways to expand global R & D functions? (2) How does the management ensure effective communication in diverse cultural settings of business? (3) How do firms integrate design and engineering databases to achieve complex customer requirements? The following literature review section suggests that the answers to these questions lie in product life cycle management. In this study we present a research model of product life cycle management that depicts three essential elements of PLM: (1) meeting the challenges of global R & D, (2) effective communication in the diverse cultural settings of business, and (3) design and engineering for effective global collaboration. Four selected case studies of large Japanese firms examine the business practices that support their global market strategy through specific PLM practices, which include data exchanges, design knowledge management, supplier integration, and BOM (bill of materials) design. These case studies suggest that PLM practices are differently implemented according to strategic focus, product, and market characteristics. Concluding remarks summarize the lessons from these case studies.

12.2 LITERATURE REVIEW

12.2.1 Global Issues of Product Life Cycle Management

Product and process design have been examined from a multitude of perspectives, not only from the perspectives of engineering, manufacturing, marketing, and industrial design, but also from the perspective of the integration of some or all of these functions. These cross-functional perspectives have led to various approaches (i.e. design for manufacturing [DFM], agile enterprise, concurrent engineering, value engineering, design for assembly [DFA], product data management [PDM], product life cycle management [PLM], and many others) (Bordoloi and Guerrero, 2008). In this study, we focus on the strategic approaches of PDM and PLM (Alemanni et al., 2008; Rachuri et al., 2008; Le Duigou et al., 2009).

For the purpose of this chapter, we use a working definition of PLM as "A strategic business approach that applies a consistent set of innovative solutions in support of the collaborative creation and management of an organization's product-related information across the extended enterprises from its initial conception to the end of life" (Amann, 2002; Le Duigou et al., 2009; Park, et al., 2009c). This concept makes it possible for planning departments to access information directly from a design department and to suggest modifications, thus shortening the product development cycle beyond one successful cycle of product development and commercialization (Schuh et al., 2008). The PLM concept is gaining greater acceptance with the emerging globally networked firms. These PLM firms are quite different from the market or hierarchy-based organizations that use a transactions cost model as the basis of their organizational structure (Rachuri et al., 2008).

In this study, we examine the following four aspects of global PLM—particularly the effective flows of design data, design information, and knowledge components across organizational and national borders.

First, PLM emphasizes integration of suppliers in the global market by vastly improving the information flows of project management, product development, and engineering processes (Ebert and Man, 2008). The automotive OEM has adopted supplier integration into its complex product development processes (Tang and Qian, 2008). The PLM system explores innovative ways to support the collaboration and partnership management between the automotive OEM and associated suppliers. The application of modularity in collaborative product development is to improve product R & D quality, development productivity, and mass customization. The PLM integration framework is related to the unusual convergence of three important developments (Ming et al., 2008): (1) standardizing of product- and meta-data models, and streamlining the engineering and business processes; (2) emerging service-oriented architecture for sharing information; and (3) implementing robust communication middleware across organizational boundaries. These flexible modular software pieces are reconfigured according to the changing business conditions. In the subsequent section, Case A explores how effective information flows are achieved for product development processes that include suppliers in the global market.

Second, PLM builds on the strengths of knowledge management. As the nature of the work of enterprises is becoming more knowledge intensive, the integration of complex knowledge systems becomes a huge challenge (Huang and Diao, 2008). Significantly large numbers of knowledge requirements, widely scattered application systems, and heterogeneous design automation systems all make it difficult to manage and maintain a flexible integrated system for PLM. The Alcatel-Lucent case study shows how challenging it is to achieve the effective integration of engineering processes, tools, and people on the basis of knowledge-centric product life cycle management (Ebert and Man, 2008).

Diverse organizations (e.g., contractors, suppliers, partners, and customers) operate with different business architectures and organizational structures. The challenges of PLM are how to identify and integrate different information systems and support activities related to product development (Kemmerer, 1999; Alemanni et al., 2008). Furthermore, timely assessments of the changing requirements of global customers and effective incorporation of this information into the design and manufacturing processes of new products and services are essential aspects of PLM (Elgh, 2008). Such PLM supports product-centric business solutions and unifies product life cycle through online sharing of product knowledge and business applications (Sudarsan et al., 2005; Ming et al., 2008). In the case study section, Case B illustrates how different information systems are integrated for effective knowledge and business applications.

Third, today's global firms require new technologies to address increasingly complex product development processes in satisfying the high expectations of customers. Computer-supported collaborative design (CSCD) has emerged in response to these dynamic requirements (Shen et al., 2008). Project management information systems have also supported the entire life cycle of projects, project programs, and project portfolios (Elgh, 2008). PLM systems support the management of a portfolio of products, processes, and services throughout the development processes, including initial concept, design, engineering, launch, production, delivery, use, and final disposal. Thus, the scope of global collaboration includes the motivation of the design and deployment of PLM, integration of business and technical information systems, and the creation and delivery of innovative products throughout the entire product value chain among various players, internal and external to the enterprise (Ming et al., 2008; Srinivasan, 2009). Case C examines how new technologies are used to meet the requirements of PLM.

Fourth, it is essential for engineers to have timely access and to understand a variety of information resources in carrying out a high level of design work (Giess et al., 2008; Hong et al., 2005; Doll et al., 2010). PLM engages the creation, storage, and retrieval of data, information, and knowledge throughout the life cycle of a product (i.e., from its concept and inception to its final disposal and recovery) (Wognum and Trappey, 2008). For the integration of global data, the BOM is a critical component of the product life cycle. It lists the subassemblies, intermediate parts, and raw materials that go into a parent assembly (Goel and Chen, 2008). Manufacturing activities associated with the BOM include material resource planning, inventory control, and production scheduling. Any problem in the BOM may cascade down through subsequent processes and cause cost overruns and delays in shipment. The requisition team worked on designs for the GE Wind 2003–2004 production run. With delay-causing problems in their BOM, more than 150 engineering change requests (ECR) were generated during this period (Goel and Chen, 2008). In this way, a reliable BOM process is essential for global product life cycle integration. Case D explores the issues related to BOM processes for PLM implementation.

12.2.2 A Research Framework

This section presents the business context of Japanese firms and the PLM research framework. Since the early 2000s, Japanese firms have rapidly expanded their R & D investment in East Asian countries.

Figure 12.1 presents a research framework which shows four areas of strategic business process priorities (A, B, C, D) which are product architecture construction, design process improvement, global operations improvement, and global BOM construction.

These four strategic business process priorities recognize numerous challenging issues that include complexity of problem solving, information leaks, work sharing problem, modularity, reduction of nonvalued workload requirements, and integration of BOM production basis. The macromanagement challenges, microbusiness problems, and global production issues also impact the nature of these strategic business process priorities (ABCD). Based on this research framework, the focus of this study is to examine Japanese PLM practices in the global context. Specifically, we explore specific practices on: (1) global market access through product module design and global data exchanges, (2) design engineer workload reduction through design knowledge management, (3) global operation management through supplier integration, and (4) design of a global BOM.

12.3 CASE STUDIES

Table 12.1 shows the plans for establishing R & D centers in Japan and the Asian region. The drivers of such investment plans are: (1) collaboration with the local production factories, (2) quick response to the changes in local markets and customer requirements, and (3) ease of securing competent local engineers.

With such rapid expansion of R & D centers for growing global markets, it is quite challenging for firms to integrate design information. Faster production development accelerates the rate of accumulation of product development information. Management of design information is critical for R & D centers. Global competitiveness assumes the integration of both domestic and overseas suppliers. Therefore, a study of bill of materials (BOM) management requires practice details on how the huge amount of design information is to be made easily accessible to functional specialists in product planning, design, purchasing, manufacturing, and marketing.

In the following section, four cases are selected to address four specific issues: (1) Case A illustrates how effective information flows are achieved

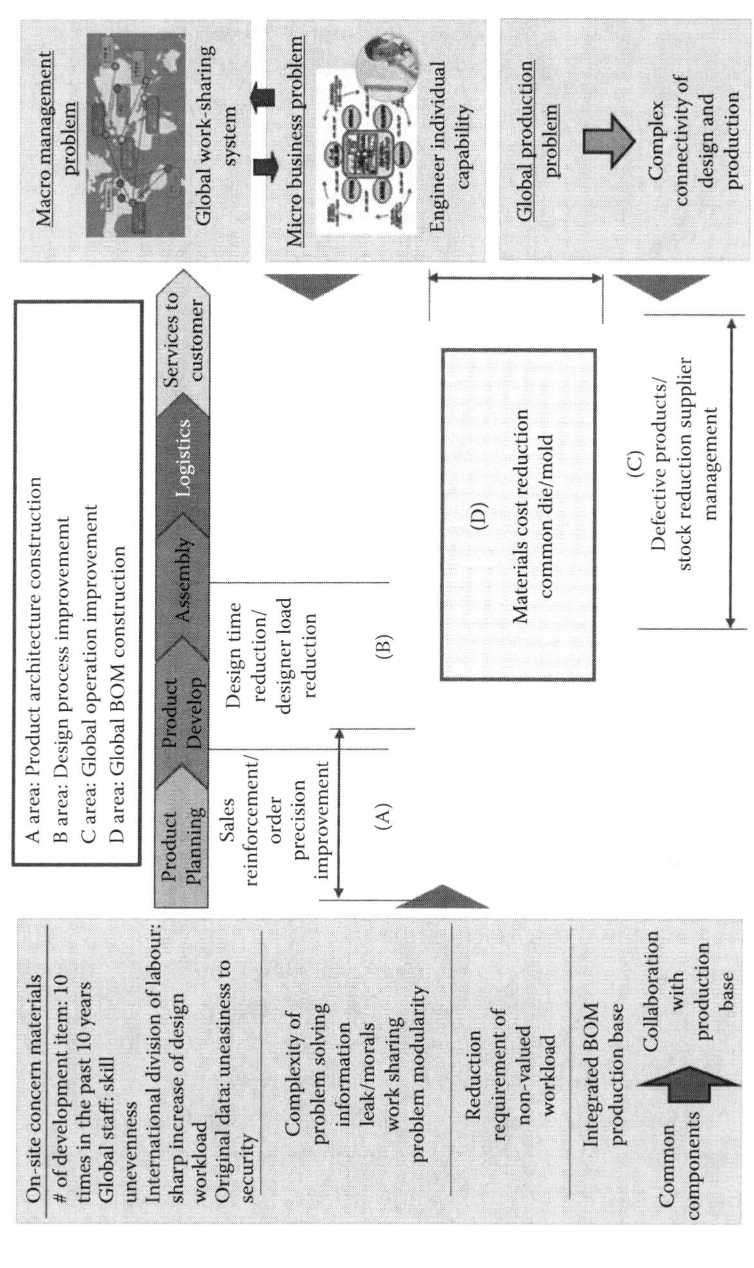

FIGURE 12.1
Research framework.

TABLE 12.1

Growth Rates on Planned R & D Centers of Japanese Firms (in Next 5 Years)

	Growth Rate on Future Planned R & D Center for Japanese Firms (in Next 5 Years)	
	For Local Market	**For Global Market**
Japan	-7%	0%
China	51%	76%
NIEs	42%	133%
ASEAN4	27%	71%

Source: Park et al., 2009c.

for product development processes that include suppliers in the global market; (2) Case B shows how different information systems are integrated to bring about effective knowledge and business applications; (3) Case C examines how new technologies are used to meet the requirements of PLM; (4) Case D explores the issues related to BOM processes for PLM implementation.

12.3.1 Case A

12.3.1.1 Conversion of Product Architecture in Response to Global Marketing

In the past, Firm A did not seriously apply their manufacturing and marketing methods to improve short-term delivery issues; instead, their production was based on forecasting of customer demands, and therefore they usually carried a high level of inventory of goods. Specifically, because Firm A manufactured machineries in advance and kept them as inventories in anticipation of customer demands, the increasing level of the long-term and short-term inventory of machinery (for domestic and overseas sales) was a real management concern. The four months of delivery cycle unnecessarily extended design and production up to the point of order receipts. The reduction of delivery time from four months to two months would start production after a few weeks of order receipts and lower the required inventory level as well. In the past, the forecast volume of machineries was substantially different from the actual customer orders. Besides, the integral product architecture made the product pattern changes and component reconfigurations quite difficult. Usually big losses occurred in the environment of such process challenges, which required constant relocking and rerunning even after reconfiguration.

To resolve these inventory problems, Firm A adopted a specific reduction target for delivery time by two months. For the 35% reduction of inventories (work in progress and component parts), Firm A decided to move their product design and production toward modularity. Figure 12.2 shows the evolution of product architecture from integral to modular. In this way, the interdependence between parts was becoming simplified.

Firm A carefully defined product structures and common components (base parts) to make pattern changes easier. Thus, in modular product architecture, design changes required fewer reconfigurations and the tasks became easier to handle. Table 12.2 is a summary of the comparison of Firm A's past and emerging product structures. This change of architecture did not immediately reduce the number of components, production methods, and production volume. The next section discusses the results

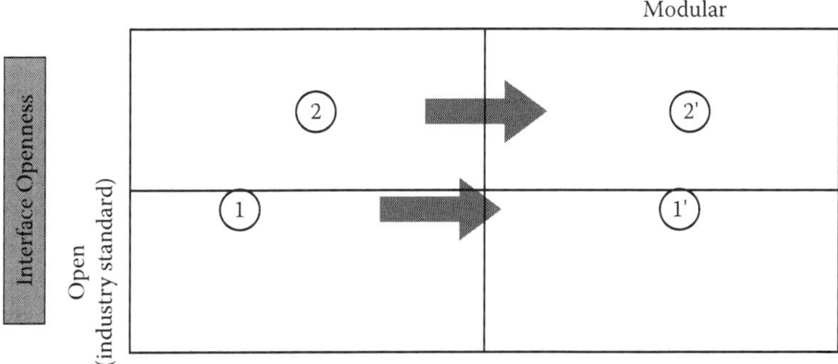

FIGURE 12.2
Changes from Integral to modular product architecture.

TABLE 12.2

Comparison of Firm A's Past and Emerging Product Structures

Product Classification	Industrial Machinery
Production methods	Forecast production
Production volumes	300 per year
Product patterns	Many
Past product architecture	Integral
Emerging product architecture	Integral + modular
Number of components	About 10,000 components

of changing product architecture from integral to a mixture of integral and modular.

12.3.1.2 The Results of Changing Product Architecture

Figure 12.3 shows Firm A's process toward modularity. In the past, the three components were interrelated, and therefore the distinction between the optional, variant, and common components was not so obvious.

This change of the product architecture from integral to modular enabled Firm A to convert its mixed product system that contained complex interrelated components (i.e., specific, optional, variant, and common) into a simplified building block system. By changing variant components into common ones, Firm A drastically reduced the number and the level of component parts. By simplifying a high specification base to common patterns, the reduction level of parts and mixed modules (i.e., common component + variance component) was 10% and 71%, respectively. Through using the building block model, delivery time was reduced to two months as well. Figure 12.4 shows that, with the change of product architecture, the component structure was becoming simpler, clearer, and easier from the design, production, and delivery standpoints.

Table 12.3 is the summary of project management outcomes. In the past (under integral product structure), the number of assembly steps was 24. In the new outcomes (under modular + integral), the total assembly steps were 16 (decrease by 8). Besides, more tasks were classified as easy (3 to 10), there were fewer difficult tasks (12 to 6), and tasks that were not feasible disappeared entirely (9 to 0).

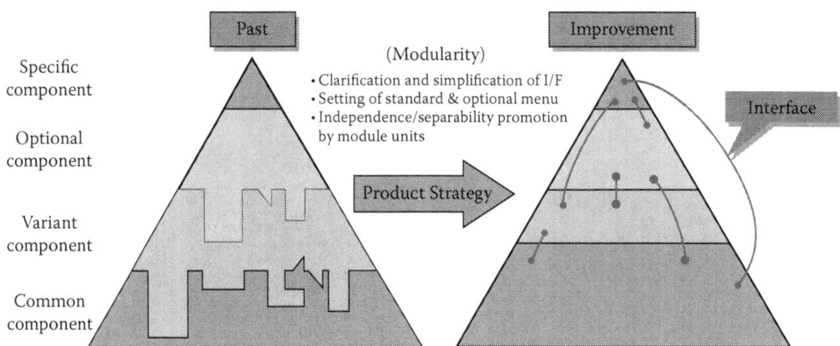

FIGURE 12.3
Firm A's process toward modularity.

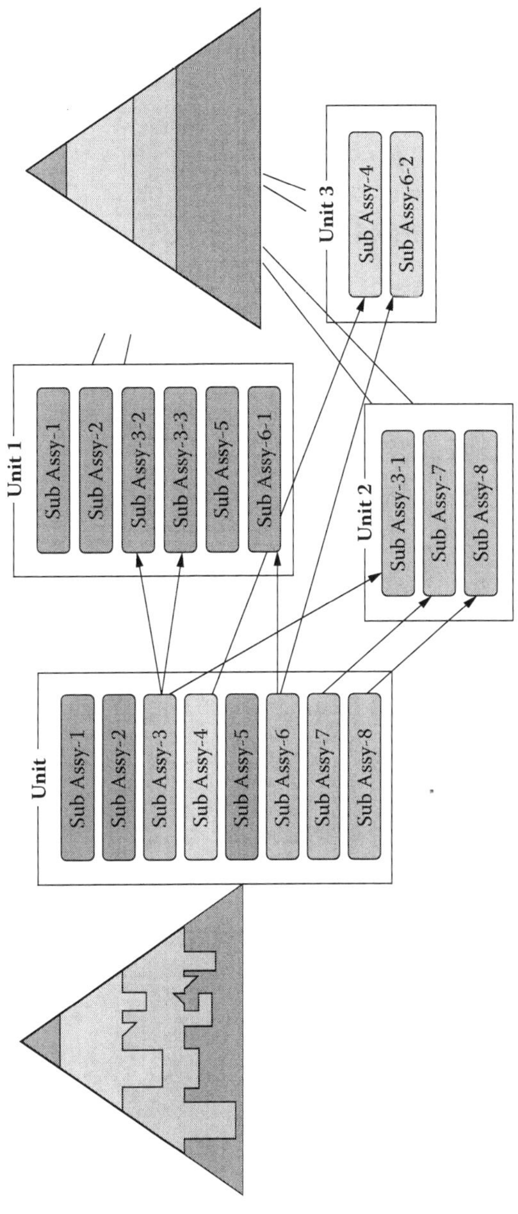

FIGURE 12.4
From duplicate component structure to redefinition by building blocks.

12.3.2 Case B

12.3.2.1 Adoption of a Design Navigation System

Company B is an automotive manufacturing firm. In 2007, it adopted PLM for the product and process development of engine components. The purpose of PLM is to improve product development processes (e.g., quality and productivity) and to reduce time for engine development. Specifically, it is to build up data management for engine parts and achieve a lean production system, and implement visualization know-how and design process improvement with a design navigation system.

The goals of this project are to (1) maximize process improvement through modeling simulation and (2) achieve design cycle time reduction through better design methods.

Figure 12.5 shows past waste design processes prior to the implementation of PLM. The three waste design processes involve design, production

TABLE 12.3

Project Management Outcomes

Task Difficulty	Past Outcomes	New Outcomes
Easy (o)	3	10
Difficult (Δ)	12	6
Not Feasible (×)	9	0
Assembly Total	24	16

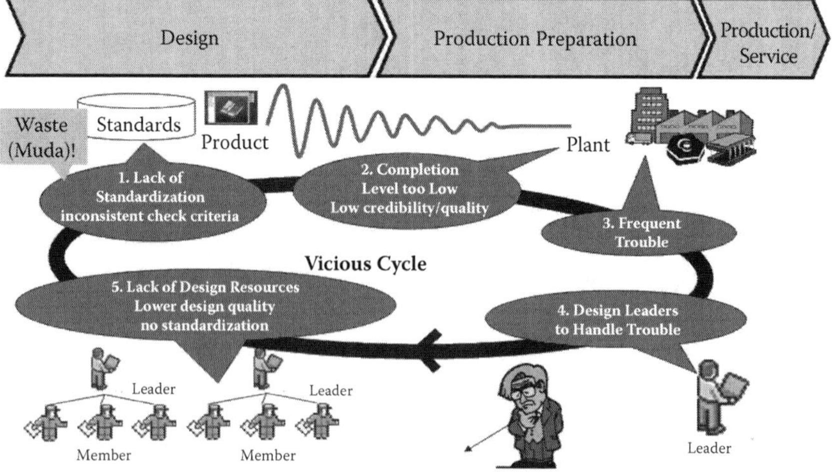

FIGURE 12.5
Past waste design process.

preparation, and production service. Inefficient wastes occur because of five reasons: (1) lack of standardization with inconsistent check and inspection criteria for products; (2) too low a level of completion and therefore low credibility and quality levels in the plant; (3) frequent troubles and shutdowns in the plant; (4) design leaders are expected to handle troubles for which they have little understanding of the process details; and (5) lack of design resources with lower design quality and no real reliable standardization criteria. The combined effects of the above mentioned five socio-technical issues perpetuate the system with unresolved vicious cycles of wastes.

Figure 12.6 is the system mechanism of design NAVI (embedded know-how into the process) through which recycling of knowledge is being accomplished. The process layer defines each task by specific details (e.g., instruction, input, reference, and output). Instead of a vicious cycle of wastes, the new system process recycles knowledge. A dataset generated from a business process is organized by the appropriate data layer. Then, at the needed time, these datasets produce approved current data and current notice of information to create relevant knowledge (including management tips and other technical details). This extracted knowledge is further creating credible reference knowledge. Such recycling of

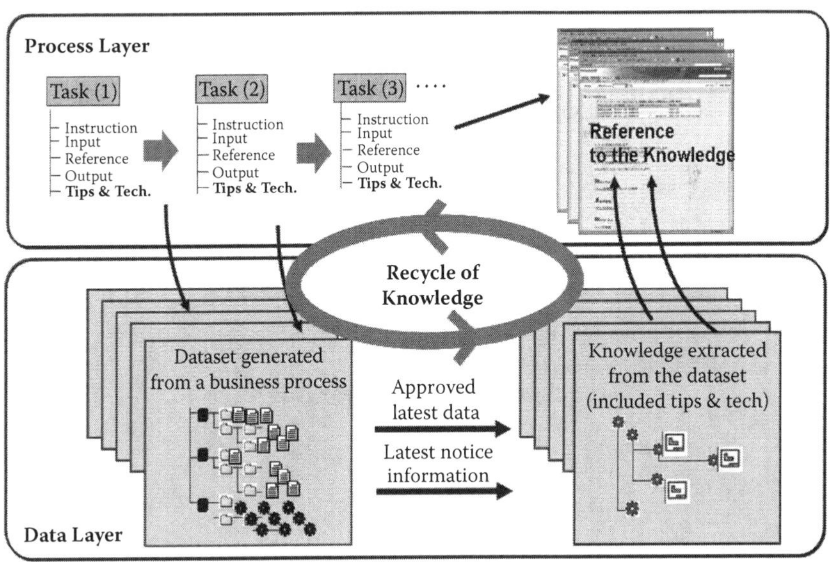

FIGURE 12.6
System mechanism of design NAVI (embedded know-how process).

knowledge continues to improve process efficiencies and to attain waste reduction by providing a healthy business cycle.

12.3.2.2 System Adoption Results

After the adoption of the new system, the outcome measures are quite obvious: (1) realization of unneeded work reduction by 25%, (2) time required for search to collect information reduced by 30%, (3) time for meetings/reporting sessions to communicate information improved by 20%, (4) design time reduced by 25% by reusing design information and knowledge, (5) substantial enhancement of process productivity of handling issues of greater than 20%.

Figure 12.7 shows how this healthy business process works. The process of design, production preparation, and production services remains the same. However, the workflow cycles show sound business practices in the form of (1) rich standards, (2) knowledge-leveraged design, (3) improved and standardized quality, (4) solve issues and challenges early in the plant level, (5) effective information feedback for design and manufacturing standards, (6) development of people through improved member and leader relationships, and (7) finding issues early with progress management.

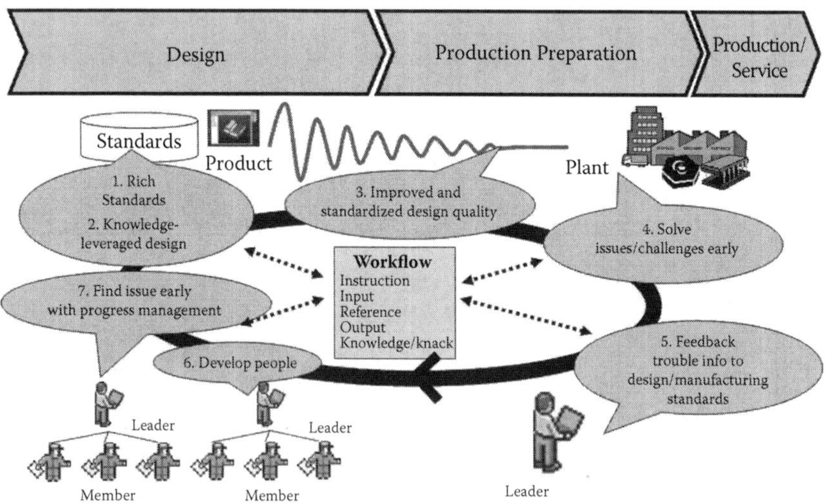

FIGURE 12.7
Healthy business cycle after implementing a design NAVI system (lean product development process).

12.3.3 Case C

12.3.3.1 Design Localization for Local Product

Firm C pursued design localization for the integration of domestic and overseas production development efforts. Prior to the localization efforts, some of the limitations were obvious. (1) It was not possible to deliver the most recent domestic design data to the overseas R & D center; (2) the updated overseas design data was not available to the domestic center; (3) the changes in domestic base patterns were not immediately translated for the overseas branch patterns; (4) overseas designers used the previous design data because they were not allowed to check the most updated design data; (5) in spite of frequent access to the telephone, e-mail, CD, and FTP sites, the revision status of overseas development design data was not usually confirmed, and therefore no effective design review was possible based on the overseas design data; (6) there was little communication from overseas designers in the form of reports, inquiry, or any discussions in regard to the project status and overseas project members.

Figure 12.8 is the model of Firm C's global collaboration environment. The firm defines its strategic priority of building a global collaboration development environment that involves Japanese, Chinese, and Latin American design centers. The key functions of these centers are to provide (1) check-in and check-out functions; (2) access, resume, speed, and assembly management functions; and (3) examination and communication functions. Two specific implementation goals are (1) to build design

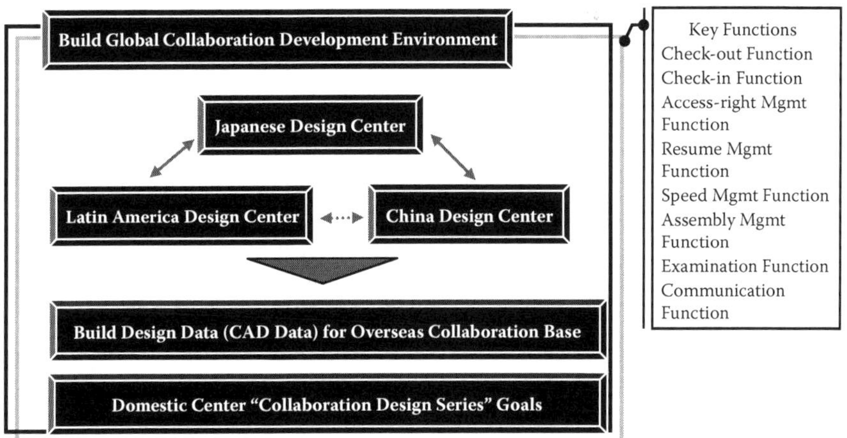

FIGURE 12.8
A model for building a global collaboration environment.

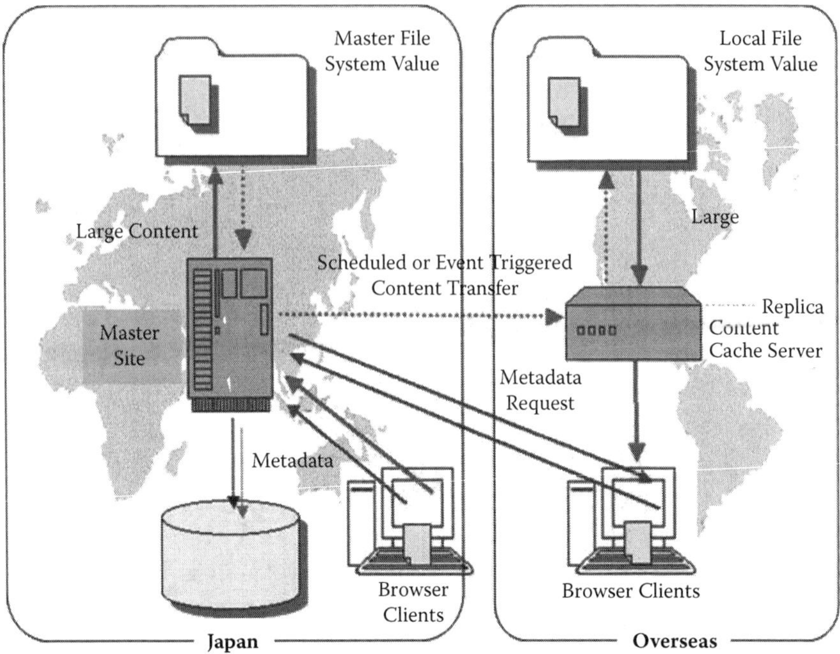

FIGURE 12.9
Conceptual diagram for Japanese and overseas systems integration.

data (CAD data) for overseas collaboration and (2) to clarify domestic center "collaboration design series" goals.

Figure 12.9 is the conceptual diagram for Japanese and overseas systems integration. This details how the Japanese design center and overseas design centers communicate. The Japanese design center is positioned as the master site that maintains the master file system, supports the overseas local sites, and provides relevant data for the local file system. The file transfer either occurs in a scheduled/planned manner or is triggered by a content request in response to situations, events, or needs. Because browser clients are located throughout the world, they may access data through the master site in Japan. In this way, both Japanese and local research centers collaborate in the form of intra- and interorganizational data access and a client browser system.

12.3.3.2 Results of Adoption

Firm C could resolve all the above design data exchange by centralizing design data management with a new global integration system.

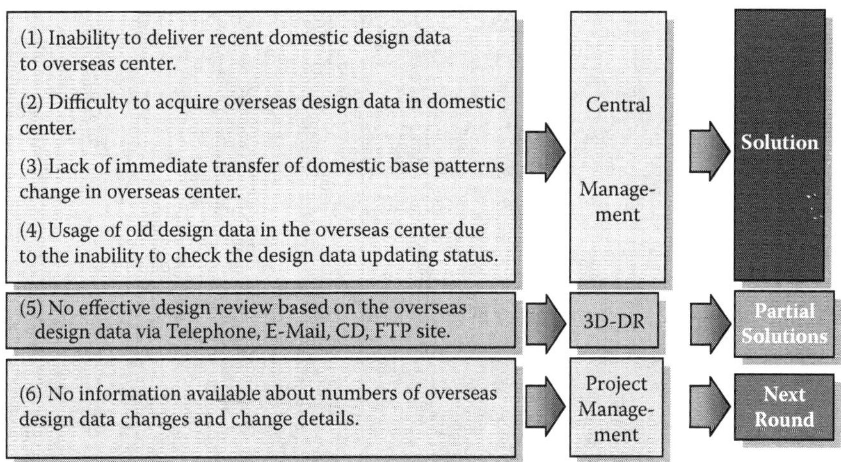

FIGURE 12.10
Adoption results.

Figure 12.10 is a summary of the adoption results. The first column is a list of problems identified before the PLM project adoption. The second column contains the practices of central and local design centers. The third solution column shows how problems are specifically resolved. However, the information sharing issue of (5) via telephone, e-mail, CD, or FTP site was partly resolved through the usage of 3D-design review (3D-DR). Other issues (e.g., determining the number of design data revisions and the names of change agents) were not resolvable, and therefore the project was extended to the next round. These results suggest that the goals of the Japanese firm's global development integration are not necessarily easily and quickly attainable.

12.3.4 Case D

12.3.4.1 Global BOM (Bill of Materials)

Prior to 2000, Firm D focused on internal product development and successfully built diverse infrastructures including a BOM system. However, with the lack of a collaborative development environment (through interorganizational information sharing) and poor integration between development design and production, it did not effectively meet its customer requirements. For example, the development system did not fit the task environment in terms of consistency and reliability. The diverse systems from development and production were mostly autonomous, and therefore total system effectiveness was fairly low. Development design did not support global response needs. The existing organizational structure and system would not be able to accomplish reduction in production development time either. Thus, each business unit independently pursued IT innovation and system improvement. The duplication of efforts was common, and the overall project productivity did not support the goals of its business strategy.

Figure 12.11 is the conceptual model of collaborative product development (CPD). This shows how the Internet and intranet support both the front end and back end needs of data, information, and knowledge. The model of this newly built system has some important features: (1) In the system front end products of Firm D, users may have access to information about when, where, and whom to access through CPD that connects and integrates diversely located systems (e.g., intra-Web server, Note-CAD server, legacy system like BOM, CRM, MR) without being conscious of the system in the Web. The new PLM system unified E-BOM (engineering bill of materials) and M-BOM (manufacturing bill of materials) through global CPD (collaborative product development).

This figure also suggests that by building a PLM system (including design process innovation) this firm could implement the specific strategic priority of "bottom line enhancement through cost structure innovation" and accomplish overall cost reduction targets. As the result of completing such systems, the firm no longer depends on the BOM legacy system which was developed internally in the past.

12.3.4.2 Outcomes of Implementation

Firm D defined concrete targets that would accurately measure such process innovation outcomes. The examples of such targets include (1) 20% development cost reduction, (2) elimination of one-third of the undesirable development expenses, and (3) increase of soft development project numbers by 30%. Specific real outcome results after the completion of the systems are reductions in (1) development time by one-third, (2) prototype preparation time by three months, and (3) study flows by 30%.

As a part of its globalization policy, the firm also developed a product development environment that allows access to information at anytime, anywhere, and to anyone through strategic IT services for total customer satisfaction. In this way, the firm achieved joint development with Chinese firms, smooth production transfers, and efficient global procurements.

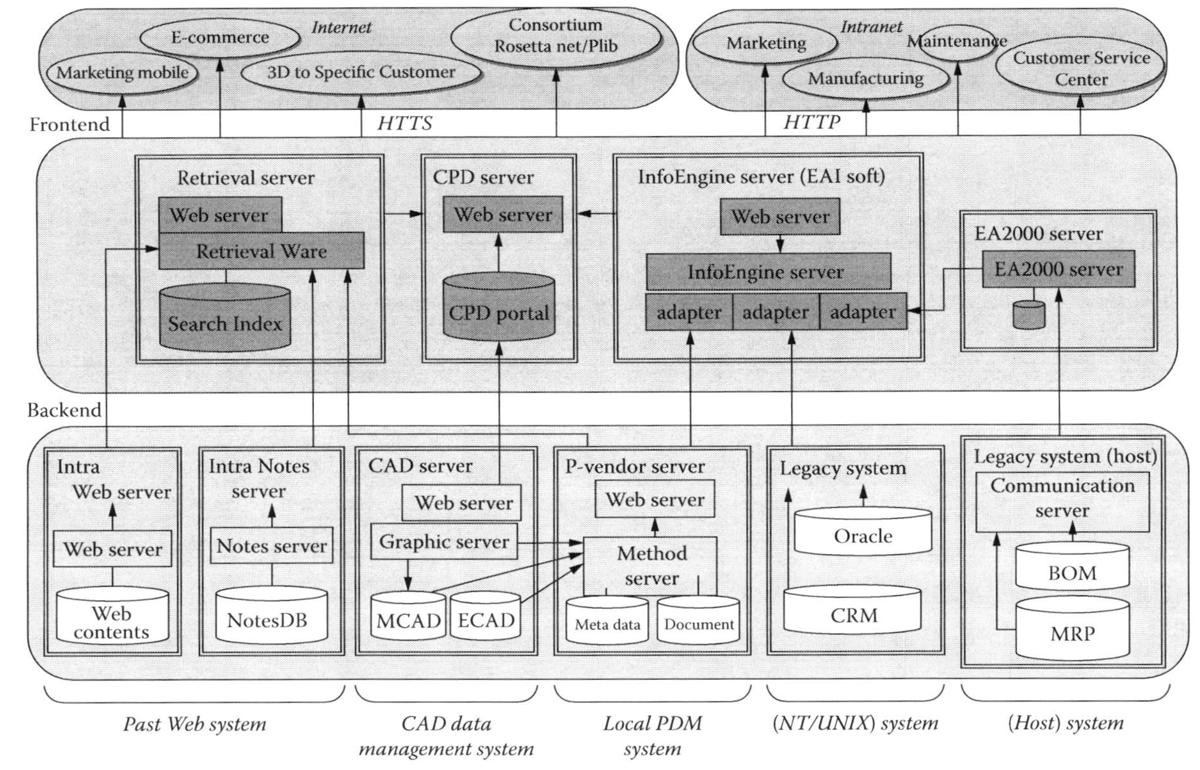

FIGURE 12.11
A model of CPD (collaborative product development).

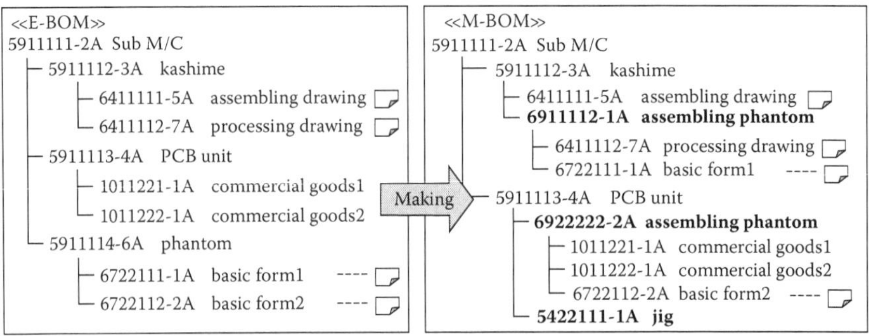

FIGURE 12.12
Process changes from E-BOM to M-BOM.

Besides, each business unit is allowed to determine the desirable level of security, English response codes, standardization of component masters, and integration of component structures. Figure 12.12 shows the changes of E-BOM to M-BOM. The new system reflects changes in the BOM system—E-BOM to M-BOM. The useful design (e.g., M-BOM) is not feasible for branch model construction. Naturally, with the old system it used to experience long delays or occasional mistakes in times of construction. However, in the new system, the useful designs of E-BOM include functions of M-BOM compatible to manufacturing processes.

12.4 CONCLUSION

In this study, we examined PLM issues of Japanese firms with four cases which examined (1) global market access through product module design and global data exchanges, (2) design engineer workload reduction through design knowledge management, (3) global operation management through supplier integration, and (4) global BOM (bill of materials) design.

This study focuses on examples of successful PLM integration of Japanese firms, particularly Toyota's *Oobeya* ("big conference room") approach, which requires "all-related-members" affected by or contributing to the project to participate for attaining creativity, innovative problem solving, and outstanding results. Therefore, front-end automotive product development (front loading) is much more effective than its American counterparts (Fujimoto and Nobeoka, 2006). From the standpoint of product architecture, Japanese firms have a development environment that is more fitting to integral architecture than modular architecture (Fujimoto, 2003). Therefore, Firm A shows some level of success in changing the previous integral product architecture to modular architecture. Most Japanese firms are somewhat weak in this area. More weaknesses are obvious from the standpoint of global BOM integration. In Japan, the distance between components is fairly large; therefore, it is not easy to integrate whole business organizations. Electronic products with unique elements of product characteristics are not easy to integrate with other nonelectronic products. Therefore, integration issues for diverse design information data invite additional challenges for Japanese firms. However, as shown in the Japanese automotive industry, the integration between assemblers and suppliers is well accomplished. Based on these successful experiences, firms need to experiment in different industries. What is obvious from this study is that global collaboration (between domestic and overseas) involves strategic priorities for building PLM. Successful formulation and implementation of PLM should focus on identifying critical problems and adopting innovative problem solving in the context of complex global supply chains. As global firms wrestle with these complex sets of issues, more researchers and practitioners find PLM as quite relevant and useful for practical solutions.

In brief, the research model and case studies presented in this study suggest the dynamic nature of product life cycle management for a global market which requires concerted efforts and due diligence to evaluate one's internal capabilities with interorganizational collaboration in the rapidly changing market environment. The findings of this study are based on interviews with executives of four Japanese firms. The intent of this study is not to present a general model for product life cycle management practices. Instead, this study is intended to provide a useful insight on how to formulate and implement life cycle management with resource constraints. Future research would explore complex life cycle management challenges and opportunities in view of rapidly changing global market environments, suggest effective life cycle management practices in diverse business contexts based on more robust PLM models, and empirically test the key constructs and interrelationships.

13

Integrated Manufacturing and IT Strategy for Futuristic PLM: A Conceptual Framework from Japanese Firms

Different from traditional IT systems, a futuristic IT system requires fast utilization of design information in new product development according to customer value requirements. This chapter presents a conceptual framework of futuristic product life cycle management (PLM) from the standpoint of integrated manufacturing. This futuristic PLM model, in contrast to the traditional PLM model, translates customer values into product development and emphasizes the importance of integration of product design reflecting customer needs, design feedback, and management strategy. Three case studies illustrate the practical applications of this research framework. Managerial implications are discussed as well.

13.1 INTRODUCTION

Integrated manufacturing information system (IMIS) refers to effective utilization of IT systems that integrates all the functional processes including product concept, system and detail design, purchasing, production, marketing, logistics, and services. In a sense, IMIS is quite similar to PLM. Three aspects of IMIS are emphasized from the University of

Tokyo research team at Manufacturing Management Research Center (MMRC).

1. IMIS is a total system approach that integrates strategic management, production activities of manufacturing, production development processes, marketing, maintenance, and service activities.
2. IMIS includes a broad view of design information that encompasses production processes, product development activities, management, marketing, and maintenance/services.
3. The purpose of IMIS focuses on "competitive advantage based on customer value perspective."

Different from traditional IT systems, a futuristic IT system requires quick utilization of design information in new product development according to customer value requirements. For example, firms may use claim information from customers through a customer relationship management (CRM) system. Most of the IT system for PLM has focused on only design information for developing and manufacturing new products, including specifically quality assurance, cost reduction, effective design, production efficiency, standardization, data management, and product information management. However, futuristic IMIS (integrated manufacturing information system) emphasizes design information for customer value creation and delivery. Thus, IMIS pays more attention to incorporating customer-valued information to front-loading capability, which enhances the overall product development effectiveness. This paper presents a conceptual framework of futuristic PLM from the standpoint of integrated manufacturing (*monozukuri* in Japanese). It examines the IT system strategy that considers product architecture and front-loading capability (Ueno et al., 2007). Through case study of three Japanese firms, we further suggest a futuristic PLM model and its implications as well.

13.2 LITERATURE REVIEW

13.2.1 Past and Future of Product Life Cycle Management

From the Japanese perspective, it is important to consider the future of product life cycle management (PLM). In the global business environment, firms are required to fulfill diverse market requirements. For the purpose of this paper, our focus here is on Japanese firms.

First, recently many Japanese firms are losing their competitive advantage with the increasing deterioration of their profit levels (Chang, 2008; Shintaku and Amano, 2009). Although they produce new products with premium value, they are not necessarily connected to generate customer values and thus business growth. The heart of the issue is the gap between business strategies and design specifications—particularly with the lack of congruence among design engineers, management, and IT functions (Park et al., 2009b). The critical failures lie in the systematic gap between product development and IT system utilization.

Second, Japanese manufacturers experience troubles in integrating business strategy and technological capabilities (Park et al., 2008b; Itami, 2009; Park, 2009; Shintaku and Amano, 2009). Compared to Japanese businesses, Korean and Chinese firms are not necessarily better in their technological and product development capabilities. Yet, the difference in their market performance occurs in the ways business strategies are executed. Japanese firms do not have clear performance evaluation parameters that measure the management effectiveness through integration of *monozukuri* and IT systems. In this respect, it is critical to evaluate the comprehensive capabilities that integrate product architecture, business system, process technology, and design engineering-manufacturing-IT capabilities (Park et al., 2007a; Park et al., 2009b,c; Park et al., 2010b).

Third, key issues related to product development process need to be mentioned here. In front loading of product planning (prior to new product development process), it is critical to coordinate the key task processes such as customer needs identification, processes clarification, post-evaluation of product development, know-how accumulations, and standardizations (Tomke and Fujimoto, 2000; Fujimoto, 2003, 2006; Fujimoto and Nobeoka, 2006; Park et al., 2007a; Ueno et al., 2008).

Fourth, the issues of platform and modularity are to be considered. There are enormous challenges to implementing appropriate product architecture that is based on a platform/modular base that enhances customer values. The point is not merely to sell products like Apple and Google. Rather, it is to conduct comprehensive solutions businesses according to the customer needs (Christensen, 1997; Christensen et al., 2002).

Fifth, another real challenge is about design capabilities (Park et al., 2007a; Ueno et al., 2008). Thus, before making prototypes, it is critical to enhance digital prototype capability (i.e., simulation functionality). Compared to previous ones, new product development capability requires more design information for customer values.

Sixth, the scope of international division for new product development has been extended through globalization (Park et al., 2009c). Division and international cooperation among technology, new product development, design engineering, and manufacturing are not clearly defined; thus it remains unclear what particular aspects need to be globalized.

Seventh, we must not ignore supplier management through sharing design information (Park et al., 2009a). Supplier integration is increasingly critical for customer value creation and timely introduction of new products in keeping with market changes.

Eighth, manufacturing management capability is also important. With the continuing gaps between enterprise resource planning (ERP) and manufacturing information systems, too often improvement efforts in the manufacturing field are not properly communicated to senior management (Park, 2009).

Finally, we have to consider cost planning capability. The gap between design cost and production cost prevents the integration of cost design idea and managerial practices. Current Japanese manufacturing challenges require all the more new framework that separates from the existing PLM concept.

The PLM concept is gaining acceptance with the emergence of the globally networked firms in contrast to the market- or hierarchy-based organizations that use a transaction cost model as the cornerstone for the choices of organizational structure (Rachuri et al., 2008). Park et al. (2009c) suggested two aspects of global PLM—particularly the effective flows of design data, design information, and knowledge components across organizational and national borders. First, PLM emphasizes integration of suppliers and global market by vastly improving information flows of project management, product development, and engineering processes (Ebert and Man, 2008). Second, PLM has recently been recognized as a new strategic business model to support collaborative creation, management, dissemination, and use of product assets (e.g., data, information, knowledge) from concept to end of life by integrating people, processes, and technology across extended enterprises (Ming et al., 2008).

This study argues for a new PLM concept that reflects customer values in a timely manner. In general, the most important factor that determines the changing product and service values is the customer assessment. In the cases of failing to meet the functionality requirements of customers in the market, constraining contexts related to intellectual property appropriation, lock-in, asset specificity, and the challenges of coordinating interdependent investments, firms compete to make better products (Chandler, 1977; Klein et al., 1978; Williamson, 1979; Teece, 1986; Christensen et al., 2002). By using any available technologies, design engineers adopt integral architecture type products to make the most outstanding products that customers assess (Fine, 1998; Christensen et al., 2002; Nobeoka, 2006; Ueno et al., 2008). On the other hand, if firms offer products that exceed the functionality expectations of customers in the market, stiff cost-based competition arises due to the standardization requirements for the component parts. In such cases, firms tend to move toward modular types of products that emphasize the time-to-market requirements (i.e., speed, flexibility, and customization) to secure customer segments that value functionality of products according to their purchasing motives (Christensen, 1994; Christensen et al., 2002; Ueno et al., 2008). Thus, in view of the fact that product life cycles are determined in the market according to customer evaluations, the critical aspects of futuristic PLM are in connecting customer needs assessments into product planning and development.

13.2.2 A Framework of Futuristic PLM

For a long time "manufacturing system" (*monozukuri* system in Japanese context) has focused on design information for new product development and commercialization. This system encompasses all other business processes, including quality assurance, cost reduction, design productivity, production efficiency, standardization, data management, and product information management.

However, a future integrated manufacturing system focuses on more design information for customer value/business activities than others and explores such questions as "What are the products that the customer highly values?" "What are customer needs?" "How to determine the battle grounds for the new market penetration?" "What market would maximize profit potential?" "How to achieve competitive cost reductions?" "If it was possible to gain product market advantage in the past, why not now?" and "Was the product cost planning appropriate?" The

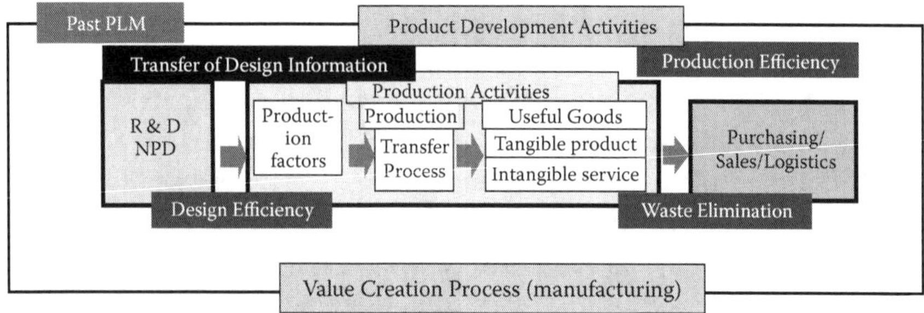

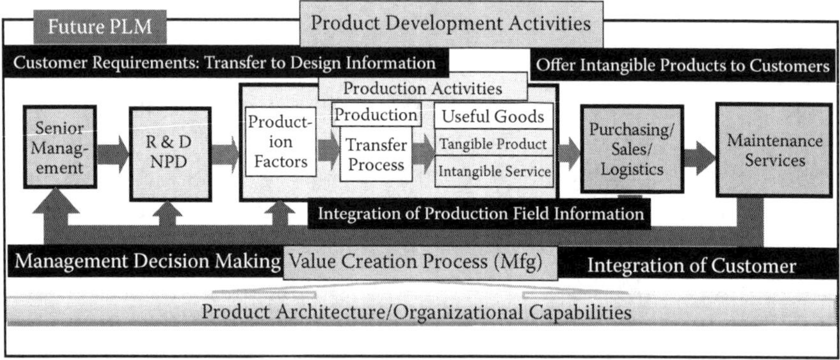

FIGURE 13.1
Research framework: Past PLM (top); future PLM (bottom).

clarity of design information is essential for creation and delivery of customer values through business processes. Thus, life cycle management from the customer perspective will be more and more important in harsh global competitive environments. This paper presents a futuristic PLM system from a customer perspective. This new system is to visualize the transfer processes of design information from customer needs based on the integrated standpoints of product architecture and organizational capabilities.

Figure 13.1B proposes a new futuristic PLM system that is somewhat different from the past PLM system (Figure 13.1A). The customer value feedback mechanism is denoted in red color. It is related to product planning, product design, and marketing management in contrast to the past PLM model. Based on such framework, in the next sections three cases highlight the product development processes.

13.3 CASE STUDIES

13.3.1 Case A

Firm A produces household electronic products, of which the video camera is the primary one. Here, our focus is video camera product development. From the product architecture standpoint, video cameras are open integral type. Therefore, most of the component parts are standardized, but because of miniature requirements integral architecture is applied for video camera development and production.

Let us consider the background of video camera development at Firm A. For new product development Firm A wrestled with the issue of self-contradiction in its product features. For example, for high-quality video recording the firm needs to install high-powered zoom functionality. Since its rival Sony succeeded with its "huge hit products," the industry was stuck with past product development practices instead of innovative new product development. Thus, it was not quite easy to develop a new model of products, which is the essence of new product development. Because the goals of product concept planner, designer, and end-user are not integrated enough, it is quite challenging to introduce new excellent marketable products. For these reasons, the firm was somewhat behind in its product development efforts compared to its rival firms, and the aim of core technology development was not easy to attain.

In this competitive context, Firm A established the following two objectives for product development. First, by strengthening the applied product development capability, it strives to take the number one position in the industry. To survive as the product development leader and manufacturer, its strategic intent is to focus on rapid new product development. Second, the firm moves toward securing a sustainable core advantage through the enhancement of its internal product development capability. The specific strategic initiatives include new product development efforts based on product design priority that goes beyond previous complacent and routine ways of utilizing market information and technology capability.

Figure 13.2 shows the product development processes of a video camera. For the business design axis, the business unit executive (BUE) takes full charge in the areas of product planning and marketing management. The BUE is also responsible to formulate and execute his business unit

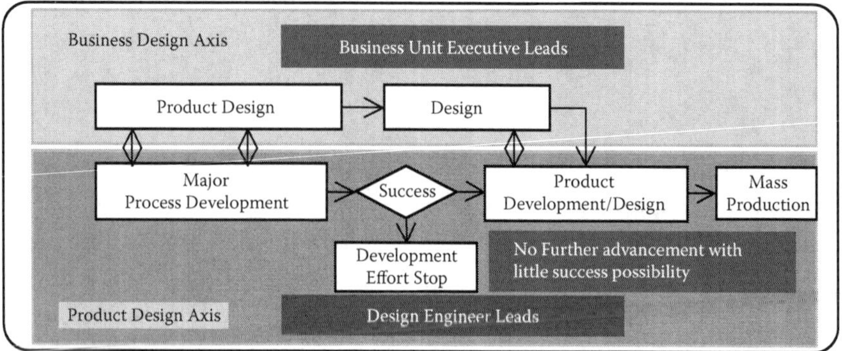

FIGURE 13.2
Firm A's product development process.

goals in terms of profit level and accordingly must manage product design planning, component parts purchasing, and production planning. In the product design axis, design engineers take charge of the overall business processes that integrate major process development, product development design, and mass production. In this way, the business unit executive and design engineer collaborate, with clearly defined responsibilities that cover all the relevant processes in integrative and systematic manners.

Now let us consider the two critical success factors of Firm A's video camera product development. First, to commercialize a new product idea with the cutting-edge technology, the firm set the decision space of the business unit executive (BUE). The BUE was able to study about a new technology that might be a seed for new product development and then implement a new idea through the commercialization project system, which even considers an initial low-market-success-probability idea. In addition, the design engineer determined core technologies as the base of product concept, which is connected to product development and design engineering and then a specific business plan. Second, through decision making space (DMS) and learning mechanism, the firm developed product development routines which can apply core technology to other products. Specifically, other design engineers also learn about the new mechanism that connects the new technology acquired through DMS to design engineering. By sharing core technologies (e.g., device technology and manufacturing technology) the firm continued to apply these technologies to other product development efforts. With the common structures that share product roadmaps and device roadmaps, Firm A accelerated product development time and thus secured new product development patterns which are quite different from its rivals.

13.3.2 Case B

Firm B is about the power train development case. From product architecture, the vehicle power train is a typical closed integral product type. Such development is done based on its original standards. Its life cycle is 10 to 15 years in the case of the power train platform and 30 years for engine parts.

The background of power train platform development suggests a few practical issues. Because the real development of a power train considers quality and cost after making the prototype of the power train, it was quite challenging to reduce the development time period. It was difficult to move the subsequent steps or to respond on functionality evaluation results. The power train is influenced by the competitors' patterns as well. Because the question is "how to surpass the competitors' design patterns," the firm has to change its product development planning (engine planning) if any competitor introduces high-performing engines in the market.

In this competitive context, Firm B focused on two points. First, it targeted on creating customer values through power train planning. It engaged in development plans by constantly benchmarking and comparing with the new products of its competitors with one consuming passion, "Surpass the rivals!" This was not about specification additions but customer value enhancement. For the purpose of using power trains for long term, it implemented power train platformization. Second, by strengthening digital development, it cultivated product development capability. By using digital prototypes based on 3D, it applied zero defect standards for performance evaluation.

Figure 13.3 shows the digital development process of Firm B. By applying digital development prior to vehicle development, this firm built a system that found innovative problem solutions through digital prototypes rather than actual prototypes. The firm removed various constraints (e.g., quality, delivery, and cost) through such digital connectivity, which covers diverse processes such as prototype unit development, prototype vehicle evaluation, power train development, and vehicle development.

The two success factors of Firm B's power train are as follows. First, the firm created a long-term power train according to the customer needs.

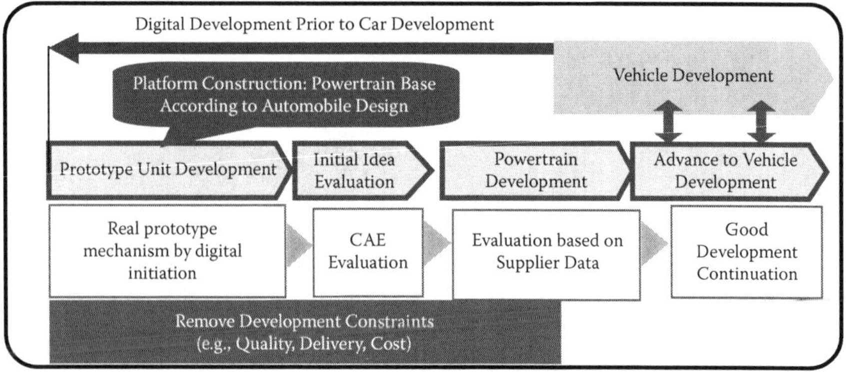

FIGURE 13.3
Firm B's digital product development processes.

Recently the global vehicle market has experienced intense competition, with changing market environment requirements (e.g., CO_2, lifestyle changes, fuel-efficiency and energy cost reduction, compact design). The firm was successful in overcoming these market requirements, by building a new power train platform based on new product concepts, and started power train planning based on the power train platform and managed its life cycle. Second, the firm devised a system mechanism in which design engineers utilized their maximum technological capabilities in the planning process stage. Specifically, the firm adopted a new development process that effectively uses 3D CAD (computer-aided design) and CAE (computer aided engineering) simulation. For example, Firm B constructed the system that 3D CAD incorporated the power train elements defined by sets of functions (i.e., technical knowledge). It also strengthened the coordinative relationships with its suppliers based on 3D data, by which design engineers engage in product development easily by applying common design rules. For the additional needs of design engineers the firm outsourced some parts of design tasks as well.

13.3.3 Case C

Firm C is in the housing industry. From the standpoint of product architecture, Firm C's products are closed modular architecture. In general, housing products adopt the closed integral type. However, Firm C entered this market somewhat late. Thus, it modularized the component processes just as with electronic products for an efficient production system. Since

Firm C's products are houses, the life cycle is about 40 to 50 years, which is fairly long compared to any other average products.

Firm C has constructed customer-oriented PLM for three reasons. First, with the drastic reduction in new housing market demand, there was a crowding-out effect in the house products supply. In recent years, demand for the new houses seriously declined. For this reason, it was not possible to continue this business based on the old 1990s' business model, and a new business model was needed instead. Second, with the changing market reality, the nature of demand also changed as well. The new demographic patterns (i.e., environmental concerns, reduction in younger population, and increase in older population) have resulted in the changes in demand curves. Third, the internal organizational improvement efforts have reached their limits. Operational improvement was not enough to generate a substantial sales increase. For example, every year the firm implemented new product development ideas with no real noticeable performance improvement in terms of sales increase. In this context, Firm C focused on developing customer-based PLM.

The development objectives of Firm C's customer-based PLM are, first, enhancement of PLM efficiency through the integration of all business processes from order receipt to maintenance. Specifically, it is to reduce contract- and delivery-time periods and improve cash flows and increase sales. With the implementation of modular processes, the assembly processes are much more simplified. Accordingly, Firm C achieved substantial reductions in total cost and time requirements. Furthermore, the firm endeavored to secure an adequate level of highly competent workers and financial resources. Second, in terms of internal operation the firm changed its focus into customer and end-user perspective and expanded a new market segment. The firm explored the new market opportunities (e.g., reform market, product repairs, maintenance, and services) based on field information.

Figure 13.4 presents the PLM process of Firm C. The first important process focused on the pursuit of modularity of the components, modular systemization in the initial design, and production preparation for new product development. Then, the firm incorporated this module systemization into real house order receipts and production processes. Furthermore, the integration efforts of diverse modules are rule-based and thus the order delivery time was drastically reduced. Finally, by modularizing after service and maintenance processes, the firm also constructed a customer information system from order receipts to final product delivery.

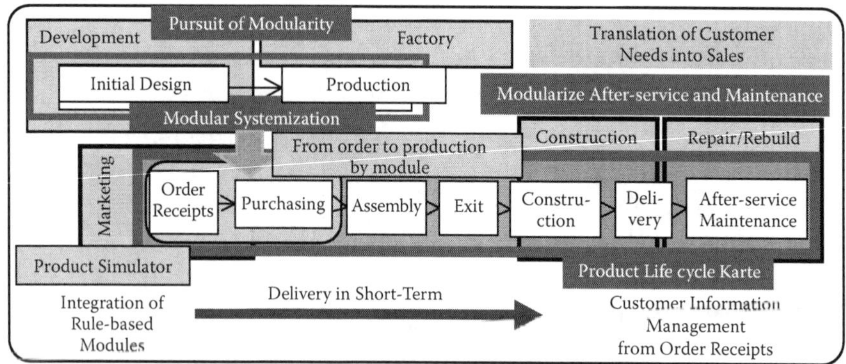

FIGURE 13.4
Firm C's product life cycle management processes.

Two success factors of Firm C's PLM processes are noteworthy. First, it made its structure conducive to IT investment for creating customer values. Specifically, (1) it pursued modular processes in business processes that cover from order receipts all the way to maintenance and thus achieved an efficient PLM based on customer values; (2) it constructed the system from product planning which incorporated systematic applications of rules that cover design, production, purchasing, and services product concept; (3) it utilized quality enhancement and a cost reduction system through reduction of contract and delivery time and realized module-based free design (e.g., marketing design for better customer responsiveness); and (4) for integration purposes, it incorporated PLM information (e.g., customer, maintenance, and design and trouble-shooting information) into management decision making.

Second, through after-maintenance modules it also expanded into a new growing market. From order receipts, it built life cycle *karte* that utilizes customer information that considers maintenance needs from the very beginning of order receipts and thus facilitated the house remodeling (reform) business by utilizing customer information and design information about the reform market.

13.4 DISCUSSION

This paper proposes a futuristic PLM model that may make a real impact in life cycle management in Japanese contexts. Based on this model, three case studies of Japanese firms illustrate the practical implications. The first case suggests the practical possibility to enhance applied product development capability. Senior management and business unit leaders need to constantly learn about new technologies that are essential for developing new products that are not available in the current market. To commercialize the new technologies, product development organizations (1) create forum space for CEO's decision making (core technology creation), (2) share the core technological information for the sake of incorporating core technology in product design, and (3) manage core technology in relation to product and device roadmap.

The second case provides an insight on how design engineers may exert the best possible technological competence in the product planning stage. To clear up the planning constraints such as delivery, quality, and cost, it is important to: (1) construct a digital development system that effectively utilizes platforms and 3D CAD/CAE simulations, (2) design a knowledge rule by which designers may flexibly develop products, and (3) consider outsourcing options that contract out some aspects of design tasks to overcome the shortage of qualified designers.

The third case is useful in understanding how to expand and develop new market segments in mature markets. In mature markets it is critical to create new customer values. Therefore, a few specific paths need to be carefully considered, such as (1) value chain efficiency through system integration of IT investment from order receipts to service delivery; (2) modularity of all the key processes including design, production, delivery, and service based on product concept and realizing free design based on modularity (i.e., enhancement of customer responsiveness through marketing design); (3) improvement of business model which forecasts market demands.

Development capabilities of Japanese firms are not inferior to those of world-class firms. From the perspective of front loading that determines the lead time in new product development, Japanese firms maintain a comparative advantage over those of the United States and Europe (Fujimoto, 2003; Fujimoto and Nobeoka, 2006). Yet the real challenge of many Japanese firms is the business reality that these outstanding new product development capabilities are not necessarily connected to customer values. A futuristic PLM model that connects customer needs and values into front-loading processes is the practical answer to the current Japanese business dilemma. Implementation of this new initiative requires fundamental changes in business and organizational processes. Yet such drastic change initiatives may result in adverse outcomes because of serious interfunctional conflicts and rivalry. To many organizations such measures might be too shocking for organizations to handle. This paper suggests practical alternatives of creating customer values by information integration through IT infrastructure (without involving external drastic organizational changes). This paper, through specific case studies, suggests futuristic PLM models, and yet IT system construction details need to be further described in another paper.

14

Conclusion

The final conclusion summarizes the key difference between Korean and Japanese firms in terms of their competitiveness. The critical difference lies in their selection of catch-up objects and timing. Japanese firms experienced catch-up in analog periods and thus utilized Japanese skilled workers for the enormous scope of process innovation. On the other hand, Korean firms engaged in catch-ups in the digital age and thus drastically shortened their learning cycle for product innovation and utilized IT system capability for their global market penetration.

For future research issues, the emerging challenges that Korean and Japanese firms face are mentioned as well. Both Japanese and Korean firms need to excel in ways that demonstrate their market leader capability to create and deliver products and services that meet the changing needs of customers in the ever-expanding global market. These customers continue to seek innovative, noble, and fantastic cultural and innovative values that fit their cultural, social, and technological norms and thus enhance what they define as the outstanding quality of life.

Particularly in the areas of product architecture framework, Japanese firms focused their strategic attention on closed integral industries (e.g., automobiles and electronics). At first, Japanese firms applied integral architecture for their electronic products, which are now manufactured by open modular product architecture. Korean firms thus were able to accomplish rapid catch-up for the open modular electronic products. Yet in the areas of products that use closed integral architecture, the product development patterns still use analog elements. In contrast, open modular architecture has very short product life cycle, and speed is quite critical in their product development. Korean firms constructed organizational and decision making processes that fit to this open modular and speed-based product and processes. This is what might explain how Korean firms have attained competitive advantage in the global market.

Japanese firms value technological capability–based strategy, while Korean firms focus on building brand value strategy based on open modular products (Figure 14.1). On the other hand, Korean firms build their competitive advantage by utilizing leadership styles and management systems that achieve a broad range of differentiation in terms of design, functionality by market segment and timely product introduction, and IT integration that facilitates effective global SCM strategy implementation. In other words, the Korean growth mechanism is characterized by rapid investment decision making and organizational execution capability through cross-functional integration of product planning, development, manufacturing, and marketing for global market expansion. Global learning effect is also achieved through an integrative information system that standardizes product development, manufacturing, marketing, and distribution.

Such phenomenal success is reflected in the modular architectural products with very short product life cycles. It is highly probable that even the current closed integral architectural products may evolve into more open modular architectural products. Global automobile manufacturers will

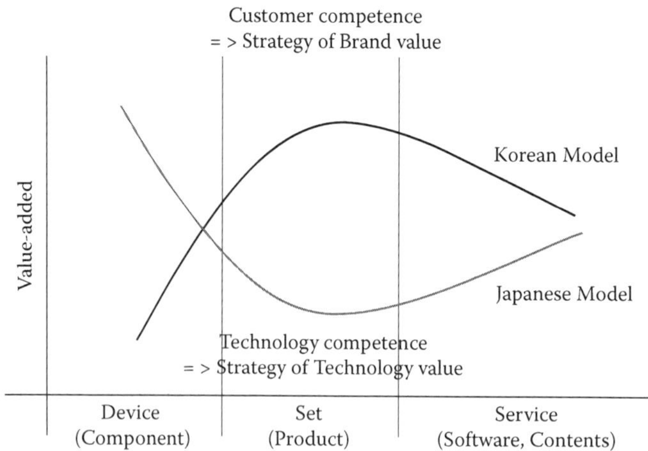

FIGURE 14.1
Comparison between Korean and Japanese competitiveness.

adopt more open modular architecture as they produce more electrical cars with rapid digitization in the innovation processes. In this case, it is critical to understand and respond with the rapid product development and delivery in the global scale according to the changing customer requirements. Such capability is a key for network capability.

A firm's core competencies are effective only when it integrates customer and technological core competence. The critical linkage of such integration of customer needs and technological capability is the essence of network capability management. The emerging customer needs are too often now so visible. Thus, the market leaders constantly recognize the unmet intangible customer needs. Many global firms fail in this aspect because they tend to focus on current successful products in the market. They too often lose the steadily appearing emerging opportunities. In the global market, particularly in rapidly expanding emerging markets, network capability is about such sensing ability of these growing market needs.

For future research issues, it is worth mentioning about the potential weaknesses of Korean firms as well. Different from U.S., European, and Japanese firms, long-term technological competence is not a particular strength of many Korean firms. Korean firms, like Japanese counterparts, do not have obvious advantage on software aspects of businesses, either. As the market environment moves toward more green-friendly environments, firms are expected to integrate hardware and software infrastructures for their content development systems. Korean and Japanese firms have attained integration of hardware and IT systems for business success. Yet software dimensions of business (i.e., cultural and emotional aspects of business and intangible customer needs) will become increasingly important. The continuing competitive challenge is thus how both Japanese and Korean firms excel in ways that demonstrate their market leader capability to create and deliver products and services that meet the changing needs of customers in the ever-expanding global market. These customers continue to seek innovative, noble, and fantastic cultural and innovative values that fit their cultural, social, and technological norms and thus enhance what they define as the outstanding quality of life.

References

Abe, M. 2006. "The Growth of Korean Handset Industry." In *IT industry of East Asia: Dynamics of Cooperation, Competition, and Coexistence*, (Eds.) K. Imai and M. Kawakami, pp. 17–53. Institute of Developing Economies (in Japanese).

Abernathy, W. J. 1978. *The Production Dilemma*. Johns Hopkins University Press.

Abernathy, W. J. and Clark, K. 1985. "Innovation Mapping the Winds of Creative Destruction." *Research Policy*, Vol. 14, pp. 3–22.

Abernathy, W. J. and Utterback, J. M. 1978. "Patterns of Industrial Innovation." *Technology Review*, Vol. 80, No. 7, pp. 40–47.

Akira, Y. 2006. A *Semiconductor Industry to Understand Well.* Japanese business publishing company. (In Japanese)

Alemanni, Marco, Grimaldi Alessia, Stefano Tornincasa, and Enrico Vezzetti. 2008. "Key Performance Indicators for PLM Benefits Evaluation: The Alcatel Alenia Space Case Study." *Computers in Industry*, Vol. 59, Issue 8, October, pp. 833–841.

Amann, K. 2002. "Product Lifecycle Management: Empowering the Future of Business." *CIM Data Inc.*

Amsden, Alice H. 1989. *Asia's Next Giants South Korea and Late Industrialization*, New York: Oxford University Press.

Amsden, A. H. 1990. "Third World Industrialization: Global Fordism or a New Model." *New Left Review*, Vol. 1, No.182 (July-August), pp. 5–31.

Aoki, M., and H. Ando. 2002. *Modularity: The Essence of New Industry Architecture*, Toyokeizai (in Japanese).

Aoshima, Y., and T. Kato. 2003. *Strategic Management*, Toyokeizai (in Japanese).

Aoshima, Y., K. Nobeoka, and Y. Takeda. 2001. "Introduction of Three Dimensional CAD and Organizational Process in New Product Development Process." In *Organizational Restructuring in the Age of Digital Innovation: Tracing the Evolution of Japanese Workplace and Firm*, (Eds.) K. Odaka and T. Tsuru. Yuhikaku (in Japanese).

AP. 2006.12.29. HKMC *Expands Supplier Collaboration and Support Efforts.* Yonhapnews (29th December). (In Korean)

Arthur, W. B. 1988. "Competing Technologies: An Overview." in Dosi, G., Freeman, C., Nelson, R., Silverberg, G. and Soete, L. (eds.). *Technical Change and Economic Theory.* London, Printer Publishers, pp. 590–607.

Asanuma. B. 1989. "Manufacturer-Supplier Relationships in Japan and the Concept of Relation-Specific Skill." *Journal of the Japanese and International Economics*, Vo.3, pp. 1–30.

Asanuma, B., 1997, *Mechanism of Innovative Adaptation in Japanese Company organization.* Toyo Keizai Shinposha.

Asanuma, B. 2006. "Relationships between OEM and Suppliers in Japan." In Fujimoto. T., Ito, H. and Nishiguchi, T. (eds.) *Readings Supplier System: Construction of New Business Relationships*, Yuhikaku, pp. 1–39. (In Japanese)

Baba, Y., and K. Nobeoka. 1998. "Towards Knowledge-Based Product Development: The 3D CAD Mode of Knowledge Creation." *Research Policy*, Vol. 26, No. 6, pp. 643–659.

Baldwin, C. Y., and K. B. Clark. 2000. *Design Rules: The Power of Modularity*, Cambridge, MA: MIT Press.

Barney, J. B. 2002. *Gaining and Sustaining Competitive Advantage*. Pearson Education, Inc.

Beatty, C. A. 1992. "Implementing Advanced Manufacturing Technologies: Rules of the Road." *Sloan Management Review*, Vol. 33, No. 4, pp. 49–60.

Bordoloi, Sanjeev, and Hector H. Guerrero. 2008. "Design for Control: A New Perspective on Process and Product Innovation." *International Journal of Production Economics*, Vol. 113, No. 1, pp. 346–358.

Brusoni, S. and Prencipe A. 2001. "Managing Knowledge in Loosely Coupled Networks: Exploring the Links between Product and Knowledge Dynamics." *Journal of Management Studies*, Vol. 38, No. 7, pp. 1019–1035.

Buxey, G. 1990. "Computer-Assisted Design/Computer-Assisted Manufacturing (CAD-CAM) and Its Competitive Advantage." *Journal of Manufacturing Operations Management*, Vol. 3, pp. 335–350.

Chandler, A. D. 1977. *The Visible Hand*. Cambridge, MA: The Belknap Press of Harvard University Press.

Chang, Byunghwan. 2005. *Dynamism of Korean Electronics and IT Industry: Global Industry Alliance and Business Strategy of Samsung*, Souyou (in Japanese).

Chang, S. J. 2008. *Sony vs. Samsung*, John Wiley & Sons.

Changchien, S., and H. Y. Shen. 2002. Supply Chain Reengineering Using a Core Process Analysis Matrix and Object-Oriented Simulation. *Information and Management*, Vol. 39, No. 5, pp. 345–358.

Chase, R. B. 1998. *Production and Operations Management: Manufacturing and Services*. Irwin/McGraw-Hill.

Che, Z. H. 2009. "Pricing Strategy and Reserved Capacity Plan Based on Product Life Cycle and Production Function on LCD TV Manufacturer." *Expert Systems with Applications*, Vol. 36, No. 2, pp. 2048–2061.

Chesbrough, H. W. 2004. "Managing Open Innovation: Chess and Poker." *Research Technology Management*, Vol. 47, No. 1, pp. 23–26.

Chesbrough, H. W. 2007. "Why Companies Should Have Open Business Models." *MIT Sloan Management Review*, Vol. 48, No. 2, pp. 22–28.

Chesbrough, H. W. and Appleyard, M. M. 2007. "Open Innovation and Strategy." *California Management Review*, Vol. 50, No. 1, pp. 57–76.

Chesbrough, H.W. and Kusunoki, K. 2001. "The Modularity Trap." in Nonaka, I. and Teece, D.J. (Eds.) *Managing Industrial Knowledge*, Sage Publications, London, pp. 202–230.

Chiang, T-A. and Trappey, A.J.C. 2007. "Development of Value Chain Collaborative Model for Product Lifecycle Management and Its LCD Industry Adoption." *International Journal of Production Economics*, Vol. 109, pp. 90–104.

Cho, D. S., and J. U. Yoon. 2005. *Technology Capability Construction Strategy of Samsung: Technology Learning Process for Global Company*, Yuhikaku (in Japanese).

Cho, H. J., H. R. Jun, and S. K. Lim. 2005. *Digital Conqueror Samsung*, Maeil Business Newspaper (in Korean).

Choi, Y. S. 2010. *iPhone and iPad: Apple's Strategy*. Arachne (In Korean).

Christensen, C. M. 1994. "The Drivers of Vertical Disintegration." Harvard Business Working Paper.

Christensen, C. M. 1997. *The Innovator's Dilemma: When New Technologies Cause Great Firms to Fail*. Boston, MA: Harvard Business School Press.

Christensen, C. M. 2006. "The Ongoing Process of Building a Theory of Disruption." *Journal of Product Innovation Management*, Vol. 23, No. 1, pp. 39–55.

Christensen, C. M. and Bower, J. L. 1996. "Customer Power, Strategic Investment, and the Failure of Leading Firms." *Strategic Management Journal*, Vol. 17(3), pp. 197–218.

Christensen, C. M., M. Verlinden, and G. Westerman. 2002. "Disruption, Disintegration and the Dissipation of Differentiability." *Industrial and Corporate Change*, Vol. 11, No. 5, pp. 955–993.

Chun, K. J. 2000. "CDMA Evolution in Korea." *The 5th CDMA International Conference and Exhibition, Proceeding*. Vol. 1. pp. 1–15.

Chung, K. M., and K. R. Lee. 1999. "Mid-Entry Technology Strategy: The Korean Experience with CDMA." *R&D Management*, pp. 353–363.

Clark, K. B. 1985. "The Interaction of Design Hierarchies and Market Concepts in Technological evolution." *Research Policy*, Vol. 14, pp. 235–251.

Clark, K. B., and T. Fujimoto. 1991. *Product Development Performance: Strategy, Organization, Management in the World Auto Industry*. Boston, MA: Harvard Business School Press.

Coase, R. 1937. "The Nature of the Firm." *Economics*, Vol. 4, pp. 380–405.

Cohen, W. M. and Levinthal, D. 1990. "Absorptive Capacity: A New Perspective on Learning and Innovation." *Administrative Science Quarterly*, Vol. 35, pp. 128–152.

Danneels, Erwin. 2002. "The Dynamics of Product Innovation and Firm Competencies." *Strategic Management Journal*, Vol. 23, pp. 1095–1121.

David, A. P. 1985. "Clio and Economics of QWERTY." *American Economic Review*, Vol. 75, pp. 332–337.

Demeter, K., Gelei, A. and Jenei, I. 2006. "The Effect of Strategy on Supply Chain Configuration and Management Practices on the Basis of Two Supply Chains in the Hungarian Automotive Industry." *Industrial Marketing Management*, Vol. 104, No.2, pp. 555–570.

de Treville, Suzanne, Roy D. Shapiro, and Ari-Pekka Hameri. 2004. "From Supply Chain to Demand Chain: The role of Lead Time Reduction in Improving Demand Chain Performance." *Journal of Operations Management*, Vol. 21, No. 6, pp. 613–627.

Digital Times. 2006. "Not Successor but Pioneer (2): Old Effective Competition Policy." March 28, 2006.

Digital Times. 2006. "Is There Method Lowering Qualcomm' s CDMA Loyalty." May 10, 2006.

Digital Times. 2005.2.3. *Main Focus on Large Firms-SMEs Cooperation Support*. Digital Times (3rd Feb). (In Korean)

DisplaySearch. 2010. LCD Trend Report.

Doll, W., P. Hong, and A. Nahm. 2010. "Antecedents and Outcomes of Manufacturability in Integrated Product Development." *International Journal of Operations and Production Management*, Vol. 30, No. 8, pp. 821–852.

Dougherty D. 1995. "Managing Your Core Incompetencies for Corporate Venturing." *Entrepreneurship Theory and Practice*, Vol. 19, No. 3, pp. 13–135.

Dougherty, D. and Heller, T. 1994. "The Illegitimacy of Successful Product Innovations in Established Firms." *Organization Science*, Vol. 5, pp. 200–218.

Ebert, Christof, and Jozef De Man 2008. "Effectively Utilizing Project, Product and Process Knowledge." *Information and Software Technology*, Vol. 50, Issue 6, May, pp. 579–594.

Edaily. 2008.12.4. HKMC *Aggressive Global Sales Target of 3.05 Million Cars*. Edaily (4th December). (In Korean)

Edaily. 2009. *The Principle of the First Class Quality: Hyundai Motor Company-Hyundai Mobis, Double Teams of Illusion Go* (November 26, 2009).

Elgh, Fredrik. 2008. "Supporting Management and Maintenance of Manufacturing Knowledge in Design Automation Systems." *Advanced Engineering Informatics*, Vol. 22, No. 4, pp. 445–456.

ETNEWS. 2005. "Success and Crisis of IT Industry—Next Round." Dec. 26, 2005.

ETNEWS. 2006. "10 years of CDMA and Future: Communication Change History, and Future Strategy." Apr. 20, 2006.

ETNEWS. 2006. "10 years of CDMA and Future: How Has Mobile Phone Been Changed." Apr. 20, 2006.

ETNEWS. 2006. "10 years of CDMA and Future: Korean Mobile Phone Admitted by World." Apr. 20, 2006.

ETNEWS. 2006. "10 years of CDMA and Future: People Unearthing CDMA." Apr. 20, 2006.

ETNEWS. 2008. "LG Electronics Targets the Sales of 17 Million Units of Flat Panel TV." Jan. 8, 2008 (in Korean).

ETRI. 2002. "Technology Development of CDMA, Industry Success Factors, and Future Assignment." *ETRI Report*, July 4, 2002 (in Korean).

Feitzinger, E., and Lee, H. L. 1997. "Mass Customization at Hewlett-Packard: The power of postponement." *Harvard Business Review*, Vol. 75, No. 1, pp. 116–121.

Fine, C. H. 1998. *Clockspeed: Winning Industry Control in the Age of Temporary Advantage*. Reading, MA: Peruseus Books.

Fitzgerald, K. 1987. "Compressing the Design Cycle." *IEEE Spectrum*, Vol. 24, No. 10, pp. 39–42.

Foster, R. N. 1986. "Timing Technological Transitions." in Tushman, M. L. and Moore, W. L. (eds.) *Readings in the Management of Innovation*. New York, NY, Harper Business, pp. 215–227.

Foster, R. N. and Kaplan, S. 2001. *Creative Destruction: Why Companies That Are Built to Last Underperform the Market and How to Successfully Transform Them*. Mckinsey and Co., Inc.

Fujimoto, T. 1997. *The Evolution of a Manufacturing System*. Yuhikaku.

Fujimoto, T. 2001a. "Business Architecture: Strategic Design of Products, Organizations, and Processes." Yuhikaku, Tokyo (edited with A. Takeishi and Y. Aoshima, in Japanese).

Fujimoto, T. 2001b. *Introduction to Production Management 1&2*. Nihon Keizai Shinbunsha, Tokyo (in Japanese).

Fujimoto, T. 2002. "A Note on the Product Architecture Concept, Measurement, and Strategy." Discussion Study, CIRJE-J-78, Faculty of Economics, University of Tokyo (in Japanese).

Fujimoto, T. 2003. Noryoku kochiku kyoso (Capability-Building Competition), Chukousinsyo (in Japanese). English translation: Competing to Be Really Good (Translated by Brian Miller), Tokyo: International House of Japan.

Fujimoto, T. 2004. "Japan's Manufacturing Philosophy." Nihon Keizai Shinbunsha, Tokyo (in Japanese).

Fujimoto, T. 2005. "A Note on Architecture-Based Comparative Advantage" *MMRC Discussion Study* 24 (in Japanese).

Fujimoto, T. 2006a. "Architecture-based Comparative Advantage in Japan and Asia." Tokyo University, *MMRC Discussion Study*, No. 94, pp. 1–8 (in Japanese).

Fujimoto, T. 2006b. "Product Architecture and Product Development Capabilities in Automobile." Tokyo University, *MMRC Discussion Study*, No. 74, pp. 1–12 (in Japanese).

Fujimoto, T., and K. Nobeoka. 2006. "Power of Continuance in Competitive Power Analysis: Product Development and Evolution of Organizational Capability." *Organaizational Science*, Vol. 39, No. 4, pp. 43–55 (in Japanese).

Fujimoto, T., K. Nobeoka, Y. Aoshima, Y. Takeda, and J. H. Oh. 2002. "Information Technology and Company Organization: in the Viewpoint of Architecture and Organization Capability." In *Electronic Society and Market Economy*, (Eds.) M. Okuno, A. Takemura, and Z. Shintaku. Shinseisya (in Japanese).

Fujimoto, T., and T. Oshika. 2006. "Empirical Analysis of the Hypothesis of Architecture-based Competitive Advantage and International Trade Theory." *MMRC Discussion Study* 71, pp. 1–21.

Fujimoto, T., T. Oshika, and N. Kishi. 2005. "Empirical Analysis on Product Architectural Measurements." *MMRC Discussion Study* 26 (in Japanese).

Fujitshu. 2007. *Monodukuri Which Does Not Make a Thing*. JUSE Press.

Garwood, Dave. 2006. *Bills of Material: Structured for Excellence,* (Ed.) Taro Yamada. Nikkei BP (in Japanese).

Gawer, A., and M. A. Cusumano. 2002. *Platform Leadership: How Intel, Microsoft, and Cisco Drive Industry Innovation*. Boston, MA: Harvard Business School Press.

Giess, M. D., P. J. Wild, and C. A. McMahon. 2008. "The Generation of Faceted Classification Schemes for Use in the Organisation of Engineering Design Documents." *International Journal of Information Management,* Vol. 28, Issue 5, October, pp. 379–390.

Goel, Sanjay, and Vicki Chen. 2008. "Integrating the Global Enterprise Using Six Sigma: Business Process Reengineering at General Electric Wind Energy." *International Journal of Production Economics*, Vol. 113, Issue 2, June, pp. 914–927.

Government Authorization Briefing Special Project Team. 2008. *Participation Government Economy 5 Years, Hanseu Media,* pp. 176–185 (in Korean).

Gunasekaran, A., and E. W. T. Ngai. 2004. "Information Systems in Supply Chain Integration and Management." *European Journal of Operational Research*, Vol. 159, pp. 269–295.

Gunpinar, Erkan, and Soonhung Han. 2008. "Interfacing Heterogeneous PDM Systems Using the PLM Services," *Advanced Engineering Informatics*, Vol. 22, Issue 3, July, pp. 307–316.

Hamel, G. and Prahalad, C.K. 1994. *Competing for the Future*. Harvard Business School Press.

Hamel, G. and Prahalad, C. K. 1990. "The Core Competence of the Corporation." *Harvard Business Review*, Vol.68, No.3, pp. 79–91.

Han, J. 1995. "Korean Big Companies' Macro-Management and Corporate Strategic Characteristics," *Management Characteristics of Korean Big Companies*, Segyon.

Han, J. 2002. "Korean Firms' Management Innovation and CEO," *Management Characteristics of Korean Big Companies,* Dosan Books.

Hattori, Tamio. 1996. *Korea's Management Development,* Bunsindou.

Helfat, C.E. and Raubitschek, R. S. 2000. "Product Sequencing: Co-evolution of Knowledge, Capabilities and Products." *Strategic Management Journal,* Special Issue, Vol. 21(10/11), pp. 961–979.

Henderson, R. 1991. "Of Life Cycle Real and Imaginary: The Unexpectedly Long Old Age of Optical Lithography." *Research Policy*, Vol. 24, pp. 631–643.

Henderson R. 1993. "Underinvestment and Incompetence as Responses to Radical Innovation: Evidence from the Photolithographic Alignment Equipment Industry." *The Rand Journal of Economics*, Vol. 24, No. 2, pp. 248–270.

Henderson, R., and K. B. Clark. 1990. "Architectural Innovation. The Reconfiguration of Existing Product Technologies and the Failure of Established Firms." *Administrative Science Quarterly*, Vol. 35, pp. 9–30.

Henderson, R., and I. Cockburn. 1994. "Measuring Competence? Exploring Firm Effects in Pharmaceutical Research." *Strategic Management Journal*, Vol. 15, pp. 63–84.

Hoek, R. I. and Weken, H. A. M. 1998. "The Impact of Modular Production on the Dynamics of Supply Chains." *The International Journal of Logistics Management*, Vol. 9, No. 2, pp. 35–50.

Hong, P., W. Doll, and A. Nahm. 2004a. "Project Target Clarity in an Uncertain Project Environment Uncertainty of Project." *International Journal of Operations and Production Management*, 24(12), 1269–1291.

Hong, P., William Doll, Abraham Nahm, and X. Li. 2004b. "Knowledge Sharing in Integrated Product Development." *European Journal of Innovation Management*, Vol. 7, No. 2, pp. 102–112.

Hong, P., H. Kwon, and J. Roh 2009. "Implementation of Strategic Green Orientation: An Empirical Study of Manufacturing Firms." *European Journal of Innovation Management*, Vol. 12, No. 4, pp. 512–532.

Hong, P., and J. Roh. 2009. Internationalization, Product Development and Performance Outcomes: A Comparative Study of Ten Countries. *Research in International Business and Finance*, Vol. 23, No. 2, pp. 169–180.

Hong, P., J. Roh, and W. Hwang. 2006. "Global Supply Chain Strategy: From a Chinese Market Perspective." *Journal of Enterprise Information Management*, Vol. 19, No. 3, pp. 320–333.

Hong, P., M. Vonderembse, D. William, and A. Nahm. 2005. "Role Changes of Design Engineers in Integrated Product Development." *Journal of Operations Management*. Vol. 24, No. 1, pp. 63–79.

Hong, Paul, David D. Dobrzykowski, and M. Vonderembse. 2010a. "Effective Integration of E-Technologies and Lean Practices: Supply Chain Performance in Product and Service Focused Firms." *Benchmarking: An International Journal*. Vol. 17, No. 4, pp. 561–592.

Hong, Paul, Oahn Tran, and Kiyun Park. 2010b. "Electronic Commerce Applications for Supply Chain Integration and Competitive Capabilities: An Empirical Study." *Benchmarking: An International Journal*, Vol. 17, No. 4, pp. 539–560.

Hong, Paul, SunHee Youn, and Abraham Nahm. 2008. "Supply Chain Partnerships and Supply Chain Integration: The Mediating Role of Information Quality and Sharing." *International Journal of Logistics Systems and Management*. Vol. 4, No. 4, pp. 437–456.

Hong, S. 2004a. "Disintegration of Korea Incorporated and Political Economy of Semi-Conductor Growth Process." In *Nation and Industrial Competitiveness: Political Economy for Information Communication Industry Development*, pp. 47–113. Kookmin University Press (in Korean).

Hong, S. 2004b. *Display Industry and Industrial Competitiveness. In Nation and Industrial Competitiveness: Political Economy for Information Communication Industry Development*. Kookmin University Press. pp. 114–152 (in Korean).

Huang, N., and S. Diao. 2008. "Ontology-Based Enterprise Knowledge Integration." *Robotics and Computer-Integrated Manufacturing*, Vol. 24, Issue 4, August, pp. 562–571.

Hyundai Mobis. 2007. "30 Years History of Hyundai Mobis" (in Korean).

ICA. 2003. "IT Export Specials." *Monthly IT Export*.

iNews24. 2005.2.2. "Taking All Power for Large Firms - SMEs Cooperation Support: Concerned Organizaitons Meeting. " *iNews24* (2nd Feb). (In Korean)

inews24. Sep. 2, 2007. "Flat TV, Design Plus α: Best Effort for Satisfaction—an Interview with LD DD Director" (in Korean).

inews24. Dec. 18, 2007. "Not yet in sight of PDP Breakthrough" (in Korean).

inews24. Jan. 25, 2008. "A VIZIO 81 cm PDP TV Release Start: LG Electronic Module Deployment—Second Quarter" (in Korean).

inews24. Feb. 1, 2008. "LG Electronics: Attain PDP No 2 Position with the Support of 81 cm" (in Korean).

ISBI. 2006. "Mobile Internet Series 2006." March 2006.

Ishikura, Y. 2003. "Significance and Use of the Cluster from Viewpoint of Firms." In *Strategy for Cluster Initiatives in Japan*, (Eds.) Y. Ishikura, M. Fujita, N. Maeda, K. Kanai, and A. Yamasaki, pp. 1–41. Yuhikaku (in Japanese).

Itami, H. 1987. *Mobilizing Invisible Assets*. Boston, MA: Harvard University Press.

Itami, H. 2009. *Objection against Technology Management in Japan*. Nihon Keizai Shinbunsya (in Japanese).

Itami, Hiroyuki. 2000. *Three Waves of Japanese Industry*. NTT Press (in Japanese).

Itohisa, M., Y. Igari, and R. Yoshioka. 2009. "Korean Firms: Architecture Positioning and Strategy." In *Monozukuri International Management Strategy: Asian Industrial Geography*, (Eds.) J. Shintaku and H. Amano, pp. 232–259. Yuhikaku (in Japanese).

Itoh, M. 2005. *Construction of Product Strategy Management: Competitive Strategy of Digital Device Company*. Yuhikaku. (In Japanese)

Jang, Sungwon and Bum-Sik Kim. (2005). Semi-Conductor and Korean Economy. Samsung Economic Research Institute Issue (in Korean).

Javidan, M. 1998. "Core Competence: What Does It Mean in Practice?" *Long Range Planning*, Vol. 31, No. 1, pp. 60–71.

Johnson, Chalmers. 1982. *MITI and Japanese Miracle:The Growth of Industrial Policy, 1925–1975*. Stanford: Stanford University Press.

Joins. 2009. *When Losing a Job, It Is Refunded, Marketing of Hyundai Motor Company in America*. Feb. 4, 2009 (in Korean).

Joo, D.Y., Sue, D.H. and Cho, H.S. 2003. "World Share Change of Electronic Industry and Korean Choice." *Korea Institute for Industrial Economics and Trade*. (In Korean)

Jun, Y., and J. Han. 1997. *Japanese Firms for New Asian Age: Firms That Stretch toward China*. Chukoshinsyo (in Japanese).

Kappel, T. A., and A. H. Rubenstein. 1999. "Creativity in Design: The Contribution of Information Technology." *IEEE Transactions on Engineering Management*, Vol. 46, No. 2, pp. 132–143.

Karube, M. 2004a. "Resources and Competition: Two Dynamics." In *Strategy and Logic of Invisible Assets*, (Eds.) H. Itami and M. Karube, pp. 73–103. Nikkei (in Japanese).

Karube, M. 2004b. "Induction and Drive: Resources Accumulation and Utilization Mechanism." In *Strategy and Logic of Invisible Assets*, (Eds.) H. Itami, and M. Karube, pp. 104–138. Nikkei (in Japanese).

Katahira, H. 2005. "New Management from Brand Marketing Perspective." In *Samsung Study: A Study of its Outstanding Competitiveness*, (Eds.) Global Firm Research Association and Nikkei Biztech, pp. 256–260. Nikkei BP (in Japanese).

Kayama, Susumu. 2006. "Innovation in Semi-Conductor Industry and Tasks of Business Management." In *Innovation and Competitive Advantages*, (Eds.) Sakakibara Kiyonori and Kayama Susumu, pp. 198–237. NTT Press (in Japanese).

Katz, M. L. and Shapiro, C. 1985. "Network Externalities, Competition and Compatibility." *American Economic Review*, Vol. 75, No.3, pp. 424–440.

Kemmerer, S. 1999. "STEP: The Grand Experience." Gaithersburg, MD: National Institute of Standards and Technology, NIST special publication 939.

KETI. 2007a. "General Condition of Mobile Communication Components and Camera Phone Module." KETI (2007.8a), pp. 1–21 (in Korean).

KETI. 2007b. "General Condition of Portable Convergence Phones and Handsets." KETI (2007.8b), pp. 1–18 (in Korean).

Kim, Jungeon and Jung, Hyunjun. 2005. "IT Industry Polarization and Policy Direction." KISDI Issue Report (12.5) (in Korean).

Kim, Kihong. 2004. "The Study of Strategy for Promoting High-have Type Industry Based IT", Kyonggi University, Information Telecommunication Study 03-01.

Kim, M. S. 2002. "Information Communication Industry Movement—Section 1 Information and Communication Phones." KISDI (2002.10), pp. 3–4 (in Korean).

Kim, M. S. 2003. "Information Communication Industry Movement—Section 1 Mobile Phones." KISDI (2003.12), pp. 139–171 (in Korean).

Kim, Y. J. 2006. "Large Firms-SMEs Coexistence Cooperation Plans: Die Purchasing Strategy of 4 Large Firms." *CAD & Graphics* (Feb). (in Korean)

Kim, S. H., and Lee, S. M. 2005. *Challenges of Mongu Chung*, God's Win (in Korean).

Klein, B., R. Crawford, and A. Alchian, A. 1978. "Vertical Integration, Appropriable Rents, and the Competitive Contracting Process." *Journal of Law and Economics*, Vol. 21, pp. 297–326.

Ko, J. M., Lim, Y. M. and Park, S. B. 2006. "The 20th Anniversary Special Issues of Samsung Economic Research Institute foundation: (1) Step of Korea Industry 20 Years." *SERI CEO Information*, Vol.560 (7.5) (In Korean)

Kobayashi, Osamu. 2000. "Case Study: Samsung Electronics." *Nikkei Business* (November 6th), pp. 67–69. (In Japanese).

Kogan, K. and Tapiero, C. S. 2009. "Optimal Co-investment in Supply Chain Infrastructure." *European Journal of Operational Research*, Vol. 192, pp. 265–276.

Korea IT Research Report. 2001. "Why Was Japan Caught-Up." Nikkankougyo-sinbun.

Koufteros, X. A., M. A. Vonderembse, and W. J. Doll. 2001. "Concurrent Engineering and Its Consequences." *Journal of Operations Management*, Vol. 19, No. 1, pp. 97–115.

Krause, Daniel R., Thomas V. Scannell, and Roger L. Calantone. 2000. "A Structural Analysis of the Effectiveness of Buying Firms's Strategies to Improve Supplier Performance." *Decision Sciences*, Vol. 31, No. 1, pp. 33–55.

Ku, S. H. 2003. "Introduction of 3D-CAD and its Effects in Automobile Industry: 3D-CAD, Communication among Firms, Efficiency of Development, Cause and Effect Model." *Organizational Science*, Vol. 37, No. 1, pp. 68–81 (in Japanese).

Kuhn, T. 1970. *The Structure of Scientific Revolutions*. Chicago, IL, University of Chicago.

Kukminilbo. 2006. "Samsung Electronics Defeated by Netizen's Opinion." May 5, 2006.

Lambert, D. M., and M. C. Cooper. 2000. "Issues in Supply Chain Management." *Industrial Marketing Management*, Vol. 29, No. 1, pp. 65–83.

Latour, A. 2001. "Trial by Fire: A Blaze in Albuquerque Sets Off Major Crisis for Cell-Phone Giants." *The Wall Street Journal*, Eastern Edition (January 29).

Le Duigou, J., A. Bernard, N. Perry, and J. C. Delplace. 2009. "Global Approach for Technical Data Management: Application to Ship Equipment Part Families." *CIRP Journal of Manufacturing Science and Technology*, Vol. 1, pp. 185–190.

Lee, B. C. 2003. "Global Semi-Conductor Industry and Korean Semi-Conductor's Competitive Strategy–In the Case of Samsung Electronics." Youngnam College of Business.

Lee, C. K. M., H. C. W. Lau, G. T. S. Ho, and W. Ho. 2009. "Design and Development of Agent-Based Procurement System to Enhance Business Intelligence." *Expert Systems with Applications*, Vol. 36, pp. 877–884.

Lee, C. Y. 2005. "New Management from Brand Marketing Perspective." In *Samsung Study: A Study of its Outstanding Competitiveness*, (Eds.) Global Firm Research Association and Nikkei Biztech, pp. 54–70. Nikkei BP (in Japanese).

Lee, D. H. 2005. "Development of Mobile Communication Service and Phone Industry." Information Communication and Change of Korea, Communications Books, pp. 277–293.

Lee, Eunkyong. 2003. "Socio-Economic Impacts of Successful R&D Results in Korea." *Ministry of Science and Technology, Policy Study*, 2002–2023 (April) (in Korean).

Lee, I. G. 2008. *Mongu Chung and His Drive for Hyundai and Kia*, Map of Thought Leadership (in Korean).

Lee, Keun. 2004. "Emerging Digital Technology as a Window of Opportunity and Technological Leapfrogging: Catch-up in Digital TV by the Korean Firms." *Akamon Management Journal,* Vol. 3, No. 9.

Lee, KunHee. 1997. *Lee KunHee Essay: See the World Thinking*. DongA-Ilbo (in Korean).

Lee, M. H. 2005. "Industrial Spreading Effects of Mobile Communication." Information Communication and Change of Korea, *Communications Books*, pp. 294–310.

Lee, Sanghun. 2007. "Factory without Chimneys and Semi-Conductor IP Industry." *Embedded World 2007*, Techworld, pp. 72–81 (in Korean).

Leonard-Barton, D. 1992. "Core Capabilities and Core Rigidities: A Paradox in Managing New Product Development." *Strategic Management Journal*, Vol. 13(1), pp. 111–125.

Levitt, B. and March, J. G. 1988. "Organizational Learning." *Annual Review of Sociology*, Vol. 14, pp. 319–340.

Levary, R. 2000. "Better Supply Chains through Information Technology." *Industrial Management*, Vol. 42, No. 3, pp. 24–30.

Levinthal, D. A., and J. G. March. 1993. "The Myopia of Learning." *Strategic Management Journal* ,Vol. 14, pp. 95–112.

LG Economic Institute. 2006a. "LCD Industry! Be Prepared to Japanese-Oriented Crisis." *LG Weekly Economy* (Dec 13, 2006) (in Korean).

LG Economic Institute. 2006b. "Threats to the Strategic Positioning of Display Power." *LG Weekly Economy* (April 19, 2006) (in Korean).

LG Economic Institute. 2007a. "Display Industry: How Long LCD Monopoly in Display Industry?" (March 14, 2007) *LG Weekly Economy* (in Korean).

LG Economic Institute. 2007b. "Display Component Parts Industry: Move Beyond the Trap of Wider Application Illusion." *LG Weekly Economy* (May 16, 2007) (in Korean).

Li, X. and Wang, Q. 2007. "Coordination Mechanisms of Supply Chain Systems." *European Journal of Operational Research*, Vol. 179, pp. 1–16.

Liao, Ying, Paul Hong, and Subba Rao. 2010. "Supply Management, Supply Flexibility and Performance Outcomes: An Empirical Investigation of Manufacturing Firms." *Journal of Supply Chain Management,* Vol. 46, No. 3, pp. 6–22.

Liker, J. K. and Choi, Y. I. 2004. "Building Deep Supplier Relationships." *Harvard Business Review*, Vol. 82, No. 12, pp. 104–113.

Liker, J. K., M. Fleischer, and D. Arnsdorf. 1995. "Fulfilling the Promises of CAD." In *Productivity in the Office and the Factory,* (Eds.) P. Gray and J. Jurison, pp. 176–191. New York: Boyd & Fraser Publishing Co.

Liua, Jianxun, Shensheng Zhang, and Jinming Hu. 2005. "A case Study of an Inter-Enterprise Workflow-Supported Supply Chain Management System." *Information and Management*, 42, pp. 441–454.

Lim, Y. T. 2007. *People without Vision Perish. Daily Economic Newspaper* (eBook). (In Korean)

Lippman, S. A. and Rumelt, R. P. 1992. "Demand Uncertainty, Capital Specificity, and Industry Evolution." *Industrial and Corporate Change*, Vol. 1, No. 1, pp. 235–262.

Lummus, Rhonda R., and Robert J. Vokurka. 1999. "Defining Supply Chain Management: A Historical Perspective and Practical Guidelines. *Industrial Management and Data Systems,* Vol. 99, No. 1, pp. 11–17.

Maeil Economics. 2007.5.19 (in Korean).

Maeil Economics. Dec 25, 2007. "Is It True That LCD TV Cheaper Than PDP?" (in Korean).

March, J. G. 1991. "Exploration and Exploitation in Organizational Learning." *Organization Science* Vol. 2, pp. 71–87.

Masuyama, S. 2002. "Asian Multinational Enterprise." Yoshihara, H. (eds.) *Invitation to International Business Theory*. Yuhikaku, pp. 279–299. (In Japanese)

Matthews, John A., and Dongsung Cho. 2000. *Tiger Technology: The Creation of a Semiconductor Industry in East Asia*. Cambridge, UK: Cambridge University Press.

Miller, W. L. and Morris, L. 1999. *Fourth Generation R&D: Managing Knowledge, Technology, and Innovation*, Wiley, New York.

Ming, X. G., Yan, J. Q., Wang, X. H., Li, S. N., Lu, W. F., Peng, Q. J., and Ma, Y. S. 2008. "Collaborative Process Planning and Manufacturing in Product Lifecycle Management." *Computers in Industry*, Vol. 59, Issues 2–3, March, pp. 154–166.

Ministry of Knowledge Economy. 2009. "Policy Issue1- IT Innovation Business for Large Firms-SMEs Coexistence: Achievement Expectation of Active IT Led by SMEs." *Moazine* (2009.6), pp. 1–5. (In Korean)

Ministry of Information and Communication. 2008. (http://mic.news.go.kr/).

Mintzberg, H., Ahlstrand, B., and Lampel, J. 1998. *Strategic Safari*. FreePress.

Mintzberg, H. and J. A. Waters. 1985. "Of Strategies, Deliberate and Emergent." Strategic *Management Journal,* Vol. 6, pp. 257–272.

Miwa, Seiji. 2001. "Architecture Innovation in Semi-Conductor Industry." In *Business Architecture,* (Eds.) Fujimoto Takahiro, Takeishi Akira, and Aoshima Yaichi, pp. 73–100. Yuhikaku (in Japanese).

Monczka, Rober M., Kenneth J. Peterson, and Robert B. Handfield. 1998. "Success Factors in Strategic Supplier Alliances: The Building Company Perspective." *Decision Sciences*, Vol. 29, No. 3, pp. 553–577.

Morone, J. 1993. *Wining in High Tech Markets*. Boston: Harvard Business School Press.

Nagai, Satomi. 2003. "Reality and Challenges of Semi-Conductor Industry: Can It Revive with Business Integration and Specialization?" Review of TBR Industrial Economy, No. 03 (March), Toray Corporate Business Research (in Japanese).

Narayanan, V. G. and Raman, A., 2004. "Aligning Incentives in Supply Chains." *Harvard Business Review*, Vol. 82, No. 11, pp. 94–102.

Nelson, R. R. and Winter, S. G. 1982. *An Evolutionary Theory of Economic Change*. Belknap Press, Cambridge, UK.

Nikkei Electronics. 2004.2.6. "Sony Makimoto's Makimoto Waves: Next Waves in 2007" (in Japanese).

Nikkei Microdevices. 2006. "Ever Leaping Forward." *Japanese Device Industry*, Vol. 255 (Sept 1, 2006).

Nishimura, K. 2004. *Invisible Structure Change of Japanese Economy*. Nihon Keizai Shinbunsya.

Nobeoka, K., M. Ito, and H. Morita. 2006. "Failure of Value Capture by Commodity; A Case of Digital Consumer Electronic." In *Innovation and Competitive Advantage: Digital Consumer Electronic in Commodity*, (Eds.) K. Sakakibara and S. Kohyama, NTT Press (in Japanese).

Nobeoka, T. 2006. *Introduction to MOT*. Nihon Keizai Shinbunsya.

Nonaka, I., and Takeuchi, H. 1995. *The Knowledge Creating Company: How Japanese Companies Create the Dynamics of Innovation*, Oxford University Press.

Ogasawara, A., and Y. Matsumoto. 2006. "Competition of TV Industry and Diversification of a Profit Acquisition Method." In *Innovation and Competitive Advantage*, (Eds.) Sakakibara Kiyonori and Kohyama Susumu. pp. 163–196 (in Japanese).

Ogawa, K. 2007a. "Business Model Innovation of New Japan Type Management (1)—Rebuilding of a Japanese Model Innovation System Assuming Dynamism of the Product Architecture." Tokyo University, *MMRC Discussion Study*, No. 184 (in Japanese).

Ogawa, Koichi. 2007b. "Platform Formation Mechanism in Japanese Electronics Industry: Toward the Revitalization of Electronics Industry by Architecture-Based Platform Approach." *MMRC Discussion Study*, No. 146, (in Japanese).

Ogawa, Koichi. 2008a. "Modular Evolution Mechanism in Japanese Electronics Industry: Business Environment's Historical Transition on Micro-Computer and Firmware." *Akamon Management Review*, Vol. 7, No. 2 (in Japanese).

Ogawa, Koichi. 2008b. "A Suggestion for Standardized Business Model Based on Product Architecture Dynamism: Japanese Style Management of Business Model Innovation." *MMRC Discussion Study*, No. 205 (in Japanese).

Ogawa, Koichi, Y. W. Park, Hirofumi Tatsumoto, and Paul Hong. 2009. "Architecture-Based International Specialization: Semiconductor Device as an Artificial Genome in Global Supply Chain." Third International Symposium and Workshop on Global Supply Chains (Jan 6–7).

Oh, G. H. 2004. "Success Factors of CDMA Technology Development and Industry." In *Competitive Power of Nation and Industry: Political Economics of ICT industry Development*, pp. 191–240. Dosan Books, Kookmin.

Ootaki, Seiichi, Kazuyori Kanai, Hideo Yamada, and Satoshi Iwato. 2003. *Strategy Management: Toward Creation and Sociality*. Yuhikaku ARMA.

Oshika, T., and T. Fujimoto. 2006. "Positive Analysis of the Product Architecture Theory and International Trade Theory." *Akamon Management Review*, Vol. 5, No. 4, pp. 233–271.

Park, S. 2006. "Korean Flat Panel Display Industry—Another Semi-Conductor Miracle Possible?" Samsung Economic Research Institute (2006.8) (in Korean).

Park, S., and Y. Gil. 2006. "How Samsung Transformed Its Corporate R&O Center." *Research-Technology Management* (July-August), pp. 24–29.

Park, S. H., and W. K. Park. 2007. Samsung VS LG, Their War, Future Window (in Korean).

Park, Y. W. 2004 "Outsourcing of Information System and Core Competence in Small and Medium-Sized Enterprises: A Case Study of a Japanese Company Compared with a South Korean Company." The Japan Association for Social Informatics, Vol. 16, pp. 31–44 (in Japanese).

Park, Y. W. 2005. "Relationships between Strategic Alliances and Organizational Capabilities—A Case Study of STLCD." *Proceedings of International Business Studies Conference*, pp. 165–182 (in Japanese).

Park, Y. W. 2006. "Platform Leadership in Korean Digital Contents Industry—Case Studies of SK Telecom and KT." *13th International Business Studies Conference*, pp. 212–215 (in Japanese).

Park, Y. W. 2007. "Organizational Capabilities of Korean Telecommunication firms and Platform Leadership in Digital Contents Industry—Case Studies of SK Telecom and KT. " *Journal of International Business Studies*, Vol. 13, pp. 39–56 (in Japanese).

Park, Y. W. 2008. "History of Korean Semi-Conductor Industry and Business Strategy." *Worldwide Business Review*, Vol. 9, No. 2, pp. 186–207. Doshisha University (in Japanese).

Park, Y. W. 2009. *Core Competence and IT Strategy*, Waseda University Press (in Japanese).

Park, Y. W., and P. Hong. 2006. "Korean IT Industry and Platform Leadership: A Comparative Study with Japanese Experiences." Asia Academy of Management Fifth Conference in Waseda University (December 2006).

Park, Y. W., T. Fujimoto, R. Yoshikawa, P. Hong, and T. Abe. 2007a. "An Examination of Computer-Aided Design (CAD) Usage Patterns, Product Architecture and Organizational Capabilities: Case Illustrations from Three Electronic Manufacturers." Portland International Conference on Management of Engineering & Technology Conference in Portland, USA (August 5–9, 2007).

Park, Y. W., P. Hong, and T. Fujimoto. 2007b. "Product Architecture and Global Supply Chain Management of Liquid Crystal Display (LCD): Case Illustrations from Korean LCD Manufacturers." International Symposium and Workshop on Global Supply Chain, USA (October 25–26, 2007).

Park, Y. W., and Koichi Ogawa. 2008. "Comparative Analysis of Japan-Korea Semi-Conductor Industry." The Institute of Image Information and Television Engineers 2008 Conference in Fukuoka Institute of Technology (in Japanese).

Park, Y. W., S. H. Ham, K. Ogawa, and H. Tatsumoto. 2008a. "History and Corporate Strategy of the Korean Semi-Conductor Industry in a Viewpoint of Product Architecture: A Comparison Study with Japanese Semi-Conductor Industry." *MMRC Discussion Paper* 224 (in Japanese).

Park, Y. W., G. W. Moon, and H. Tatsumoto. 2008b. "A Success Factor and a Corporate Strategy of Korea Mobile Communication Industry from a Product Architecture Viewpoint." Tokyo University, *MMRC Discussion Study*, No. 195 (in Japanese).

Park, Y. W., P. Hong, and W. Hwang. 2009a. "Suppliers Support of manufacturers for Supply Chain Integration: A Case Study of Korean Hyundai-Kia Firms." The 3rd International Symposium and Workshop on Global Supply Chain Management, Jan. 6–7 in PSGIM, Coimbatore, India.

Park, Y. W., T. Fujimoto, J. Shintaku, M. Yasumoto, and T. Abe. 2009b. "Product Architecture and Computer Aided Design: An Empirical Investigation in Japanese Electronic Industry." Asia Pacific Conference on Information Management (APCIM) 2009, in Peking University, Beijing, China) March 27–29, pp. 447–460.

Park, Y. W., P. Hong, T. Abe, and S. Goto. 2009c. "Product Lifecycle Management for Global Market: Case Studies of Japanese Firms." International Conference on Product Lifecycle Management, in Papers presented at PLM'09 [CD-ROM], OR: PLM, July 2009.

Park, Y. W., K. Ogawa, H. Tatsumoto, and P. Hong, 2009d. "The Impact of Product Architecture on Supply Chain Integration: A Case Study of NOKIA and Texas Instruments." *International Journal of Services and Operations Management,* Vol. 5, No. 6, pp. 787–798.

Park, Y. W., P. Hong, and T. Shimizu. 2010a. "Role of Owner/CEO on Development of Organizational Capability: A Case Study of Korean Global Firms." Fuji Conference, Hitotsubashi University, JP (Jan 9–10, 2010).

Park, Y. W., Fujimoto, T., Hong, P. and Abe, T. 2010b. "Integrated Manufacturing and IT strategy for Futuristic PLM: A Conceptual Framework from Japanese Firms." *International Conference* on *Product Lifecycle Management*, in Papers presented at PLM'10 [CD-ROM], Bremen, Germany: PLM, July 2010.

Park, Y.W., Hong, P. and Moon, G.W. 2011a. "Implementation of Product Strategy with Differentiated Standards." *International Journal of Technology Management* (forthcoming).

Park, Y.W., Hong, P., Kim, J. H and Hwang, W. S. 2011b. "Building Supply Chain Capabilities: A Case Study of Korean Hyundai-Kia Motors Company." *International Journal of Logistics Systems and Management*,. Vol. 9, No. 2, pp. 238–250.

Park, Y.W., Oh, J. and Fujimoto, T. 2012. "Global Expansion and Supply Chain Integration: Case Study of Korean Firms." *International Journal of Procure Management* (Forthcoming).

Pascale, R. T. "Perspective on Strategy: The Real Story behind Honda's Success." *California Management Review*, Spring, 1984, pp. 47–72.

Patterson, K., C. Grimm, and T. Corsi. 2003. "Adopting New Technologies for Supply Chain Management." *Transportation Research Part E: Logistics and Transportation Review*, Vol. 39, No. 2, pp. 95–121.

Penrose, E. T. 1959. *The Theory of the Growth of the Firm*. Oxford: Basil Blackwell and Mott.

Peters, T., and R. Waterman. 1982. *In Search of Excellence*. New York: HarperCollins,.

Pinch, T. J. and Bijker, W. E. 1987. "The Social Construction of Facts and Artifacts: Or How the Sociology of Science and the Sociology of Technology Might Benefit Each Other." in Bijker, W. E. Hughes, T. P. and Pinch, T. J. (eds.) *The Social Construction of Technological Systems*. MIT Press, pp. 17–50.

Pisano, Gary P., and David J. Teece. 2007. "How to Capture Value from Innovation: Shaping Intellectual Property and Industry Architecture." *California Management Review*, Vol. 50, No. 1, pp. 278–296.

Porter, M. 1987. "From Competitive Advantage to Corporate Strategy." *Harvard Business Review*, May/June, pp. 43–59.

Porter, Michael, and Taekeuchi Takahiro. 2002. *Japanese Competitive Strategy*, Diamond Press (in Japanese).

Prahalad, C. K., and G. Hamel. 1990. "The Core Competence of the Corporation." *Harvard Business Review*, May–June, pp. 79–91.

Quinn, L., and M. Dalton. 2009. "Leading for Sustainability: Implementing the Tasks of Leadership." *Corporate Governance*, Vol. 9, No. 1, pp. 21–38.

Rachuri, Sudarsan, Eswaran Subrahmanian, Abdelaziz Bouras, Steven J. Fenves, Sebti Foufou, and Ram D. Sriram. 2008. "Information Sharing and Exchange in the Context of Product Lifecycle Management: Role of Standards." *Computer-Aided Design*, Vol. 40, Issue 7, July, pp. 789–800.

Rauniar, R., W. Doll, G. Rawski, and Paul Hong. 2008a. "The Role of Heavyweight Product Manager in New Product Development." *International Journal of Operations and Production Management*, Vol. 28, No. 2, pp. 130–154.

Rauniar, R., G. Rawski, W. Doll, and Paul Hong. 2008b. "Shared Knowledge and Product Design Glitches in Integrated Product Development." *International Journal of Production Economics*, Vol. 114, No. 2, pp. 723–736.

Reitman, V. 1997. "To the Rescue: Toyota's Fast Rebound After Fire at Supplier Shows Why It Is Tough." *The Wall Street Journal*; Eastern Edition (May 8).

Ritter, T. 1999. "The networking company - Antecedents for Coping with Relationships and Networks Effectively." *Industrial Marketing Management*, Vol. 28, No.5, pp. 467–479.

Ritter, T. and Gemunden, H. G. 2003. "Network Competence: Its Impact on Innovation Success and Its Antecedents." *Journal of Business Research*, Vol. 56, No. 9, pp. 745–755.

Robertson, D., and Allen, T. J. 1993. "CAD System Use and Engineering Performance." IEEE Transactions on Engineering Management, Vol. 40, No. 3, pp. 274–282.

Rodgers, E.1983. *Diffusion of Innovations*. New York, NY, Free Press.

Roh, J., P. Hong, and Y. Park, 2008. "Organizational Culture and Supply Chain Strategy: A Framework for Effective Information Flows." *Journal of Enterprise Information Management*, Vol. 21, No. 4, 2008. pp. 361–376.

Roh, James, Hockey Min, and Paul Hong. 2010. "A Coordination Theory Approach to Restructuring the Global Supply Chain." *International Journal of Production Research*, Vol. 49, No. 15, pp. 4517–4541.

Rumelt, R.1984. "Towards a Strategic Theory of the Firm." In Lamb, R. B. (ed.) *Competitive Strategic Management*. Englewood Cliffs, NJ: Prentice Hall. pp. 556–570.

Sahin, F. and Robinson, E. P., 2002. "Flow Coordination and Information Sharing in Supply Chains: Review, Implications, and Directions for Future Research." *Decision Science*, Vol. 33, No. 4, pp. 505–535.

Sakakibara, K. 1988. "Innovation in Production System." In *Competition and Innovation: Company Growth of Auto Industry*, (Eds.) H. Itami, T. Kobayashi, M. Ito, T. Kagono, and K. Sakakibara. Toyokeizai (in Japanese).

Sakakibara, K. 2006. "Dilemma of Integrated Company." *In Innovation and Competitive Advantage*, (Eds.) Sakakibara Kiyonori and Kohyama Susumu, pp. 49–69 (in Japanese).

Samsung. 1998. *50 Years History of Samsung Group* (in Korean).

Samsung. 2009. *Samsung Electronic 40th Anniversary*, Samsung Electronics, Special Edition (September) (in Korean).

Samsung Economic Research Institute. 1999. "The Second Semi-Conductor Miracle—TFT-LC Success." *CEO Information*, Vol. 209 (1999.9.1) (in Korean).

Samsung Economic Research Institute. 2005. "Intensifying Competition among LCD Clusters," *SERI Economic Focus*, Vol. 57 (2005.9.12) (in Korean).

Samsung Economic Research Institute. 2006. "Accelerating Trend of Monopolization of TFT-LCD Component Parts." *SERI Economic Focus*, Vol. 113 (2006.10.16) (in Korean).

Schilli, B., and F. Dai. 2006. "Collaborative Life Cycle Management between Suppliers and OEM." *Computers in Industry*, Vol. 57, Issues 8–9, pp. 725–731.

Schuh, Günther, Henrique Rozenfeld, Dirk Assmus, and Eduardo Zancul. 2008. "Process Oriented Framework to Support PLM Implementation." *Computers in Industry*, Vol. 59, Issues 2–3, March, pp. 210–218.

Schumpeter, J. A. 1934. *The Theory of Economic Development: An Inquiry into Profits, Capital, Credit, Interest, and the Business Cycle*. Harvard University Press, Cambridge, MA.

Shapiro, C. and Hal, V. 1999. "The Art of Standards Wars." *California Management Review*, Vol. 41, No. 2. pp. 8–32.

Sheffi, Y. 2005. *The Resilient Enterprise*. Cambridge, MA: MIT Press.

Shen, Weiming, Qi Hao, and Weidong Li. 2008. "Computer Supported Collaborative Design: Retrospective and Perspective." *Computers in Industry*, Vol. 59, Issue 9, December, pp. 855–862.

Shin, J. S., and S. W. Jang. 2006. "Analysis of SAMSUNG Semiconductor World 1st Secret: Strategy and Organization of First Mover Advantage Creation." SERI (in Korean).

Shin, Yoogun. 1996. *Success and Failure of Korean Firms*. Sangonhyeuso.

Shintaku, Junjiro. 2000. *Competition among Japanese Firms*. Yuhikaku (in Japanese).

Shintaku, J., Shibata, T., and Konomi, Y. (eds). 2000. *Essence of de facto Standard*. Yuhikaku.

Shintaku, J., T. Yoshimoto, and H. Kato. 2004. "Strategy of Japanese Firms in Chinese Module Type Industry." *Akamon Management Review*, Vol. 3, No. 3, pp. 95–114.

Shintaku, J. 2006. "Positioning Japanese Firms in East Asian Manufacturing Network Formation." Tokyo University, *MMRC Discussion Study* No. 92.

Shintaku, J., K. Kyo, and S. So. 2006a. "Development of Taiwanese LCD Industry and Business Strategy." Tokyo University, *MMRC Discussion Study* No. 84 (in Japanese).

Shintaku, J., K. Ogawa, and T. Yoshimoto. 2006b. "Competition in Light Disk Industry and International Alliance Model—Progress in Integral and Modular Elements." Tokyo University, *MMRC Discussion Study* No. 68 (in Japanese).

Shintaku, J., K. Ogawa, and T. Yoshimoto. 2006c. "Architecture-Based Approaches to International Standardization and Evolution of Business Models." *MMRC Discussion Paper 96*, pp. 1–21.

Shintaku, J., Y. W. Park, J. Tomita, H. Tatsumoto, and T. Yoshimoto, T. 2007. "Architecture to International Specialization in Liquid Crystal Industry." International Business Research Society Theme Session. October 28, 2007 (in Japanese).

Shintaku, J., Yoshimoto, T., Tatsumoto, H., Kyo, K., and So, S. 2007b. "Product Architecture of LCD TV and Status of Chinese Firms." Tokyo University, *MMRC Discussion Study* No. 164 (in Japanese).

Shintaku, J., Tatsumoto, H., Yoshimoto, T., Tomita, J. and Park, Y. 2008. "Architecture Based Analysis on International Technology Transfer and International Division of Labor." *Hitotsubashi Business Review* 56(2), pp. 42–61 (in Japanese).

Shintaku, J., and Amano, H. 2009. "Emerging Market Strategies: Changes in Market and Resource Strategies." *MMRC Discussion Paper* 278, pp. 1–33.

Shintaku, J., Oh, J., Park, Y. W., Amano, T., Yoshimoto, T., Fukazawa, M. and Fujimoto, T. 2010. "Oversea Monozukuri Operations of Korean Firms (2): Case Studies of Hyundai Motor Company and LG Electronics in East European Centers." *Akamon Management Review*, Vol. 9, No. 2, pp. 103–113. (In Japanese)

Shumpeter, J. A. 1942. *Capitalism, Socialism and Democracy*. New York, NY, Harper & Row.

Smith, A. 1776. *An Inquiry into the Nature and Cause of Wealth of Nations*. London: Routledge.

SMEs-Venture Study Group (eds.). 2006. *SMEs / Venture Company Support System Conspectus*, Hankuk Economic Newspaper (eBook). (In Korean)

Sohn, H. B. 2006. "Analysis of Domestic Main Mobile Phone Production Companies." *KETI* (2006.4), pp. 1–21 (in Korean).

Song, Ranok. 2005. *Technology Development and Semi-Conductor Industry*. Bunrikaku (in Japanese).

Song, W. 2006. "Korean Mobile Communication: From Catching Up to Strategic Leading." Samsung Economic Research Institute (in Korean).

Song, W. J. 1999. "The Study about Wireless Communication Technology Process: Mutual Action between Technology Politic and Learning." Science Technology Policy Management Institute (in Korean).

Srinivasan, V. 2009. "An Integration Framework for Product Lifecycle Management." *Computer-Aided Design*, doi:10.1016/j.cad.2008.12.001, pp. 1–15.

Stalk, G., P. Evans, and L. E. Shulman. 1992. "Competing on Capabilities: The New Rules of Corporate Strategy." *Harvard Business Review*, March–April, pp. 57–69.

Sudarsan, R., S. J. Fenves, R. D. Sriram, and F. Wang. 2005. "A Product Information Modeling Framework for Product Lifecycle Management." *Computer-Aided Design*, Vol. 37, pp. 1399–1411.

Sugiyama, Yasuo, Takanori Yorita, and Atushi Nagauchi. 2006. "Stopping Interest of Standardization." *International Competition and Global Standard, JIS*, pp. 155–192.

Sung, H. H. 2009. *CIOBIZ News Inside: POSCO, Large Firms-SMEs Coexistence Cooperation.* ETnews (26th October). (In Korean)

Suo, H., H. Chu, and Y. Jin. 2004. "Supply Chain Coordination under Manufacturer's Supporting Innovation Activities." In *Proceeding of Fifth World Congress on Intelligent Control and Automation*, Hangzhou, pp. 3184–3186.

Takahashi, Nobuo. 2000. *Trans-Company and Organization Theory*. Yuhikaku.

Tan, C. L., and M. A. Vonderembse. 2006. "Mediating Effects of Computer-Aided Design Usage: From Concurrent Engineering to Product Development Performance." *Journal of Operations Management*, Vol. 24, No. 2, pp. 494–510.

Tang, Dunbing, and Xiaoming Qian. 2008. "Product Lifecycle Management for Automotive Development Focusing on Supplier Integration." *Computers in Industry*, Vol. 59, Issues 2–3, March, pp. 288–295.

Teece, D. J. 1998. "Capturing Value from Knowledge Assets: The New Economy, Markets for Know-How, and Intangible Assets." *California Management Review*, Vol. 40, No. 3, pp. 55–79.

Teece, D. 1986. "Profiting from Technological Innovation: Implications for Integration, Collaboration, Licensing and Public Policy." *Research Policy*, Vol. 15, pp. 285–305.

Teece, D. J. 2007. "Dynamic Capabilities and Strategic Management." *Strategic Management Journal,* Vol. 18, No. 7, pp. 509–533.

Teece, D. J., and G. Pisano. 1994. "The Dynamic Capabilities of Enterprises: An Introduction." *Industrial and Corporate Change,* Vol. 3, No. 3, pp. 537–556.

Teece, D. J., G. Pisano, and A. Shuen. 1990. "Enterprise Capabilities, Resources and the Concept of Strategy." *Consortium on Competitiveness and Cooperation, Working Paper CCC* 90–8, Institute of Management, Innovation and Organization. Berkeley, CA: University of California.

Teece, D. J., G. Pisano, and A. Shuen. 1997. "Dynamic Capabilities and Strategic Management." *Strategic Management Journal*, Vol. 18, No. 7, pp. 509–533.

The Korea Economic Daily. 2002. *Samsung Rising*, Hankyung BP (in Korean).

Thomke, S., and T. Fujimoto. 2000. "The Effect of Front-Loading Problem Solving on Product Development Performance." *The Journal of Product Innovation Management*, Vol. 17, No. 2, pp. 128–142.

Tomino, T., Y. W. Park, P. Hong, and J. Roh. 2009. "Market Flexible Customizing System (MFCS) of Japanese Vehicle Manufacturers: An Analysis of Toyota, Nissan and Mitsubishi." *International Journal of Production Economics.* Vol. 118, No. 2, pp. 375–386.

Tomita, J., Park, Y. and Hong, P. 2011. "Process Architecture Impact: A Comparative Study of Two Glass Industries." *International Journal of Services and Operations Management.* Vol. 8. No. 3, pp. 390–403.

Toriya, K. 2006. *3D Monozukuri Innovation*, Nikkei Press (in Japanese).

Tukamoto, Kiyoshi. 2002. *Shock in Manufacturing of Korean Firms: From Field of Hyundai, Samsung, LG, SK Telecom*, Koubunsya.

Tushman, M. L. and Anderson, P. 1986. "Technological Discontinuities and Organizational Environments." *Administrative Science Quarterly*, Vol. 31, pp. 439–465.

Tushman, M. L. and Rosenkopf, L. 1992. "On the Organizational Determinants of Technological Change: Toward a Sociology of Technological Evolution." in Staw, B.M. and Cummings, L.L. (eds.) *Reseach in Organizational Behavior*. Greenwich, CT., JAI Press, Vol. 14, pp. 311–347.

Tushman, Michael L., and Charles A. O'Reilly, III. 1996. "Ambidextrous Organizations: Managing Evolutionary and Revolutionary Change." *California Management Review,* Vol. 38, No. 4, pp. 8–30.

Twigg, D., C. A. Voss, and G. M. Winch. 1992. "Implementing Integrating Technologies: Developing Managerial Integration for CAD/CAM." *International Journal of Production Management*, Vol. 12, No. 7–8, pp. 76–91.

Tyson, L. D' Andrea. 1992. *Who's Bashing Whom?*. Institute for International Economics.

Udagawa, M. and Abe, E. 1995. Morikawa, H. and Yonekura S. (eds.) *History of Japanese Management 5: Beyond High Growth*, Iwanami Books, 1995, pp. 241–295. (In Japanese)

Udagawa, Masaru, Takeo Kikkawa, and Junjiro Shintaku. 2000. *Competition among Japanese Firms*, Yuhikaku.

Ueno, Y. 2005. *Practicing the Digital Monozukuri: PLM in Electronic Industry*, Hakujitsusha (in Japanese).

Ueno, Y., T. Fujimoto, and Y. W. Park. 2007. "Complexity of Artifacts and Mechanical/Electrical Design: Mainly in CAD Use of Auto and Electronic Industry." *MMRC Discussion Study* 179.

Ulrich, K. 1995. "The Role of Product Architecture in the Manufacturing Firm." *Research Policy*, Vol. 24, pp. 419–440.

Utterback, J., and F. Suarez. 1993. "Innovation, Competition, and Market Structure." *Research Policy,* Vol. 22, No. 1, pp. 1–21.

Velocci, T., and J. Childs. 1990. "French Aerospace: Global Leadership." *Aviation Week Space Technology*, Vol. 133, No. 9, pp. 5–24.

von Hippel, E. 1986. "Lead Users: A Source of Novel Product Concepts." *Management Science*, Vol. 32, No.7, pp. 791–805.

Wakabayashi, N. 2009. *Network Organization: New Organization Image From Social Network Theory.* Yuhikaku (In Japanese).

Walsh, S. and Linton, J. D. 2002. "The Measurement of Technical Competencies." *Journal of High Technology Management Research*, Vol.13, No.1, pp. 63–86.

Walters, David. 2008. "Demand Chain Management+Response Management=Increased Customer Satisfaction." *International Journal of Physical Distribution & Logistics Management*, Vol. 38, No. 9. pp. 699–725.

Wang, Albert and Gary Banta. 2004. "Riding on the Makimoto Wave: Toward Development, Standardization and Customization for the User-based Processors." *Design Wave Magazine*, September, pp. 98–107 (in Japanese).

Weick, K. E., K. M. Sutcliffe, and D. Obstfeld. 2005. "Organizing and the Process of Sensemaking." *Organization Science,* Vol. 16, pp. 409–421.

Wernerfelt, B. 1984. "A Resource-Based View of the Firm." *Strategic Management Journal*, Vol.5, No.2, pp. 171–180.

Whipple, M., and R. Frankel. 2000. "Strategic Alliance Success Factors." *The Journal of Supply Chain Management,* 36 (3), pp. 21–28.

Williamson, O. 1979. "Transactions Cost Economics: The Governance of Contractual Relations." *Journal of Law and Economics,* Vol. 23, pp. 233–261.

WISEINFO. 2007.10. "Summary of a Mobile Communication Market and Handset Production Companies." KETI (2007.10), pp. 1–15 (in Korean).

Wognum, Nel, and Amy Trappey. 2008. "PLM Challenges." *Advanced Engineering Informatics*, Vol. 22, No. 4, pp. 419–420.

Wolf, Charles, Jr. 1988. *Market or Governments: Choosing between Imperfect Alternatives.*The Rand Corporation, 1988 (Jun, Sangil. Market and Government, Kyomun).

Yamazaki, H. 2004. Business History Society of Japanese (Ed.), *Japanese Business History: Basic Facts and Concepts,* Yuhikaku (in Japanese).

Yasumoto, M. (2010) "Final Product Manufacturers and Interfirm Labor Division under the Global Market Differentiation: Lessons from Mobile Handset Industries." *MMRC Discussion Paper* 300, pp. 1–35.

Yoon, Jongrok. 2006. "Be Prepared to Inter-Industry Collaboration." *TTA Journal*, Vol. 103, No. 2, pp. 8–9.

Yoshimoto, T. 2007. "Business Strategy by Sections and Modularity in Cathode-ray Tube Television: Decentralization Management of Integrated Firms." Doshisha Commercial Science, Vol. 58, No. 4–5, pp. 27–52. (In Japanese)

Yoshioka, Hidemi. 2007. "The Competitive Power of Korean Semi-Conductor Industry: Changes in DRAM Industry and Superior Position of Samsung Electronics." In *A Study of Competitiveness of Korean Major Industries*, (Ed.) Okuda Satoru, pp. 19–47. Institute of Developing Economics, JETRO (in Japanese).

Youn, S., P. Hong, and A. Nahm. 2008. "Supply Chain Partnerships and Supply Chain Integration: the Mediating Role of Information Quality and Sharing." *International Journal of Logistics Systems and Management*. Vol. 4, No. 4, pp. 437–456.

Yu, H., A. Z. Zeng, and L. Zhaoa. 2009. "Single or Dual Sourcing: Decision-Making in the Presence of Supply Chain Disruption Risks." *Omega*, 37, pp. 788–800.

Yunhap News. Feb 15, 2009. "Samsung and LG: A Reason without Monday of Blood."

Zhang, D. Z., A. I. Anosike, M. K. Lim, and O. M. Akanle. 2006. "An Agent-Based Approach for E-Manufacturing and Supply Chain Integration." *Computers & Industrial Engineering*, Vol. 51, pp. 343–360.

Index

A

B

C

D

E

L

M

N

Q

R

S

T

U

V

W

X

Y